Causes of War

To students of war everywhere

Causes of War

Jack S. Levy

and

William R. Thompson

WILEY-BLACKWELL

A John Wiley & Sons, Ltd., Publication

This edition first published 2010
© 2010 Jack S. Levy and William R. Thompson

Blackwell Publishing was acquired by John Wiley & Sons in February 2007. Blackwell's publishing program has been merged with Wiley's global Scientific, Technical, and Medical business to form Wiley-Blackwell.

Registered Office
John Wiley & Sons Ltd, The Atrium, Southern Gate, Chichester, West Sussex, PO19 8SQ, United Kingdom

Editorial Offices
350 Main Street, Malden, MA 02148–5020, USA
9600 Garsington Road, Oxford, OX4 2DQ, UK
The Atrium, Southern Gate, Chichester, West Sussex, PO19 8SQ, UK

For details of our global editorial offices, for customer services, and for information about how to apply for permission to reuse the copyright material in this book please see our website at www.wiley.com/wiley-blackwell.

The right of Jack S. Levy and William R. Thompson to be identified as the authors of this work has been asserted in accordance with the UK Copyright, Designs and Patents Act 1988.

Wiley also publishes its books in a variety of electronic formats. Some content that appears in print may not be available in electronic books.

Designations used by companies to distinguish their products are often claimed as trademarks. All brand names and product names used in this book are trade names, service marks, trademarks or registered trademarks of their respective owners. The publisher is not associated with any product or vendor mentioned in this book. This publication is designed to provide accurate and authoritative information in regard to the subject matter covered. It is sold on the understanding that the publisher is not engaged in rendering professional services. If professional advice or other expert assistance is required, the services of a competent professional should be sought.

Library of Congress Cataloging-in-Publication Data
Levy, Jack S., 1948–
  Causes of war / Jack S. Levy and William R. Thompson.
    p.   cm.
  Includes bibliographical references and index.
  ISBN 978-1-4051-7560-9 (hardcover : alk. paper) – ISBN 978-1-4051-7559-3 (pbk. : alk. paper)
  1. War–Causes. 2. International relations. I. Thompson, William R. II. Title.
  JZ6385.L48 2010
  355.02′7–dc22

                                                                              2009030166

A catalogue record for this book is available from the British Library.

Set in 10 on 12 pt Sabon by Toppan Best-set Premedia Limited
Printed in Singapore by C.O.S. Printers Pte Ltd

7   2015

Contents

Acknowledgments

A number of people provided valuable feedback at various phases of this project, and we want to acknowledge our appreciation. Five anonymous reviewers provided helpful comments on our initial proposal. Tim Knievel read the entire manuscript and offered detailed suggestions for improvements in both substance and style. Kim Marten gave us insightful comments on chapter 1 and provided additional feedback on questions arising in later chapters.

We also want to thank the people at Wiley-Blackwell for making this book a reality. Nick Bellorini, the Senior Commissioning Editor for Philosophy and Politics, provided the initial encouragement. Liz Cremona, the Senior Production Editor, supervised all phases of the project and kept the process running smoothly. Paul Stringer did a nice job of copyediting, and then flawlessly incorporated our last-minute changes into the final product. We thank them all for their patience in dealing with us throughout the process.

The authors would also like to thank each other for tolerating each other's idiosyncrasies without escalating to warfare.

1

Introduction to the Study of War

War has been a persistent pattern of interaction between and within states and other political units for millennia. In its many varieties, it is probably the most destructive form of human behavior. War kills people, destroys resources, retards economic development, ruins environments, spreads disease, expands governments, militarizes societies, reshapes cultures, disrupts families, and traumatizes people. Preparation for war, whether for conquest or for protection, diverts valued resources from more constructive social activities, and it often undermines security rather than enhances it.

War also has a profound impact on the evolution of world politics and the behavior of states. Over the years it has been one of the primary mechanisms for change in the world system, through its impact on both the distribution of military power and wealth and the structure of the world economy. War also has a profound impact on the institutional structures and cultures of states, and it has played a key role in the birth and death of many states. We cannot understand the development of the modern nation-state system four or five centuries ago, or of earlier or more recent states, in the absence of patterns of warfare. As Tilly (1975:42) argued, "war made the state, and the state made war."

It is hard to imagine what life would have been like in the late twentieth century in the absence of World War I and World War II, which had such profound effects on the global system and on domestic societies. The same can be said for the Cold War. For nearly a half century it shaped both international and domestic politics and cultures, not only in the United States and the Soviet Union but also in Western Europe and the Third World (Weart, 1989). The development of new states in the contemporary era continues to be influenced by warfare and preparations for war. With the proliferation of nuclear weapons, and with the threat of the acquisition of nuclear weapons by terrorist groups and "rogue states," new threats to the security of even the most powerful states in the system have emerged.

The proliferation of civil wars and conflicts involving "non-state" actors has changed life throughout the developing world. A better understanding of the causes of war is a necessary first step if we are to have any hope of reducing the occurrence of war and perhaps mitigating its severity and consequences.

The unquestioned importance of war as a social phenomenon has led scholars, journalists, and others to devote enormous amounts of intellectual energy in attempt to better understand the nature of war and its causes. Ever since Thucydides (1996) wrote his *History of the Peloponnesian War* over 2,400 years ago in an attempt to explain the great war between Athens and Sparta (431–404 BCE), scholars from a wide range of disciplines – philosophy, history, political science, theology, anthropology, sociology, psychology, economics, mathematics, biology, literature, and others – have engaged the questions of what causes war and how humankind might eliminate war or at least bring it under greater control. Their efforts have led to a proliferation of theories but to no consensus as to the causes of war or of other forms of social violence.

Scholars disagree not only on the specific causes of war, but also on how to approach the study of war. It is not surprising that there are divisions between scholars in different countries (Wæver, 1998) and in different disciplines – that psychologists generally emphasize psychological factors, that economists emphasize economic factors, that anthropologists emphasize cultural factors, and so on. We also find enormous differences within each discipline. Scholars debate not only what the causes of war are, but also what theoretical approaches and methodologies are best suited to identifying those causes. The only consensus that seems to be emerging is that the question of the causes of war is enormously complex, although a minority of scholars question even that. Scholarly debate goes on, but the scourge of war continues.

The complexity of the question of the causes of war is compounded if we consider the many different forms of war. Most of the scholarly research on war since the time of Thucydides has focused on wars between states. Interstate wars dominated the study of war in political science until the last couple of decades, even though civil wars have actually been more frequent than interstate wars during most periods (Levy and Thompson, 2010b), and dramatically so in the last half century (Sarkees, Wayman, and Singer, 2003; Human Security Centre, 2005; Hewitt, Wilkenfeld, and Gurr, 2008). If we broaden our focus from interstate war to include civil war, colonial war, ethnic war, tribal war, and other forms of warfare, the question of the causes of war becomes even more complex. Although each of these forms of warfare shares some common elements (for example, the use of military force is usually seen as a strategy for advancing group interests), there are important differences as well.

Differences across types of war are particularly clear in the scholarly literature on interstate war and civil war. As we demonstrate later in this book, theories of interstate war emphasize fundamentally different factors than do theories of civil wars. To take just one example, the emphasis on the distribution of military power in the international system that is so common in discussions of the causes of interstate war, particularly great power wars, is given relatively little emphasis in theories of civil war. Similarly, the key variables of levels of economic and social welfare, which are critical in much of the literature on civil war, are given much less attention by scholars who study interstate war. As a result, most of the contemporary literature on war focuses either on interstate war or on civil war, but not on both.

With the changing nature of warfare, we believe that no general book on war is complete without some treatment of both interstate war and civil war. For that reason we break with the scholarly norm and include discussions of both. Still, we give most of our attention to interstate war, for a variety of reasons. More than any other form of warfare, interstate wars have shaped the evolution of the modern international system. This has made them the central focus of scholarly attention and debate for several centuries. Thus the literature on the causes of interstate war is intimately tied to the literature on international relations theory that has developed during the past 60 years. It is only recently that international relations theorists have engaged the question of the causes and consequences of civil war. Prior to that, students of comparative politics had a monopoly on the study of civil war, and for many years their approach was more descriptive than theoretical. The fact that little consensus has emerged on the causes of interstate war is another strong argument for continuing to study it.

There are other considerations as well. Though it has been declining in frequency, interstate war continues to have a profound effect on the contemporary world. The United States has already fought two interstate wars in the first decade of the new century – against the Taliban government of Afghanistan in 2001 and against the Iraqi government in 2003 – and each war evolved into an internationalized civil war in which the United States was deeply involved. The Iraq war contributed to enormous human costs, a significant decline in US prestige around the world, political divisions at home, and economic costs that contributed to its declining economic fortunes. As we write in summer 2009, analysts debate whether it will be possible for the US to win the ongoing internationalized civil war in Afghanistan. Elsewhere, the Russian–Georgian war of fall 2008 signaled a renewed Russian assertiveness in international politics and sent shock waves through the West.

In addition, a brief survey of the world suggests a number of "flash points" that could trigger an interstate war, and some of these carry a significant risk of escalation to a broader conflict. We have almost certainly not seen the end of Palestinian–Israeli conflicts, which recently led to short wars in Lebanon involving Hezbollah in 2006 and in Gaza involving Hamas in 2008–09, and the potential for one of these conflicts to draw in other Arab states cannot be discounted.

The prospective proliferation of nuclear weapons involves other possible flash points. When Israel suspected that Syria was in the early stages of developing a nuclear program, it launched a limited preventive strike against a Syrian facility in September 2007.[1] In response to the development of Iran's nuclear program, which most observers believe is within a few years of becoming operational, and to Iranian President Ahmadinejad's open call for the destruction of Israel, Israel has threatened to launch a preventive strike against Iran. The United States strongly prefers non-military means of preventing Iran from acquiring nuclear weapons, but it has thus far refused to take the military option "off the table."

One also thinks of the Indo–Pakistani rivalry, which has already led to three major wars in the past 60 years (1948, 1965, 1971) and which is increasingly dangerous because both sides have nuclear weapons and because of domestic instability within Pakistan. The rivalry led to a war over Kargil in 1999 and to high levels of tensions at other times, including after the deadly terrorist attack on Mumbai in 2008. It is known that Pakistani citizens led the attack, and India charges that Pakistani security forces trained and equipped the terrorists. Other possible danger points are located in the Far East. One is the Korean Peninsula, with a nuclear-armed North Korea often acting in unpredictable ways. Still another danger is the dispute between China and Taiwan over the political status of the latter, which has enormous implications for US–China relations, particularly in the context of the possibility of a "power transition" involving the ascendancy of China over the United States within a few decades.

Thus while interstate war is not likely to be the most frequent form of warfare in the upcoming years, it has the potential to be the most destructive in human and economic terms. A war involving advanced nuclear states could be the most catastrophic war in history and fundamentally change human life as we have known it. Thus we devote most of our attention to interstate war, while reserving some attention to the phenomenon of civil war, which continues to occur on a regular basis.

We proceed as follows. In the rest of this chapter we provide a theoretical and historical context for our study of the causes of war. We define war and identify some of its primary characteristics. We then attempt to describe the changing nature of war over time, in order to put our extensive treatment of interstate war and briefer discussion of civil war in a broader historical context. Next we summarize the levels-of-analysis framework that we use for organizing our survey of the causes of war. Then in subsequent chapters we examine some of the leading theories of interstate wars. Our aim is not to present our own theory of war, but rather to survey some of the most influential theories advanced by scholars over the years and to point out some of the limitations of each of those theories. We give particular attention to the theories developed by international relations scholars in political science, but we also include important theoretical work from other disciplines as well.

What is War?

If our aim is to explain the causes of war, we must begin with a brief definition of the subject of our inquiry. We define war broadly as *sustained, coordinated violence between political organizations*.[2] Such a definition includes great power wars like World War I, colonial wars like those fought by the European great powers in Africa and Asia from the eighteenth century to early twentieth century, civil wars like those in the United States in the nineteenth century or in the Congo or in Yugoslavia in the 1990s,[3] organized insurgencies like the one against American forces in the Iraq War, tribal wars among pre-modern societies, and a wide variety of other forms of violence. This definition has several component parts, and it would be useful to examine each of them individually.

First, and most obviously, war is violent. It involves the use of force to kill and injure people and destroy military and economic resources. The German military theorist Carl von Clausewitz ([1832]1976:89) ended the first chapter of his famous book *On War* by identifying "primordial violence" as the first element of a "trinity" of "dominant tendencies" of warfare.[4] That violence has the potential to be quite extreme. Earlier in the same chapter Clausewitz argued (p. 77) that "war is an act of force, and there is no logical limit to the application of that force."

The element of violence in warfare separates it from other forms of intergroup and interstate conflict. Conflicts of interests – over power, territory, resources, and more symbolic issues – are common in world politics. Rivalries involving sustained and hostile competitions between actors are also common, as are threats of force by actors in an attempt to resolve disputes in their own favor.[5] But conflicts of interests, rivalries, disputes, and threats of force do not become a war unless they involve sustained violence. The "Cold War" between the United States and the Soviet Union was a rivalry, not a war.[6] Indeed, one of the distinctive features of the Cold War was the fact that the US–Soviet rivalry, unlike most previous rivalries between the leading states in the system, did not escalate to war. This is something that many scholars have spent a great deal of time trying to explain, with little agreement (Gaddis, 1987).

To take another example, the Arab–Israeli conflict goes back to the founding of the state of Israel in 1948 and beyond. Yet we would not describe it as a continuous war. Rather, it is a conflict or rivalry that has involved frequent low-level military activity, including armed incursions across borders and subsequent retaliations, but that has also been punctuated by a number of well-defined wars. The most prominent of these are the wars of 1948, 1956, 1967, 1973, and 1982, though we would probably also include as wars the Israeli conflicts in Lebanon in 2006 and in Gaza in 2008–09. The point is that conflicts of interests and rivalries are fairly common, whereas wars are not. Explaining why some rivalries, conflicts, or disputes lead to war while others do not is an important question. This makes it all the more important to define war as a separate concept, distinct from conflict or rivalry.

Another component of our definition of war involves the apparently innocuous word that follows violence in our definition – "between." Yet this element of the definition is far from trivial. It indicates that violence must be reciprocated for it to qualify as war. A war is *between* two political organizations. If the target of the initial violence does not fight back, we do not normally call it a war. The Hungarian army forcibly resisted the Soviet invasion in 1956, and consequently scholars refer to the violent struggle that followed as the Russo–Hungarian War (Singer and Small, 1972). The Czechoslovakian army did not forcibly resist the Soviet invasion in 1968, and consequently we describe this as the Soviet invasion of (or intervention in) Czechoslovakia, but not as a war. To take another example, in 1981 Israel bombed an Iraqi nuclear reactor, with the aim of destroying the facility before it could become operational. Iraq did not respond militarily, in part because it was already engaged in a war with Iran. For that reason, scholars refer to the Israeli action as a preventive strike but not as a war.

Thus we treat war as the joint outcome of the behavior of two or more actors. In an alternative use of the concept, scholars sometimes talk about war as a strategy rather than as an outcome (Vasquez, 1993: chap. 1). Here the question is why a state or other political organization adopts a strategy involving the substantial use of military force rather than some other strategy. In speaking of war as a strategy, it is generally assumed that military action will be resisted. If it is not resisted, however, most scholars would not refer to the outcome as a war.

This brings us to the actors who engage in war. The actors are organizations, not individuals. Individuals do the actual fighting, but they fight on behalf of a larger collective political unit, under the direction and coordination of political and/or military leaders, to advance the goals of the collectivity, or at least of its leadership. An individual who acts on his own to kill a border guard, or who crosses a border to kill citizens of another political system, is not engaging in war. But if that individual is part of a political system's formal military organization, and that military organization engages in a sustained campaign of violence against the military organization of another state or another organized group, we would call it a war.

Most books on the history of war in the modern era (which historians date from about 1500 on) focus on interstate wars, with particular attention to interstate wars between the great powers, the most powerful states in the system.[7] These wars were the primary focus of Clausewitz ([1832]1976), who wrote after the experience of the French Revolutionary and Napoleonic Wars (1792–1815) and who emphasized the importance of major battles between the armies of the leading states in the system.[8] Interstate wars, however, constitute only one manifestation of the wide variety of sustained, coordinated violence that we observe over the millennia.

In addition to fighting other states in interstate wars, states fight domestic challengers in internal or civil wars for the control of the state or for secession from the state. Those domestic challengers may fight each other. States may also fight non-state entities in their external environments, as illustrated by the current US wars against al Qaeda and against the Taliban insurgency in Afghanistan, and by the frequent armed conflicts between the state of Israel and the Palestinian authority and other non-state actors such as Hezbollah and Hamas. Wars may involve many of these elements simultaneously. The Iraq War started out as an interstate war (between the United States and the Iraqi government of Saddam Hussein) but then involved a domestic insurgency against an external state (the US), a civil war (between Shia and Sunni) for the control of Iraq, a war for secession from – or at least independence within – Iraq (by the Kurds), and international intervention in the civil war by state and non-state actors (the United States, Iran, and al Qaeda).

We must also remember that the nation-state, or even the broader category of the territorial state, is a relatively modern phenomenon. Before the rise of the state in early modern Europe, life was organized around kings and nobles, before that around "city-states," and long before that around looser forms of social organization, including agricultural communities and groups of hunter-gatherers.[9] During each of these periods organized violence between groups was fairly frequent. It differed in many respects from organized violence in later eras, but one thing that much of that violence had in common was that it involved the sustained, coordinated use of armed force by one political organization against another.[10] We define war broadly enough to include those phenomena.

Thus far we have said nothing about the purpose of violence. Although political leaders' motivations are not technically part of our definition of war, implicit in our discussion is the idea that violence is usually driven by a purpose. The political organization, as represented by its authoritative leadership, has goals, and one of the strategies they sometimes adopt in pursuit of those goals is the use of force. The purposeful nature of violence was most famously captured by Clausewitz ([1832]1976: 87), who repeatedly emphasized that war is a "political instrument, a continuation of political activity by other means. ... The political object is the goal, war is the means of reaching it, and means can never be considered in isolation from their purpose."[11]

A good example of an appreciation of the Clausewitzian view of the fundamentally political nature of war is an exchange between an American colonel and his North Vietnamese counterpart a couple of years after the end of the Vietnam War, which was widely regarded as a major defeat for the United States. The American colonel stated that, "You know you never defeated us on the battlefield." The North Vietnamese colonel replied, "That may be so, but it is also irrelevant" (Summers, 1984:21).

It is the diplomatic and political outcomes of war that are important, and they are not always congruent with military outcomes on the battlefield. Egypt was in a stronger diplomatic position after the 1973 Arab–Israeli War than it was before the war, even though it was on the verge of a major military defeat at the end of the war until the United States forced Israel to withdraw its forces rather than crush the Egyptian army that it had surrounded. Egypt was militarily defeated but politically successful in the 1973 war.[12]

When political actors resort to military force, the goal is usually to influence the adversary's behavior in ways that advance their own interests. As Clausewitz ([1832]1976:75) emphasized on the first page of *On War*, "War is thus an act of force to compel our enemy to do our will." War is fundamentally coercive, driven by the aim of influencing the behavior of other actors. The Greek historian Polybius recognized this nearly two millennia before Clausewitz wrote, when he stated in his *Histories* (second century BCE) that "It is not the object of war to annihilate those who have given provocation, but to cause them to mend their ways."

Sometimes the immediate goal of the use of force is not to influence the enemy's behavior directly but instead to destroy or weaken his military forces or economic resources.[13] This is usually an instrumental strategy, however, since weakening the adversary militarily and economically reduces its future battlefield performance and therefore its coercive bargaining leverage. In their use of force and conduct of war, state leaders aim to change the adversary's expectations of the outcome of the war if the war were to continue, and presumably to make the adversary more willing to make extensive concessions to avoid that outcome.

In most cases, of course, political leaders would prefer to achieve their goals through non-forceful means, including diplomacy and economic pressure, which are generally less costly and less risky than the use of military force. Political leaders may use threats of force to reinforce their demands, but they generally prefer that their adversaries comply with those threats and concede what is demanded, so that the actual use of military force is unnecessary. In fact, the most effective uses of military power are often found in those situations in which military force is not actually used but where the mere threat of force is sufficient to change the adversary's behavior. Deterrence, or the dissuasion of an adversary from taking an action that would be harmful to one's own interests, is a good example. If the adversary is unwilling to make sufficient concessions, however, and if political leaders are convinced both that they can achieve more through military force than through negotiation and that they have no other option that would work as well, then the use of force often becomes an attractive option.

It is sometimes argued that diplomacy stops when war begins, that diplomacy and military force are two alternative strategies for preserving or advancing state interests. That view is quite misleading. The use as well as the threat of force is often an integral part of an actor's bargaining strategy. It is a highly coercive activity, aimed at influencing the cost–benefit calculus of the adversary and persuading the adversary to change its behavior. The goal is to convince the adversary that the costs of continuing the war will be sufficiently great that it is preferable to make concessions now through a negotiated settlement. Referring to the subtitle of a recent book, this is "bargaining with bullets" (Sisk, 2009). The American use of the atomic bomb against Japan in 1945, for example, was driven by the goal of coercing Japan to end the war quickly, by sending a signal that additional violence would follow if Japan did not surrender. US leaders wanted to avoid the casualties that would be involved in the prolonged warfare that would otherwise be necessary to defeat the Japanese army. Thus diplomacy and force are often inseparable. As Frederick the Great of Prussia is widely reputed to have said, "Diplomacy without force is like music without instruments."

This argument about the coercive nature of military force applies to nearly all political organizations, including terrorist groups. Terrorism against Israel is almost always motivated by the goal of imposing high enough costs on Israeli society to convince Israeli leaders that the benefits of occupying Arab territories are exceeded by the costs of doing so and that Israel would be better off by changing its policies. In initiating attacks against US military barracks and naval vessels overseas and against the World Trade Center in New York City, al Qaeda had many political goals, including using the threat of further terrorist attacks to try to persuade the US to remove its troops from Saudi Arabia and to reduce its support for other conservative Arab regimes (Pape, 2005b).[14]

Although we have emphasized that the use of military force is generally purposeful, we have not formally incorporated that into our definition of war. This contrasts with the approach of scholars like Malinowski ([1941]1968:523), an anthropologist who defined war as an "armed contest between two independent political units, by means of organized military force, in the pursuit of a tribal or national policy." Our argument is that cases of sustained, coordinated violence between political organizations that are not driven by a clear sense of the political interests of the organization, but instead by personal or domestic political interests or perhaps by an insubordinate military leader, still qualify as wars. Our definition of war is based on the *behavior* of two adversarial political organizations, not on their motivations. In most cases, we believe that the use of military force is purposeful, but that is ultimately an empirical question rather than a definitional one.[15] Identifying the motivations behind the use of force is a key task in explaining the causes of a particular war.

Finally, let us turn to the "sustained" element of the definition. Our aim is to differentiate war from organized violence that is more limited in its magnitude or impact. A minor border incident involving opposing armies may result in casualties on one or both sides, but we want to preserve the term "war" for those incidents that escalate and cross a certain threshold of violence. Border clashes between Chinese and Indian forces in 1962 continued to escalate and involved sustained fighting, and we refer to the "Sino–Indian War." Border clashes between Chinese and Soviet forces over disputed areas around the Ussuri River occurred in March 1969 and then again six months later, but successful crisis management soon ended the crisis without further escalation. Thus we generally refer to that conflict as a "border clash" rather than a war (A. Cohen, 1991). States can mass armies on their borders for weeks or months, as each side attempts to demonstrate its resolve while at the same time seeking some formula for de-escalating tensions. The Indo–Pakistani "Brasstacks crisis" in 1986–7 is a good example (Ganguly 2002:85–8). Unless such an incident involves the sustained use of violent force, however, it does not constitute a war.

The question is what threshold of violence to use. Some scholars use the criterion proposed by the "Correlates of War Project" (Singer and Small, 1972). The "COW" project requires at least 1,000 battle-related deaths among all participating states and an annual average of 1,000 battle deaths for wars lasting more than a year. That criterion is quite reasonable for COW's purposes of analyzing wars during the last two centuries. It is less useful for earlier periods when populations and armies were much smaller and when fewer battle deaths reflected a larger relative proportion of the army or of the population. Since we want our definition to apply to the organized violence between much earlier political systems as well as contemporary ones, we prefer a different criterion than battle deaths.[16]

Note that a precise (or "operational") threshold is particularly important if the analyst is compiling lists of wars, which requires that s/he has explicit and replicable criteria for determining whether a violent conflict gets included in or excluded from a list of wars. We are not compiling a data set on wars, however, so more general criteria will suffice for our purposes. The main point is that our analysis of the causes of war is limited to those violent conflicts that cross some kind of threshold of magnitude. The fighting must be sustained rather than sporadic in order to differentiate war from "lesser" uses of military force. By sustained we mean not only duration but magnitude. There must be a fairly regular use of force of a certain magnitude during the period of the war.[17]

The Changing Nature of Warfare[18]

Human warfare has changed significantly over time. There is substantial evidence of warfare going back roughly ten thousand years to the beginning of agricultural societies (Keeley, 1996; Haas, 1999; Cioffi-Revilla, 2000), and growing evidence of war between hunter-gatherer groups before that (Gat, 2006), though archaeological evidence about warfare is more plentiful for the last 5,000 years (Ferrill, 1997). By that time there is evidence of full-fledged armies equipped with armor and organized into formations. Gradually, these armies became larger in size and more lethal in weaponry, and war became increasingly deadly. If we examine major battles, which admittedly are not representative of all wars, deaths per war more than doubled between the fifth century BCE and the fourteenth century CE, more than doubled again between the fourteenth and early nineteenth centuries CE, and then increased by as much as a factor of 10 between the early nineteenth and twentieth centuries (Levy and Thompson, 2010b).

This enormous increase in the severity of war, defined in terms of battle-related deaths, is countered by another trend, at least for the great powers over the past five centuries. There has been a steady decline in the frequency of great power war during this period, from about 22 in the sixteenth century to five in the nineteenth century and five or six in the twentieth century, depending on one's precise definitions.[19]

These opposite trends for the last five centuries are probably related in a causal sense: the increasing destructiveness of great power wars has reduced the incentives of great powers to fight them. This may help to explain another interesting pattern: the world has experienced no great power war in the last half century. This is by far the longest period of peace between the great powers in the last five centuries of the modern era. Many scholars trace this absence of great power war to the development of nuclear weapons and their deterrent effects (Jervis, 1989), but other arguments have also been advanced (Gaddis, 1987; Kegley, 1991).

The absence of great power war for over half a century have led some to refer to this period as "the long peace" (Gaddis, 1987). This is quite misleading, since the period since World War II has witnessed a proliferation of smaller wars and other forms of armed conflict.[20] Interstate wars have continued to occur, initially at about the same rate as in the period prior to 1945 (Levy and Thompson, 2010b), though in the last two decades the frequency of interstate war has begun to decline (Hewitt, Wilkenfeld, and Gurr, 2008).

One noticeable change in interstate war, however, is where these wars are fought. We do not have a perfectly reliable database on global wars, but what evidence we have suggests that for most of the last five centuries of the modern era a disproportionate number of interstate wars were fought in Europe (Wright, 1965:641–51).[21] The global system was centered in Europe, and the world's leading powers were all located in Europe until the beginning of the twentieth century. Those great powers fought each other, expanded by fighting weaker European states, and engaged in colonial wars throughout the world. Since 1945, however, we have witnessed a dramatic shift in warfare (both interstate and civil) away from Europe to other parts of the world (Singer, 1991). The Yugoslav wars of the 1990s were the first in Europe since 1945.

Another significant trend is a significant increase in the frequency of civil wars and other forms of intrastate conflict (K. Holsti, 1996).[22] The ratio of internal to external wars increased from about two to one before 1945 to nearly five to one after 1945 (Levy and Thompson, 2010b). There was a particularly strong increase in the number of civil wars beginning in the 1970s after the period of decolonization, and civil wars continued at a relatively high frequency until the late 1990s. After that, there has been a decline in the frequency of civil wars. This pattern may be surprising given the constant images of warfare seen on the television and elsewhere, but it is well-documented (Hewitt, Wilkenfeld, and Gurr, 2008; Human Security Centre, 2005; Harbom and Sundberg, 2008). Whether this decline in civil wars and other forms of armed conflict is likely to continue is a source of considerable debate (Gleditsch, 2008).

These patterns suggest that there has been a shift in the nature of warfare over time – away from the great powers, away from Europe, and, increasingly, away from state-to-state conflict and toward civil war, insurgency, and other forms of intrastate and trans-state warfare. It is a kind of warfare that differs in many respects from the wars that have dominated the past five centuries of the modern international system. The wars of most interest to scholars have been interstate wars that were "symmetric" in the sense that the two sides were of roughly equal strength and fought with similar types of weapons. The primary actors were states that possessed a monopoly of legitimate force within their borders, a description that characterized most of the leading states of Europe by the mid-seventeenth century. This was the basis for Clausewitz's ([1832]1976) image of war as militarized conflict between state armies, directed by state leaders on behalf of state interests, and resolved by decisive battles.[23]

With the increasing shift from interstate war to civil wars, and with the changing character of civil wars themselves, scholars have begun to question whether the conventional "Westphalian" model of warfare continues to be relevant for the contemporary era.[24] Fewer and fewer wars involve conventional clashes of two opposing armies. The Russian–Georgian war of 2008 is a recent exception, though it was a highly asymmetric conflict.

Civil wars themselves have changed. Unlike the American civil war of the nineteenth century, the army of the state often faces not a single rebel army but instead a coalition of rebel soldiers representing different groups with different interests (Horowitz, 1985). Many of these central players in civil wars are ethnic or religious groups, and the wars are sometimes referred to as "ethnic wars" or "identity wars." Some question, however, whether most of these wars are primarily about ethnicity or identity, or whether ethnicity and identity mask underlying conflicts that are driven primarily by security goals, economic resources, political power, or private interest (Gagnon, 2004).[25] Warlords, aiming to protect or advance their own parochial interests, play a key role in many of these conflicts (Marten, 2006/07). Globalized criminal networks have also come to play a significant role in the funding of civil wars and insurgencies, and wars are often sustained by illicit black markets (Mueller, 2004; Andreas, 2008). Armies have increasingly "outsourced" many of their traditional functions, and in many respects wars have become more privatized (Avant, 2005).

Strategy and tactics have also changed, along with the norms of warfare. Warfare is increasingly "asymmetric." Rebel groups are often outmatched by the state in organization and military technology, and they respond by adopting strategies of guerrilla warfare, insurgency, and terrorism. Tactics increasingly include the direct targeting of civilians, and massacre and ethnic cleansing have become more common. This has led some to talk of the increasing "barbarization of warfare" (Kassimeris, 2006). Most of this behavior is purposeful, driven by the aim of persuading and coercing people to shift their political loyalties by demonstrating that the state is unable to protect its citizens. Contemporary civil wars are rarely settled by decisive battles, but instead by protracted struggles.

This is the image of the "new wars," which are often contrasted with the "old wars" of the Westphalian era (van Creveld, 1991; Kaldor, 1999;

Münkler, 2004). A major debate has emerged, however, as to whether the "new wars" are really new, or whether elements of the new wars can be found in past historical periods (Kalyvas, 2001; Duyvesteyn and Angstrom, 2005; Malešević, 2008).[26] That debate focuses more on how war is conducted than on the varied causes of war, which is our primary concern in this book, with primary attention to interstate war but with some attention to civil war, which we address in chapter 7.

The Levels-of-Analysis Framework

Any survey of the causes of war needs an organizing framework that helps to make sense of the many varied causes of war. We need a typology that groups similar causes together. One framework that many international relations theorists have found useful for the analysis of war and of foreign policy behavior is the "levels-of-analysis" framework. This framework goes back to Kenneth Waltz's book *Man, the State, and War* (1959), which identified three "images" of war. These images referred to sources of causation associated with individuals, the nation-state, and the international system, respectively. Following Singer (1961), scholars began to refer to these images as "levels" of analysis. The levels-of-analysis framework is not a theory of war but instead a typology of the causes of war. More accurately and more generally, it is a framework for classifying the different causal factors influencing the policies and actions of states and of other actors.[27]

The individual level of analysis aims to explain the foreign policy decisions made by the political leaders of the state (or other political unit). It includes characteristics shared by all individuals, such as "human nature" and its hypothesized predispositions toward aggression. The individual level also includes factors that vary across individuals, including belief systems, personalities, psychological processes, political socialization, lessons learned from history, management styles, and similar variables. The presumption of individual-level theories is that the particular individual or individuals in power have an important causal impact. The implication is that if another individual had been in power the outcome might have been different. Many interpretations of World War II, for example, focus on German Chancellor Adolf Hitler, and argue that if Hitler had not come to power the war might have been avoided (Mueller, 1989).

The national level or nation-state level of analysis includes both factors associated with the government and factors associated with society. The former include variables like the institutional structure of the political system and the nature of the policy-making process, and the latter include variables like the structure of the economic system, the influence of economic and noneconomic interest groups, the role of public opinion, and political culture and ideology. At the national level, for example, there is considerable evidence that because of democratic institutions and political cultures, democracies behave differently than authoritarian regimes with respect to war. At a minimum, democracies rarely if ever go to war with each other (Doyle, 1983). At the societal level, one hypothesis is that some political cultures are more warlike than others, although many scholars have concluded that there is not much evidence to support this argument (Wright, 1965). Diversionary theory suggests that political leaders sometimes decide on war when they anticipate that war against an external adversary will increase their domestic political support by generating a "rally round the flag" effect. Certain governmental bureaucracies may push for higher military budgets as part of a strategy to increase their power and influence within the government, or domestic economic groups may push for more aggressive foreign policies because it serves their own parochial interests. Each of these factors would be encompassed by the nation-state level of analysis.

System-level causes include the anarchic structure of the international system,[28] the number of major powers in the system, the distribution of military and economic power among them, the pattern of alliances, and other factors that are closely related to the distribution of power, including the structure of the system's political economy.[29] Most realist theories, including balance of power theory, are system-level theories, as are theories of hegemonic order and power transitions. The system level also includes other factors in the external environment common to all states, including the structure of international institutions, the nature of international norms, or system-wide ideologies or cultures.[30]

Waltz's (1959) conception of three images or levels has been extremely influential in the study of international relations and foreign policy. While many scholars adopt Waltz's three-level framework, others modify it. Following Rosenau (1966), some scholars disaggregate state (or governmental) and societal sources of causation into two separate levels. Jervis (1976: chap. 1) modifies Waltz's framework by distinguishing the levels of decision-making, the bureaucracy, the state and domestic politics, and the international environment. Others simplify Waltz's framework and identify two levels of causation, one internal to the state (which Waltz (1979) labels "unit level") and one external.[31]

There is no single "correct" number of levels. Levels-of-analysis frameworks are analytic constructions to help us make sense of the world, and they are best evaluated in terms of their theoretical utility rather than seen as a direct reflection of "reality." For the purposes of summarizing theories of the causes of war, we find it most useful to distinguish among theories that emphasize sources of causation at the system, state and societal, and decision-making levels of analysis, and to divide the latter into individual and organizational levels.[32]

We also introduce an additional level, commonly referred to as the "dyadic" or "interactional" level, which reflects the bilateral interactions between pairs of states. The past history of interactions between two states would be included in this category, as would territorial conflicts and bilateral bargaining between states. Some scholars include this factor in their system-level category, and thus define the system level broadly to include everything in a state's external environment. We find it more useful to distinguish between causal variables that reflect the entire international system (polarity, for example) and those that reflect the relationship and interactions within a particular pair of states within that system.[33] It is also useful, for certain questions, to distinguish between the international system and various regional systems nested within it. The Middle East system and the South American system have different characteristics and dynamics, though both exist within a single global system. Crisis dynamics between two states can be influenced by the structure of power in the global system, by the structure and culture of the regional system within which they interact, and by the characteristics and history of the dyad itself.

The levels-of-analysis question has important normative implications, particularly in terms of evaluating moral responsibility. If the primary causal factors leading to war or a state's decision for war arise from systemic or dyadic-level threats to the national interest, so that any reasonable state or individual in that situation would have responded in roughly the same way, we would not ordinarily attribute moral responsibility for the war to that state or its leaders. Political leaders understand this, of course, and we often hear political leaders say, whether they had a choice or not, that "I had no choice." Assessing the causal weight of various factors is an important step in evaluating blame, and differences in assessments of causality complicate efforts to attribute blame.

After World War I, for example, the victorious Western allies forced a defeated Germany to sign a "war guilt" clause in the Treaty of Versailles (1919). This may have just been victors' justice, however, as within a decade many historians began to shift to the view that the primary causes of the war were more systemic, based on the system of power politics and secret alliances (Fay, 1928) and not on the actions of particular governments or states. After Fritz Fischer's publication of *Germany's Aims in the First World War* in 1961 and the English translation six years later, and Fischer's argument that Germany's aims went beyond security to world power, opinion on responsibility for the war shifted back.[34] Political scientists are often less interested in questions of "war guilt," or moral responsibility for war, than are historians (Schroeder, 2001), but it is clear that any such evaluation rests on an empirical analysis of the causes of the war.

It would be useful to illustrate our levels-of-analysis framework with respect to various explanations that analysts have proposed to explain the

US decision to invade Iraq in 2003. Although some explanations emphasize causal variables at a single level of analysis, others combine variables from several different levels. Some argue that the US intervention was the product of President George W. Bush's worldviews and religious beliefs, his determination to finish the job begun by his father in the 1990–91 Gulf War, or Bush's confidence in the correctness of his beliefs or his disregard for information running contrary to his beliefs and policy preferences. These are all individual-level causal factors, which we discuss in chapter 5 on decision-making at the individual-level. The implication of these theoretical arguments is that if someone else besides Bush had been president, the probability of US military action would have been different.

Others attribute the US decision to the nature of the American political system and society. They emphasize the traditional US commitment to democracy and the promotion of democracy abroad, the impact of the September 11 attacks on American political culture and on public opinion (which created a permissive environment for an aggressive policy toward Iraq), the hesitancy of members of Congress to argue or vote against the war for fear of possible political repercussions,[35] and the influence of the US oil industry or perhaps of the "Israeli lobby" (Mearsheimer and Walt, 2007) on US policy. Still others focus on decision-making at the bureaucratic/organizational level, and emphasize the influence of neoconservatives on the policy-making process, the influence of Vice-President Cheney and Secretary of Defense Rumsfeld and the political marginalization of Secretary of State Colin Powell from the inner circle of decision-making, and the flaws in an intelligence process (including the "politicization of intelligence") that generated grossly misleading estimates about Iraqi weapons of mass destruction.[36]

Another set of interpretations argue that the US intervention was driven primarily by system-level threats and opportunities (at the regional as well as global level) and the calculations about the national interest related to them. They point to the George W. Bush Administration's aim to destroy what they perceived as Iraq's existing or developing weapons of mass destruction, which was the administration's primary public rationale for the war. Other system-level causes include the impact of the 9/11 terrorist attacks on Americans' perceptions of their vulnerability and on the assumed link between al Qaeda and Saddam Hussein; the aim of bringing democracy to Iraq or perhaps to the Middle East as a whole, both as an end in itself and as a means of enhancing US security by creating like-minded regimes; or the permissive conditions created by the collapse of Soviet power and the end of the Cold War over a decade earlier.

The levels-of-analysis framework is normally applied to states and to interstate relations. It can also be applied to the behavior of non-state actors, where it leads us to ask similar questions about the sources of causality. Does a particular ethnic group act the way it does because of external threats and opportunities in its environment, because of internal politics among various subgroups within it, or because of the particular beliefs and charisma of an individual leader? Similarly, are the actions of a terrorist group aimed primarily to advance the interests of the group as a whole, or are they the product of infighting between competing factions within it or of the beliefs and preferences of a particular leader?

The levels-of-analysis framework is useful for organizing the varied sources of conflict into categories that help simplify and impose some structure on the way we think about war and foreign policy more generally. Although we prefer this framework to others as an organizing device, we should acknowledge some of its limitations. Ideally, a typology should have categories that are both exclusive and exhaustive – causal factors should fit into one and only one category, and there should be some category for all causal factors. The levels-of-analysis framework (like most typologies) falls short of this ideal-type standard. The important factor of misperceptions, for example, can result from system-level uncertainty or adversary strategic deception, national-level ideologies that predispose leaders to interpret the behavior of others in certain ways, and individual-level personalities that contribute to further distortions in incoming information. Economic factors include both national economic interests such as the stability of a society's economic system and the influence of private economic groups (e.g., arms manufacturers) on state foreign policies.

We should also note that the levels-of-analysis framework is better for classifying causal variables than for classifying theories. Although some theories incorporate variables from a single level of analysis (most psychological theories, for example), most theories combine variables from multiple levels of analysis. In these cases, we classify the theory based on the level of its variable of greatest causal weight. For example, although neoclassical realist theory incorporates domestic and individual-level variables, it gives primacy to the international system, and we classify it accordingly. Multiple-level theories sometimes complicate the use of the level-of-analysis framework. At the same time, however, by distinguishing among different levels the framework is useful in identifying the different kinds of factors that operate within a particular theory and how they interact with each other in the processes leading to war and peace.

Although causal variables at any level of analysis can be used to help explain individual beliefs, state behavior, and dyadic or systemic outcomes, we need to point out a potential logical problem associated with certain types of explanations for war. One concerns individual-level explanations for war. Although analysts often trace the outbreak of a particular war to the beliefs or personalities of a single individual (Hitler and World War II, for example), that does not constitute a logically complete explanation of war.

We have defined war in terms of the behavior of political organizations, whether the state, a rebel group, or a terrorist organization. War is institutionalized, not individual. This means that to explain a state's decision to adopt a strategy of war, we need to know more than the preferences, beliefs, and personality of the leader. It is incumbent upon us to explain how the leader's preferences, along with the preferences of other decision-makers, are translated into a foreign policy decision for the state. Since war is made by states, not individuals, an individual-level theory of war has to be linked to a broader theory of foreign policy.

It might seem that in a dictatorship such additional variables might not be necessary for a complete explanation for war, but in fact the dictatorial structure of the regime is part of the explanation. The politically centralized nature of the regime helps to explain how a leader who wants war actually gets war implemented as policy.[37] In more decentralized regimes, including democratic regimes (especially parliamentary regimes), sometimes political leaders who want war are prevented from implementing that strategy by domestic constituencies or by the cabinet. Alternatively (but less frequently), political leaders who believe that war is contrary to the national interest and who prefer to avoid war are sometimes pushed into war by a xenophobic public opinion or by powerful domestic groups. US president William McKinley hoped to avoid war with Spain in 1898, but because of domestic pressures McKinley "led his country unhesitatingly toward a war which he did not want for a cause in which he did not believe" (May, 1961:189).

There is a second logical problem. War involves violence *between* political organizations. A theory of war must explain how both sides get to the brink of war in the first place and why both are willing to fight. Since war is a dyadic or system-level outcome resulting from the joint actions of two or more states, understanding the causes of war requires an explanation of the strategic interaction of the two (or more) adversaries. For this reason individual-, societal-, and state-level causal factors cannot by themselves provide a logically complete explanation for the outbreak of war. That is, they are not jointly sufficient for war. We need to include dyadic or system-level causal variables (a theory of bargaining, for example) for a complete explanation. This does not necessarily mean that dyadic and system-level variables have a greater causal influence than do individual or domestic variables, only that the former cannot be logically excluded from the analysis.

An example will help illustrate the point. Consider the hypothesis that the primary cause of a particular war is the existence of a state or political leader with particularly aggressive intentions. This hypothesis is not a logically complete explanation for war. Nazi Germany, for example, behaved quite aggressively in the mid-1930s. It violated international treaties by rearming, remilitarizing the Rhineland, annexing Austria, and demanding the incorporation into Germany of the Sudetenland. For several years, however, none of these actions led to war, because the West chose to pursue a policy of appeasement rather than stand up to Germany and thereby risk war. Many historians conclude that Hitler actually wanted war over Czechoslovakia, and was forced to abandon that goal, at least temporarily, when the West responded with enough concessions to make war politically infeasible (Taylor, 1961). War eventually came, of course, but only after the West changed course after further aggression by Hitler. A complete explanation for World War II, and for any war, requires that we not restrict the analysis to the behavior of a single individual or state.

Similarly, it is not enough to explain a peaceful outcome by showing than one side pursues a conciliatory policy. A strategy of extensive concessions often leads to a peaceful outcome, but it is also possible that it might create the image of weakness and lead the adversary to increase its demands in the hope of coercing further concessions. British and French appeasement of Hitler in the 1930s illustrates this point as well. Britain and France each sought peace, but peace was not the outcome because Hitler responded to their concessions with further aggressive moves and demands for further concessions. In fact, some argue that appeasement actually made war more likely, though that proposition makes the problematic assumption that a more confrontational policy would have deterred Hitler. Again, the broader theoretical argument is that theory of war requires a theory of bargaining or strategic interaction that explains how states respond to each other's actions and how they act in anticipation of each other's responses.

Other Conceptual Issues in the Analysis of War

Another conceptual issue relates to our earlier discussion of the changes in war over time, which reminds us that war is a variable, not a constant. War varies in terms of who fights, where they fight, how often they fight, with what intensity, and so on. Thus the primary phenomenon that most international relations scholars want to explain is variations in war and peace over time and space. Why does war occur between some states rather than other states, at some times rather than other times, under some conditions rather than other conditions, by some political leaders rather than other leaders. As Bremer (2000) asked, "Who Fights Whom, Where, When, and Why?"

The variable nature of war and peace has important but often-neglected implications for the study of war. Any theory that predicts that war is a constant must be rejected, or at least modified to include additional variables that explain variations in war. An "independent variable" that is constant cannot explain a "dependent variable" that varies.

This logic is what led Waltz (1959), in his discussion of "first image" or individual-level explanations, to reject *human nature* as a cause of war. If human nature is conceived as a set of traits or predispositions common to all people at all times, it is a constant and it cannot explain variations in war and peace. We can "unpack" human nature into a number of more specific factors, such as cognitive ability, personality, emotional makeup, propensity to take risks, etc. These factors do vary across individuals and thus can in principle explain some of the variation in war and peace. Even if this were true – and it would have to be demonstrated empirically – the source of causality would be these specific variables, not "human nature" in the aggregate.[38]

An aggregate concept of human nature might serve as a "permissive condition" for war, in the sense that it allows war to happen, but that does not tell us too much. Despite the frequent recurrence of war in human history, and the fact that somebody is at war with somebody somewhere most of the time, in fact peace is more common than war. Considering the number of dyads in the international system, most of these dyads are at peace most of the time.[39] Does human nature explain peace as well as war? Does it explain the long great power peace since World War II, or the sustained peace between the United States and Canada? The argument that human nature explains both war and peace is unsatisfactory (unless it could explain the conditions under which each outcome is likely to occur).

A central characteristic of a scientific theory is that it be "testable," in the sense that there must be some empirical evidence that would lead us to conclude that the theory is false.[40] Theories that cannot be tested have little explanatory or predictive power, and they cannot differentiate between what actually happens and what might have happened but did not.

The idea that one cannot explain variations in war and peace with a constant has other implications as well. If a factor persists over a period of time that includes periods of peace as well as periods of war, we cannot include that factor in an explanation for war without including other variables that explain when the factor contributes to peace and when it contributes to war. For example, it has become popular to explain the explosion of ethnic violence in the past two decades in terms of "ancient hatreds" between rival ethnic or religious groups. While this factor might contribute to ethnic wars, it does not provide a sufficient explanation. It does not explain why wars have broken out between some ethnic communities but not between others who also have "ancient hatreds" (Kalyvas, 2006). Nor does it explain the timing or severity of those wars. The ancient hatreds factor might serve as an underlying cause of the war, and perhaps a necessary condition for war, but it is not sufficient for war, and whether or not war occurs depends on more proximate variables or trigger causes.[41]

Consider the Bosnian wars of the 1990s. Serbs and Croats had a long-standing rivalry, but prior to the twentieth century they had fought relatively few wars. We must include additional variables to explain why they fought each other during the 1990s and not before (Gagnon, 2004; Woodward, 1995). The Iran–Iraq War (1980–88) is another example. Some explain the war by emphasizing the long-standing ethnic differences between Persians and Arabs. Yet there was relatively little armed conflict between Arabs and Persians during the previous two centuries. There was even a treaty in 1975 that settled many outstanding issues. Thus a satisfactory interpretation of the Iran–Iraq War must explain what specific factors, by themselves or in combination with the underlying ethnic rivalry, occurred after 1975 to trigger the war.[42]

The fact that many important wars are preceded by lengthy periods of peace also raises a methodological issue about how we should study war. For those who analyze individual historical cases or who compare several historical cases, it is important to examine the wars that do not occur as well as those that do occur. For one thing, as Sherlock Holmes suggested, the dogs that don't bark may reveal as much information as those that do. In addition, looking at cases with different values on the key variables is critical for any comparative methodology. If a hypothesized causal factor (ethnic differences, for example) is present in two crises that occur under very similar circumstances, and if the outcome is war in one crisis and peace in the other, then under most circumstances that factor is not a primary cause of war.[43]

Having put our study of the causes of war in context, and considered some of the conceptual problems that complicate the study of war, we turn in subsequent chapters to a review of the leading theories of the causes of war, organized by the levels-of-analysis framework outlined in this chapter. We begin with theories of interstate war, starting with a discussion of leading system-level theories and continuing with dyadic-level interactions. After examining state- and societal-level causes of war, we turn to the role of decision-making at the individual, organizational, and small-group levels. We then look at some of the leading theories of civil war. We conclude our study with reflections on the levels-of-analysis framework, causation, and war.

Notes

1. We discuss prevention and preemption in chapter 2.
2. For surveys of definitions of war see Levy (1983b:50–3) and Vasquez (1993: chap. 2). On civil wars see Sambanis (2004).
3. The Congo and Yugoslav wars each had an international component, and might be called "internationalized civil wars." Another example of an internationalized civil war was the Russian Revolution in 1917, which attracted outside intervention by the United States and other great powers.

4. The two other elements of Clausewitz's trinity are "chance and probability" (the "fog of war") and the primacy of politics. We discuss the second of these below, and the first later in the book. For interpretations of Clausewitz, see Paret (1976), Howard (1983), Aron (1985), and Strachan and Herberg-Rothe (2007). Clausewitz is sometimes compared to Sun Tzu (1963), the Chinese military theorist who wrote *The Art of War* over 2,000 years ago. Some observers regard them as history's two greatest military theorists.

5. We discuss international rivalries in chapter 3.

6. The US and the USSR each funded and equipped the military forces of other countries to fight some of their battles for them, and thus supported "proxy wars," but the organized military forces of the two superpowers did not engage each other in sustained combat.

7. For three different conceptions of the great powers, see Levy (1983b: chap. 2), Thompson (1988), and Black (2008).

8. Although Clausewitz ([1832]1976) wrote mainly about large wars, he was also intrigued by the guerrilla campaign in Spain against the French invaders during the Napoleonic Wars, and he wrote several works on small or "irregular" wars (Daase, 2007). That aspect of Clausewitz is neglected by most of his interpreters. For a useful analysis of the contemporary relevance of Clausewitz, see Strachan and Herberg-Rothe (2007).

9. Some might question whether hunting–foraging bands can be viewed as political organizations. But once they acquire group identities and some type of leadership hierarchy, these bands have a rudimentary level of political organization. Scholars debate exactly how to define "political," but one standard definition refers to politics as the authoritative allocation of resources for a society (Easton, 1953). By that definition, hunter–gatherer groups qualify.

10. On the changing nature of warfare, see Archer et al. (2002), Gat (2006), and Levy and Thompson (2010b).

11. To say that an action is purposeful does not necessarily imply that it is rational. We discuss the criteria for rationality in chapter 5 on theories of individual decision-making.

12. Military outcomes are sometimes ambiguous, leading to domestic political debates over how to interpret the outcome of the war (Johnson and Tierney, 2006). See also Martel (2007) on the meaning of victory.

13. Some use the term "brute force" to refer to the use of force to degrade an adversary's military power and potential (Schelling, 1966: chap. 1). Brute force is defined in terms of the immediate objectives of military force rather than in terms of its resulting destruction.

14. Some of the 9/11 hijackers may have had more nihilistic goals of damaging a way of life they despised, without having any specific political objectives in terms of changing US policy. Given our definition of war in terms of a violent conflict between political organizations, it is the goals of the al Qaeda leadership that count, not those of individuals whom it recruits to serve its interests.

15. By purposeful, we mean purposeful for the political organization. As we will see later in this book, war can also be purposeful for an individual leader or for an organization or group within the state, but not for the state itself.

16. For similar reasons, we prefer to avoid a legalistic definition that separates war from the use of force short of war depending on whether there is a declaration of war (for example, Wright 1965:8). Declarations of war were common for several centuries, and were consistent with the norms of the European system, but were less common in earlier historical eras and even today. None of the many American wars since 1945 have been accompanied by a formal declaration of war. Plus, declarations of war were limited to interstate wars and were not used for civil wars or other forms of organized violence.

17. Duration by itself is not an adequate criterion. Egypt and Libya had artillery exchanges for four days in 1977, while Egypt and Israel fought for six days in 1967, but only the second (the Six Day War) is treated as a war.

18. This section builds on Levy and Thompson (2010b).

19. It is important to note that the substantial increase in the number of battle-related deaths from war is not matched by a comparable trend in the relative number of deaths as a proportion of population, which is the *intensity* of war. Among all interstate wars, the intensity of war has actually declined slightly during the past five centuries (Levy, 1983b:124). The Thirty Years' War (1618–48) resulted in a decline of 15–20 percent in the population of Germany, and far more in particular German states (Parker, 1984). By this measure, the intensity of war for many wars among hunter-gatherer groups was much greater (Keeley, 1996). See Levy (1983b: chap. 3) for data and for a discussion of problems of exactly which wars to count as great power wars in the twentieth century. Note that there is a more general tendency for the frequency of wars to be inversely related to their severity (Morgan and Levy, 1990).

20. The "long great power peace" might be a more appropriate label, though this was a "cold" peace, characterized by the ongoing Cold War rivalry between the US and the USSR and the constant threat of war, rather than a stable peace (Boulding 1978; Kacowicz et al., 2000) or a "warm" peace (Miller, 2007).

21. We need to qualify this statement by noting that the identification of wars gets more and more difficult as we go back in time because of the limitations of information, especially for wars outside of Europe. Consequently, Wright's ([1942]1965) data reflects a European bias, one that is exacerbated further by the fact that the data on interstate wars were undoubtedly based on a Eurocentric conception of what constitutes a "state." As a result, Wright probably underestimates the number of non-European interstate wars and consequently overestimates the ratio of European to non-European interstate wars. In the absence of a reliable database on global wars, however, we cannot know the extent of this distortion. (But see Zhang et al. (2007:19215) and its link to the article's supplemental material, which refers to a broader database.) We suspect, however, that the bias is not great enough to affect our statement that a disproportionate number of interstate wars in the early years of the modern system (sixteenth and seventeenth centuries) were fought in Europe.

Note that these biases diminish as wars become more serious and consequently more visible. Thus our earlier statement about the increase in major battles is less affected by measurement error, and our statement about great powers wars is minimally affected by measurement error because most great powers in the modern system have been European. Other regional systems had their own great powers (Black 2008) but, unlike Europe, other regions did not have a spiral of intensive wars between multiple great powers between 1500 and 1945.

22. The traditional distinction between interstate wars and civil wars, while never perfect, is beginning to blur. The Bosnian wars of the 1990s, for example, were both civil wars within a disintegrating Yugoslavia and interstate wars between Serbia, Bosnia, and Croatia (Woodward, 1995).

23. As we noted earlier, Clausewitz also wrote about small wars.

24. The Treaty of Westphalia in 1648 formalized the sovereign state system, and the several centuries since then are often referred to as the Westphalian era.

25. These factors are not necessarily independent. Laitin (2007) and others argue that national cultural homogeneity helps produce public goods and economic growth. Leaders attempt to influence the formation of identities in order to mobilize their peoples for war and/or to enhance their own hold on political power.

26. The privatization of war, for example, is not entirely new. See Howard's (1976: chap. 2) discussion of the "wars of the mercenaries" in the sixteenth and seventeenth centuries. As to the "barbarization of warfare," one can certainly find systematic violations of the norms of war, in terms of the proper treatment of prisoners of war and of civilians, in the two World Wars of the twentieth century (Hull, 2005) and in pre-historic warfare (Gat, 2006).

27. Some scholars in other disciplines utilize similar frameworks. Hinde (1993) organizes his study of aggression and war around "levels of social complexity." The historian A.J.P. Taylor (1961) offers an interesting analogy by referring to an automobile accident. Taylor suggests that we can classify causes in terms of the individual driver, the car, or the road and other environmental conditions. The driver may have fallen asleep or been otherwise impaired. The car may have had poor brakes or other defects. Alternatively, the weather may have been poor or the road may have been treacherous.

28. International relations scholars refer to anarchy as the absence of a legitimate authority in the international system. Whereas states have governments, the legitimate authority to resolve conflicts between domestic groups and/or citizens, and a monopoly of force within its borders, there is no legitimate authority to adjudicate disputes between states or other actors in the international system. If states cannot resolve their disputes peacefully (as they usually prefer to do), they must rely on their own military forces, or those of their allies, to protect them from another state's attempt to resolve conflicts through the use of force. This is why power is regarded as so important in international politics. Anarchy and power are central to realist theories of international conflict, which we discuss in chapter 2.

29.   Closely related to the distribution of power in the system is the polarity of the system. Scholars distinguish among unipolar, bipolar, and multipolar systems, and argue that each generates a different set of strategic dynamics.
30.   Some historians, for example, trace World War I to the role of Social Darwinist ideology (Koch, 1984) or to the "unspoken assumptions" and the "mood of 1914" (Joll, 1984: chap. 8).
31.   See also Singer (1961) and Wolfers (1962: chap. 1).
32.   In chapter 6 we include a brief discussion of the "small group" level of analysis, which emphasizes the social–psychological dynamics of interaction among individuals in small decision-making units.
33.   While we use the levels-of-analysis framework to classify the causal variables influencing decisions and outcomes, some scholars use the framework in a different way. Instead of using the level of analysis to refer to the independent causal variable, they use it to refer to the unit whose policy preferences or actions are being explained, or the dependent variable. Rather than treat individual-level beliefs and policy preferences as the independent variable, they treat it as the dependent variable to be explained. In this usage the individual level refers to the beliefs or actions of individuals; the organizational level refers to the behavior of organizations; and the state level refers to state foreign policies. The dyadic level refers to patterns of interaction of two states, and the system level refers to broader patterns in the international system. Sometimes the state level is called the "monadic level."

   These two different uses of the levels of analysis have created a great deal of confusion in the field. To minimize this confusion, we use the term "level" of analysis to refer to causal variables and the term "unit" of analysis to refer to what we are trying to explain. Note that causal variables from one level can be used to explain unit behavior at another level. Thus nation-state level democratic institutions or cultures can be used to explain the preferences of individual political leaders, the behavior of organizations, the foreign policies of democratic states, and the patterns of interactions of democratic states. The only constraint is that any outcome at one level must incorporate a variable at that unit or higher level of aggregation. We explain the rationale for this later in the chapter.
34.   Albertini ([1942]1957) made a strong case for a similar argument in 1941. For a recent review of what we know and what we do not know about World War I, see Williamson and May (2007).
35.   Some Democrats who had voted against the authorization US intervention in the first Persian Gulf War in 1991 were defeated in the 1994 Congressional election.
36.   Powell was skeptical about the wisdom of the war (DeYoung, 2006). On intelligence see Pfiffner and Phythian (2008). For various interpretations, see Mann (2004), Gordon and Trainor (2006), Ricks (2006), and Haass (2009).
37.   Saddam Hussein's beliefs and personality may be central to an explanation of the origins of the 1990–91 Persian Gulf War, but only in conjunction with the highly centralized structure of the Iraqi regime that allowed Saddam Hussein to make policy in the absence of any significant internal constraints. The same argument applies to Hitler's Germany in the 1930s.

38. The concept of human nature is over-aggregated in another sense – it treats male and female as indistinguishable and neglects any possible impact of gender on the causes of war. As suggested by a book entitled *Demonic Males* (Wrangham and Peterson, 1996), perhaps males are programmed for violence through an evolutionary process. The traits that helped hunter–gathers survive and reproduce are the traits that evolved and that characterize modern man, since the hunter–gatherer period constitutes over 99% of human existence. Perhaps, but this would not explain variations in war and peace over time and space during the past 5,000 years. It might explain different proclivities toward violence in different species (Wrangham, 2006), but that is not our focus here. The relationship between gender and war (which is not identical to the relationship between gender and aggression) is an extraordinarily complex question, one that attracted interest from evolutionary theorists, primatologists, feminist theorists, and other scholars from a variety of disciplines. For a nice summary of evolutionary perspectives, see Gat (2006: Part I). For work in political science see Elshtain (1987), Cohn (1987), Tickner (2001), Goldstein (2001), and Rosen (2005).

39. Bennett and Stam (2004:204) estimate that the "base-line" frequency of interstate war per dyad per year in the international system is about 1 per 14,000.

40. On the "falsifiability" of theories, see Popper (1989) and King, Keohane, and Verba (1994). Evidence to falsify or disconfirm a theory must exist in principle, but it need not be immediately available. When Einstein developed his theory of general relativity, scientists had to wait several years until certain astronomical conditions (a solar eclipse) were present to allow the collection of evidence (about light bending around the sun) that confirmed the theory.

41. On necessary and sufficient conditions and different forms of causal explanation see Goertz and Levy (2007) and Mahoney, Kimball, and Koivu (2009).

42. One key factor was the Iranian revolution, which brought a fundamentalist Islamic regime to power and threatened the domestic security of the secular Baathist regime of Saddam Hussein in Iraq (Hiro, 1991).

43. On the methodology of "controlled comparison," see George and Bennett (2005).

2

System-Level Theories

The study of the causes of war in political science has traditionally been dominated by realist theories, which emphasize states' competition for power and security in a high-threat international environment. In this chapter we summarize some of the key concepts in realist theories of international conflict, including anarchy, the security dilemma, the spiral model, and the deterrence model. We then identify varieties of realist theories and their hypotheses about the causes of war. These theories include classical realism, neorealism, defensive realism, offensive realism, and neoclassical realism. After examining balance of power theory in greater detail, we turn to hegemonic theories of conflict, including power transition theory, hypotheses on preventive war, and long-cycle theory.

Realist Theories

The realist school of thought goes back to Thucydides' (1996) account of the Peloponnesian War between Athens and Sparta in the fifth century BCE. Realist international theories were further shaped by Machiavelli, Hobbes, Rousseau, and a number of other prominent philosophers and social theorists.[1] After the rise of idealism and an emphasis on international law after World War I, and after the failure of those efforts to prevent the aggressions of the 1930s, Morgenthau's book *Politics Among Nations*, first published in 1948, led a resurgence of realist thinking after World War II.

Realism is not a single theory but instead a constellation of theories, each of which shares a common set of assumptions but also includes some distinctive elements.[2] All realist theories emphasize that the key actors in world politics are sovereign states (or other territorially defined groups) that act rationally to advance their security, power, and wealth in an anarchic international system.[3] Realists (and most other international relations

theorists) define anarchy in structural terms as the absenc[
governmental authority to regulate disputes and enforce agr[
states or other actors.

For most realists, anarchy, in conjunction with uncer[
intentions of other states, has enormous consequences. It i[
and a continuous competition for power, which makes t[............
system inherently conflictual. Given omnipresent threats, political leaders
tend to focus on short-term security needs and adopt worst-case thinking.
They often utilize coercive threats to advance their interests, influence the
adversary, and maintain their reputations. Anarchy does not automatically
lead to war, but it creates a permissive environment for war by creating a
system of insecurity, conflicts of interest, and international rivalries. Realists
tend to have a pessimistic worldview, and they tend to be skeptical of grand
schemes for creating and maintaining a peaceful international order.[4]

Realists generally accept the core hypothesis that a primary determinant
of international outcomes, including both wars and the peaceful settlement
of crises and disputes, is the distribution of power in the international
system or within a particular dyad. As Thucydides (1996:352 [5.89])
famously said in the "Melian dialogue," "... the strong take what they can
and the weak suffer what they must." Different conceptions of power and
of the specific dynamics of power relationships, however, lead to different
realist theories and to different predictions about the results of particular
distributions of power.

Another thing that nearly all realist theorists agree upon is the view that
wars can occur both through deliberate and inadvertent processes, though
different strands of realism differ on which of these processes occurs most
often. In the first path to war, two states have a direct conflict of interests
and at least one decides that it is more likely to achieve its interests through
military force than through a negotiated settlement. The image here is one
of predatory states. Most historical conquests fit this model of deliberate,
unprovoked aggression. Hitler's initiation of a European war in 1939 is a
classic example (Weinberg, 1994), as is Iraq's invasion of Kuwait in 1990
(Freedman and Karsh, 1993). In this view, a predatory, "revisionist" state
makes a deliberate decision to initiate war to change the status quo in its
favor.

Equally important, however, is a second path to war that involves
states that are content with the status quo and that are more interested in
maintaining their current positions than in extending their influence. Such
"security-seeking" states can end up in war, often an *inadvertent war* that
neither side wants or expects at the onset of the crisis. International anarchy
induces a competition for power driven by the inherent uncertainty about
the intentions of others (Jervis, 1976: chap. 2) and by the fear that others
might engage in predatory behavior. If one's adversary is growing in strength

forming alliances, the inherent uncertainty about the adversary's intentions often leads one to conclude that the worst outcome is the failure to build up one's own power, leaving one's interests exposed if the adversary turns out to have aggressive intentions.

States may take these actions for purely defensive purposes, but adversary states often perceive these actions as threatening. Compounding this is the fact that most weapons systems can serve offensive as well as defensive functions. The result is a tendency toward worst-case analysis in the context of extreme uncertainty. The threatened state responds with measures to protect itself, and those measures are in turn perceived as threatening by the other. This can generate an action–reaction cycle and a conflict spiral that leaves all states worse off and that can sometimes escalate to war. This is the core of the *security dilemma*: actions that states take to increase their security often induce a response by adversaries and actually result in a decrease in their security (Herz, 1959; Jervis, 1978; Glaser, 1997). It is worth noting that although an inadvertent war is inadvertent in the sense that neither side wants war or expects war in the early stage of a crisis, such wars can actually begin with a deliberate step at the end of an inadvertent process (George, 1991).[5]

The security dilemma and conflict spiral are the core of the *spiral model* of war and peace (Jervis, 1976: chap. 3). These concepts are important in part because they explain how wars can occur even if states prefer peace to war and even if they behave rationally, since conflict spirals can be structurally induced by the system. Conflict spirals can also be exacerbated further by non-rational psychological processes, which we describe in chapter 5 on individual decision-making and war. Spiral theorists often point to World War I or to the 1967 Arab–Israeli War as examples of spiral dynamics that escalated to war when one side decided to take preemptive action.[6] Another good example of a conflict spiral is the process leading up to the Seven Years' War between Britain and France in North America (1756–63), which Americans know as the "French and Indian War" and which Smoke (1977: chap. 8) describes as involving "no offensive steps by any player at any time."

The spiral model is sometimes contrasted with the *deterrence model*, which suggests that wars occur when deterrence fails – when one side either lacks the military capabilities to threaten a sufficiently costly response to aggression, or when its threat lacks credibility (Jervis, 1976: chap. 3).[7] Deterrence theorists generally assume that predatory behavior is the primary path to war and minimize the importance of inadvertent processes. They adopt the adage "*si vis pacem para bellum*" (if you seek peace, prepare for war), argue that military build-ups and coercive strategies reinforce deterrence and maintain the peace, and contend that the appeasement of aggressors only encourages future aggression. Deterrence theorists often invoke the British and French attempt to appease Hitler at Munich as an example of the futility of appeasement.[8]

Spiral and deterrence theorists each argue that the policy prescriptions of the other make war more likely rather than less likely. Deterrence theorists argue that the more conciliatory policies advocated by spiral theorists increase the probability of war by undermining deterrence, and spiral theorists argue that the hardline policies advocated by spiral theorists only provoke conflict spirals and war. Each theory is flawed, however, because each makes unconditional predictions that ignore the specific contexts of a dispute or crisis. In some situations, hardline policies work to induce compliance, whereas in other situations they backfire and provoke counter-responses and escalation. The key question is the conditions under which coercive threats are effective and the conditions under which they are not (Jervis, 1976: chap. 3).

We noted earlier that realist international theory is more of a school of thought than a single theory, and that there are a number of varieties of realism. Scholars divide up realist theories in different ways, but one common distinction is between "classical" realism and "structural" realism. Structural realism is often equated with the "neorealism" of Waltz, but it also includes "defensive" realism and "offensive" realism. A fifth variation of realism, which formed in response to structural realism, is "neoclassical" realism.

Classical realism

Classical (or traditional) realists believed that there are multiple sources of state behavior and hence of the causes of war. In addition to the importance of the absence of central authority in the international system, which was central to the theories of Hobbes and to a certain extent of Rousseau (Doyle, 1997), classical realists emphasized the role of human nature as a source of aggressive behavior and war. They pointed to aggressive instincts, selfishness, greed, pride, and passion as key factors leading to human aggression. It is also important to note that classical realists were interested in explaining not only wars and other international outcomes, but also the foreign policies and grand strategies of states and the art of statecraft. This led them to develop more detailed but less "parsimonious" theories of international relations.[9]

Waltzian neorealism

As we noted in chapter 1, Waltz (1959) was very critical of the classical realist idea of attributing causality to "human nature," since a constant human nature cannot explain the obvious variations in war and peace over time and space. In a later book, Waltz (1979) argued more strongly that classical realists did not adhere to social science methodology, and that they were not interested in constructing theories and hypotheses that were mutually consistent and subject to empirical test against the empirical evidence. These considerations led Waltz (1979) to develop neorealism as an alternative realist theory.[10] His aim was to give realism a stronger social science orientation and to construct a parsimonious realist theory.

Whereas traditional realists emphasized the pursuit of power as an end in itself, Waltz (1979) emphasized the pursuit of security, with power serving as a means rather than an end. Waltz placed particular emphasis on international anarchy and the distribution of power in the system. Given the limited variation in anarchy across time and across international systems, and hence its inability to explain the enormous variation in war and peace over time and space, the distribution of power in the system, especially among the leading powers, carries most of the explanatory power in Waltzian neorealism. Waltz argued that the distribution of power has far more impact on state behaviors and international outcomes than do the internal characteristics of states or the characteristics of individual political leaders. Differently constituted states under similar configurations of power will act similarly, and similarly constituted states under different configurations of power will act differently.

Waltzian neorealism is a form of balance of power theory. Waltz (1979) posited that hegemonies rarely form in international systems and that balances of power are the norm throughout most of international history. He also argued that the anarchic and competitive nature of the international system leads most states to emulate the successful practices of other states in providing for their security. Those who are unable to provide for their security are vulnerable to conquest by others. Thus the anarchic and competitive international system socializes states and induces certain kinds of beliefs and behaviors (a "realist culture," some might say) that reinforce the nature of the system.[11]

In his analysis of the distribution of power in the system, Waltz (1979) stressed the central importance of the "polarity" of the international system, a factor that had engaged earlier realists as well.[12] Realists argue that systems of different polarity create different threats and opportunities for states and generate different foreign policy behaviors, particularly for the great powers. Realists often disagree, however, as to the specific relationship between the polarity of the system and its stability, which is defined different ways but which usually refers to a low probability of a major war in the system.

For many years the primary debate was about the relative stability of bipolar and multipolar systems.[13] Morgenthau (1967), Gulick (1955), and other classical realists, along with Deutsch and Singer (1964) and some other non-realists, generally argued that multipolar systems were more stable than bipolar systems. They argued that multipolarity created a greater number of possible coalitions that might form against any possible aggressor, thus reinforcing deterrence against aggression. In bipolarity, by contrast, the allies of the leading powers were too weak to play a significant role in balancing against an aggressor. In addition, with several strong powers in multipolarity, each was less likely to focus all of its energies on any single rival, and cross-cutting cleavages over multiple issues tended to diffuse conflicts from escalating along a single axis. In bipolar systems, on the other hand, there is a tendency toward the polarization of the alliance system around the two leading powers, increasing the risks of escalation.[14]

Waltz (1979) and most neorealists disagreed, arguing that bipolar systems are more stable than multiple systems. There is less uncertainty under bipolarity, and thus less of a risk of war through miscalculation.[15] Each adversary is clearly focused on the other, monitors its behavior, and responds appropriately. In bipolarity, one leading power has no choice but to balance against the other. Multipolarity raises "collective action" problems (Olson, 1971), since each state has incentives to "free ride" and let others pay the costs of balancing against an aggressor. As a result, balances often fail to form against aggression, which undermines deterrence.

Theoretically, each side of the debate suggests plausible arguments, which raises the empirical question of which of these effects dominates. Historical evidence on the relative stability of bipolar and multipolar systems is mixed. The multipolar system of the nineteenth century witnessed relatively few major wars, but that of the first half of the twentieth century included two world wars. The bipolarity of ancient Greece witnessed the Peloponnesian War, and the French–Habsburg bipolarity of the early sixteenth century was quite conflictual, but the bipolar Cold War period was stable (though many argue that had more to do with the deterrence effects of nuclear weapons than with bipolarity). Mearsheimer (2001a) examines a number of historical case studies and finds that "unbalanced multipolarity" is the most war-prone type of system, but statistical analyses yield no evidence that one type of system is significantly more or less war-prone than the other (Sabrosky, 1985; Bueno de Mesquita and Lalman, 1992; Bennett and Stam, 2004).

Waltzian neorealism is one of the most influential international relations theories of the last half century. It reinvigorated the realist research program and gave it a more solid social scientific grounding. The norms of the field soon required that any new theory be tested against a realist alternative. At the same time, however, Waltz's theory became a central target for criticism. One of the most basic criticisms was that the key explanatory variable, the distribution of power in the system, does not vary enough to explain the enormous variations in war and peace. Nor can neorealist theory explain fundamental changes in key structural characteristics of the international system (its polarity, for example) or in the behavior of the actors in that system.[16] Thus critics charged that neorealism could make very general predictions, but not more specific predictions, about international politics (Keohane, 1986; Buzan, Jones, and Little, 1993; Ruggie, 1998).

Waltz (1979) conceded this point to a certain extent. He acknowledged that his theory is limited to explaining international outcomes, and that it cannot explain the specific foreign policy behaviors of states or specific wars. He said that "although neorealist theory does not explain why particular wars are fought, it does explain war's dismal recurrence through the millennia" (Waltz, 1988:620). Most scholars argue that this is too limiting, and that we need a theory that explains both international outcomes and foreign policy behaviors (Elman, 1996) and the conditions under which wars are most likely. Most recent developments in realist theory can be seen as attempts to introduce additional causal variables in order to formulate a more nuanced theory (though admittedly a less parsimonious one) that explains more of the complexity of international relations. The different ways they do this has defined different variations of realist theory. In addition, contemporary realists have made a much greater effort than earlier realists to test their theories against the empirical evidence, largely through historical case studies (e.g., Walt, 1987; Mearsheimer, 2001a; Elman, 2004).[17]

Defensive realism

Defensive realists agree with neorealists that the anarchic structure of the international system creates potential security threats, but they do not believe that anarchy in itself forces states into conflict and war. If all states seek only security, and if there are no predatory states seeking expansion, and if all states know that, then states can avoid war. This raises the question of the importance of perceptions of the intentions of other states. Whereas Waltz (1979) emphasized the central importance of power and argued that states balance against the leading power in the system, defensive realists emphasize the importance of actual threats, of which intentions are an important component. Some strong powers can be benign. Following Stephen Walt's (1987) development of "balance of threat" theory, defensive realists argue that states balance against the greatest threats to their interests rather than against the strongest power in the system.

Defensive realists also depart from Waltzian realism in their conception of power. Whereas Waltz (1979) focused primarily on the overall distribution of power, defensive realists emphasize a more "fine-grained structure of power" (Van Evera, 1999). One key component of threat is geography.

The impact of military power declines over distance (the "loss of strength gradient" (Boulding, 1962:262)), and spatially distant states pose less of a threat than do proximate states. Defensive realists also emphasize the importance of technology, particularly as it affects the "offensive–defensive balance" (Jervis, 1978; Van Evera, 1999). The more technology contributes to the ease of conquest and gives an advantage to those who strike first, and the greater the proximity of strong states, the greater the threat to the security of others, the greater the competition for power and security, and the higher the probability of conflicts and war. If strong states are distant and if military technology favors the defense, however, security competition is less intense and the probability of war declines. Similarly, the probability of war is reduced if states adopt defensive doctrines and military postures. This relates to state intentions and perceptions of intentions. Through defensive doctrines states can signal their peaceful intentions to their adversaries (Jervis, 1978; Glaser, 1997; Kydd, 1997).

Of all realists, defensive realists are the most confident about the effectiveness of balance of power mechanisms in restraining aggression. This combines with other factors to limit the utility of territorial expansion except under relatively rare conditions. All of this makes defensive realists guardedly optimistic about the possibilities for cooperation under anarchy, at least under certain conditions (Jervis, 1988).

Defensive realists recognize, however, that states are sometimes aggressive, that great powers occasionally make bids for hegemony, and that war frequently occurs. To explain this, defensive realists supplement system-level structural variables with domestic variables. If states behave aggressively, it is not because of anarchy-induced systemic pressures but instead because of malevolent leaders, hostile regimes, and decision-making pathologies. Defensive realists argue that war will not arise in a world of purely security-seeking states in the absence of domestically induced revisionist goals or extreme misperceptions of external threats (Snyder, 1991; Glaser, 1997; Kydd, 1997; Van Evera, 1999).

Offensive realism

Offensive realists do not doubt the existence of predatory states and predatory leaders, but they argue that the sources of predation can be traced to the structure of the international system, the inherent uncertainty about adversary intentions, and anarchy-induced tendencies towards worst-case analysis, without invoking domestic variables. The international system is so hostile and unforgiving that uncertainty about the future intentions of the adversary combined with extreme worst-case analysis lead even status quo-oriented states to adopt offensive strategies, which often lead to war (Zakaria, 1992; Labs, 1997; Mearsheimer, 2001a; Elman, 2004). Even if the adversary has currently benign intentions, there is no guarantee that such intentions will not turn belligerent in the future, either through a change in orientation of those in power or a change in regime that brings a more hostile regime to power (Copeland, 2000). States often act aggressively because they perceive that expansion is the best way to provide for security in a competitive and uncertain world. Contrary to defensive realists, offensive realists contend that aggression sometimes pays and contributes to the accumulation of power that facilitates further aggression.[18]

Mearsheimer (2001a), for example, contends that the best way for a state to provide for its security is to achieve hegemony. He argues, however, that no state has the resources to create a truly global hegemony, especially given the difficulties of projecting power over the oceans (the "stopping power of water"). Consequently, leading states limit their aims to hegemony over their own region. In contrast to defensive realists, who argue that regional hegemony is unrealistic because of the formation of blocking coalitions, Mearsheimer and other offensive realists argue that balancing often fails. Balancing is costly, and states prefer to "pass the buck" and let others pay the costs of balancing against an aggressor. As a result, balancing coalitions are slow to form, creating opportunities for aggression. Although balancing has ultimately worked to prevent hegemony in Europe, it often arises too late to deter aggression in the first place, as illustrated by the delayed formation of a counterbalancing coalition against Nazi Germany in the 1930s.

The clearest example of a successful bid for regional hegemony, at least in the West during the past five centuries, is the United States in North America. This raises the puzzle of why the United States has been able to succeed while others have not. One answer is that the United States is unique among continental powers because it has faced no peer competitors. The absence of balancing is due to the absence of balancers, and to the fact that potential balancers in other regions, such as France in the early nineteenth century, were more preoccupied with local issues, like the struggle for hegemony in Europe (Elman, 2004).

Another point of contention is the defensive realist emphasis on the offensive–defensive balance of military technology as an important variable. Defensive realists argue that some weapons systems and some military strategies are inherently defensive, and that by carefully developing defensive military postures states can provide for their own security without threatening others. Offensive realists reject that argument. They insist that it is nearly impossible to distinguish defensive weapons from offensive weapons, since weapons systems can serve multiple purposes (Levy, 1989a; Lynn-Jones, 1995; Betts, 1999; Lieber, 2005; Mearsheimer, 2001a). They argue that it is also difficult to distinguish aggressive intentions from more defensive intentions, and that the uncertainty inherent in the system induces a tendency toward worst-case analysis towards both adversary weapons systems and intentions.[19] Thus offensive realists argue that the security dilemma cannot be diminished, and that any weapons build-up is likely to generate counter-responses and conflict spirals.

To summarize, offensive realists offer a strictly structural theory of war and peace and emphasize the role of the pursuit of power in the context of anarchy and uncertainty. Defensive realists emphasize the pursuit of security in a context in which anarchy is present but not always compelling and where technology, geography, and state strategies can mitigate the effects of anarchy. Defensive realists also depart from a strict structuralist perspective and incorporate domestic variables in an attempt to explain why wars occur. What defensive realists fail to do, however, is to offer a complete theory of exactly *how* domestic factors influence decisions for war and peace, in what kinds of states and under what conditions. During the past 10 years or so, another variation of realism has emerged, one that departs from structural realism by constructing a more complete theory of foreign policy behavior that pays more attention to domestic structures and processes. This is neoclassical realism.

Neoclassical realism

Neoclassical realists (Rose, 1998; Schweller 2006; Lobell, Ripsman, and Taliaferro, 2009) recognize the importance of anarchy, argue that material capabilities are the single most important determinant of state strategies, and give causal primacy to system structure. They emphasize, however, that there is an imperfect "transmission belt" between systemic opportunities and constraints and the foreign policy decisions of states. System-level pressures affect foreign policy choices through intervening domestic processes. Most important are political leaders' perceptions and misperceptions of the distribution of material capabilities; the autonomy of the state from society; the state's capacity to extract resources from society and to build military power, which often involves bargaining with societal actors; and the influence of domestic societal actors and interest groups on the process (Lobell, Ripsman, and Taliaferro, 2009).

Whereas structural realists and some classical realists implicitly assume that a country's human and economic resources translate directly into national power, neoclassical realists emphasize the need of state leaders to mobilize societal resources and covert them into power that can be used to support security policies of the state (Christensen, 1996; Zakaria, 1998; Schweller, 2006). The ability of state leaders to extract and mobilize societal resources varies as a function of state strength and its autonomy from society. Weak states are more divided, influenced more strongly by societal groups, less expansive in the scope of their responsibilities, and poorer.

Thus Zakaria (1998) argues that the rise of the United States to great power status in the world was delayed because of the relative weakness of its state structures relative to societal groups, resulting in a lag between the rapid expansion of American economic resources and its effective power from 1865 to 1889.[20]

This example suggests a challenge for neoclassical realist theory. Neoclassical realists emphasize that they give causal primacy to system structure and that material capabilities are the primary determinant of state strategies. It is not clear how the causal primacy argument can be reconciled with the propositions that weak state structures limit the ability of political leaders to mobilize societal resources to create effective national power, that political leaders need to bargain with social groups, and that political leaders' perceptions of military power often play an important role in the formation of state grand strategies. It is not clear where to draw the line between a neoclassical realist model that emphasizes the primacy of system structures and material capabilities – as they are perceived by domestic actors and operate through domestic processes – and an *"innenpolitik"* model that emphasizes the primacy of domestic politics (Kerr, 1965).

Since each of these realist theories emphasizes to varying degrees the centrality of the balance of power in their theories of conflict and war, we now turn to a more detailed look at balance of power theory. Before doing so, we should note that while nearly all balance theories are realist theories, not all realist theories are balance of power theories. Although "balance of power realism" is the most common form of realist thought, one can also identify a form of "hegemonic realism" (Levy, 2003b). Whereas balance of power realism posits that hegemony is rare but dangerous and that the avoidance of hegemony is the highest goal of states, hegemonic theories (realist and otherwise) posit that hegemony or hierarchy, not balance, is commonplace and in fact less war-prone than other distributions of power. After examining balance of power theories, we then turn to hegemonic theories.

Balance of Power Theory

The balance of power is one of the oldest concepts in international politics. Historians and political scientists often speak of the eighteenth and nineteenth centuries as the "golden age" of the balance of power, and they occasionally apply the concept to other historical systems and to the contemporary era as well. The concept, however, is quite ambiguous (Claude, 1962). The balance of power has been used to refer to the actual distribution of power in the international system, to a distribution of power favorable to one's own state, or to any distribution of power. That usage refers to the balance of power as an international outcome. Some scholars use the balance of power as a synonym for power politics or *realpolitik*, and thus refer to the balance of power as a state strategy. Others treat the balance of power as a theory, but those who do so disagree on what the key assumptions and propositions of balance of power theory are and on what the theory claims to explain. The different ways scholars use the term balance of power led Richard Cobden ([1903]1969) to describe it as "a chimera – an undescribed, indescribable, incomprehensible nothing."[21]

Here we treat balance of power as a theory, and use the term distribution of power to refer to the actual or desired distribution of power in the system. We do not try to summarize all of the many versions of balance of power theory, but to identify what they share in common and to specify the core propositions that all balance of power theorists would accept. This facilitates a minimal empirical test of balance of power theory. All balance of power theories share the basic core assumptions of realist theory: the system is anarchic, the key actors are territorial states (or other territorially based groups) who aim to maximize their power and/or security, and they act reasonably rationally to promote those goals.[22] Different balance of power theorists then add empirical content to these basic assumptions by suggesting additional assumptions and hypotheses. This leads to different versions of balance of power theory, some with conflicting propositions (about the relative stability of bipolar and multipolar systems, for example).

Although some balance of power theorists argue that balance of power systems have the goal of maintaining the peace (Wolfers, 1962: chap. 8; Claude, 1962:55), that view is problematic. First of all, systems do not have goals. Only actors (individuals, organizations, states) have goals. Second, balance of power theories generally posit that most states, particularly the great powers, define other goals as more important than peace and regard war as an acceptable instrument of policy to achieve those goals if other strategies fail to achieve them.

The primary aim of all states is their own survival, defined as a combination of territorial integrity and autonomy from outside rule. States also have a nested hierarchy of additional goals that are instrumental goals for survival. The most important of these is the avoidance of hegemony, a situation in which one state amasses so much power that it is able to dominate over the rest and thus put an end to the multistate system. Polybius (1960) wrote that "we should never contribute to the attainment by one state of a power so preponderant, that none dare dispute with it. ..." Vattel ([1758] wrote that, "The balance of power is an arrangement of affairs so that no State shall be in a position to have absolute mastery and dominate over others." Finally, Winston Churchill (1948: 207) stated that, "For four hundred years the foreign policy of England has been to oppose the strongest, most aggressive most dominating Power on the Continent. ..."

Other state goals are instrumental to the prevention of hegemony. One is maintaining the independence of other states in the system, or at least the independence of the other great powers, which facilitates the formation of balancing coalitions against potential aggressors. Another is maintaining an approximately equal distribution of power in the system, defined in terms of some combination of individual state capabilities and the aggregation of state capabilities in coalitions. This also facilitates the formation of a number of possible blocking coalitions if one state grows too strong.

Peace is also an important goal of states. It usually advances security, prosperity, social welfare, justice, and a range of other goals. In balance of power theory, however, the goal of peace is conditional on the avoidance of hegemony and perhaps the achievement of other instrumental goals. If those goals are threatened, states are often willing to go to war if necessary to secure their interests.

Balance of power theorists specify two general strategies that states can adopt in their efforts to prevent hegemonies from forming. Waltz (1979) distinguishes between "external balancing" and "internal balancing." The former involves the formation of counterbalancing alliances in order to block the expansion of an aggressor or to deter a potential aggressor from initiating aggressive policies.[23] Internal balancing is the internal mobilization of military power and a build-up of the economic and industrial foundations of military strength.

Balance of power theorists are far from agreement on which strategies states adopt under what conditions, though many argue that external balancing is often the preferred strategy in multipolar systems, in part because for many states alliances are cheaper than the mobilization of men, money, and materials (Barnett and Levy, 1991). Internal balancing is generally preferred in bipolar systems, since there are no other states to serve as potential allies. Although some have argued that states tend to adopt one strategy or another, there is little evidence of the "substitutabilty" of arms and alliances (Most and Starr, 1987; Palmer and Morgan, 2006), and these strategies can be mutually reinforcing. The pre-World War I period was characterized by both coalition formation (the Triple Entente and the Triple Alliance) and by arms races on land and on sea (Kennedy, 1982; Stevenson, 1996). In the Cold War, the United States balanced against the Soviet Union both by forming the NATO alliance and also by building up its own military capabilities.

It is useful to recall that balance of power theory is a theory of system-level outcomes. Sometimes scholars confuse balance of power theory with the *power parity hypothesis*, which predicts that an equality of power between two states is more likely than a preponderance of power to lead to peace. The power parity hypothesis is a dyadic-level hypothesis that assumes that alliances play no role, while balance of power theory is a systemic-level theory in which alliances are central. A finding at one level does not always hold at the other level.

In fact, most quantitative studies of the relationship between the dyadic distribution of power and war/peace demonstrate that a preponderance of power is more likely than an equality of power to be associated with peace (Kugler and Lemke, 1996; Bennett and Stam, 2004). This is the *power preponderance hypothesis*. The logic is that under preponderance the strong are satisfied and do not have the incentives for war, and the weak, though dissatisfied, lack the capability for war. Evidence that parity is conducive to war at the dyadic level does not logically imply that an equality of power is conducive to war at the system level.

Balance of power theorists also argue about the impact of alliances on war and peace. Some argue that alliances deter war by increasing the probability of balancing against an aggressor (Gulick, 1955:61), while others argue that alliances generate counter-alliances that sometimes lead to conflict spirals and war.[24] In terms of overall tendencies, there is some evidence that alliances on average tend to increase the probability of war (Senese and Vasquez, 2008). Indeed, alliances have historically often been followed by war. That does not necessarily mean, however, that alliances cause war. An alternative interpretation for the correlation between alliances and war is that alliances form when states anticipate that war is likely, so that underlying conditions are the cause both of alliance formation and the outbreak of war, with alliances themselves having little causal impact (Levy, 1989b).[25]

Despite their many disagreements, most balance of power theorists make some common predictions. Two propositions in particular stand out. (1) If any state threatens to gain a position of hegemony over the system that would enable it to dominate over others, a balancing coalition of other states will form against it. As a result, (2) hegemonies rarely if ever form in world politics. The first is a proposition about state strategies, and the second is a proposition about international outcomes (Levy, 2003a).

With regard to the first, balance of power theorists point to the balancing coalitions that formed against a succession of states that grew so strong that they threatened to dominate Europe: Spain under Philip II in the sixteenth century, France under Louis XIV in the seventeenth century, France under Napoleon at the beginning of the nineteenth century, and Germany under the Kaiser and then under Hitler in the twentieth century. Each led to a "hegemonic war" involving most of the great powers in the system and lasting many years.

The above-mentioned propositions and examples all refer to threats of hegemony over the system and to "counter-hegemonic balancing" by great powers in response. Balance of power theorists are divided over the question of balancing against other kinds of threats. Most classical realists and neorealists argue that states balance against the strongest power in the system, without explicitly specifying whether or not there is a threat of hegemony; defensive realists argue that states balance against the greatest threat (but not necessarily a hegemonic threat); and offensive realists emphasize balancing against power but argue that balancing often breaks down. Few theorize about the balancing behavior of weaker states vis-à-vis stronger powers. Given the vulnerability of weaker states, particularly those sharing borders with stronger states, and given their lesser impact on outcomes, weaker states are likely to join the strongest coalition.

One thing all balance of power theorists agree upon, however, is that great powers generally balance against hegemonic threats. Offensive realists, who argue that states balance against the strongest power, and defensive realists, who argue that states balance against the strongest threat, both reach this conclusion. Only the strongest power in the system can threaten hegemony, and the threat of hegemony is almost always the strongest threat to other states, certainly to other great powers. In fact, there is systematic statistical evidence that great powers usually balance against a leading state that is strong enough to threaten hegemony but not against a leading state that has lesser margins of advantage, at least for the last five centuries of the European system (Levy and Thompson, 2005).

At this point in the discussion of balance of power theory and the absence of hegemony, some readers will be thinking "what about the United States today?" The relative economic and military power of the United States is historically unprecedented,[26] yet no great power balancing coalition has formed against it. This is a puzzle for many scholars, who argue that balance of power theory predicts balancing in such situations (Zakaria 2001; Ikenberry 2002:3; Walt, 2005).

Realists disagree on how to explain the absence of absence of "hard balancing" against the United States, defined as the formation of formal military alliances or substantial increases in military spending, but their explanations can be grouped into five categories.[27] Some argue that balancing will still occur and argue that it is just a matter of time before it does (Waltz, 2000; Layne, 2006). A second group argues that states, and particularly the great powers, have not balanced against the United States because they recognize that the US has benign intentions and does not pose a threat to the vital interests of other states.[28] They claim that the US differs from the dominant powers of the past because it has no interest in territorial conquest, in part because of its geographical isolation from other leading powers (Pape 2005a; Paul, 2005a; Walt, 2005).

Brooks and Wohlforth (2008:35) offer a third explanation: that balance of power theory predicts balancing against an aspiring hegemon but not against a state that has already achieved a hegemonic position, and that consequently the theory does not apply to the United States in the period following end of the Cold War. They trace the absence of balancing to the enormous material capabilities of the United States, both military and economic, which make it too dangerous to balance against the US.

Mearsheimer (2001a) advances a fourth explanation. He argues that states that have achieved regional hegemony (global hegemony being out of reach) attempt to prevent the rise of peer competitors in other regions by playing the role of an "offshore balancer."[29] Weaker states in these other regions are more worried about threats to their interests emanating from within their region than from outside the region, and hence do not generally see the offshore balancer as the primary threat to their interests. These considerations lead Mearsheimer (2001b:49) to conclude that "Offshore balancers do not provoke balancing coalitions against themselves." The United States plays the role of an offshore balancer in other regions, and hence does not provoke balancing coalitions.[30]

Levy and Thompson (2005, 2010a) offer an alternative interpretation for the absence of great power balancing against the US, one that overlaps with Mearsheimer's (2001a) view but that (we think) goes beyond it. The failure of a balancing coalition to form against the United States does not contradict balance of power theory because the theory, as it has been developed in the West over the last three centuries, has generally been applied to land-based continental systems but not to maritime systems. Dominant land powers with large armies are far more threatening to other leading states than are dominant sea powers with large navies, and consequently great power coalitions tend to form against the former but not against the latter.[31] Just as other great powers rarely balanced against Britain at the peak of its global power in the nineteenth century, or against the Dutch when they were the leading global power in the late seventeenth century, great powers do not balance against the United States in the contemporary system.[32] Thus the absence of balancing is not a puzzle for balance of power theory.[33]

While some argue that balance of power theory works well in explaining the dynamics of past international systems but not the contemporary system, others argue that the theory fails in earlier periods as well. They argue that an alternative theory, based on the idea that hierarchy and hegemony are more common than balance, more accurately captures the strategic dynamics both of the contemporary world and the world of the past. To these we now turn.

Hegemonic Theories

Whereas balance of power theories posit that states fear hegemony, that they balance against any state threatening hegemony, and that counter-hegemonic balancing makes hegemony rare and great power war common, hegemonic theories argue that strong concentrations of power in the hands of a single power in the international system are historically common and stabilizing. Hegemonic theories share realist assumptions about the primacy of rational and unitary states and their primary concern with power, but they de-emphasize the importance of anarchy while emphasizing the leading state's management of the system within a hierarchical order.

Power transition theory

Organski (1958) was the first modern scholar to advance a hegemonic theory (though he avoided the term hegemon). Organski believed that balance of power theory was too static, too narrowly focused on military power, and inattentive to the sources of changes in relative power. He argued that international systems are frequently dominated by a single powerful state that uses its strength to create a set of political and economic structures and norms of behavior that enhance both the security of the lead state and the stability of the system as a whole. Some other states are satisfied with the existing order, ally with the leading state, and receive economic and security benefits from doing so. Other states are dissatisfied, but they are usually too weak to challenge the dominant state.

In this dynamic theory, differential rates of growth, based largely on different rates of industrialization, lead to the rise and fall of states (Organski and Kugler, 1980).[34] The most dangerous and war-prone situation is one in which a state that is rising and dissatisfied with the status quo begins to approach the strength of the leading state in the system and threatens to surpass it in power. The rising challenger has a motivation to overturn the existing order, which was set up by the dominant state when it was at the peak of its power and which serves the interests of the dominant state and its allies. Power transition theorists argue that the challenger initiates a war in order to accelerate the power transition and bring its benefits from the system into line with its rising military power (Organski and Kugler, 1980; Kugler and Lemke, 1996, 2000; Tammen et al., 2000). Thus the three key conditions for war in power transition theory are power shifts, approximate equality of power, and dissatisfaction with the status quo. War is unlikely to occur before the challenger approaches the strength of the leading state (operationally defined as 80 percent of the strength of the leader) and after it has surpassed the former leader (by 20 percent).

Unlike balance of power theorists, who focus primarily on military power, power transition theorists define power as the product of population, economic productivity, and the political capacity of the state to mobilize the resources of society to support its international policies.[35] A state's power follows an S-shaped growth curve. Power grows rapidly during industrialization and then levels off to a more modest but sustained growth. This growth of power is irreversible, and consequently power transitions are unavoidable. The only question is whether the transformation of the international order is peaceful or violent.

Many attempts to explain power dynamics in the contemporary world, even by scholars who do not define themselves as power transition theorists, adopt many key elements of the theory. Many scholars writing about the causes and consequences of unipolarity, for example, argue that American hegemony contributes to stability in the contemporary world, although there is disagreement as to how long American hegemony will last. Posen (2003) and Brooks and Wohlforth (2008) each argue that American hegemony is fairly stable, while Layne (2006) argues that the current unipolar system is transitory and that differential rates of growth will eventually lead to the rise of new leading powers, with destabilizing consequences for the international system.[36]

Power transition theory is also the basis of many arguments about the rise of China and its consequences for the international system. In particular, many fear the consequences of the continued rise of Chinese power and the dangers of a Sino–American conflict as the point of power transition approaches. Based on contemporary growth rates, that point was estimated to occur in about three decades, though it is not clear how that prediction will be affected by the global economic crisis that began in 2008. Scholars debate the ability of the Chinese economy to sustain its recent growth rate and whether its political system will be conducive to the kinds of technological innovation that are necessary for a lead economy (Rapkin and Thompson, 2003). Thus the likelihood and timing of a future Sino–American transition are more uncertain than power transition theorists imply.

One theme of power transition theory that many find useful, however, is that the key variable determining the peaceful or violent nature of any transition is the extent to which China will be satisfied or dissatisfied with the international system during and after the power transition. Many argue that the more China is engaged in an interdependent world economy, the more satisfied it will be with the current international system, and the lower the probability of a militarized Sino–American conflict over Taiwan or some other issue. Less useful, however, is the argument by power transition theorists that nuclear weapons have no deterrent effect on conflict. Most theorists argue that nuclear deterrence was a central stabilizing feature of the Cold War (Jervis, 1989) and that nuclear weapons will also significantly reduce (though not eliminate) the danger of a Sino–American war in the future.

Let us return to the question of the *timing* of war during a power transition. Power transition theorists have not reached a consensus on this important question. Organski (1958) initially argued that the rising power initiates a war before the point of transition, for the purpose of accelerating the transition. Organski and Kugler's (1980) empirical analysis suggested that the war was likely to occur after the point of transition, but Kugler and Lemke (2000) question that finding.[37] A more recent formulation of power transition theory (Tammen, et al., 2000) suggests instead that the challenger initiates a war after the point of transition.

The hypothesized timing of the war has important theoretical implications and requires further research. Organski's argument that the rising state initiates a war before a power transition is problematic because at that point the rising power is weaker and it is likely to lose any war. It would make more sense for it to wait and initiate the war when it is stronger and more likely to win, as Tammen et al. (2000) argue. But if that were the case, why would the declining state wait for challenger to increase in strength and fight on the challenger's terms? Why wouldn't the declining state initiate a war to defeat its rising challenger while the opportunity is still available?

Such a war is often referred to as a *preventive war*, a concept familiar to historians and to balance of power theorists. A preventive war is motivated by the perception of a rising adversary, a shift in power, and by the fear that once the adversary is stronger it will attempt to exploit its advantage through coercion or war (Van Evera, 1999; Copeland, 2000; Levy, 2008a), and is driven by "better-now-than-later" logic. Faced with a rising adversary, especially a potentially hostile one, a state may be tempted to fight now, when it is stronger, rather than later, when conditions are less favorable. The danger of waiting, however, is not just the risk of a future war. States fear a decline in bargaining leverage associated with their relative decline in power. If the adversary makes greater demands once it is stronger – and most realists argue that state interests expand with the relative power of the state – the question is the extent of the concessions the declining state would have to make in the future in order to avoid the unwanted war.

It is important to emphasize that strategies of prevention are different than strategies of preemption. Preemption involves a military attack in response to the virtual certainty that the adversary is about to strike and by the motivation of gaining the advantages of striking first. Prevention is motivated not by the anticipation of an imminent attack, but instead by the anticipation of an adverse power shift over the next few years and the fear of its consequences. Israel launched a preemptive strike against Egypt to begin the 1967 war and a preventive strike against Iraqi nuclear facilities in 1981.[38]

Historians and political scientists have identified numerous cases in which power shifts and better-now-than-later logic have led to war. When Thucydides (1996:16) argued that the "real cause" of the Peloponnesian War was "the growth of the power of Athens and the alarm which this caused in Sparta," he was invoking preventive logic. The historian A.J.P.

Taylor (1954:166) claimed that, "Every war between Great Powers [in the 1848–1918 period] started as a preventive war, not a war of conquest." Scholars have given particular attention to the role of the preventive motivation in the outbreak of World War I. The argument is that German leaders, recognizing the rising power of Russia and the likelihood any war with Russia would invoke the Franco–Russian alliance, and fearing that by 1917 Germany could not longer be confident of winning such a war, acted preventively to fight before its relative power continued to slide (Levy, 1990/91; Van Evera, 1999; Copeland, 2000; Stevenson, 2004).

Perhaps the clearest example of a preventively motivated attack is the Israeli strike against the Iraqi nuclear reactor in 1981. Israel was driven by the fear that Iraq was on the way to acquiring a nuclear capability that would enormously increase its ability to damage or coerce Israel (Nakdimon, 1987).[39] Similarly, the fear of many in the second Bush Administration that Iraq was about to cross the nuclear threshold was one important factor leading to the US-led war in Iraq in 2003. Although the causes of the war are quite complex, the preventive motivation was the main rationale the administration used to help mobilize American public opinion in support of the war (Rich, 2006; Levy, 2008a).[40]

Although impending shifts in relative power sometimes lead to war through preventive logic, more often such power shifts do not lead to war.[41] The United States surpassed Britain as a global power at the beginning of the twentieth century, but the transition was peaceful. Few states have grown in power as rapidly as Nazi Germany in the 1930s, but Britain and France responded with a strategy of appeasement rather than preventive war (Ripsman and Levy, 2007, 2008). This raises the critical question of the conditions under which adverse power shifts (and perceptions of such) do and do not lead declining states to adopt preventive war strategies. This is a major task for scholars interested in the question of preventive war strategies.

We now return to power transition theory's hypothesis that strong concentrations of power in the international system (or in a dyad) inhibit war. Balance of power theory posits that hegemony rarely occurs and that concentrations of power are destabilizing, while power transition theory posits that hegemony frequently occurs and is stabilizing. The two theories therefore appear to be diametrically opposed. One can argue, however, that these theories are more "incommensurable" (Kuhn, 1962) than contradictory, in the sense that they provide different answers to slightly different questions than different answers to the same question. Balance of power theory and power transition theory are each theories of power dynamics within international systems, but they focus on different systems and different kinds of power (Rasler and Thompson, 1994; Levy, 2003a; Levy and Thompson, 2005).

Most balance of power theories implicitly conceive of power in terms of land-based military power, and their examples of hegemonic threats and balancing are generally based on the European experience, where high concentrations of power often triggered balancing coalitions and major wars. Applications of power transition theory, on the other hand, tend to focus on the global system and define power in terms of wealth and other forms of economic dominance (though it is worth noting that Lemke (2001) applies power transition theory to regional systems). Their standard indicator of power, for example, is gross national product (Kugler and Lemke, 1996, 2000). They predict that concentrations of power and wealth in the global system are stabilizing, while power transitions in that system are destabilizing. The same is true for other hegemonic theories. Most versions of "hegemonic stability theory" (Keohane, 1984), for example, are theories of the stability of the international political economy and say little about war and peace.

Since they focus on different systems and on different bases of power in the system, balance of power theory and power transition theory could each be correct within its own domain. It is conceivable, for example, that the European system has been most stable under an equilibrium of military power and that hegemonies rarely if ever form in that system, whereas the global system is most stable in the presence of a single dominant economic and naval power (which occurs frequently). The most destabilizing situation would be one characterized by the combination of the diffusion of power at the global level (to the point of an impending global power transition) and an increasing concentration of power in Europe (Rasler and Thompson, 1994).

Several of history's "hegemonic wars" fit this pattern. The two world wars of the twentieth century (1914–18 and 1939–45) occurred as Britain's global dominance was rapidly waning while Germany's power on the European continent was rapidly increasing. The French Revolutionary and Napoleonic Wars (1792–1815) occurred after an earlier eclipse of Britain's global power while France was growing on the Continent. These patterns are predicted by long-cycle theory, to which we now turn.

Long-cycle theory

Long-cycle theory, as developed by Modelski and his colleagues, was not designed for the primary purpose of explaining warfare. It is a theory about the emergence of global leadership or management of trans-regional interactions such as trade.[42] Global war does, however, have a prominent place in the theory because it has been a mechanism for consolidating new leadership over the last 500 years. Global wars – which have been fought in 1494–1516, 1588–1608, 1688–1713, 1792–1815, and 1914–1945 – are lengthy periods of crisis and conflict, generally lasting between 20 and 30 years, that draw in most the major powers of the era on opposing sides. One side defeats the other and ushers in a new period of global system leadership. These periods of intensive combat serve as selection devices for leadership in the global system, with the leading state in the victorious alliance ascending to a position that facilitates developing new rules and policies for global transactions.

To explain the infrequent but increasingly intensive global wars (Rasler and Thompson, 1994, 2000b; Modelski and Thompson, 1996), the theory relies primarily on two structural dynamics: regional–global dissychronization and the "twin peaks" model. An important distinction is first made between global and regional politics. Global politics are about managing long-distance commerce, especially after the 1490s, while regional politics center around attempts to create and stave off continental hegemonies. Over the past 500 years, the elite states in the world system have tended to give greater priority to one or the other of these two types of activity. Sea powers have specialized in intercontinental trade and, later, industry, while land powers, particularly those based in Europe, have focused on territorial expansion in the home region. The dissynchronization element is that deconcentration of resources and leadership in the global system encourages concentration of power in the regional system and vice versa. Thus, European land powers have tended to be at their strongest when global sea powers have been at their weakest.

Territorial expansion in Europe threatens leading global powers either directly or indirectly, depending largely on the location of the global powers in question and how much insulation they possess from land attacks. For instance, Portugal (sixteenth century) and the Netherlands (seventeenth century) were adjacent to expanding Spain and France, respectively. Britain (eighteenth and early twentieth centuries) and the United States (late twentieth century) enjoyed some maritime insulation from French, German, and Soviet attack. Regardless of the insulation, the threat of hegemonic expansion in Europe galvanizes the leading sea powers into organizing a coalition of land and sea powers to thwart the threat and into rebuilding the capabilities of global powers to withstand expansionary attack.

The "twin peaks" model refers to the assertions that long-term economic growth is discontinuous. It comes in spurts, tends to be monopolized initially by a single state from the global power ranks, and is most evidently manifested in commercial (prior to the late eighteenth century) and industrial "leading sectors" that, once introduced, tend to radically change the way the world economy works. The economy that pioneers the innovation of these leading sectors is rewarded by a predominant position in global politics because it possesses the system's strongest economy and technology and is able to develop great wealth as a consequence.

Each of these lead economies experiences at least two growth spurts. The first one destabilizes the pecking order of the world economy but also generates the resources needed to finance the suppression of the threat of regional expansion (as in Western Europe between 1494 and 1945). Victory in global war exhausts the opposition but tends to be beneficial to the relative position of the leading global power. Resources are highly concentrated in the global sphere of activities immediately post-global war and highly deconcentrated in the primary region. Conditions are right for a second growth spurt in the post-war era. But this state of affairs is highly transitional. The leading global power's relative position tends to decay. New (and sometimes old) regional challengers and global rivals emerge with the passage of time. The structural combination of global decline and regional ascents tend to re-create the potential for global war – a war fought to determine who will make post-war rules and policy in global politics.

Balance of power theory, power transition theory, and long-cycle theory are clearly system-level theories that emphasize the importance of the overall structure of the international system for state behaviors and international outcomes.[43] The same is true for offensive and defensive realism, though the latter introduces a dyadic component by focusing on the intentions and proximity of the adversary, and in the end it invokes domestic causal variables to help explain variations in war and peace. Other realist theories are more difficult to classify. Classical and neoclassical realism each incorporate individual-, state-, and societal-level factors, though neoclassical realists insist that the system level is still primary. Each is as interested in explaining state strategies as well as international outcomes like wars. The spiral model and deterrence model focus primarily on the interactions between pairs of states and consequently are more properly seen as dyadic-level theories, but we introduced them in this chapter because they are central to structural realist theories of war and peace. There are other theories of war and peace that focus primarily on the dyadic-level interactions of states, though sometimes within a systemic context. We turn to those theories in the next chapter.

Notes

1. On the realist tradition in international politics, see Doyle (1997) and Haslam (2002). For alternative interpretations of the Peloponnesian War, see Lebow (2001) and Kagan (2003).
2. Realism is a label, not a fact. To call a theory "realist" does not necessarily imply that it is a "realistic" theory in the sense that it accurately describes and explains international behavior. That must be determined by theoretical and empirical investigation.

3. This is a conventional view of realism, but particular realist theories loosen some of these assumptions. Some realists downplay the importance of anarchy and emphasize the hierarchical nature of the international order within a nominally anarchic system, as we will see in our analysis of "hegemonic theories" later in this chapter. Many contemporary realists who study civil war have relaxed the state-centric assumption by applying the concept of the ethnic security dilemma to intrastate communal conflicts (Posen, 1993; Snyder and Jervis, 1999).

4. For good summaries and assessments of realist theory see James (1995), Keohane (1986a), Gilpin (1986), Brooks (1997), Jervis (1998), Van Evera (1999), and Walt (2002). For a summary of early philosophical theories of the conditions conducive to a peaceful international order, see Hinsley (1967: part I).

5. The inadvertent war concept also applies to some civil wars. This is reflected in the view of the American Civil War advanced by Abraham Lincoln in his Second Inaugural Address (March 4, 1865): "All dreaded it, all sought to avert it ... And the war came."

6. Views of World War I are changing, and many historians and political scientists now emphasize Germany's deliberate drive for Continental or world power (Fischer, 1967, 1974; Levy, 1990/91; Copeland, 2000). For a summary of changing interpretations of World War I, see Mombauer (2002). For alternative interpretations of the 1967 Arab–Israeli War, see Stein (1991), Oren (2002), and Segev (2007). On the puzzle that preemptive strikes are relatively rare, see Reiter (1995).

7. The spiral model and deterrence model might be better classified at the dyadic–interactional level, since the key variables are the interactions between two states rather than the properties of the international system as a whole. These concepts are central to realist theories, however, and they are best discussed here.

8. This assumes that a strong stand by Britain and France would have led to a conciliatory response by Hitler and to peace. Most historians question this counterfactual assumption (Murray, 1984).

9. The parsimony of a theory is best conceived in relational terms. One theory is more parsimonious than another if it explains the same empirical phenomena but with fewer theoretical assumptions, or explains more with the same number of assumptions. The parsimony criterion calls for "explaining more with less." Scholars disagree on the importance of parsimony compared with other criteria for evaluating theories. For an alternative conception of parsimony, one based on the idea that the world is simple, see King, Keohane, and Verba (1994).

10. Neorealism is sometimes called "structural realism," but other scholars have constructed alternative versions of structural realism (Buzan, Jones, and Little, 1993).

11. On realist cultures, see Johnston (1995) and Wendt (1999). See also Vasquez (1993). For an argument about how belief change can lead to systems change, see Schroeder (1994).

12. If power is concentrated in the hands of a single state in an international system, the system is unipolar. If two states of roughly comparable capability

stand far above the rest, the system is bipolar. If power is more widely distributed, the system is multipolar. The nineteenth century European system was multipolar; the Cold War period (1945–89) was bipolar; and the contemporary system of American dominance is unipolar.

13. Until the end of the Cold War and the American dominance, Waltz and other realists gave relatively little attention to unipolarity. They drew largely on the European experience of the past several centuries, which had not witnessed unipolarity.

14. Here we distinguish between polarity, or the number of major centers of power, and polarization, which refers to the clustering of alliance patterns around those centers of power (Rapkin and Thompson, with Christopherson, 1979).

15. The implication here is that uncertainty is destabilizing, while proponents of multipolarity suggest that uncertainty is stabilizing, since uncertainty about coalition formation to oppose aggression helps to deter aggression. This suggests that risk propensity and hence responses to uncertainty are key variables intervening between polarity and war-proneness (Bueno de Mesquita, 2003). We return to risk propensity in chapter 5.

16. Thus many criticize realist theory for its failure to predict the end of the Cold War, the collapse of the Soviet Union, and the transformation from bipolarity to unipolarity (English, 2000). A leading historian (Gaddis, 1992/93) makes the same criticism of international relations theory as a whole. For a realist explanation of the end of the Cold War, see Wohlforth (1994/95).

17. The introduction of additional causal variables to explain the enormous variation in war, peace, and other aspects of international politics has led some critics to argue that realism is a "degenerative research program" in the sense that the additional variables simply patch up theoretical and empirical inconsistencies in existing theory without adding new explanatory power (Vasquez, 1997). For debates on this issue, see Vasquez and Elman (2003). On the concept of "degenerative" and "progressive" research programs see Lakatos (1970). Another line of criticism is that neorealist theory remains a narrowly materialist theory that neglects important cultural variables (Wendt, 1999).

18. While some have argued that territorial conquest became less and less useful in an era of industrial economies and mass politics (Knorr, 1966), Liberman (1996) presents evidence to the contrary for German expansion in the 1930s.

19. Even an immobile fort might facilitate a state's offensive actions by reducing the costs to the state of a counter-offensive by the adversary. For perspectives on "offense–defense theory," see Brown et al. (2004). In the Cold War the United States started to build an anti-ballistic missile system designed to intercept incoming Soviet missiles. Many Americans saw this as a purely defensive weapons system. To the Soviet Union, however, it was an offensive security threat because it created the possibility that an effective missile defense might eliminate the Soviet retaliatory threat and therefore undermine Soviet deterrence against a US first strike.

20. As we discuss in a later chapter, state weakness is seen as a major cause of civil wars because it denies states a monopoly of violence, undercuts a state's ability to satisfy the needs of its people, and creates an opportunity for rebel groups.

21. For useful treatments of the balance of power, see Gulick (1955), Claude (1962), Morgenthau (1967), Bull (1977), Waltz (1979), Sheehan (1996), Paul, Wirtz, and Fortmann (2004), and Little (2007). Our interpretation draws on Levy (2003a).

22. There are important exceptions. Hegemonic realists like Gilpin (1981) give little weight to anarchy. Morgenthau (1967) and Waltz (1979) each reject the rationality assumption, but for different reasons.

23. External balancing includes other strategies as well, such territorial compensations or partitioning states for the purposes of redistributing power and satisfying grievances. It can also include military intervention or preventive war (Gulick, 1955).

24. Alliances also increase the likelihood that if war occurs it will spread to include additional actors (Vasquez, 1993).

25. Whereas balance of power theorists emphasize the "capability aggregation" function of alliances, Schroeder ([1976]2004) and Pressman (2008) each argue that states use alliances to restrain their allies. This suggests an additional possible path between alliances and war or peace. Alliance norms (Kegley and Raymond, 1990) may also be important.

26. For data, see Brooks and Wohlforth (2008: chap. 2). Posen (2003) emphasizes the United States' "command of the commons" – air, sea, land, and space. Each argues that US dominance will persist for many years.

27. True, American dominance has led to various forms of resistance to and non-cooperation with the United States, as illustrated by the lack of support by leading European states for the American invasion of Iraq in 2003. Such behavior is often referred to as "soft balancing" (Paul, 2005a; Pape, 2005a). Soft balancing is important, but does not fit into the same category as "hard" balancing behavior. For critiques of the concept of soft balancing, see Lieber and Alexander (2005) and Brooks and Wohlforth (2008: chap. 3).

28. The emphasis on intentions reflects a defensive realist view.

29. Britain historically played this role with respect to the continental European system.

30. The US intervention in Iraq in 2003 goes beyond an offshore balancing role.

31. The most widely invoked examples of counter-hegemonic balancing, as noted above, are all against land powers: Spain in the sixteenth century, France in the seventeenth century and late eighteenth century, and Germany in the twentieth century.

32. This hypothesis about land powers and sea powers explains why other great powers in the late 1940s balanced against the Soviet Union, the leading continental power in Eurasia, and not against the United States, the leading global power. It may be true that over time Europe has become less central in global politics, but on the other hand there is little doubt that the future of Germany was the central issue in the Cold War (Trachtenberg, 1999).

33. Levy and Thompson's (2005, 2010a) broader argument is that the European system upon which balance of power theory is based may not be representative of all international systems, and that hypotheses based on the European experience are not automatically transferable to other historical systems. This point is reinforced by the fact that although a sustained hegemony has not formed in Europe for at least 1,500 years, hegemonies have been more common in

non-Western historical systems (Hui, 2004; Kaufman, Little, and Wohlforth, 2007).

34. There are other closely related theories. Gilpin's (1981) "hegemonic transition theory" focuses on the rise and fall of the leading states in the system and their consequence for war and peace. Gilpin's important theoretical contribution did not lead to a sustained research program because it was followed by few empirical studies to test the theory. Doran's (1991) "power cycle theory" developed the argument that states go through a power cycle of rise and decline and that they are more prone to warfare at some stages of the power cycle than at others. Kennedy's (1987) historical treatment of the rise and fall of the great powers during the last five centuries included concepts of "imperial overstretch," relative decline, and the rise and fall of great powers. Long-cycle theory also emphasizes the rise and fall of states, and we discuss it below. For more liberal conceptions of hegemonic order, see Ikenberry (2000) and Lake (2009).

35. One could imagine a power transition theory that gave primary emphasis to military power, but theorists associated with the power transition research program have chosen not to do so.

36. For analyses of the dynamics of the contemporary unipolar system under American primacy, see Ikenberry, Mastanduno, and Wohlforth (2009) and other articles in the January 2009 issue of *World Politics*.

37. In critiques from outside the power transition research program, Thompson (1983:110–11) found wars before transitions and Kadera (2001) generated mixed findings. See also DiCicco and Levy (2003:137–44).

38. Note that prevention as defined here differs from strategies designed to avert war or humanitarian disasters, such as "preventive diplomacy," "preventive deployment," and "preventive intervention."

39. In the 1981 case, the result was not war because Iraq did not respond militarily, in part because it was already involved in a war with Iran. Any future Israeli strike against Iran to interrupt its apparent development of a nuclear program would reflect a strategy of preventive war.

40. The Bush Administration probably referred to its actions as "preemptive" because preemptive attacks in response to imminent threats are easier to justify in international law than are preventive strikes in response to future threats, since the latter but not the former provide some time for the target to implement alternative strategies in response to the threat. On the ethical and legal dimensions of preemption and prevention, see Doyle (2008).

41. For statistical evidence, see Lemke (2003).

42. Goldstein (1988) also proposes a long-cycle theory based on changes in the global political economy, but he gives less attention to system management within a hierarchical order.

43. For a summary of additional system-level theories and evidence on war, see Rasler and Thompson (forthcoming).

3

The Dyadic Interactions of States

Although structural realist theories dominated the study of war in political science for many years, scholars gradually became more and more skeptical as to whether system-level theories, and realist theories in particular, provided a sufficiently complete explanation for war. They questioned whether system structures could explain enough of the variance in war, peace, and other international behaviors and outcomes. That disillusionment has led in several directions, including a growing interest in dyadic-level theories focusing primarily on the interactions of pairs of states rather than on broader system-level structures and patterns. The interest in dyadic-level theories derived in part from the success of theories of the democratic peace in uncovering some very strong empirical regularities (the near-absence of war between democratic states) that had previously been neglected. The hope was that by focusing on dyads rather than on the system as a whole, researchers might uncover additional patterns that had previously been obscured. Quantitative researchers were also encouraged by the success of early work at the dyadic level that used regime type, territorial conflicts, and the dyadic balance of power to explain the frequency of war between pairs of states (Bremer, 1992; Bennett and Stam, 2004). Contributing further to interest in dyadic-level phenomena was some new work on international rivalries. This work emphasized the impact of the history of the interactions between pairs of states on their evolving relationships, and introduced a new dynamic element in the study of international interactions.

There are many dyadic-level theories, just as there are many system-level theories, and we cannot survey them all here. Among the most important are theories of international rivalry, the "steps-to-war" model, the bargaining theory of war, and theories of economic interdependence and peace. None of these is exclusively dyadic in character, but each places primary emphasis on causal variables relating to the interactions of pairs of states. We consider each in turn.[1]

International Rivalries

The explicit study of rivalries is a fairly recent phenomenon to emerge as a distinctive approach to war causation.[2] Although scholars have often made distinctions among different types of wars – as in the difference between general wars involving all of the great powers and wars between small powers – the modal assumption in war studies is to assume that, other things being equal, all states have some similar propensity to go to war. Of course, there are some obvious caveats on the "other things being equal" modifier. States that cannot reach each other are certainly less likely to fight. Paraguay and Burkina-Faso are two examples. Assuming they had some reason to become involved in a conflict, neither state has the capability to project armed force across the Atlantic that a war would require. But since they are unlikely to have much contact with each other in the first place, they are also not too likely to have conflicting interests. Thus, proximity, or lack thereof, can be significant.

Another reasonable caveat is that very weak states do not usually take on very strong states. Readers will quickly think of exceptions to this rule (for example, Vietnam and the United States in the 1960s and 1970s), but that is the point – there are exceptions to what is a norm. We could make the situation even more extreme by matching states that lack an army (Iceland, Costa Rica) with states that have large armies and forecast fairly safely that states without armies are unlikely to attack states with armies. Relative capability, therefore, normally makes some difference.

Two of the main reasons for examining rivalries are similar to the observations immediately above. First, the historical pattern of warfare is such that, at any given point in time, most states in the international system are not involved in war, and many have never participated in interstate warfare. In contrast, there is a relatively small group of states that go to war and often do so repetitively with the same opponents. Although Israel has never fought Cambodia or Peru, it has gone to war repeatedly against Egypt and Syria. The tendency toward warfare recidivism is the first tip-off that we might not want to assume that all states are equally likely to fight with one another.

A second tip-off is that states do not gear their diplomatic networks, security preparations, and intelligence activities to cover all possible opponents. Instead, they tend to operate with a prioritized schedule of which states are most likely to represent threats and focus a disproportionate amount of attention on these enemies. Alliances are constructed to contain or deal with these threats. NATO and the Warsaw Pact, for instance, were not designed to cope with future unidentified threats. They were aimed at each other. War and military contingency plans are often modeled on fighting the specific states that are thought to be the most likely opponents in a future war. That is one of the reasons major power military forces have problems shifting orientations from fighting conventional wars in, say, Europe, to fighting unconventional wars in Asia or the Middle East. They train to fight the armed forces of other most-threatening, major powers and then find that their doctrines and tactics do not work well against other types of foes. Intelligence agencies have similar problems. In the Cold War, the CIA and KGB were fixated on the Soviet Union and the United States, respectively. When required to focus on other problems and antagonists, they had problems making the switch.[3]

If states prioritize their security environment and focus selectively on the states that appear to represent the greatest threat, it is conceivable that this type of information can also be useful for explaining which states are most likely to go to war with one another. Rivals are states that foreign policy decision-makers single out as most likely antagonists. Rivalries can last for decades. They persist in part because states have conflicting interests that go unresolved. Rivals wish to occupy the same territory, control the same markets, or monopolize overlapping positions of influence. Once rivalries are underway, it may not matter much that some of the contested objectives are no longer in conflict. Intense rivals will find new sources of conflict as time goes by.

Not surprisingly, then, rivals are found to be involved in a disproportionate number of wars – ranging from roughly 50 to 75 percent of all warfare of the past two centuries – depending on how one defines rivalry. There are two main approaches to identifying which states are involved in rivalries. One school of thought (see, for example, Diehl and Goertz, 2000; Klein, Goertz, and Diehl, 2006), which looks at "enduring rivalries," thinks that the most objective approach is to focus upon conflict patterns. When states are involved in multiple militarized disputes within a designated period of time, the density of conflict will identify which states should be regarded as rivals. A problem, however, is that not all rivalries are constantly engaged in militarized conflict, and are so only rarely. Another problem is that some states are in nearly constant conflict but the capability asymmetries that are involved make it difficult for one or both sides to treat the other seriously as a source of intense threat, as compared with, say, a persistent nuisance. If US troops are sent on missions to Haiti with some frequency, does it mean that Haiti and the United States are rivals?

These problems led a second school of thought (Thompson, 2001a; Colaresi, Rasler, and Thompson, 2007) to look at "strategic rivalries" and argue that rivals should be identified by examining foreign policy histories and attempting to discern who decision-makers regarded as their most threatening enemies. This school also stipulates that rivals should regard each other as competitors. This usually means that the antagonists possess similar capabilities. Again, there are exceptions. States sometimes promote weaker states to rival status just as weaker states sometimes behave as if they were not weak states. The US–Cuban relationship represents both situations. The United States initially bestowed a great deal of threat potential on Cuba, in part because Cuba conducted foreign policy and military activities in the Caribbean, Latin America, and sub-Saharan Africa that were not appreciated by US decision-makers. Yet the rivalry limps on long after Cuban foreign policy activity subsided.

The fact that a disproportionate number of wars involve international rivals reinforces the idea that a focus on repetitive war behavior and processes of rivalry that lead to war could be profitable explanatory paths. Information on rivalries can therefore help separate some of the chaff from the wheat of intensive conflict participation. Yet there is more that can be gained by looking at rivalry as a conflict process. Rather than assume, for instance, that every dispute, crisis or war is an event with no relevant history, we can examine whether the outcomes of earlier confrontations have some impact on subsequent interactions. This is all the more the case if two rivals engage in a long series of confrontations. Empirical findings do suggest that (a) earlier disputes make later disputes more probable, and (b) the greater the number of disputes or crises between rivals, the greater the probability that any subsequent dispute or crisis between them will escalate to war (Leng, 1983; Hensel, 1994; Colaresi and Thompson, 2002). What this means is that any specific conflict usually has a history and that history influences how serial conflict plays out.

There may be several different processes at work (Leng, 2000). The state that secures the most concessions in a dispute often attributes its success to a hardline negotiating strategy, and repeats the strategy in the next dispute. The state that perceives itself to be the loser in a dispute often attributes its failure to weak negotiating strategy, so it adopts a more hardline strategy in the next dispute. The increasingly hardline bargaining strategies in the numerous crises leading to World War I are a good example. On the other hand, the scare of the Cuban missile crisis (1962) induced greater caution in both the United States and the Soviet Union (though the USSR undertook a major military build-up). Whatever the mix, the probability of conflict escalation in the next confrontation is to some degree a consequence of the history of previous interactions. If we ignore the history of a rivalry, therefore, we are apt to misinterpret not only what is happening in the present, but also what is likely to happen in the immediate future. Certainly political leaders of adversarial states do not ignore their past interactions.

There is also evidence that rivalries make a variety of international processes – territorial disputes, arms races, opportunities to divert populations from domestic problems – more dangerous (Huth, 1996a). Disputes, preparedness competitions, and diversionary targets seem to work differently if rivals are involved than if they are not.[4] This process is probably very similar to conflict escalation processes. If the antagonist is a hated and mistrusted rival of longstanding hostility, decision-makers try harder not to be bested in disputes and competitions. If one wishes to divert a mass public from domestic problems, emphasizing the threats from a rival works much better than if the target is a state with little history of hostility towards one's own state.

Another reason why we might want to know more about rivalries involves the question of historical dynamics in a different way. Given time and rivalry maturation, there is a good possibility that the issues that intense rivals fight about become less important than the fact of their rivalry. The alchemy of rivalry works in such a way that objects of limited value can become important symbols of which side is moving ahead or falling behind. Rivalries also become weighted down with mutual suspicion and mistrust that make attempts at accommodation become perceived as something sinister. As a consequence, rivalries are generally quite difficult to terminate.

Rivalries can also have impacts on domestic processes that make external conflict more probable.[5] Decision-makers, to maintain their political positions, must be concerned about the appearance of a rival getting ahead or somehow beating them in international competition. The security of their jobs may well depend on how their manner of dealing with the international competition is perceived (Colaresi, 2004). The process of participating in a rivalry is also likely to have repercussions on other domestic political processes. One argument (Thies, 2004) is that states that participate in rivalry improve their state infrastructure by expanding their ability to collect taxes and build up the state's financial foundation.[6] But it may be that other rivalry byproducts – for instance, increased military expenditures and negative tradeoffs with economic growth – may prove to be more significant. If so, weaker states engaged in rivalry may be more likely to remain weak states. Whether that makes them more or less likely to engage in warfare remains to be seen.[7]

Rivalry analysis remains promising, which may be another way of saying that the promise of this particular analytical approach has not yet been delivered in full. There is no question that rivals exist and predominate in war activity. We have good reason and strong empirical evidence that the existence of rivalry contributes to conflict escalation. We know less about precisely how rivalry processes contribute to heightened probabilities of war outbreaks. Do they affect all wars similarly, or do different types of rivalries influence wars through different paths?[8] We also know much less about how rivalries begin, how they evolve over time, and how they end.[9] Thus, the jury remains out on just how far information about rivalry relationships can take us in explaining the causes of war.[10]

The "Steps-to-War" Model

The theories we have examined so far all emphasize the central role of power and security as state motivations. One thing that is striking about so many of these theories is that they say so little about the specific issues over which states fight. Thirty years ago, Mansbach and Vasquez (1981) developed an "issues" paradigm that gave more emphasis to the issues of contention between states than to the power relationships between them. This framework did not have an immediate impact, but international relations scholars started to pay more attention to issues when quantitative empirical research began to show that there was a much stronger tendency to fight over some kinds of issues – and territorial issues in particular – than over other kinds of issues (Huth, 2000; Hensel, 2000).

Meanwhile, Vasquez (1993) was developing a model of war that combined territoriality with some other variables traditionally associated with realist theory (including alliances, arms races, and rivalries), along with domestic divisions between hardliners and accommodationists. He then collaborated with Senese to more fully develop and test a "steps-to-war" model. Senese and Vasquez (2008) acknowledged that there are many paths to war, and many kinds of war, but they focused their attention on delineating a closely related set of paths to war that involve a series of steps between states that are roughly equal in power. They were less interested in asymmetrical conflicts between stronger and weaker states, which they assumed follow a different dynamic.[11]

Whereas structural realists focus on anarchy and the struggle for power, Senese and Vasquez (2008) gave more attention to the resolution of disputes about issues. Disputes commonly arise. The primary factors determining war and peace are the foreign policy practices or strategies adopted by states to deal with their disputes. These strategies are adopted as a series of steps in a conflict sequence. Senese and Vasquez (2008) analyzed the impact of each of these steps on the probability of war.

The initial step involves the occurrence of an interstate dispute.[12] The most commonly used frameworks for classifying different kinds of disputes are those that focus on disputes about *territory*, about the kinds of *policy* the adversary is pursuing, and about the adversary's *regime type*. Senese and Vasquez (2008) build on recent empirical research and show that disputes about territory are more likely to escalate to war than are disputes about the specific policies the adversary is pursuing or about the nature of the adversary's regime type (democratic or authoritarian, for example).[13]

This line of argument is slightly different than the plausible proposition, backed by substantial evidence (Bremer, 1992), that contiguous states sharing borders are more likely to go to war than are non-contiguous states. Senese and Vasquez (2008) demonstrate that contiguity may increase the likelihood of a dispute occurring between two states, but that, once a dispute occurs, whether or not that dispute is likely to escalate to war depends primarily on whether it is about territory and on the kinds of foreign policy practices states adopt. Most territorial disputes do not escalate to war, but those that do are the ones in which states adopt *realpolitik* strategies, including coercive threats, military build-ups, and alliances. That is, the strategies that many realists prescribe for states to provide for their security in fact make war more rather than less likely. Senese and Vasquez refer to this as the "realist road to war."[14]

We have seen this path to war before, of course, in the form of the spiral model. The steps-to-war model is more specific, however, about the particular behavioral patterns that are likely to increase the probability of war. Paths to war are triggered by an issue dispute, with territorial disputes being the most war prone. Although most territorial disputes can be resolved by diplomacy, those disputes are more likely to escalate if states adopt realist strategies. The formation of alliances and military build-ups are key elements of the process. If states have been involved in a rivalry, war is more likely still. What is important is not the particular sequence of these steps to war, but rather the fact that they are mutually reinforcing.

Senese and Vasquez (2008) provide an impressive array of statistical evidence to support their steps-to-war theory. They show that each "step" increases the probability of war, and that the process is cumulative. First, the occurrence of a dispute between two states increases the probability of war, with territorial disputes having the greatest impact. A territorial dispute also increases the probability of another territorial dispute. If one of the states in the dispute responds by forming an alliance with another state, the probability of war increases, especially if there is already a territorial dispute.[15] If the adversary responds with a counter-alliance, the probability of war increases further still. A build-up of armaments that leads to an arms race increases the probability of war even more.[16] If the dispute occurs between two states that have been engaged in a rivalry, the probability of war is still greater. Crises tend to generate subsequent crises (Leng, 1983, 2000).[17] The impact of each step on the probability of war is cumulative, so that the combination of two or more steps makes the relationship even more war-prone. Whether the order of the steps makes a difference is an interesting question but one that remains to be investigated.

The evidence provides particularly strong support for the steps-to-war model for the period between 1816 and 1945 (from the end of the Napoleonic Wars to the end of World War II). Although the Cold War period is not fully consistent with the model, the period since 1989 fits the model reasonably well. This leads Senese and Vasquez (2008) to conclude that the fundamental nature of international politics did not change with either the advent of nuclear weapons or the emergence of American hegemony.

The steps-to-war model is an important contribution to our understanding of the causes of interstate war. Scholars have conducted earlier work on the impact of alliances, arms races, rivalries, and other factors on war, but they usually treated these factors individually. Senese and Vasquez (2008) provide a more systematic treatment that demonstrates the cumulative and interactive effects of these variables in the processes leading to war. Their emphasis on the role of disputes over issues, their demonstration that territorial disputes are more likely to escalate to war than are other types of issues (but usually only if combined with the other factors mentioned above), and their conception of one key path to war as involving a series of steps, each of which increases the probability of war, constitute an important advance in the study of the causes of war.

Senese and Vasquez (2008), like many others, argue that realism is not just an explanatory theory that attempts to explain why states behave the way they do, but also a normative or prescriptive theory that suggests to political leaders how they *ought* to behave in order to advance their interests. One of the main points of their book is that these policy prescriptions become part of a set of foreign policy practices or culture that itself makes war more likely. This is why they call it the "realist road to war" and why they regard realist practices as a proximate cause of war. Senese and Vasquez argue, however, that there are alternative ways of dealing with disputes that are more likely to promote peace. That is, there are alternative strategies to power politics or *realpolitik*.

Although Senese and Vasquez (2008) provide substantial evidence that realist practices like coercive threats, alliance, and arms races contribute to war, we think that their description of realist theories is misleading in one important respect. In particular, they strongly imply that *all* realists believe that realist practices help to safeguard the peace. This is true of some realists but not of others. It is true that many realists adopt some version of the deterrence model, and argue that coercive strategies help to promote peace and security.[18] Many other realists, however, believe that under some conditions there is a tradeoff between peace and security. Their policy prescriptions are not aimed at maximizing peace but instead at maximizing security. They recognize that under some conditions realist strategies end up in war, but they see that as a tragic outcome induced by the structure of the international system.

This is particularly true of offensive realists, who recognize that under many conditions *realpolitik* strategies can sometimes lead to war, but who argue that the failure to adopt those strategies would leave those states even worse off (Mearsheimer, 2001a).[19] It is not the strategies themselves that increase the probability of war, but the international structures, along with the uncertainty induced by those structures, that create the incentives to adopt realist strategies. If the adversary builds up its arms or forms an alliance, the threatened state has little choice but to respond with its own arms build-up or counter-alliance. The alternative is to leave the adversary in a stronger position and able to make even more coercive threats. Both adversaries would be better off pursuing more conciliatory strategies, but neither trusts the other to follow through on its agreements, and each fears being exploited more than it fears escalation. Conflict spirals are undesirable, but they are preferred to unilateral advances by the other side. By failing to differentiate among different varieties of realist theories, Senese and Vasquez attribute to all realists views that are shared only by some.

Senese and Vasquez (2008) also differ from realists in a more fundamental philosophical way. Whereas most realists have a pessimistic view about the possibilities of avoiding interstate war and other forms of intergroup violence, Senese and Vasquez are much more optimistic about that possibility. Contrary to the structural realist (and particularly offensive realist) argument that *realpolitik* strategies are induced by the anarchic structure of the international system and uncertainty about the intentions of adversaries, Senese and Vasquez argue that those strategies constitute learned behavior that is passed on from one generation to the next and that becomes part of a realist strategic culture.[20] Since those strategies are learned, they can be unlearned. Political leaders can adopt other strategies that are less war-prone, and the impact of war on the human condition can be reduced.[21] Structural realists, on the other hand, argue that such strategies flow naturally from the structure of the system and are difficult to change.

The "Bargaining Model of War"

In the last chapter we noted the argument, shared by some classical and neoclassical realists as well as by non-realists, that Waltzian neorealism and other structural realist theories cannot explain enough of the variance in war and peace over time and space. This critique focuses primarily on the empirical deficiencies of structural realist models. Another line of argument grows out of game-theoretic models of economic and social behavior (Schelling, 1960; Morrow, 1994). Such models posit that human behavior is both rational and strategic, in that actors make decisions based not only on their own preferences and the constraints under which they operate, but also on their anticipations of how other states are likely to behave.[22]

Rationalists focus on the interactions between actors. They attempt to explain all behavior in terms of the preferences of actors, their beliefs about others and the world, the structure of the system that imposes constraints on their actions and those of the adversary, and the information that is available. Rationalists (and some other scholars as well) argue that realist theories linking the distribution of power at the systemic or dyadic levels to the likelihood of war are theoretically incomplete because they fail to specify the causal mechanism that leads from system structure to war or peace. The bargaining theory of war provides such a link between micro motivations and macro processes and outcomes.

The bargaining theory of war begins with the obvious point that war is costly. War and other forms of violent conflict are inefficient ways to resolve conflicts because they destroy resources that might be distributed among adversaries. In principle, there must be some negotiated settlement short of war that is mutually preferred to fighting. This argument, long familiar to economists, entered the international relations literature with Blainey's (1988: chap. 8) argument that disagreements about relative power are the central cause of war. If adversaries have similar expectations about the likely outcome of war, they should be able to reach a negotiated settlement based on those shared expectations about how war will end.

The assumption is that the military and political outcome of the war shapes the bargaining leverage of each side and thus the kind of settlement they would be able to negotiate. A settlement based on the likely outcome of war is preferred to actual war because the settlement would give each adversary the same outcome it would expect to get from war without having to pay the economic and human costs of fighting. If either side expected that it could gain more by war than by negotiation, however, it would choose war. Since the primary determinant of the outcome of war is the relative power of two states, the question is whether states agree on their relative power. Blainey went on to argue that the course of fighting clarifies the nature of relative power, which leads to a convergence of expectations about the consequences of additional fighting, and which facilitates a settlement that terminates the war. For Blainey, the termination of war is shaped by the same factors that determine the outbreak of war.

Blainey's (1988) argument was a powerful one, though it had some limitations. Though Blainey used the fact that war is costly as a point of departure for his model, he did not incorporate the magnitude of those costs into the analysis. Nor did he incorporate the importance of the issues that are being contested, and hence the value of the stakes to each of the actors. In Blainey's model, the outbreak of war (and its termination as well) is determined only by disagreements about relative power. Actors' expected costs of fighting or evaluations of the stakes of the issues involved do not affect their calculations.

Thus Blainey's argument, while based on an important insight, was in some respects theoretically incomplete. Rational choice theorists in political science (Fearon, 1995; Powell, 2002; Wagner, 2000) took Blainey's basic idea, expanded on it, and developed it into a logically consistent theory of war. The theory has come to be known as the "bargaining model of war." Scholars have applied it to the outbreak of war, the conduct of war, the termination of war, and a variety of other important questions in the study of conflict. It applies to wars between ethnic groups (Cetinyan, 2002) and between other types of actors as well as to wars between states.

Fearon (1995) began with the puzzle of why war occurs despite the fact that it is so costly, and thus an inefficient means of resolving disputes between states. He argues that any theory of the causes of war must answer the question of what prevents actors from reaching a negotiated settlement that spares each the costs and risks of war. Fearon acknowledged that psychological variables might provide one answer, and that the personalities or cognitive or emotional biases of political leaders might lead them to choose war over a negotiated settlement. He also acknowledged that leaders' domestic political interests might also explain a choice of war over a negotiated settlement.[23]

Putting aside these paths to war, Fearon (1995) focused on unitary rational actors (that is, on actors with a single set of homogeneous interests that they try to maximize) and asked how they might end up in war despite the costs and inefficiency of war as a mechanism for conflict resolution. He made some very basic assumptions and then used the analytic techniques of game theory to prove that when these assumptions hold there is always a set of negotiated settlements that both sides prefer to war. Fearon demonstrated that there are only three sets of conditions under which two rational unitary actors could end up in war with each other: private information and incentives to misrepresent that information, commitment problems, and indivisible issues. Fearon demonstrated that if none of these conditions is present, there must be a "bargaining space" of outcomes that are mutually preferred to war.

The *private information* mechanism builds on Blainey's (1988) argument that disagreements about relative power, and hence about the likely outcome of war, are a central cause of war. Whereas Blainey (1988) traced these disagreements to psychologically driven (and hence non-rationalist) misperceptions, Fearon (1995) emphasized the more general concept of private information along with incentives to misrepresent that information. If one side has information that the other side does not about factors that might affect the outcome of the war – about its military capabilities, new weapons systems, military strategies, the intentions of its allies to provide military or economic support, its own resolve (and those of its citizens) to fight a lengthy and costly war if necessary, etc. – then the two sides' estimates of the likely outcome of the war will differ. If the difference is substantial relative to the expected costs of war, the informed actor is likely to make greater demands or grant fewer concessions than the other side is willing to accept, and war is likely.

True, actors could avoid the risks of war through the private information mechanism by revealing their private information, which would lead to shared information and therefore shared expectations about the outcome of war. The problem is that states have incentives not to reveal private information about military capabilities, doctrines, strategies, or other considerations that might affect the outcome of war and consequently their relative bargaining power.

If a state recognizes that it is actually weaker than the adversary believes, it has no incentives to undercut its bargaining power by revealing its weaknesses. If a state is actually stronger than others perceive, it fears that revealing specific information would give the adversary the incentives and the opportunity to take countermeasures – building up arms, mobilizing, securing an ally, or changing its military strategy. Such countermeasures would presumably reduce the military advantages of the first actor, decrease its chances of victory, and impose additional costs regardless of the military outcome, each of which would reduce the bargaining leverage of the first actor. Revealing information might also create the temptation for the adversary to initiate a preemptive attack in the hope that the first-mover advantage might compensate for its military disadvantages. Thus states generally have incentives not to reveal private information, which narrows the bargaining space of mutually agreeable outcomes and increases the probability of war.[24]

The private information argument has been applied to the conduct and termination of war as well as to the outbreak of war. Rational choice theorists have developed Blainey's argument that the process of fighting a war reveals information about the relative military strength and resolve of the two sides and hence about the likely outcome of war, contributes to a convergence of expectations about the consequences of future fighting, and thus increase the likelihood of a negotiated settlement (Wagner, 2000). This central idea is the core of rationalist theories of war termination (Goemans, 2000; Slantchev, 2003).[25]

A second causal mechanism that might lead two rational actors to fight a costly war involves the *commitment problem* (Fearon, 1995; Wagner, 2000, 2007; Powell, 1999, 2006), which can operate even in the presence of complete information. If the relative distribution of power between two states is shifting (more accurately, if one or both states perceive that relative power is likely to shift in the future), expectations of shifts of power may make it difficult to reach a settlement that is mutually preferred to war.

Consider a situation in which the power of one actor is growing and expected to surpass the power of its adversary. Even if information about military capabilities is public rather than private, so that both sides have shared expectations about the likely outcome of a war and that neither expects to gain more from war than from a negotiated settlement, it may be difficult for the two states to reach a settlement that avoids a costly war. The state that is weaker but growing has incentives to reach a settlement,

because it is likely to lose any war fought now. In add
it will be in a better position to fight (or to get what it w
ing) in the future. The state in relative decline, however, .
about whether a negotiated settlement would last. Th
knows that if power shifts as expected in the adversary's fav
the adversary would then have incentives to initiate a new s
ask for additional concessions, and resort to force if those cc
not granted.

Even if the adversary wants to settle now, and even if it promises to honor the present settlement, how can the declining actor be confident that the adversary will honor that agreement after underlying conditions have changed and once the adversary has the coercive power to extract greater concessions and the military power to enforce those concessions? In the absence of a legitimate and reliable authority external to the two states with the power to enforce any agreement, there is no way an adversary that is increasing in power can commit itself to a settlement based on the existing balance of power. This is the commitment problem. The only concessions that would work to satisfy the declining power are those that would restrict the growth of the rising power, but the latter is not likely to find that acceptable. This narrows the bargaining space and increases the probability of war.

The third rationalist mechanism leading to war involves *indivisible issues* (Fearon, 1995). Any settlement that is mutually preferable to war must be based on a compromise that reflects shared expectations of the likely outcome of war and hence the distribution of power between two states. Such a settlement requires a proportionate division of the stakes in dispute, which may require that those issues are infinitely divisible. If issues are not divisible, such a proportionate division of the issues in conflict may not be possible. Material goods are often divisible, since actors can accept less than the whole. Territory is sometimes divisible, though peoples are often reluctant to part with territory that has historically been part of the nation. But issues of principle, including many religious issues, are often not easily divisible. Scholars often refer to the status of Jerusalem as an example of an indivisible issue. As Israeli Foreign Minister Tzipi Livni once said, criticizing actions by some to "theologize" the Arab–Israeli conflict, "I cannot solve a religious strife ... but I can solve a conflict between nations."

On the other hand, even if a particular issue is indivisible it may nevertheless be possible to construct a mutually agreeable settlement if the issue in question is linked to another issue (Morgan, 1994) or if one side makes "side payments" to another. In addition, the source of indivisible issues is often domestic in nature (uncompromising religious parties, for example), which moves the problem out of the domain of bargaining between rational and unitary actors. For these reasons, Fearon downplays the importance of

..civisibility of issues and emphasizes the role of private information ...nd incentives to misrepresent that information) and commitment problems in impeding negotiated settlements and contributing to war.[26]

The logic of private information and the commitment problem is inherent in many of the theories of war discussed above. It parallels, but in a more sophisticated and formalized way, the realist argument about the difficulties of cooperation under anarchy, given uncertainties about the future intentions of the adversary and the logic of the security dilemma. Fearon's (1995) formulation of the commitment problem is particularly relevant to theories of power transition and preventive war strategies, because it helps to explain the difficulty that rising and declining states have in finding a mutually agreeable negotiated settlement that avoids war, even if there is no private information about military capabilities. The very fact that the declining state knows that the rising adversary would probably be able to demand concessions later and back its threats with its then-superior military capabilities – regardless of any promises the adversary makes now – reduces the incentives for the declining state to accept any concessions the adversary offers now (Levy, 2008a). This is why negotiated settlements are so difficult under conditions of shifting power.

These rationalist paths to war apply as much to conflict between small states and to civil wars as they do to traditional interstate wars. The ethnic security dilemma (Posen, 1993a) is based on uncertainties about other ethnic groups' current and future intentions, and information-based models based on rational responses to asymmetric information are now common in the literature on civil war (Fearon and Laitin, 1996, 2003; Snyder and Jervis, 1999; Rose, 2000). A leading explanation of ethnic conflict emphasizes the impact of changes in the relative power of communal groups (whether driven by demographic change, the differential impact of globalization on different regions, or by other variables) on the likelihood of conflict or cooperation, and these arguments are often framed explicitly in terms of commitment problems (Fearon, 1998). If one demographic group is growing considerably faster than another, power sharing agreements that make sense at one point in time might not be politically stable once the demographic balance has shifted. Lebanon is a good example.

The bargaining model of war has been very influential among international relations scholars. It emphasizes that a good explanation of the causes of war requires a good answer to the question of "why can't they settle?" We must remember, however, that the three rationalist paths to war are not the only answers to this question. As Fearon acknowledged, psychological or domestic political factors can also explain why states end up in war despite the fact that negotiated settlements were feasible that would have left all actors better off than they were with war (Tarar, 2006). In addition, psychological or domestic factors might also help to explain the existence of private information or indivisible issues. One state's strategic assessment of the strength of another might be influenced by psychological biases, bureaucratic impediments to information processing, cultural distortions, and other domestic factors. As Fearon noted, issues are often indivisible only because of the role of domestic publics.

It is also worth noting that one of the assumptions underlying Fearon's model is that actors are risk neutral or risk averse but not risk acceptant.[27] If actors are risk acceptant, they might prefer to gamble on war rather than take a negotiated settlement based on *ex ante* assessments of relative power and expectations of the likely outcome of war. They would be less deterred by the costs of war. As we discuss in our later chapter on individual decision-making, some theories in social psychology (and prospect theory in particular) suggest that actors tend to be risk acceptant when all of the likely outcomes are undesirable. They are willing to take risks to eliminate losses, even at some risk of incurring even greater losses.

The previous chapter and most of this chapter have focused on theories that emphasize the primacy of the security goals of states. One of the many challenges to political realism comes from liberal international theory. Liberals have long argued that with proper domestic structures, international institutions, and economic interchange among themselves, states can mitigate the effects of international anarchy, minimize the violence-prone tendencies of the international system, promote further cooperation, and reduce the frequency of war. Until recently, however, it was hard to identify an integrated liberal theory of peace and war.

This is no longer the case. With the development of a substantial line of research on the democratic peace, a renewal of interest in the old argument that economic interdependence promotes peace, the beginning of more systematic work on the role of international institutions in peacemaking and peacekeeping, and preliminary attempts to combine these into a single integrated theory, we now have the outlines of a liberal *theory* of peace and war (Doyle, 1997; Russett and Oneal, 2001). Some see this as a continuation of the classical liberal tradition and the systematization of Kant's ([1795]1949) conception of perpetual peace based on democratic institutions, free trade, and international law and institutions. Scholars sometimes refer to theories of the effects of democracy, economic interdependence, and international institutions as "republican liberalism," "commercial liberalism," and "institutional liberalism," respectively (A. Stein, 1993).[28]

It is difficult to classify liberal theories of economic interdependence and peace based on our levels-of-analysis framework. Those theories include causal variables from all levels of analysis, but the most influential explanations give primary emphasis to factors relating to the interactions of states, including interstate bargaining, and we discuss those theories in this chapter. We can imagine an alternative classification of liberal theories of peace and war, but given our use of the levels-of-analysis framework to focus on the independent causal variables, this classification works reasonably well.[29]

Theories of Economic Interdependence and Conflict

Liberal theorists since Adam Smith and David Ricardo have argued that trade and other forms of economic exchange promote peace between states. As Montesquieu ([1748]1989: I, Bk. 20, chap. 1) argued, "peace is the natural effect of trade." Thomas Paine ([1791/92]1969) stated it more strongly: "If commerce were permitted to act to the extent it is capable, it would extirpate the system of war." These classical liberal arguments form the basis of what Doyle (1997: chap. 7) calls the tradition of "commercial pacifism" and what some call the "capitalist peace" (Weede, 2003; Gartzke, 2007).

The liberal view that trade promotes peace was in part a response to the mercantilist economic ideology that dominated most of the seventeenth and eighteenth centuries. Mercantilists were economic nationalists who believed that economic policy was an instrument of state policy for the promotion of state interests, and that the state should regulate trade with that aim in mind. With respect to domestic politics, the mercantilist system aimed to enhance state power against decentralized sources of economic power in society, which had been strong in the Middle Ages before the rise of the state. With respect to foreign policy, mercantilist policies aimed to strengthen the power of the state against other states in the system.[30]

Mercantilist economic ideology led to closed trading systems, not open, liberal, free-trading systems. Most of a state's trade was conducted with its own colonies, not with its competitors, who were excluded from a state's economic sphere. State leaders feared that trade with competitors would only enrich their adversaries and increase their long-term military power and potential. The closed trading systems of the mercantilist were significantly different than the free-trading systems that emerged with liberal economic ideologies.

Mercantilists widely believed that commerce and war were mutually reinforcing. Commerce contributed to the wealth that provided the economic foundations of military power, and military power could be used to seize territory, resources, and colonies that strengthened the economic foundations of state power. In Howard's (1976:47) words, "War, to paraphrase Clausewitz, was a continuation of commerce with an admixture of other means." An important qualification, though, is that although the pursuit of power and the pursuit of wealth were usually mutually reinforcing in mercantilist thought, whenever they diverged the state must give priority to advancing state power over advancing wealth (Viner, 1948).

Adam Smith and other liberals were highly critical of the mercantilist view that international economic relations constituted a "zero-sum game," that a gain for one state was a loss for its adversary. Liberals believed that there is a natural harmony of interests both between and within states. Trade based on specialization and comparative advantage could create an ever-expanding pie that would make all states better off. The imposition of tariffs, quotas, and any other forms of interference with market mechanisms reduces economic prosperity and consequently increases the likelihood of war (Silberner, [1946]1972). Smith and other liberals criticized the mercantilist emphasis on national economic monopolies and the protectionist and colonial policies that served those monopolies. They believed that those practices, combined with mercantilism's assumptions of a zero-sum world, contributed to expansionist and militaristic policies of autarkic mercantilist states, of which they were highly critical.

By the late nineteenth century, Cobden, Mill, and other liberal theorists were arguing that with changes in the nature of production and the size of the market, war was becoming less and less useful as an instrument of state policy for the accumulation of wealth. Norman Angell ([1910]1972) made a particularly strong statement to this effect in his book on *The Great Illusion*. More and more, industrial economies were increasingly dependent on factors that were more easily acquired through trade than through conquest. Angell also emphasized that economic globalization enhanced financial interdependence as well as commercial interdependence. It was not just the producers and the great trading firms whose interests were more and more served by peace rather than by war, but international bankers as well (Kirshner, 2007). As production and wealth became increasingly dispersed, mobile, and less tied to territory, the strategies of political coercion and control advocated by economic nationalists became less and less effective. Trade was becoming a more efficient strategy for the accumulation of wealth, and war was becoming too costly for advanced industrial economies (Rosecrance, 1986; Brooks, 2005; Gartzke, 2007).

The outbreak and expansion of World War I only two years after the publication of *The Great Illusion* was widely regarded as a repudiation of Angell's thesis (though Angell never actually said that a major war would be impossible, only that it would be devastating). That, plus the decline of economic interdependence in the 1930s, the outbreak of World War II, and then the US–Soviet rivalry of the Cold War period, dampened theoretical interest in the trade-promotes-peace hypothesis, though some argued that the autarky of the 1930s contributed significantly to the outbreak of World War II (Kindleberger, 1973). It was not until the 1990s that social scientists – equipped with new methods, models, and data, and also interested in expanding the liberal international theory associated with the democratic peace – turned again to the question of the relationship between economic interdependence and peace.

Liberal theorists suggest a number of more specific causal mechanisms to explain why trade and other forms of economic interdependence promote peace.[31] One of the most influential is the "economic opportunity cost" hypothesis, sometimes also referred to as the "trade-disruption hypothesis" (Polachek, 1980). Trade generates economic advantages for both parties based on specialization, efficiency, and comparative advantage. Political leaders anticipate that war will disrupt trade and lead to a loss or reduction of the benefits of trade, and this loss of the gains from trade deters them from initiating militarized conflict. On the other hand, lower levels of trade between states generate fewer economic opportunity costs of war and consequently reduce economic incentives for political leaders to avoid war. These tendencies are reinforced by domestic political considerations. Trade increases the influence of economic groups who benefit most from trade, and who, consequently, have incentives to use their influence to pressure the government to maintain the peace that helps promote trade (Rogowski, 1989; Solingen, 1998; McDonald, 2009).

The profits generated by capitalist economies make those states both strong and committed to a peaceful international order that creates optimal conditions for further trade. Capitalist states with democratic regimes are "powerful pacifists" (Lake, 1992) that are both relatively secure from foreign threats and lacking in the incentives for external aggression, at least against trading partners. They have shared interests in a stable international economy. This leads some to argue that democratic capitalist states have common interests, that those shared interests minimize the issues that might trigger violent conflicts, and that it is these common interests, rather than trade interdependencies per se, that minimize conflicts between capitalist states (Morrow, Siverson, and Tabares, 1998; Mousseau, 2000, 2009; Gartzke, 2007).

Some liberal theorists support their arguments about capitalist states' lower propensity to war by referring to factors at the societal level. This goes back to the arguments of Comte, Spencer, and others that the underlying spirit of industrial societies runs counter to the spirit of military societies because industrialism brings prosperity to the masses as well as to the business classes and diverts their interests from external expansion and conquest to making profits (Veblen, [1915]1966; Schumpeter, [1919]1951). As Blainey (1988:10) argues, people are "too busy growing rich to have time for war."

Realist and rationalist critiques

Realists, who share the economic nationalism and statist orientation of the old mercantilists, criticize the liberal economic theory of peace on a number of grounds. First of all, they argue (as do some non-realists) that even if it were true that trade has a pacifying effect, the magnitude of the impact of trade on decisions for war and peace is small relative to that of military and diplomatic considerations (Buzan, 1984; Levy, 1989b). Realists, like mercantilists, argue that states are motivated primarily by power and that economic opportunity costs of war are minor in the context of the long-term struggle for power. Were the Western liberal democracies seriously concerned about the short-term loss of trade when they made decisions to go to war against the hegemonic threats posed by Germany in 1914 and again in 1939?

Realists also argue that trade and other forms of economic interdependence can actually increase the level of militarized conflict rather than reduce it (Barbieri, 2002). As Rousseau (cited in Hoffmann, 1963:319) argued, "... interdependence breeds not accommodation and harmony, but suspicion and incompatibility." Among other things, interdependence creates increased opportunities for conflict. The greater the interdependence between states, the greater the number of things to argue about. In addition, whereas liberals argue that economic interdependence creates mutual dependence and incentives to avoid war, realists argue that interdependence may also be asymmetrical. Each is dependent on the other, but the degree of dependence is uneven. The less dependent party may be tempted to use economic coercion to exploit the adversary's vulnerabilities and influence its behavior relating to security as well as economic issues.[32] These can lead to retaliatory actions, conflict spirals, and war.[33]

The temptation to exploit asymmetries of interdependence is enhanced by the realist view that political leaders are concerned with "relative gains" and that they aim to maximize their power relative to that of their adversaries.[34] Whereas liberals focus on absolute gains and ask how much states gain from trade, realists focus on relative gains and ask who gains more. Liberals are more interested in the size of the pie, while realists are more interested in who has the larger slice. With respect to economic gains, realists assume that a state can convert any disproportionate economic gains into military power (Huntington, 1993a). Realists argue that in relations between adversaries or rivals, political leaders on at least one side will fear that the adversary will gain more from trade and convert those gains into further economic gains, political influence, and military power. This leads realists to argue that leaders' concerns about relative gains will lead to reductions in trade in intense international rivalries and to the termination of trade if war breaks out between trading partners (Gowa, 1994).

Concerns about the effects of asymmetric interdependence (and even symmetrical interdependence) are also shared by many rational choice theorists. One analytic problem with the economic opportunity cost model is that its causal logic focuses only on the costs and benefits to individual states and ignores strategic bargaining between states. If states are mutually dependent and fear the economic opportunity costs of escalation and war, it is quite possible that both might make concessions to avoid war, as the opportunity cost model predicts. It is also possible, however, that one side might conclude that its adversary has more to fear from war and more to lose in terms of opportunity costs of war, and that the adversary can be coerced to make concessions to avoid war. This is particularly likely if interdependence is asymmetrical. One state might actually increase its demands during a crisis, and engage in threats of force to back those demands, something that is even more likely to occur if one side is more risk acceptant than the other.

In a crisis between interdependent states, then, it is unclear whether states will make concessions to avoid the opportunity costs of war or whether they will attempt to exploit their adversary's fear of war through increased coercion. Depending on the magnitude of the increased demands, war might be more rather than less likely under conditions of interdependence. In the absence of more information, the outcome is indeterminate (Morrow, 2003:90).

This line of argument leads some rational choice theorists to suggest another mechanism through which economic interdependence contributes to peace. The advantage of high levels of economic interdependence is that it provides states with a greater range of options for sending credible signals of their resolve in a dispute. Trade and financial instruments serve as additional mechanisms (economic sanctions, for example) through which states can emphasize their evaluation of the issues at stake and their determination to hold firm, but with less cost and risk of escalation (Morrow, 1999, 2003; Gartzke, Li, and Boehmer, 2001). Economic sanctions are costly to the initiator as well as to the target. Only states that are highly resolved will be willing to incur those costs, so cutting back on trade or financial flows helps a state to signal its resolve in a dispute. Other states understand this, and the result is to reduce uncertainty about adversary intentions and consequently to reduce the danger of a war through miscalculation. Economic signaling also avoids (or at least delays) the resort to military threats that might also induce compliance but that are also more likely to induce counter-threats and escalation.

Realists also question the standard liberal assumption that trade is always more efficient than military coercion in expanding markets and investment opportunities and in promoting state wealth. Realists argue that for much of human history military force has been a useful instrument to promote state wealth as well as power. Many liberals concede this point, but argue that as the foundations of wealth and power have historically shifted from territory to industrialization and now to knowledge-based forms of production, the economic value of territorial conquest has diminished, at least for advanced industrial states. The greater the mobility of production and of capital, the less is the utility of war as a means for acquiring wealth (Hirschman, [1945]1980; Brooks, 2005). Strategies of enhancing wealth through conquest have been replaced by strategies of enhancing wealth through trade, finance, and other forms of economic exchange. This line of argument leads Rosecrance (1986) to argue that the military state has gradually given way to the trading state.[35]

Both the trade-promotes-peace arguments and some of the realist critiques sound plausible in principle. Whether the deterrent effects of the gains from trade outweigh the potentially destabilizing effects of economic asymmetries and economic competitions, and whether the latter escalate to trade wars and militarized conflicts, is ultimately an empirical question that analysts began to systematically analyze in the 1990s.[36] The evidence so far suggests that, on average, trade tends to reduce the probability of war (Polachek, 1980; Russett and Oneal, 2001; but see Barbieri, 2002), but that the strength of the relationship is relatively modest. Contrary to both liberal and realist expectations, however, there are numerous instances in which trade continues between warring parties (Ripsman and Blanchard, 1996/97; Barbieri and Levy, 1999).

Most empirical analyses of the relationship between economic interdependence and peace have focused on the impact of trade on peace.[37] Some theorists have suggested, however, that trade is less important than other elements of global capitalism in mitigating the effects of violence. They emphasize the greater effects of financial markets, the coordination of monetary policy, economic development, and the mobility of production, and they attempt to incorporate these factors into their models (Crescenzi, 2005; Brooks, 2005). Gartzke (2007), looking at the period from 1950–92, finds no wars between capitalist states (or between democratic states). His other analyses, along with those of Mousseau (2000, 2009), Hegre (2000), and Mousseau et al. (2003), suggest that the combination of integrated economic markets and economic development is a more powerful source of peace than is democracy. The debate over whether we are witnessing a "democratic peace" or a "capitalist peace" is now a lively topic of scholarly debate.

Although the liberal economic theory of peace, like so many other theories of international conflict, was developed with the experience of the European great powers in mind, the trade-promotes-peace hypothesis, along with the realist critique, has enormous relevance for the contemporary world. The enormous increases in globalization during the last couple of decades have involved increasing degrees of economic interdependence. The pacifying effects of trade have undoubtedly contributed to the condition of stable peace among the advanced industrial democracies of the European Union. Whether China's engagement in the world economy will continue to contribute to its "peaceful rise" remains to be seen. Whether the lure of prosperity through trade will have a comparable effect in the Middle East or other regions, or whether it will be too weak to overcome long-standing hostilities between Arabs and Israelis or between other peoples, is a critical question for the future.

We might also note that economic nationalist ideologies are not entirely a thing of the past. Russian economic relationships with some East European states appear to be driven more by considerations of political influence than the market rationality of supply and demand. Russian manipulation of natural gas supplies and price to the Ukraine in 2008–09 and to Europe is a good example. Another question is whether the global financial crisis beginning in 2008 will lead states to adopt more protectionist "begger-thy-neighbor" policies, as they did in the 1930s, contributing, some argue, to the outbreak of World War II (Kindleberger, 1973).

Realists and other critics of the liberal trade-promotes-peace hypothesis often point to World War I as a glaring anomaly in the liberal argument, since war occurred despite high levels of interdependence. Let us return to this question, since it engages the levels-of-analysis theme that runs throughout this book. As we have argued, most explanations for the trade-promotes-peace hypothesis are basically dyadic in terms of both the level and unit of analysis. Its proponents usually ignore the systemic context in which trade and financial flows take place, particularly the pattern of diplomatic alignments and alliances. This is a critical omission, because the logic underlying the dyadic economic opportunity cost model does not necessarily imply that economic interdependence always promotes peace at the system level when third parties are involved.

At the dyadic level, economic interdependence between A and B may help to reduce the probability of war between A and B. But if B threatens C, and if A simultaneously has an economic or security interest in maintaining C's security against B, A's economic ties with B may dissuade A from attempting to deter B's attack on C. As a result, economic interdependence between A and B may *increase* the probability of war between B and C. That war could even escalate to draw in A.

This contributes to our understanding of how economic interdependence failed to prevent World War I. Britain's failure to make a formal commitment to join France and Russia if they were attacked by Germany, which many historians argue was a critical factor leading to the German decision for war (Fischer, 1967, 1988), derives in part from the extensive economic ties between Britain and Germany prior to the war and by Britain's hesitation to alienate its key trading partner by attempting to restrain that partner's strategic ambitions (Papayoanou, 1999). This reduced Germany's expected costs of going to war with France and Russia, since there was no certainty of British intervention against them. At the dyadic level, the trade-promotes-peace hypothesis actually worked in the sense that it led to closer ties between Germany and England. At the system level, however, those close ties undermined deterrence and made a European war more likely.[38]

There are other economic theories of war and peace besides liberal and realist theories of economic interdependence. Most of the others are framed at the societal level, to which we turn in the next chapter.

Notes

1. Scholars often classify theories of the democratic peace as dyadic-level. This is based on the fact that the observed absence of war between democracies reflects a dyadic-level outcome. But the closely related hypothesis (with less supporting evidence) that democracies are more peaceful than are other states (regardless of their regime type) has a state-level dependent variable. In addition, and as noted in chapter 1, we are following Waltz (1959) and defining the levels of analysis in terms of causal variables rather than the dependent variables or outcomes they are invoked to explain. Most theories of the democratic peace focus on internal causal factors that are unique to democracies and that lead them to behave differently than other states. For that reason, we defer a discussion of the democratic peace until the next chapter on state and societal theories of war.

2. Some of the book-length studies in this area include Diehl (1998), Thompson (1999), Diehl and Goertz (2000), Leng (2000), Maoz and Mor (2002), Colaresi (2005), Paul (2005b), and Colaresi, Rasler, and Thompson (2007). One of the main purposes of these books is to establish the significance of focusing on rivalries as an explanatory path. To do that it is necessary to identify who have been rivals and to document the extent to which they have monopolized interstate conflict (see especially, Diehl and Goertz (2000) and Colaresi, Rasler, and Thompson (2007) on these questions). Once that foundation is constructed, the more conventional tasks of explaining how rivalries escalate or terminate becomes the focus. Dreyer and Thompson (forthcoming) describes each of the strategic rivalries in effect between 1816 and 2005 and those of the major powers back to the 1490s.

3. American intelligence on al Qaeda and on Iraq is a good example.

4. On territorial disputes, see Huth (1996b), Vasquez (1996), and Colaresi, Rasler, and Thompson (2007); on arms races, see Gibler, Rider, and Hutchison (2005); on diversionary theory, see Levy (1989a) and Mitchell and Prins (2004). Another topic that has been viewed from the rivalry lens is the democratic peace. See, for instance, Bennett (1997), Hensel and Goertz (2000), and Rasler and Thompson (2005)

5. It is also possible to extend the concept of rivalries to domestic rivals in civil wars. DeRouen and Bercovitch (2008) find that extended domestic rivalries are fairly common and make resolving civil wars more difficult.

6. This is reminiscent of Tilly's (1975, 1990) argument that war contributed to state-building in early modern Europe. For critiques of the war-makes-the-state hypothesis, see Spruyt (1996) and Centeno (2002).

7. We argue elsewhere that weak states are less likely to participate in interstate wars and more likely to experience intrastate wars (Levy and Thompson, 2010b).

8. On different paths from rivalry to war involving spatial and positional issues, compare Vasquez (1996) and Rasler and Thompson (2000a). Alternatively, Thompson (2003) contends that multiple, "ripe" rivalries make systemic wars more probable. See also Vasquez (1998a).

9. For arguments about the beginning and ending of rivalries, see Goertz and Diehl (1995), Bennett (1998), Colaresi (2001), Thompson (2001b), and Maoz and Mor (2002). For a different view of rivalry dynamics and a comparison of the "punctuated equilibrium" versus "evolutionary" models, see Diehl and Goertz (2000:202–206).

10. People who study the connections between rivalries and war think the relationship is indispensable. Critics say that one is only using information about conflict histories to explain, rather tautologically, the probability of more conflict. One key question is whether (1) one set of causal variables fully explains both past conflict and current conflict within a rivalry or (2) past conflict itself has an additional causal impact on current conflict, by creating or reinforcing intractable hostility, by generating incidents that one side wants to avenge or losses that it wants to recover, by bringing to power new elites committed to a more confrontational strategy, or more generally by "locking in" the conflict at a higher level. Past conflict has an independent causal impact on current conflict in the second path but not in the first. Neither path technically involves a tautological relationship. For a critique of rivalry analysis and a direct response, see Gartzke and Simon (1999) and Colaresi and Thompson (2002).

11. Partial support for this assumption comes from Sample's (2002) finding that in the period from 1816–1992 military build-ups have increased the likelihood of dispute escalation for major power dyads and for minor power dyads but not for mixed dyads.

12. Like most researchers using statistical methods to study international conflict, Senese and Vasquez (2008) adopt the Correlates of War project's definition of a militarized interstate dispute (or MID) as "cases of conflict in which the threat, display, or use of military force short of war by one member state is explicitly directed towards the government, official representatives, official forces, property, or territory of another state. Disputes consist of incidents that range in intensity from threats to use force to actual combat short of war" (Jones, Bremer, and Singer, 1996:163). Data on MIDs can be found at www.correlatesofwar.org.

13. The emphasis on territorial disputes raises the interesting question of *why* territory is so important. Senese and Vasquez (2008:9–10) make no attempt to fully answer this question, since they are more interested in the consequences of territoriality than its sources. They suggest, however, that it probably has something to due to humankind's biological inheritance, since the threat and use of violence to defend territory is something that humans share with other vertebrates.

14. Scholars often confuse *realpolitik*, which is a state strategy or set of practices often equated with "power politics," with realist theory, which is a theory

constructed to explain those practices. One can in principle observe power politics practices yet develop a non-realist theory in order to explain those practices.

15. For earlier research on the relationship between alliances and war, and particularly on the question of whether alliances tend to deter war or provoke war, see Singer and Small (1968), Holsti, Hoppman, and Sullivan (1973), Walt (1987), Oren (1990), G. Snyder (1997), Gibler (2000), and Leeds (2003).

16. For research on arms races and war, see Huntington (1958), Richardson (1960), Wallace (1982), Diehl (1983), Kennedy (1983), Morrow (1989), Sample (2000, 2002), and Glaser (2004).

17. We discuss crisis decision-making in chapter 5.

18. Coercive threats sometimes succeed in inducing compliance, and they sometimes backfire and trigger counter-threats and escalation. Most empirical research suggests, however, that bullying strategies generally do not work and that strategies of reciprocity are more effective (Leng 1993; Axelrod 1984). The key question is the conditions under which military threats succeed and when they fail (Jervis, 1976: chap. 3). The question of defining success and failure is quite complex, however, because it involves not only the outcome of the current crisis but also the generation of reputational effects that might influence future beliefs and behavior. The literature on reputation is itself quite complex. There is some evidence that political actors usually attempt to build up their reputation for resolve on the assumption that it will influence others' perceptions and behavior in future interactions, but that other actors usually pay little attention to those reputations. They generally base their expectations of their adversary's likely behavior on their judgments of its interests in the current crisis rather than on its behavior in past crises (Press, 2005). There is also evidence that actions to establish reputations for resolve have a different impact on allies and on adversaries (Mercer, 1996). See also Jervis (1970), Snyder and Diesing (1977), and Crescenzi (2007).

19. Defensive realists, who believe that the anarchic structure of the international system does not compel aggressive behavior and that security-seeking states can live in peace, are more likely to agree with many of the points in Senese and Vasquez (2008). But even defensive realists recognize the dynamics of action–reaction cycles.

20. For an influential statement that war is learned behavior, see Mead (1940). For another perspective on realist strategic culture, see Johnston (1995).

21. In arguing that territorial behavior is part of humankind's biological inheritance, however, Senese and Vasquez (2008) imply that such behavior cannot be easily unlearned. Thus the first stage of the steps-to-war model will be the most difficult to eliminate. The implication is that territorial disputes are likely, and that what is critical is what kinds of foreign policy practices states adopt to handle those conflicts.

22. We return to the concept of "rationality" in chapter 5 on individual decision-making. While many structural realists argue that states and other actors generally select those strategies that they believe will maximize their interests, rational choice theorists would argue that structural realists have an underdeveloped conception of rationality. They focus on structures and either ignore preferences or simply assume that preferences are induced by the structure of

the system, and they also downplay the importance of specific details of the informational environment. For a useful introduction to strategic choice theory, see Lake and Powell (1999).

23. We deal with psychological explanations for war in chapter 5 and domestic explanations in chapter 4.

24. Another problem is that it is not at all clear that the revelation of private information would be seen as credible, as opposed to a bluff designed to coerce the adversary into greater concessions.

25. The private information mechanism is a general theory of conflict and is not restricted to war and peace. In labor–management negotiations, for example, a breakdown in bargaining might take the form of a strike or a lockout, either of which would be costly for both parties. Strikes and lockouts, like wars, do not last forever, and the dispute is eventually settled. If, at the onset of the dispute, both sides had similar views of what the final settlement was likely to look like, they could go straight to that settlement and spare themselves the cost of lost wages and revenues. So the question is: "why can't they settle?" The bargaining model suggests that the answer is disagreements about what the likely settlement would look like, based on different views of how resolved each side is and how well each side could endure a strike or lockout, along with incentives not to reveal that information. That is, costly conflicts are the product of disagreements about relative "power"; the "fighting" (strike, lockout, or war) is an attempt to demonstrate relative power, to impose costs on the adversary, and to convince the adversary that a settlement on one's own terms is preferable to a continued conflict; and conflicts are settled when adversaries agree on their relative power. A similar argument applies to plea bargaining. If the prosecutor and defendant each has similar perceptions of the strength of the evidence (their relative power), they can reach a settlement and avoid a costly trial.

26. One possible way of circumventing the indivisibility of an issue is for the actors to agree to alternate in sharing the good. If the issue is control over territory X, and if the territory cannot be divided or if shared control is not possible, states can trade off controlling the territory. The problem, of course, is that once one state controls the territory it might renege on its promise to give it back. Or at least the second state might not believe the promise is credible. This shifts us back to the commitment problem. This problem reinforces the argument that private information and commitment problems are the two primary paths to war for rational unitary actors.

27. We can illustrate what this means by a monetary example. If given a choice between $5 for certain or a gamble that yield an outcome of $10 with 50 percent probability and $0 with 50 percent probability, a risk-neutral actor would be indifferent between the two (since the expected value of the certain outcome is equivalent to the expected value of the gamble). A risk-averse actor would prefer the certain $5. A risk-acceptant actor would prefer the gamble.

28. The constructivist emphasis on a community of nations with shared values and/or international norms is often referred to as "sociological liberalism."

29. As we said in note 1, we will deal with republican liberalism and the democratic peace in chapter 4. We do not cover the effects of international law and

institutions on the causes of war. There are some important books on international institutions going back many years (Claude, 1971), and an emerging literature (Russett and Oneal, 2001: chap. 5; Pevehouse and Russett, 2006) on the impact of international institutions on interstate war. Scholars have devoted a great deal of attention to the influence of the United Nations, the World Bank, and other international institutions on the outbreak, termination, and consequences of civil war (Collier et al., 2003) and on the impact of regional institutions on regional orders (Lake and Morgan, 1997; Solingen, 1998). International institutions have less of an impact on great power conflict, however, though research on security regimes (Jervis, 1982, 2002; Haftendorn, Keohane, Wallander, 1999) is an important exception. For a good sense of liberal–realist debate on the impact of international institutions, see Mearsheimer (1994/95, 1995) and Keohane and Martin (1995). On the law of war, see Neff (2005) and O'Connell (2005).

30. For different perspectives on mercantilism, see Minchinton (1969).
31. For a summary of liberal arguments and of the realist critique, see Doyle (1997), Russett and Oneal (2001), Mansfield and Pollins (2003), and Schneider, Barbieri, and Gleditsch (2003).
32. Marxists and neo-Marxists also emphasize the coercive element in asymmetrical relationships. They argue (at the systemic level) that the historical dominance of the West over the rest of the world for the last five centuries was an important source of conflict between the "core" and the "periphery" (Semmel, 1981).
33. The US oil embargo against Japan in 1941, motivated by American attempts to exploit Japanese dependence on American oil to compel Japan to stop its expansionist behavior in Asia, set off a conflict spiral that led to the US–Japanese war in the Pacific (Sagan, 1988). On the possibility of increased Sino–Indian conflict in the future due to economic interdependence, see Rapkin and Thompson (2006).
34. On debates regarding the importance of relative gains, see Waltz (1979), Grieco (1990), Snidal (1991), and Powell (1991).
35. Some have questioned the argument that the benefits of conquest through war is a thing of the past and that territorial conquest is no longer feasible for advanced industrial states in the modern era. Liberman (1996) argued that modern economies make both coercion and repression more efficient. Milward (1977) found that Germany effectively exploited the French economy it occupied during World War II. In the Pacific War between Japan and the United States (1941–5), Japan's need for oil and other resources in Southeast Asia in the face of an American oil embargo was a key motivation leading to Japan's war of conquest in Asia and then to its war against the United States (Iriye, 1987). That was an extraordinarily high-risk war for a great power, however, and the development of nuclear weapons magnifies those risks many times over. It is hard to imagine that the political leaders of advanced industrial states in the contemporary era might conclude that their economic interests would be better served by a strategy of military conquest than a strategy of free trade.
36. One potential problem that empirical analysts need to contend with is the possibility that the causal arrow between trade and peace might be reversed.

Rather than trade promoting peace, it is peace that creates conditions for trade and prosperity (Reuveny and Kang, 1996). In this view, peace is the cause of increased trade rather than the consequence of increased trade. In fact, the relationship between trade and conflict is probably a reciprocal one, with each having some positive impact on the other. There is some support for this argument in the quantitative literature (Keshk, Pollins, and Reuveny, 2004).

37. For the argument that scholars should not focus on the total amount of trade, or trade as a proportion of gross domestic product, but instead on trade in strategic goods (reflecting a realist argument), see Ripsman and Blanchard (1996/97).

38. Crawford (2003) makes the system-level argument that British leaders were deliberately ambiguous about their intentions to intervene in continental war in an attempt to maintain the peace between Germany and Russia. Glenn Snyder (1997) refers to this as a "saddle strategy." Copeland (1996) applies a "trade expectations" model to the July 1914 crisis, and McDonald advances a domestic political economy model.

4

The State and Societal Level

Explaining war in terms of causal factors internal to states is an old tradition in the study of international relations. In his influential book *Man, the State, and War*, Waltz (1959) traces a long line of "second-image" theorists who locate the causes of war in the conditions and processes within states. He examined theories that focused on the international political and economic structures of states and societies, with particular attention to liberal theories and to Marxist–Leninist theories. As we noted earlier, however, Waltz (1979) believed that the fundamental causes of war were located at the systemic level, so he was critical of most nation-state-level theories of war and their prescriptions for a more peaceful world.

There is a wide range of more specific arguments through which state structures, conditions, and processes are said to increase the likelihood of war. Some cultures or ideologies may be particularly warlike, though Wright ([1942]1965) found little evidence to support that popular argument. Kant, Bentham, and other Enlightenment philosophers believed that the warfare that had plagued Europe for centuries could be traced to the personal and political interests of the aristocratic leaderships that ruled territorial states. These scholars argued that states with representative institutions would be much less likely to wage war because those systems invest ultimate political authority in the hands of those who must suffer the hardships of war (Kant, [1795]1949).

Marx and his followers focused attention on the economic rather than political organization of societies, and argued that modern war arises from the economic imperatives of capitalist societies and the inequitable distribution of wealth within them (Lenin, [1916]1939). A world of socialist states based on classless societies, they argued, would suffer little war. Other scholars have focused on domestic political institutions, cultures, ideologies, and religions as sources of war.[1] In the past half century more attention has been given to nationalism as a leading cause of war, with particular attention to the role of ethnonationalism in civil war.

The degree of emphasis on the state and societal level of analysis in the causes of war has varied over time. It has also varied by discipline. Especially beginning in the 1960s, contemporary historians began to place enormous emphasis on the role of these societal-level factors.[2] At that time, however, international relations theorists in political science continued to focus on system-level realist variables in their study of war (Morgenthau, 1967; Waltz, 1979), as Vasquez (1998b) and Walker and Morton (2005) have shown in their systematic assessment of the field. International relations scholars began to develop new decision-making paradigms at both the organizational (Allison, 1971) and individual levels (Jervis, 1976; Lebow, 1981) in the 1970s and early 1980s, but they gave relatively little attention to societal-level variables (Levy, 1989b).

The focus of international relations scholars began to change in the late 1980s, and today there is as much attention devoted to societal sources of war as to any other level. A major factor leading to this shift was the growing interest in the "democratic peace," after scholars realized that democracies rarely if ever go to war with each other. The study of the democratic peace has been one of the most influential lines of research in the international relations field for the last two decades, and it has generated enormous interest in other aspects of the security behavior of democracies. Scholars have also devoted a lot of attention to the diversionary theory of war and, more recently, to the impact of the domestic political economy on incentives and opportunities for war and peace. In the study of civil war, to which we return in chapter 7, there is enormous scholarly interest in ethnic and religious identity, the political capacity of states, levels of economic welfare, migration, and other factors that operate at the societal level or that include societal factors as a major step in the hypothesized causal chain leading to war.

It is important to recall at this point that domestic-level theories, if they consist exclusively of variables internal to the state, cannot provide a theoretically complete explanation of the causes of war and peace. As we emphasized in the introductory chapter, war and other forms of strategic interaction are the joint product of the actions of two or more states at the dyadic or systemic levels. Internal-level variables – whether at the societal, bureaucratic/organizational, or individual levels – are not logically sufficient to explain the outcomes of strategic interaction between states. Such explanations require the inclusion of dyadic or systemic-level causal variables. This is what Waltz (1979) meant when he argued, in the course of his critique of Marxist–Leninist theories, that a theory of foreign policy is not a theory of international politics.

It is quite useful for many purposes to distinguish between state-level and societal-level variables. This practice is standard among scholars in international political economy (Ikenberry, Lake, and Mastanduno, 1988), but is also common in many analyses of war, peace, and international security (Rosenau, 1966). For the purposes of organizing our survey of theories of the causes of war, however, we follow Waltz's (1959) original formulation and combine state and societal variables in a single category. Our rationale is that in many theories it is extraordinarily difficult to disentangle state- and societal-level variables. Many explanations of the democratic peace, for example, combine the institutional structure of democratic states with the role of democratic political cultures that leave publics averse to war and particularly to the casualties of war. Similarly, some scholars who focus on political elites emphasizes both the structure of power within the state and the nature of the societal interests that form the ruling coalitions.

With these considerations in mind, we turn to some of the leading state/societal theories of interstate war. We begin with Marxist–Leninist theories of imperialism, which trace international conflict to the interests and influence of the capitalist class within society. After a brief examination of Schumpeter's critique of Marxist–Leninist theory and his emphasis on the dominant influence of a military rather than an economic elite, we then consider a number of coalitional theories that argue that decisions for expansion or other grand strategies are the product of the actions of coalitions of different actors that act on the basis of their own parochial interests. These include Snyder's (1991) theory of logrolled coalitions and the theories of the political economy of grand strategy advanced by Narizny (2007) and Lobell (2006). Next is a discussion of the democratic peace, the evidence behind it, and theories constructed to explain it. We end with an examination of Huntington's (1993b, 1996) "clash of civilizations" thesis.

Marxist–Leninist Theories of Imperialism and War

One of the oldest and most comprehensive of all societal-level approaches to international conflict can be found in the Marxist–Leninist theory of imperialism. Implicit in Marxist–Leninist theories, and in certain other forms of elite explanations of imperialism and war, is the view that these practices are costly for society in human and economic terms, that any benefits from war fall far short of justifying those costs, and that the capitalist class benefits from war and is ultimately responsible for war. The capitalist class captures or "hijacks" the state and uses the apparatus of the state to formulate policies to advance its own parochial interests while shifting most of the costs of those policies to other societal groups. In terms of the Clausewitzian framework emphasized earlier, imperialism and war, instead of being instruments of state policy for the advancement of state interests, are instruments of the ruling elite for the advancement of class interests.[3]

Karl Marx was a nineteenth-century philosopher who argued that all social and political relationships were determined by the underlying economic structure and economic relationships, particularly the relationship between the owners of the means of production (capitalists) and the workers (the proletariat). The ongoing class struggle between the capitalists and the proletariat was, for Marx, the driving force of history. Marx himself focused primarily on domestic politics and did not develop a systematic international theory. The international component was added primarily by Lenin ([1916]1939), who built on the ideas of Hobson ([1902]1965), Hilferding ([1910]1981), and Luxemburg ([1913]1964). Given Lenin's central role we often refer to the "Marxist–Leninist" theory of imperialism, though there are in fact a number of variations of the theory (Kubalkova and Cruickshank 1980; Semmel, 1981). These theories all include the basic argument that international conflict can be traced to the nature of capitalist economic systems and the interests of the capitalist class.

In the standard Marxist–Leninist worldview, capitalist systems are not self-sufficient. They contain a number of "contradictions" that generate an inherent tendency toward stagnation and collapse in the absence of some kind of additional stimulus. That stimulus is provided by aggressive or imperialist foreign policies, which stabilize capitalist economies and enhance the profits of the capitalist class through several related causal mechanisms. This is clearly a societal-level theory, in which societal-level independent variables explain the foreign policy actions of states.

Although the vast majority of Marxist–Leninists emphasize the domestic sources of imperialism and war, it is important to note that some focus on system-level sources of international patterns, behavior, and conflict, and particularly on the structure of the world political economy. They emphasize relations of dominance and dependence between a wealthy "core" that was historically centered in Europe and a "periphery" located outside of Europe. Similar arguments are advanced by proponents of "world systems theory" in sociology. Wallerstein (1984), for example, traces such a system back to 1500 and examines hegemonic wars for the control of the system.[4]

Earlier, in chapter 2, we discussed "hegemonic" theories of international politics and general war – power transition theory (Organski, 1958; Tammen et al., 2000), Gilpin's (1981) related hegemonic transition theory, and Thompson's (1988) long-cycle theory. None of these theories prioritizes economic classes, and none can be described as Marxist. Each, however, emphasizes the hierarchical structure of the world system, the importance of the world economy, and attempts by leading states to control it. It is often hard to differentiate system-level Marxist–Leninist theories from many alternative hegemonic theories.[5] It is also difficult to analytically distinguish between versions of Marxist theory that emphasize the role of the capitalist class in stabilizing and advancing the domestic economy as a whole[6] from realist theories emphasizing power and interest.

Although recent history has not been kind to communist regimes, and although Marxist–Leninist theories have declined in influence in the social sciences, particular Marxist–Leninist hypotheses emphasizing the influence of parochial economic interests on foreign policy have been sufficiently influential to have been incorporated, with some modifications, into more conventional liberal, pluralist, and sectoral approaches to the study of international politics. Questions about the viability of Marxism as an ideology do not necessarily invalidate specific causal propositions associated with the theory. As we note below, a number of non-Marxist theories borrow some elements from Marxist–Leninist theories of imperialism, though not the philosophical underpinnings of Marxist theory.

Marxist–Leninists propose a number of motivations or causal mechanisms though which capitalist states adopt aggressive foreign policies.[7] First, capitalist economies are characterized by excess production and underconsumption, which derive from the inadequate purchasing power of the proletariat and ultimately from the inequitable distribution of wealth in capitalist societies. The result is surplus products, which generate pressures for imperialist expansion to secure external markets to absorb the surplus. This is the *underconsumptionist* theory of imperialism often associated with Hobson ([1902]1965). It is also referred to as the "surplus products" hypothesis.

A related hypothesis, one given greater emphasis by Hilferding ([1910]1981) and Lenin ([1916]1939), is the existence of *surplus capital* resulting from the declining rate of return on capital invested in the domestic economy. This line of argument suggests that capitalist economies and their inequitable distribution of wealth cannot absorb all of the profits generated by the capitalist class. Surplus capital generates pressures for external expansion in search of better investment opportunities and of higher rates of return on capital. In this view, expansionist foreign policies are necessary to secure those opportunities for investment overseas.

Lenin and others also emphasized the need of capitalist states for *raw materials* to fuel their rapidly growing industrial economies. For Lenin, however, raw materials were secondary, and the dominant factor was the need for investment opportunities abroad that provided higher rates of return on capital. Other Marxist–Leninists give more importance to raw materials and to the expansionist foreign policies necessary to secure them. Many attribute what they regard as aggressive American foreign policies in Vietnam in the 1960s to the search for raw materials (Magdoff, 1969), while most non-Marxist interpretations of the Vietnam War downplay those factors (Logevall, 1999). Similarly, arguments that American foreign policy in the Middle East and its military intervention in Iraq in 1990–91 and 2003 were driven by the goal of controlling oil at cheap prices are quite consistent with a Marxist–Leninist perspective.[8]

Another form of stimulus in capitalist economies, but one that does not necessarily involve expansion and territorial control abroad, takes the form of high levels of military spending to stimulate the economy and to compensate for the lack of demand in capitalist economies that results from underconsumption. Luxemburg ([1913]1964) first made this point, arguing that the production of armaments was the only means by which surplus capital could be re-circulated into the economy. This argument suggests that capitalist economies need war – or at least the constant threat of war in the form of arms races, rivalries, and crises – to rationalize the high levels of military spending that are necessary to maintain high levels of aggregate demand in the economy and keep unemployment low.

This causal argument is often referred to as *military Keynesianism*, which draws parallels with the role of fiscal policy in stimulating the economy in Keynesian economics. The resulting "war economy" increases the likelihood of interstate war by triggering arms races, which increases tensions and contributes to conflict spirals. Some have argued, for example, that the United States was finally able to escape the "Great Depression" of the 1930s by building up a war economy at the end of the decade to confront Nazi Germany, thus providing the American economy the stimulus it needed. Others, however, are quite critical of this historical argument (Higgs, 2006).[9]

The above-mentioned paths to war in Marxist–Leninist theory focus on the structural needs of capitalist economies as a whole. There are simply not enough markets for surplus products or investment opportunities for surplus capital, because the aggregate demand for goods and capital is too low. Another line of argument, which originated with Marxist–Leninist theories of imperialism but which have been incorporated into other materialist theories of conflict, focuses on the private economic interests of individual firms or sectors, on their willingness to put their parochial interests above the national economic interests of the state, and on their political power to get their policy preferences accepted as government policy. This approach abandons the concept of a unified capitalist class with homogenous interests and recognizes important divisions among different economic groups within the capitalist class. The capitalist class as a whole may not benefit from imperialism or war, but individual firms might have incentives to use their political influence to push for a more aggressive or expansionist foreign policy.[10]

A version of this argument gained influence among segments of the American public in the 1920s in response to the dissatisfaction with the United States' intervention in World War I. Many believed that armaments manufacturers had a disproportionate impact on the decision to enter the war. More specifically, the argument was that shipbuilders, munitions makers, the builders of tanks and trucks, and certain other firms anticipated that they would secure increased profits from war and use their influence to pressure the government to adopt increasingly hardline policies that were likely to lead to war (Tansill, 1938). This view came to be known as the *merchants of death* hypothesis.[11]

This interpretation of American entry into World War I has been rejected by most historians, who emphasize the role of balance of power considerations, American liberal ideology, the role of German submarines in attacking American commerce, and other factors. The critics argue that while arms manufacturers and shipbuilders did profit from the war, there was little evidence that they had a substantial impact on political leaders' decision to intervene in the war and that they induced President Wilson to take actions that he would not have otherwise taken.[12]

Whereas Hobson and Lenin aimed primarily to explain the imperial expansion of the European powers in the late nineteenth century, their intellectual descendants have applied many of their arguments to the United States during the last century and during the Cold War in particular (Williams, 1962; Baran and Sweezy, 1966). Theories of the *military–industrial complex* give great emphasis to the role of private economic interests in shaping policy and generating military build-ups and a "war system" that produces profits for business but that go far beyond reasonable security precautions (Melman, 1970; Rosen, 1973). Indeed, many of these arguments have been incorporated into mainstream liberal critiques of American foreign policy – without accepting the broader philosophical system underlying Marxism.[13]

Critiques of Marxist–Leninist international theory

This is not the place for a lengthy critique of the Marxist–Leninist theory of imperialism, and we refer the reader to other treatments (Aron, 1968; Cohen, 1973; Krasner, 1978: chap. 1; Waltz, 1979; Brewer, 1980). It would be useful, however, to mention a few major lines of argument. Waltz (1979), for example, questioned the Marxist–Leninist argument that economic pressures internal to capitalist states were the primary source of aggressive foreign policies. He argued that the great powers often engaged in expansionist behavior not because they were capitalist, but instead because they were powerful. Capitalism may have contributed to the power of the great imperialist states of the late nineteenth century, since it was the most efficient economic system of the time, just as mercantilism was the most efficient economic system of an earlier time. But it was power itself that led states to expand their interests and act more aggressively in pursuit of their interests.

Waltz's theory of "great power imperialism" is a more general theory of imperialism than that proposed by Lenin, since it is not restricted to a particular historical era. The fact that Lenin ([1916]1939:88–9) defines imperialism as "the monopoly stage of capitalism" has important implications, because it suggests that his theory is not able to explain imperialism that occurs before capitalism has reached the stage of monopoly.[14] This is critical, because the great period of European imperial expansion at the end of the nineteenth century took place prior to the development of monopoly capitalism or finance capital, which Lenin dated to the beginning of the twentieth century (Doyle 1997:355–6). There are also great power imperialisms going back to the ancient Greeks, the Persians, and others. These cannot be easily explained by the Marxist–Leninist theory of industrial capitalism, though class-based theories have been invoked in explanations of many past wars.[15]

Liberal theorists advance a different line of argument. They criticize the Marxist–Leninist view that the internal requirements of capitalist states for markets, investment opportunities, and raw materials leads to imperial and colonial wars to achieve those objectives. That view assumes that access to markets, investment opportunities, and raw materials requires formal political control of the relevant territories, or economic spheres of influence that were closed to competing states. This assumption neglects the fact that even without closed trading spheres, the leading economies can dominate world trade by virtue of their economic efficiencies in production, transportation, and finance. Free trade benefits the economically most efficient states, as Robinson and Gallagher (1950) recognized in their classic study of the "imperialism of free trade."[16]

It is useful to think of conquest and commerce as two alternative strategies for increasing national wealth (Rosecrance, 1986). The great sea powers of Europe, including Britain and the Netherlands, deliberately chose policies that emphasized the efficiency of production in free markets rather than political and territorial control that was more common for the leading continental states (Rasler and Thompson, 1989). While conquest was often the more efficient strategy for some states in earlier historical eras, in the last two centuries a commerce-oriented strategy has generally been more efficient for most states, and certainly for the economically advanced states, especially with the spread of globalization and the efficiency of economic exchange (Rosecrance, 1986).

Other theorists question the specific causal linkages between imperialism and war proposed by Marxist–Leninists. Just because states have motivations to expand to secure markets, investment opportunities, and resources does not necessarily imply that they will end up in war against each other. The link between imperialism and war is underdeveloped in Marxist–Leninist theory. Some of the paths from imperialism to colonial war against a subject people for markets or resources are clear enough, but the links to a war between great powers are less clear.

Many traditional balance of power theorists spoke of the benefits of an "open colonial frontier" that provided ample opportunities for great power expansion in the periphery of the system (at the expense of non-European peoples). Whereas great power conflicts in Europe directly engaged the most vital interests of the great powers, conflicts in the colonies were less likely to engage such vital interests and consequently were more easily resolved. Thus Morgenthau (1967) and many other balance of power theorists argue that imperial expansion might have actually reduced the likelihood of great power war by serving as a "safety valve" and diverting the points of conflict between the great powers from Europe to the periphery. Lenin ([1916]1939: chap. VI) implicitly recognized the validity of this point in his argument that great power wars are relatively unlikely until the world has been territorially divided among the major capitalist states (or monopolies), at which point further expansion becomes zero-sum and more likely to lead to war between the leading capitalist states.

We have relatively little systematic empirical research on the question of whether colonial expansion actually promoted great power peace in the past. Individual historical cases have been examined in considerable detail. One example is World War I. Marxists argue that World War I is a classic case of a war resulting from imperialist rivalries – between Germany and France in Africa, between England and Russia in central Asia, between England and France in Africa. Others argue that imperial expansion served as a safety-valve and that the cross-cutting nature of the imperial and European interests of the great powers dampened the pressures for war. It is significant that many of the leading colonial rivalries were between states that ended up fighting on the same side in World War I (Joll, 1984: chap. 7). Britain opposed Russia in the "great game" in Asia and opposed France in Africa, but the three states fought on the same side against Germany. In addition, most of the colonial rivalries were settled before World War I, in part because of the German threat in Europe.[17] Marxist–Leninist theories have trouble explaining these patterns.

Even some Marxists have questioned the link between imperialism and great power war. The Marxist Karl Kautsky ([1914]1970) referred to an "ultra-imperialism" (or "hyper-imperialism," in which the leading capitalist states formed a cartel to regulate their conflictual tendencies and maintain the peace. Kautsky's argument generated a major debate among Marxist theorists.

Schumpeter and military elites

In response to the Marxist–Leninist view that the primary cause of imperial expansion was capitalism, and in particular the economic interests of the capitalist class, the liberal theorist Schumpeter ([1919]1951), like the

Marxist Kautsky, argued that imperialism was harmful not only to the country as a whole but also to the capitalist class within a country. He argued that modern imperialism and war were bad for business, that capitalist leaders and industrial workers both recognized this, and that they opposed imperialist policies. Other liberal theorists had made similar arguments, but Schumpeter provided a new twist. The reason why states, including capitalist states, pursue imperialist policies, he argued, is that those policies serve the interests of a politically powerful military elite. That elite had long ago gained control of the power of the state, managed to maintain its position of dominance, and used the state to advance its interests through aggressive foreign policies.

Warrior elites first came to power, Schumpeter argued, in earlier eras when war served a useful function in the protection of empires and states against external predators. Once in power, however, warrior elites created a new military aristocracy and used war and the threat of war to justify their policies and maintain their dominant positions despite the fact that the state was secure and that aggressive military policies no longer served a useful purpose. This led Schumpeter ([1919]1951:6) to define imperialism as "an objectless disposition on the part of a state to unlimited forcible expansion,"[18] and to argue that modern military elites are "atavistic" holdovers from an earlier era when they played a useful role providing external security for the state.[19] This is a variant of the "war makes the state" argument advanced by Tilly (1975, 1990).[20] In a memorable statement of his theoretical argument, Schumpeter ([1919]1951:33) argued that "created by the wars that required it, the machine now created the wars it required."

In arguing that wars result primarily from the parochial interests of military organizations, Schumpeter ([1919]1951) seriously underestimated the real conflicts of interests between states, the difficulty of resolving those conflicts, and the escalatory pressures induced by security dilemmas, misperceptions, ideological differences, and domestic pressures. We return to the role of military organizations in chapter 6, but the recent American war in Iraq serves as a reminder that pressures from war often come more from civilian elites than from the military. The German military resisted Hitler's early policies of military expansion (H. Deutsch, 1974), and it was Stalin and the communist party, not the military, that was in back of Soviet expansionism. There is also a big gap in Schumpter's argument about how military elites initially came to power and how they have been able to hold on to power for centuries after that. Still, Schumpeter provided one of the most powerful statements of the idea of politically influential and self-interested military organizations imposing their parochial interests on states. This is an enormously influential argument, one that is central to many theories of the military–industrial complex (Mills, 1956; Rosen,

1973),[21] militarism (Vagts, 1959; Berghahn, 1982), and bureaucratic politics.

Coalitional Models

Most analysts reject the view that either the capitalist class or the military is strong enough to be able to fully capture the state apparatus and use it to advance its own economic or domestic political interests. They focus instead on the kinds of coalitions that form to gain and maintain power and to conduct domestic and foreign policy.

Snyder and logrolled coalitions

For Hobson and for Lenin, imperialism is driven by the economic interests of the capitalist class that gains control of the state. For Schumpeter, imperialism is driven by the political interests of atavistic military elites who use war and the threat of war to rationalize their hold on power. Both arguments emphasize that imperialism and war are contrary to the interests of society as a whole. This raises the question of how economic elites could maintain their hold on power for extended periods when their policies were harmful to the interests of the great majority of people. Jack Snyder (1991) attempted to answer this question in his book *Myths of Empire*, and in the process constructed an alternative theory of expansionist foreign policies.

Snyder concedes that more limited forms of expansion are often explained by system-level factors and by a rational cost–benefit calculation to advance state interests, but his primary focus is "overexpansion." These are cases of expansion – including both overly aggressive policies that trigger great power balancing coalitions and imperial overextension on the "periphery" of the international system – that generate costs that are substantially higher than any conceivable gain from expansion.[22] Snyder accepts the premise that imperialism or overexpansion is harmful to society as a whole, and notes that the only way it can be beneficial to the elite in power is if the elite is relatively small in size, so that members of the elite can reap substantial benefits from socially harmful policies while spreading the costs of such policies throughout society as a whole in the form of taxation.

In terms of collective action theory (Olson 1971), elite interests must be "concentrated" and fairly narrowly defined. But if groups are concentrated enough and narrow enough to benefit from overexpansion while passing the costs of overexpansion on to others, they are almost certainly too narrow to maintain their control over state policy. At some point the vast majority of people, who suffer from overexpansionist policies, would rebel. On the other hand, if the elite in power were broad enough to control state policy, its interests would have to be diffused over many groups, and it would not be able to reap enough of the benefits from socially costly over-expansion to make that expansion worthwhile, since they could not pass on the broader costs of those policies to society.

The solution to this dilemma, according to Snyder, is that key internal groups – each with parochial interests in limited but different forms of imperial expansion, military build-ups, or autarkic economic policies – create logrolled coalitions. The joint political strength of these coalitions is strong enough for them to be able to rule, and their joint interests are concentrated enough to be able to reap many of the benefits of expansionist policies while passing on the broader social costs to society as a whole. This comes at a cost, however, since the policies emerging from these logrolled compromises are more expansionist than either would prefer individually and often also more expansionist than can be supported by the available resources of the state.

In Snyder's view, logrolled coalitions among elites with shared interests are not sufficient to explain overexpansion or the stability of the ruling coalition behind it, because they fail to explain why the public goes along. Snyder (1991) argues that key elites justify their power and policies by promoting "strategic myths" that provide a justification for their expansionist policies. These myths include exaggeration of the current hostility of other states and of historical injustices committed by those states, of the strategic and economic value of empire, and of the likelihood that the adversary will back down in the face of hardline policies or that any war will involve minimal costs. The use of historical analogies based on lessons from the past plays an important part in the creation of national myths.

Note that in Snyder's (1991) model, political leaders are not really learn-ing from history, but instead selectively using history to rationalize their predetermined views and influence others. This "strategic" or "rhetorical" use of history runs contrary to a "learning model," in which individuals genuinely learn from historical experience (Jervis, 1976; Khong, 1992). We examine theories of learning in chapter 5.

Although elite behavior is rational and strategic in Snyder's (1991) model, the same cannot be said of behavior of the masses, since the majority of people are driven by symbolic politics and appeals to patriotism. This explains why they succumb to these myths and support the existing coali-tion even though its policies are often contrary to their interests. Snyder goes on to argue that in the end even elites depart from a pure rationality by buying into their own myths. They often internalize their own rhetoric or become politically entrapped in it. This inhibits their ability to learn from history. It also increases the obstacles to disengaging from increasingly costly expansionist policies.

Snyder (1991) further develops his theory by specifying the conditions under which these kinds of logrolled coalitions are most likely to arise. That occurs in cartelized political systems dominated by distinct concentrated interests and the lack of a centralized political leadership to minimize the role of parochial interests. This is illustrated by Germany prior to World War I. Many historians have traced German expansionism to the "coalition of iron and rye" that dominated German politics for many years (Fischer, 1975; Wehler, 1985). Snyder's theoretical model captures these dynamics quite well. Navalists and their shipbuilding allies wanted to expand the navy, but that risked alienating England. Agriculturalists in the East wanted protectionist policies to shield them from inexpensive grain from Russia, but those policies risked alienating Russia. Neither group had the political power to implement their preferred policies.

In response, these groups formed a coalition in which each backed the preferred policies of the other. The result was a policy of both naval expansion and economic protectionism against Russia. Germany could probably have handled either of these external threats individually. What they could not handle was a combination of British and Russian hostility, which was the price the coalition of iron and rye paid to secure both of their policies. This increased hostility was an important domestic factor contributing to the rise of tensions leading to World War I. It was particularly important in generating both the Anglo–German naval race (Kennedy, 1982) and the Franco–Russian Alliance, which contributed to the encirclement of Germany and the intensity of the security dilemma for Germany.

Snyder argued that overexpansion occurs in democratic political systems, but that it is less frequent and less extreme. In democracies, where political leaders are responsible to a large electorate, interests are diffuse rather than concentrated. Consequently, it is harder for a single economic interest group to gain the concentrated benefits from expansionist policies and also harder for coalitions to form. In addition, in democracies in which there is a relatively free press, the expression of multiple points of view inhibits the formation of information monopolies and the development of strategic myths that serve parochial interests. Overexpansion is less likely in unitary oligarchies, in which a small elite has clear responsibility for policy and encompassing interests in avoiding the costs of overexpansion. Snyder argues that overexpansion is less predictable in dictatorial systems (Saddam's Iraq, for example) in which there is no check on the preferences of the leader.

The theory of logrolled coalitions advanced by Snyder focuses on the foreign policy of a particular state, and particularly on state strategies that lead to overexpansion. Snyder's model is not technically a model of war, because whether or not war occurs depends on the reaction of other states. Note that even the concept of overexpansion is somewhat problematic, because whether expansion is *over*expansion depends on the reactions of other states. Presumably, if expansionist behavior is not forcibly resisted or if the expansionist state wins the war at acceptable costs, the outcome is not defined as overexpansion. Snyder's theory implies that we need one theory to explain overexpansion and a different theory to explain expansionist policies that fall short of overexpansion. It would be far preferable to have a single theory of expansion. Still, Snyder has made an important contribution to the literature by emphasizing the role of concentrated and encompassing interests and their impact on coalition formation in foreign security policy.

Other coalitional theories

While Snyder (1991) focuses on imperial expansion and gives primary emphasis to the politics and compromises within the imperial bloc, other theorists have focused on the competition between opposing coalitions for power and influence within the liberal state (Fordham, 1998; Lobell, 2006; Narizny, 2007). Like Snyder's (1991) theory of overexpansion, these are not so much theories of the causes of war as theories of the grand strategies states adopt in response to external threats. Each emphasizes the internal distributional consequences of alternative foreign policies for different groups within society (Rogowski, 1989), since the costs of increased defense spending and the policies associated with them are not borne equally by all groups within society. These theorists assume that domestic economic coalitions pressure the government based on their own economic self-interests.

Narizny (2007) presents a class-based analysis of the grand strategies of liberal democratic states, but one that departs from a Marxist framework in its theoretical foundations and in many of its predictions. He notes the conventional wisdom that leftist governments are weak on defense, and argues instead that leftist governments have historically been more likely than rightist governments to undertake major increases in military spending in response to external threats. Confronted with external threats, conservative governments are more inclined to seek external alliances or to attempt to appease their adversaries. Narizny explains these patterns by focusing on the economic interests of the primary coalition partners of left and right governments.

Conservative governments hesitate to pay for increased military spending through regressive taxation that imposes a burden on the poor because leaders fear both the electoral consequences of such taxation and possibly also some short-term mass social unrest, which might impede efforts to mobilize the economy and the country for war. Conservative governments also hesitate to raise taxes on the wealthy because the upper and upper-middle classes tied to rightist coalitions are unwilling to accept the increased taxes required for armament. They also fear the economic inflation and general monetary instability that often accompany massive increases in military spending, along with the increased government intervention in the economy and imposition of economic controls that are likely to follow.

Narizny argues that labor governments are generally more willing to support policies of massive rearmament in response to external threat. They are less constrained in taxing the rich, who are not part of their political coalition. Labor governments also see national security threats as providing an opportunity to take steps toward advancing some of their other political goals over the long term. Although a massive rearmament program usually precludes the expansion of social welfare programs in the short term, increasing taxation increases the extractive power of the state, which can eventually be used to expand social welfare programs. The economic regulation associated with rearmament programs can also be retained after the threat passes, resulting in more controls and greater regulation of the economy over the long term.

Thus Narizny concludes that leftist governments are more willing than rightist governments to build up armaments when faced with an external threat, while conservative governments prefer to avoid defense spending by securing allies against external threats or perhaps appeasing those threats. Narizny is careful, however, to suggest scope conditions that specify when the model should and should not apply.

First of all, Narizny argues that the theory applies only to states that are sharply divided by class, where one major party represents the interests of the working poor and another represents the wealthy.[23] He restricts his hypotheses to the behavior of the government, not to the party in opposition. He also argues that the theory applies to situations in which a democratic government faces a sharp increase in threat in its strategic environment, but not to situations involving only a modest increase in threat, where a massive rearmament program would not be necessary. Under such conditions, Narizny concedes that the conventional wisdom of leftist pacifism and conservative militarism might hold.[24] In addition, Narizny suggests that his theory does not apply to states at war or at the brink of war, where any government may have few policy alternatives to a rapid increase in armaments.[25] These scope conditions add to the precision of Narizny's model, and are useful for that purpose, but they significantly limit the generalizability of the model.

Narizny (2007) applies his theory to Britain and the United States since the 1860s and to France before the two world wars of the twentieth century. He concedes that one situation in which his theory fails to explain observed behavior is for the United States during the 1980s, where a conservative Reagan Administration undertook a major defense build-up against the Soviet Union. A better fit for the model is Britain in the 1930s. The conservative government of Neville Chamberlain, faced with the rising threat from Nazi Germany, adopted a strategy of appeasement rather than one of confrontation, while the opposition of the left was much more willing to support a confrontational policy against Germany. Narizny argues that the conservative Chamberlain government adopted the appeasement policy and was slow to rearm because they hesitated to impose taxes on the wealthy or to take actions that would result in increased government controls over the economy.[26]

Lobell (2006) proposes a similar political economy model that explains responses to external threat in terms of the internal distributive consequences of different policy responses to external threat. Lobell identifies two primary domestic coalitions. One group is an outward-looking internationalist coalition that consists of the internationally competitive sectors of the economy and their allies, and the other is an economic nationalist coalition consisting of less competitive sectors and domestic-oriented groups. The internationalist coalition includes fiscal conservatives, export-oriented firms, large banking and financial services, skilled labor, and finance-oriented bureaucracies. It prefers balanced budgets, low taxation, and low government spending, and it favors strong ties to the outside world and policies of conciliation and appeasement, arms control alliances, collective security arrangements. These internationalist groups oppose building up armaments except as a last resort, for fear that an arms build-up will increase the cost of capital, curtail savings and investment, and reduce foreign exchange. They also fear that an arms build-up would increase inflation, budget deficits, taxes, economic controls, and state planning.

The supporters of the economic nationalist coalition, Lobell (2006) argues, are the domestic beneficiaries from the extraction of societal resources and other policies associated with the mobilization for war. These groups include inefficient industry and agriculture, import-substituting manufacturing firms, labor-intensive industry, public sector managers and workers, and imperial bureaucracies. They prefer policies that protect domestic industry and agriculture from foreign competition, that favor greater military preparedness and rearmament in the face of external threat, and (in older times) that favor stronger links to empire and colonies.

In an application of his model to Britain prior to World War I, Lobell (2006) argues that it was the shift from an internationalist coalition in the 1912–14 period to a nationalist coalition in the 1914–16 period that led to a shift in Britain's grand strategy from one of "limited liability" to one involving a "continental commitment" and a more aggressive war plan. Lobell's interpretation of the 1930s is similar to Narizny's (2007): the Chamberlain government pursued a policy of appeasement because it was unwilling to pay for significant increases in defense spending through increased taxation, which would burden the supporters of the internationalist coalition. That coalition would also object to the increased regulation of the market economy that would follow.[27]

The domestic theories of grand strategy advanced by Narizny (2007) and Lobell (2006) are important theoretical contributions that provide alternatives to standard realist arguments that grand strategy aims to maximize state interests. In addition, their explanations of the appeasement policies of the 1930s are important contributions to the historical literature. Some have argued, however, that a realist interpretation of appeasement in the 1930s cannot so easily be dismissed. They argue that appeasement was based on the recognition that Britain was weak both in military and economic terms. Appeasement was a strategy for buying time for rearmament against Germany and for delaying a confrontation until Britain was in a stronger position to either deter Hitler from military aggression (Layne, 2008) or to prepare for a war they believed was probable (Ripsman and Levy, 2008).

Britain did in fact accelerate its defense spending beginning in the mid-1930s and then with more urgency in 1938. The primary reason that military spending did not increase more rapidly, in this view, was British leaders' fears that Britain's long-term decline and the worldwide depression left the British economy in a precarious position. More rapid spending would undermine the economic foundations that were necessary for Britain's ability to mount a sustained recovery and fight a long war, which was the only kind of war Britain would be able to win. In this view, the economic costs of excessively rapid rearmament would hurt the country as a whole, not just the upper and middle classes. The primary constraint on political leaders was the national economic interest, not pressures from particular domestic groups or classes. In this view, British appeasement policy was a realist strategy driven by the aim of advancing the national interest, not parochial private interests, but was conducted under severe internal and external constraints.[28]

Narizny (2007) and Lobell (2006) offer purely economic models of grand strategy, and posit that the willingness to accept the costs of a military build-up is a function of the economic interests of particular domestic groups. One factor they neglect is the ability of the political leader to use the symbolic politics of nationalism to unite a country facing an external threat behind his or her government. This is a key theme in the diversionary theory of war, to which we now turn.

The Diversionary Theory of War

Four centuries ago, Bodin ([1576]1955:168–9) wrote that "the best way of preserving a state, and guaranteeing it against sedition, rebellion, and civil war is … to find an enemy against whom they can make common cause." At about the same time, Shakespeare ([1596]1845) suggested to statesmen that: "Be it thy course to busy giddy minds/With foreign quarrels." Wright (1965:727) argued that a key cause of war is the belief that war is a "necessary or convenient means ... to establish, maintain, or expand the power of a government, party, or class within a state." It is now conventional wisdom that the use of force by an American president, under nearly any circumstances, generates a "rally 'round the flag" effect that boosts his popularity among the electorate, if only temporarily (Mueller, 1973; Kernell, 1978).

The tendency for foreign crises and wars to generate a "rally 'round the flag" effect that increases popular support for political leaders and often the power of the government is often explained in terms of the "in-group/out-group" (or "conflict–cohesion") hypothesis. This was first proposed by Simmel (1898), who argued that conflict with an out-group increases the cohesion and political centralization of the in-group. He extended the hypothesis to international relations, and argued that "war with the outside is sometimes the last chance for a state ridden with inner antagonisms to overcome these antagonisms, or else to break up definitely." Political leaders understand this, and leaders feeling insecure about their leadership positions may be tempted to provoke hostility with external groups in order to trigger a "rally" effect and thereby bolster their own support within the group.

Simmel recognized a need to qualify his argument, however, because under some conditions war can have the opposite effect and lead to a reduction of social cohesion. He noted that war "might either cause domestic quarrels to be forgotten, or might on the contrary aggravate them beyond reconciliation" (Simmel, 1898:832). This line of argument was developed further by Coser (1956:93–5), who argued that external conflict will increase the cohesion of the in-group only under certain conditions: if the group already exists as a "going concern," if it has some minimal level of internal cohesion, if it perceives itself as a group and the preservation of the group as worthwhile, and if it believes that the external threat menaces the in-group as a whole and not just one part of it. In the absence of these conditions, external conflict will exacerbate internal conflict rather than dampen it, perhaps to the point of rebellion. While some German leaders in 1914 were eager for war because they feared the rising tide of social democracy at home and believed that war would distract attention from social issues and unite the country around the German leadership (Kaiser, 1983), German Chancellor Bethmann-Hollweg feared the divisive and potentially revolutionary consequences of war (Berghahn, 1973).

The in-group/out-group or conflict–cohesion hypothesis has been so widely accepted among social scientists (although often without acknowledgment of the Simmel–Coser qualifications) that some have suggested that it has acquired the status of a general law of behavior. Dahrendorf (1959:58), for example, argues that: "It appears to be a general law that human groups react to external pressure by increased internal coherence." This is a major theme in social identity theory (Worchel and Austin, 1986) and in the literature on the anthropology of war (Ferguson, 1999), and it has potentially significant implications for international relations theory (Mercer, 1995).

Historians and political scientists have identified numerous cases in which political leaders' concerns about their low or falling levels of domestic support contributed, in some instances quite significantly, to their decisions to go to war. As the Russian minister of the interior supposedly said on the eve of the Russo–Japanese War in 1904, "What this country needs is a short victorious war to stem the tide of revolution" (White, 1964:38; Lebow 1981:66).[29] Similarly, the Crimean War (1853–6) has been interpreted by many in terms of Louis Napoleon's attempt to increase his political support at home, particularly among French Catholics, by aggressively supporting the Catholics in Jerusalem against the Russian-backed Greek Orthodox. As Karl Marx said of the French leader, he "has no alternative left but revolution at home or war abroad" (Mayer, 1977:225). Finally, the scholarly consensus is that a leading motivation for the Argentine invasion of the British-controlled Malvinas Islands in 1982 was the hope of maintaining the internal political power of the Argentine military junta through a major military success abroad (Levy and Vakili, 1992).[30]

Despite the numerous examples of leaders being drawn to war by the hopes of bolstering their domestic political support, it is clear that domestic political insecurity does not always lead to external scapegoating. It is also clear that the use of low-level military force for diversionary purposes does not always lead to war. Statistical studies of the relationship between domestic problems and the use of external military force – between domestic threats to regime security and the tendency of governments to respond by "bashing the foreigners" (Russett, 1990) – have generated mixed results, with most of the evidence suggesting that any relationship, if it exists, is not a strong one (Meernick, 2004).[31]

The mixed nature of the statistical evidence raises the question of the conditions under which leaders are most likely to adopt a diversionary strategy. Among the conditions that scholars have identified are low to moderate levels of domestic political support and legitimacy and poor economic performance, which is a major factor contributing to low support levels. It is also argued that democractic regimes are more prone to the "political" use of force during certain periods of the electoral cycle. Most scholars argue that the likelihood of external scapegoating is greatest in the periods leading up to an election, as long as it is not so close as to be too obvious (Russett, 1990; James and Oneal, 1991).[32] Although most studies focus on overall support levels for political leaders as a key independent variable, some scholars argue that overall political support for the leader is less important than the level of partisan support – that is, support from citizens who are members of the leader's own political party and who therefore are most likely to vote for the leader (Morgan and Bickers, 1992).

The fact that democratic leaders are more directly accountable to their constituents than are authoritarian leaders generates the common argument that external scapegoating is more likely in democratic states than in non-democratic states (Gelpi, 1997).[33] Although this is a plausible hypothesis, even non-democratic leaders must maintain domestic support from key groups in government and society – the military, internal security apparatus, financial community, or labor (Haggard and Kaufman, 1995; Geddes, 2003) – and the support of those constituencies may also be enhanced by diversionary behavior.

Many of the examples of scapegoating noted above involve external military action by non-democratic regimes. The question of whether democratic or non-democratic groups are more prone to external scapegoating is an interesting empirical question that scholars have only begun to investigate. Also interesting are the questions of whether some types of democratic regimes – presidential or parliamentary – are more prone to diversionary behavior than others (M. Elman, 2000), and whether some types of authoritarian regimes – personalist, military, or single-party (Geddes, 2003) – are more prone to external scapegoating than are others (Pickering and Kisangani, 2005; Weeks, 2008).

Another question that has received relatively little attention by scholars is that of who are the *targets* of diversionary action.[34] Presumably some states or groups make more useful targets than others for the purposes of generating a substantial and sustained domestic rally effect at minimum risk, but diversionary theory lacks a theory of targets.[35] One hypothesis is that because a leaders' domestic support is rarely enhanced by losing a war, they tend to avoid militarily superior adversaries.[36] Some might argue that weak states do not pose sufficiently serious threats to generate rally effects, but the popular response to the US military intervention against Grenada in 1983 illustrates the power of symbolic scapegoating even in the absence of a serious external threat.

Going back to the discussion of international rivalries in the last chapter, we might hypothesize that historical rivals make particularly good targets for scapegoating, especially if those rivals are not too strong (Mitchell and Prins, 2004). Another hypothesis is that because of the emotions generated by ethnic loyalties and the historical grievances associated with them, ethnic rivals, unfortunately, make particularly useful targets for scapegoating by political elites. This is well-illustrated by Yugoslavian President Milošević's manipulation of ethnic rivalries in the Yugoslav wars in the early 1990s (Gagnon, 2004).

The selection of the targets of diversionary behavior, as well as the perceived degree of hostility of the target, can also influenced by the media.

Autocratic governments can often manipulate the media to exaggerate the hostility of other states, by emphasizing historical injustices or current actions or intentions. Alternatively, in states characterized by weak central governments and strong divisions among communal groups within society, media loyal to particular groups can themselves engage in scapegoating rhetoric against external foes.

In Yugoslavia, for example, increasing liberalization during the 1980s provided an opportunity for each of the ethnic republics to form their own television stations. In the absence of centralized institutional regulation, each of these stations offered quite unflattering portrayals of the neighboring republics rather than objectively reporting the news. The lack of "strong central state institutions to promote a professional, unbiased, pan-Yugoslav mass media" encouraged the post-Tito fragmentation of popular conceptions of state identity, and contributed to the tensions precipitating the wars of 1992–5. To take another example, the Hutu majority in Rwanda responded to international pressure to democratize by quickly terminating all media censorship, which unleashed a torrent of anti-Tutsi propaganda that directly contributed to the Rwandan genocide of 1994 (Snyder 2000:219, 301–4; Knievel, 2008).

This discussion of diversionary behavior against "other" communal groups reinforces the argument made earlier about the lack of integration of the scholarly literatures on interstate war and on civil war. Scholars of interstate warfare study "diversionary behavior," and scholars of civil war study the role of "ethnic entrepreneurs" in mobilizing opinion against certain groups (often ethnic) as a means of enhancing their own legitimacy and political power. These two groups of scholars are talking about essentially the same thing, but it is striking how little each group of scholars engages the theoretical and empirical work of the other. It is symbolic of the gap between the analysis of interstate and intrastate war.

Another interesting puzzle is the gap between the findings of two different approaches to the study of diversionary behavior in interstate war. Those who look in depth at historical cases tend to conclude that diversionary behavior is fairly common and that it can have a significant impact on state behavior. Those who do statistical analyses of large numbers of cases, however, tend to find rather mixed evidence for the general theoretical argument that domestic problems contribute to the external use of military force for political purposes. From a social science perspective, these differences are troubling, as we can usually be most confident in the validity of a theoretical argument if we get the same answer by using a number of different approaches. International relations scholars are currently attempting to resolve these differences.

Earlier we noted that scholars have yet to fully resolve the question of whether democratic or non-democratic states are more likely to engage in the diversionary use of force. We also noted that scholars have paid relatively little attention to the question of what kinds of states are the most common targets of diversionary behavior. One combination that is particularly unlikely, however, is a democracy taking diversionary action involving high levels of military force against another democracy. There is strong evidence that democratic states, whatever their motivations, rarely if ever go to war with each other. Scholars refer to this as the "democratic peace," which we now examine.

The Democratic Peace

Although liberals have always argued that democracies are somehow more peaceful than are other states, and although Immanuel Kant ([1795]1949) spoke of a "pacific union" among republican regimes and Thomas Paine ([1791/92]1969) offered an even stronger conception of democratic peace a few years earlier (Walker, 2000), the dominant view of democracy among international relations scholars for many years after World War II reflected the prevailing realist orthodoxy. Hans Morgenthau (1967), who was the primary inspiration for American realism, worried that "nationalistic universalism," which included popular ideologies like democracy and communism, would detract from the effective functioning of a balance of power system. George Kennan (1951), the intellectual founder of American containment doctrine, criticized the "moralistic/legalistic approach" that characterized American foreign policy and that detracted from the pursuit of the national interest, which he defined in terms of power. The general argument was made over a century earlier by Alexis de Tocqueville ([1835]1975:243–4) in his famous book *Democracy in America*, which he wrote while visiting the United States from his native France:

> Foreign policies demand scarcely any of those qualities which are peculiar to a democracy; they require, on the contrary, the perfect use of almost all those in which it is deficient. ... a democracy can only with great difficulty regulate the details of an important undertaking, persevere in a fixed design, and work out its execution in spite of serious obstacles. It cannot combine its measures with secrecy or await their consequences with patience. ... Democracies ... obey impulse rather than prudence and ... abandon a mature design for the gratification of a momentary passion.

The argument that democracies are sometime driven more by passion than by prudence is often linked to the idea that democracies, because they often need to justify their foreign policies in terms of liberal democratic ideologies that appeal to their constituents, have a tendency to engage in ideological wars that can be particularly destructive and that are sometimes transformed into crusades to rid the world of evil.[37] US President Woodrow Wilson, for example, stated that the purpose of American intervention in World War I was to "make the world safe for democracy." President Franklin Roosevelt presented World War II to the American people as an ideological crusade. The potential destructiveness of the wars of democracies was not a surprise to some. In a speech in the House of Commons, May 13, 1901, Winston Churchill argued that "democracy is more vindictive than Cabinets. The wars of peoples will be more terrible than those of kings."

Since the 1980s, however, a new consensus has emerged about the unique features of democratic states and their foreign policy behavior. The point of departure for this new conceptualization of the role of democracy in international relations was an article published in a non-political science journal by a non-political scientist (Babst, 1972). It argued that democracies almost never go to war with each other. This was followed by an article by Singer and Small (1976) that expressed skepticism about this claim, and then by two articles by Doyle (1983), who offered systematic evidence that democracies rarely if ever go to war with each other and a plausible theoretical explanation for why this might be true.

At that point the "democratic peace" became a central focus of scholarly research in international relations (Russett, 1993; Ray, 1995; Maoz, 1997; Russett and Starr, 2000; Bueno de Mesquita et al., 2003; Russett and Oneal, 2001; Rasler and Thompson, 2005). This extraordinarily strong empirical regularity, with few if any compelling counterexamples (more on this later), was quite striking in a domain as complex as international relations, where the actions and interactions of states are influenced by so many different factors and where regularized patterns of behavior are difficult to find.[38]

Although interest in the democratic peace began with an unusually strong empirical finding, that interest was intensified by the fact that the observed pattern contradicted realist theories,[39] provided the core of an emerging liberal theory of peace and war, reinforced the ideological foundations of American foreign policy, provided some justification for an interventionist foreign policy, and gave some reason for optimism that the persistent pattern of international war might one day be broken.

One point of possible confusion regarding the democratic peace relates to our comment in chapter 1 that patterns of behavior at one unit of analysis are not necessarily replicated at, or are transferable to, another unit of analysis. Evidence that democratic states rarely if ever go to war with each other, which is what most scholars mean by the "democratic peace" and which is a dyadic-level proposition, does not necessarily imply that democratic states are more "peaceful" than other states, which is a national or "monadic"-level proposition about a state's involvement in wars, regardless of the nature of the adversary.[40]

In the early stages of research on democracy and war, most scholars believed that democracies were just as likely to get involved in wars (regardless of the adversary's regime type) as were non-democratic states. This was based on evidence that democratic–autocratic dyads were the most warprone of all dyads, which countered the peaceful nature of democratic–democratic dyads, with authoritarian–authoritarian dyads falling in between in terms of their degree of war-proneness.[41] More recently, a number of scholars have contested this assumption and argued that democracies are in fact more peaceful in their monadic war behavior (Rummel, 1995a; Benoit, 1996; Maoz, 1997; Russett and Starr, 2000), but a strong consensus has yet to arise. In part it depends on what kinds of wars one counts. The inclusion of colonial wars, many of which were fought by democracies beginning in the late nineteenth century, would increase the average frequency of war for democratic states, whereas a focus only on interstate wars would lower that average frequency.

The study of the democratic peace has gone through a number of phases. The first phase was largely descriptive, aimed at validating the statement that democracies rarely if ever go to war with each other. This phase involved carefully defining war and defining democracy (Doyle, 1983; Russett, 1993; Ray, 1995), compiling a list of wars during the nineteenth and twentieth centuries, and ascertaining whether any of the pairs of democracies ever engaged in wars.

Research on the democratic peace generally accepts the definition of war as "large-scale, institutionally organized, lethal violence" (Russett, 1993:12), with large scale defined in terms of 1,000 battle-related deaths on both sides (following the "Correlates of War Project" criteria offered by Singer and Small, 1972). Scholars vary somewhat in their definition of democracy. Common elements include regular, free, and competitive elections involving the free participation of opposition parties; a voting franchise for a substantial proportion of citizens, where the vote could be either for an executive or for a parliament to which the executive is responsible; at least one peaceful or constitutional transfer of power; and a minimal period of longevity as a democracy, which allows time for a culture of democracy to arise (Russett, 1993; Ray, 1995; Doyle, 1997).[42]

There was a fair amount of early skepticism about the validity of the democratic peace proposition, and critics identified a number of possible exceptions to the hypothesized absence of war between democracies. This led to the next stage of the democratic peace research program – a detailed examination of these hypothesized exceptions through intensive case study analysis, with particularly close attention to the definitions of democracy and of war.

One such case was the War of 1812 between Great Britain and the United States. Most scholars concluded, however, that Britain was still ruled by a king who was not responsible to parliament in the conduct of foreign policy. In addition, some emphasized that American leaders did not perceive Britain as democratic until much later in the nineteenth century (Owen, 1997). This was relevant given the argument, particularly by constructivists, that political leaders' perceptions of its adversary are critical because those perceptions strongly influence the degree of cooperation from the adversary.[43]

The American Civil War was also raised as a possible exception to the democratic peace proposition. Although its status as a civil war does not technically violate the "no war between democratic states" criterion, and although the South did not satisfy the definitional criterion of being an enduring democracy for a minimal period (usually taken to be three years), the war does violate the spirit of many of the theoretical arguments advanced in support of the democratic peace hypothesis. The Spanish–American War (1898) is also suggested as a possible anomaly in the democratic peace, but many question whether Spain met the criteria for a democracy at that time. Still other critics point to World War I, but the fact that Germany's elected Reichstag had little impact on German foreign policy violates one of the definitional criteria for democracy.[44]

The problematic nature of many of the proposed exceptions to the democratic peace have led many to conclude that it is a highly robust proposition, one that is not particularly sensitive to small modifications in the definition of democracy. That is, there are very few unambiguous cases of democracies going to war with each other.[45] Most of the proposed exceptions are genuine borderline cases, either in terms of crossing the threshold for democracy or crossing the threshold for war. Some argue that a recent exception, however, is the 1999 Kargil War between India and Pakistan. India was clearly a democracy, Pakistan is coded as democracy in 1999 by the Polity III data, and most treatments list the conflict as surpassing the minimum 1,000 battle death threshold required a war. Many South Asian specialists reject Polity III's classification of Pakistan as a democracy (though not a continuous one), however, given the influence of the non-elected Pakistani armed forces on the decisions of elected political leaders and on how long they stay in power (Tremblay and Schofield, 2005:231–3).

With the reasonably strong consensus that democratic states rarely if ever fight each other, some scholars have argued that this result is a statistical artifact that results from the limited number of democratic states in the international system (at least until recent times), from the geographic separation of democratic states (since the vast majority of wars are between contiguous states), or from the fact that democratic dyads trade a lot with each other and that trade has pacifying effects. Still others argue that the democratic peace exists primarily in the period since World War II and happens to coincide with the Cold War and American hegemonic power, which suppressed potential conflicts between democracies (Farber and Gowa, 1995; Gowa, 1999).

Another line of argument is that democracies have a distinctive set of interests, and that is the mutually compatible interests between democratic states, and not anything to do with their internal makeup, that explains the rarity of war between them (Gartzke, 2000). A variation on this theme is that the relationship between democracy and peace is not universal but applies most strongly to economically developed states, in part because market economies generate shared interests (Mousseau 2000, 2009; Gartzke, 2007). Gibler (2007) argues that many democracies are older, established states that have resolved their territorial conflicts, thus significantly reducing a potent source of violent conflict. Others agree that democratic dyads are peaceful but argue that causality runs from peace to democracy rather than from democracy to peace – peaceful conditions promote the rise and maturation of stable democratic states (Thompson, 1996; Rasler and Thompson, 2005; but see Mousseau and Shi 1999).

Debates about the democratic peace continue, but there is now a strong consensus that democracies rarely if ever fight each other and that this regularity is not the spurious result of other factors like relative power, alliances, and contiguity (Bremer, 1992; Brown et al., 1996; Doyle, 1997; Maoz, 1997; Ray, 1995, 2000; Russett and Oneal, 2001).[46] An explanation for the absence of war between democracies must have something to do with democracy, though it might involve other factors as well.[47]

The major debate now concerns what it is about democracy that contributes to the dyadic democratic peace. Scholars have proposed a number of alternative answers but there is little agreement on which one provides the best explanation. At this point most scholars would agree that the relative absence of war between democracies is an extraordinarily strong empirical regularity in search of a theory to explain it. This is significant, because in the absence of a good theoretical explanation, we cannot say with confidence that the democratic peace will persist into the future as international and domestic conditions change.

One criterion that we can use to rule out some possible explanations for the inter-democratic peace is that a viable explanation must be consistent with other empirically validated patterns of behavior involving democratic states.[48] At a minimum, any explanation for the dyadic peace between democracies must not contradict these other observed relationships, and ideally it should explain them.[49] For example, although debate continues on the monadic question as to whether democracies are more peaceful than are other states, it is clear that if there is a positive relationship, it is probably only modest in strength. Otherwise the monadic debate would have been settled by now. This suggests that any theoretical argument that implies that democracies are *significantly* more peaceful than are other states is problematic.

We also know that democracies frequently fight imperial wars; that in wars between democracies and autocracies the democracy is more likely to be the initiator than the target; and that democracies occasionally use covert action against each other (Ray, 1995, 2000; Reiter and Stam, 2002; Russett and Oneal, 2001; Bueno de Mesquita et al., 2003). In addition, democratic–authoritarian dyads are more war-prone than are pure authoritarian dyads, and democracies are much less prone to civil war or extreme human rights violations (Hegre et al., 2001; Rummel, 1995b). These are each fairly strong patterns, and an explanation for the absence of war between democracies must not violate these patterns. We must reject, for example, any hypothesized explanation of the absence of war between democracies that implies that democracies do not initiate wars.

An explanation for the democratic peace must also be consistent with evidence that democracies almost never end up on opposing sides in multilateral wars, that they win a disproportionate number of the wars they fight, that they suffer fewer casualties in the wars they initiate (Reiter and Stam, 2002), and that they engage in more peaceful processes of conflict resolution when they get into disputes with other democracies (Dixon, 1994).

At the present time there are several alternative explanations for the democratic peace and its related hypotheses, though new explanations are being offered all the time. One is the *democratic culture and norms model* (Owen, 1997; Russett and Oneal, 2001). There are several variations. One, which overlaps with the institutional constraints model, suggests that democratic societies are inherently averse to war because, as Kant ([1795]1949:438) argued, "the consent of the citizens is required in order to decide whether there should be war or not," and the people will "hesitate to start such an evil game" by voting to send themselves off to war. For these reasons, democracies are highly averse to the casualties of war.[50] In addition, democracies share norms of bounded political competition and peaceful resolution of disputes; and these internal democratic norms are extended to relations between democratic states.[51] Democracies shed norms of peaceful conflict resolution in relations with non-democratic states, however, for fear of being exploited.[52]

The plausibility of the normative model of the democratic peace is undercut by the fact that such norms have not precluded democratic states from initiating imperial wars against weaker opponents despite the absence of any threat of exploitation by the latter, or from fighting wars against autocracies with an intensity that is disproportionate to any plausible security threat. These concerns led some to supplement a democratic culture argument with a constructivist emphasis on shared identity (Risse-Kappen, 1995), which provides a more plausible explanation for democratic hostility toward non-democratic states. The argument is that other democratic states are treated as part of a shared identity group, while non-democratic states are treated as the "other," which psychologically facilitates hostile behavior. Yet democracies do engage in covert action against each other (James and Mitchell, 1995), and they occasionally use low levels of military force against each other (Bueno de Mesquita and Lalman, 1992; Bueno de Mesquita et al., 2003), which is not consistent with the idea of a shared identity of democratic states.

The *institutional constraints model* of the democratic peace emphasizes checks and balances, the dispersion of power, and the role of a free press. These institutions preclude political leaders from taking unilateral military action, ensure an open public debate, and require leaders to secure a broad base of public support before adopting risky policies. As a result, leaders are risk-averse with respect to decisions for war and can take forceful actions only in response to serious immediate threats (Morgan and Campbell, 1991; Siverson, 1995).

Although the institutional constraints model provides a plausible explanation for the relative absence of wars between democracies, like the democratic norms model it fails to explain why democracies frequently fight imperial wars despite the absence of direct and serious security threats. It also fails to explain why democracies get involved in wars just as frequently, or almost as frequently, as do non-democratic states. Proponents of the institutional and cultural models respond by arguing that because there are fewer internal constraints on the use of force by authoritarian leaders, they often attempt to exploit the conciliatory tendencies of democracies. This undermines democratic political leaders' expectations that their peaceful conflict resolution strategies will be reciprocated, reduces their internal constraints on the use of force, and provides additional incentives for democratic regimes to use force against authoritarian regimes to eliminate their violent tendencies. This does not necessarily imply that democracies fight autocracies only in defense against aggression. In fact, most of the wars between democratic and non-democratic states are initiated by democracies (Reiter and Stam, 2002).

In addition, the institutional model assumes that leaders have more warlike preferences than do their publics, which is why leaders need to be constrained by peoples who hesitate to vote to send themselves off to war, knowing that they will be the ones to suffer. The combination of hawkish rulers and pacifistic publics may often be the case, but it is not always true. Belligerent publics sometimes push their leaders into wars those leaders prefer to avoid.

A good example is the Spanish–American War of 1898, a common explanation for which is that the US was pushed into war by jingoist public opinion fueled by a "yellow press" (May, 1961).[53] To take another case, it is often argued that before his assassination in 1963, President Kennedy had come to realize that an American victory in the Vietnam War was not possible, and that he planned to withdraw American troops from the Indo-china. He was afraid to do so until after the next election, however, because he feared that he would be blamed politically for losing Vietnam to the communists (Ellsberg, 1972). Kennedy felt constrained to continue the war, at least for a time, because of what he perceived as a hawkish public opinion. There are countless other cases in which political leaders might prefer to make compromises with the adversary but conclude that it would be political suicide to do so. Negotiations between Arab and Israeli leaders often fit this pattern. Mass publics, or at least a politically influential segment of them, are sometimes more hawkish than are political leaders, which raises questions about the validity of the institutional model of the democratic peace.

Many of the patterns associated with democratic war behavior are explained by Bueno de Mesquita et al. (2003), whose general *selectorate model* of politics provides an alternative institutional explanation of the democratic peace. The selectorate model begins with the premise that the primary goal of political leaders is the maintenance of their positions of political power. A key variable in the model is the relative sizes of the "selectorate" (hence the label for the model) and of the "winning coalition" in a political system. The selectorate consists of all people who have some influence on policy. The winning coalition consists of those whose support is necessary for a political leader and his or her regime to maintain their positions of power. In the United States, the selectorate consists of all eligible voters, and a winning coalition consists of enough of the selectorate to generate a majority of votes in the Electoral College (since 1964, at least 270). In an autocracy, the winning coalition generally consists of some combination of the military, internal security forces, business, labor, or other groups. Thus the relative size of the winning coalition in an autocratic state is much smaller than that in a democracy.

The central hypothesis of the model is that the smaller the ratio of the size of the winning coalition to the size of the selectorate, the more easily a political leader can distribute "private goods" to the winning coalition but not to other members of society. Autocratic leaders can maintain the support of their small group of core supporters, and hence maintain their hold on political power, by distributing private goods to them, but that is not economically possible for democratic leaders, who require a much broader base of public support. Democratic leaders maintain their support by providing "public goods" for society as a whole through policies that benefit everybody. Thus the provision of public goods through good policies is more important for democratic leaders than for autocratic leaders, assuming their primary goal is to maintain their positions of power.

Since democratic leaders have to provide public goods for society, they are more sensitive to the outcome of wars than are authoritarian leaders.

An unsuccessful war involves greater political costs for a democratic leader than for an autocratic leader, as long as the latter continues to provide private goods to his/her smaller base of political support. This is consistent with the finding that democratic leaders are more likely than their authoritarian counterparts to be removed from office after an unsuccessful war (Bueno de Mesquita and Siverson, 1995).[54] Because of the political benefits of successful wars and the political costs of unsuccessful wars, democratic leaders tend to initiate only those wars they are confident of winning and, once in war, to devote enormous resources to win those wars. Autocratic leaders devote fewer resources to war because the costs of failure in war are less and because they need some of those resources to distribute to their key supporters at home.[55] This helps to explain the fact that democracies win a disproportionate number of their wars (Lake, 1992; Reiter and Stam, 2002; Desch, 2008; Downes, 2009).

The selectorate model posits that in a hypothetical war between democracies both sides would invest enormously in the war effort, given the political cost to leaders of defeat in war. As a result, such a war would be economically costly to both sides as well as politically costly to the loser. Democratic leaders, anticipating this outcome, have strong incentives to avoid such wars to begin with, which helps to explain the inter-democratic peace.

The selectorate model also accounts for other empirical regularities regarding democratic war behavior. It helps to explain why democracies get involved in wars fairly frequently despite the fact that they do not fight substantial wars against each other. Because democratic leaders benefit from successful wars, especially those involving low casualties, they will not hesitate to initiate imperial wars and wars against weaker autocracies. The model also explains why strong democracies sometimes initiate low levels of force against a much weaker democracy (there are few domestic political risks), why the target capitulates immediately (it anticipates that leaders in the stronger state have strong incentives to win the war), and thus why militarized disputes between democracies do not escalate to war.

The willingness of democracies to invest heavily in the war effort makes them unattractive targets of aggression, but autocrats also take greater gambles in war because the outcome of war has less of an impact on their political survival. That is, there are relatively few domestic downside risks of gambling in war to counteract the potential upside benefits of such gambles. The selectorate model predicts that autocracies will initiate wars against weak democracies but rarely against strong democracies. If *ex ante* military capabilities are approximately equal, the likelihood of a democratic–autocratic war depends on the specific values of key variables in the model. Democratic leaders will consider war if they believe that their greater investment in the war effort guarantees victory, while autocratic leaders' greater willingness to gamble might lead them to consider war if the demo-cratic effort advantage is only modest.[56]

Schultz (2001) provides an alternative institutional explanation of the democratic peace, one based on information and signaling. Schultz begins with the premise that democratic institutions and processes are more trans-parent than those of non-democratic states (J. Ritter, 2000). He also makes a number of simplifying assumptions. One is that political opposition groups have access to the same information as does the government. Another is that the opposition's primary concern is gaining power (as opposed to contributing to good public policy, even in its role in the opposition). This creates a zero-sum situation of electoral competition between government and opposition.

In a crisis with an external adversary, each state wants to maximize its bargaining leverage by convincing the adversary that it is more highly com-mitted and resolved than the adversary is. Although the government has an incentive to bluff and exaggerate its resolve, the opposition's primary goal of gaining power means that it does not always have incentives to join the government's bluff. Instead, it has incentives to support the government in a crisis only if it expects that any war resulting from the crisis would be successful and popular, because at least then it will get some of the credit for the victory. If the opposition expects an unpopular and unsuccessful war outcome, however, it has incentives to oppose the government, in order to capitalize on the political repercussions of an unsuccessful war and in doing so further its goals of gaining power. This means that the behavior of the opposition in democratic states sends a credible "signal" of the likely intentions of the government.[57] If the opposition supports the government, it expects a positive outcome of the war for the state, while if the opposi-tion opposes the government it expects a negative outcome for the state.

Schultz argues that because a free press guarantees transparency and because the political opposition has different incentives than does the gov-ernment, democracies are better able than non-democracies to send credible signals of their resolve in crises. This reduces the dangers of misperceptions in crises involving one and particularly two democratic states, and thus minimizes the dangers of crisis escalation. More specifically, the transpar-ency of the democratic process makes it obvious whether democratic politi-cal leaders involved in international crises have the support of the political opposition and the public in an international crisis. In the absence of domes-tic support the government cannot stand firm in a crisis because it cannot implement its threats. The adversary understands this and adopts a harder line in crisis bargaining. Democratic leaders anticipate their adversary's resolve and refrain from getting involved in crises in the first place. Knowing the path through which a crisis is likely to escalate makes it unlikely that actors will walk down that path.

On the other hand, if leaders expect public support, they will initiate disputes knowing they will be able to stand firm if the adversary resists. The adversary understands this and behaves more cautiously. As a result, crises involving democratic states, and particularly those between democratic states, are less likely to be characterized by misperceptions regarding the adversary's resolve and less likely to escalate to war because of misperceptions.

This reduction in misperceptions is critical if we recall, from our earlier discussion of the bargaining model of war, that misperceptions based on private information and incentives to misrepresent that information constitute one of the few paths by which rational states can end up in war with each other (Fearon, 1995). There are also non-rational paths through which misperceptions lead to war (Jervis, 1976; Lebow, 1981), and democracy reduces the likelihood of those paths arising as well. If both adversaries are democracies, misperceptions are reduced even further, though it is not clear whether this reduction is enough to account for the near-absence of war between democracies.[58]

Schultz's (2001) information-based model of democratic bargaining behavior in crisis situations is an important contribution to the literature on the democratic peace. Like most parsimonious models, however, it is based on some fairly strong assumptions. One such assumption is that in a democratic state the opposition has access to the same information as the government. The case of the second Bush Administration's distortion of information about Iraqi weapons of mass destruction in the period leading up to the 2003 American war in Iraq (Kaufman, 2004; Rich, 2006) is but one of many historical cases that contradict this assumption. This is consequential for Schultz's model. If the opposition does not always have the same information as the government does, then the adversary does not know whether the behavior of the opposition is a credible signal of the government's expectations and resolve in a crisis, or whether it reflects differences in information between the government and the opposition.

Another limitation of Schultz's (2001) rationalist model is that it assumes that the only way the government benefits from war is by advancing the national interest. This assumption ignores diversionary theory, which suggests that the leader can reap domestic political benefits from a war because war usually generates a "rally 'round the flag effect" that benefits the leader but not the country. Schultz correctly argues that rally effects are temporary, but what he ignores is that a leader can exploit his/her temporary boost in popular support by conducting policies that have far-reaching consequences, or making institutional changes that further shift the balance of power within the government in his/her favor.

Among other things, war usually results in an increased centralization of power in the executive branch of the government. As James Madison wrote to Thomas Jefferson in 1793, "War is ... the true nurse of executive aggrandizement" because it is the executive that directs war and unlocks the public treasuries in order to do so (in Hunt, 1906:174). War is a particularly severe kind of crisis, and crises enable governments to do things they might not otherwise be able to do. As Rahm Emanuel, White House Chief of Staff under President Barack Obama, said in November 2008, "You never want a serious crisis to go to waste. And what I mean by that is an opportunity to do things that you didn't think you could do before."

The opposition party often fears the growth of executive power and its consequences, and may prefer that war not occur. This implies that under certain conditions the political opposition might have incentives to oppose war not only when it anticipates an unsuccessful or unpopular war, but also when it expects a successful war, since such wars are invariably followed by an increase in popular support for government. The opposition's incentives to oppose war depend on its expectations as to whether the regime in power would be likely to exploit its advantages for political purposes, and what that might entail. Some argue that during the crisis with France in 1798 (often referred to as the "Quasi War"), the Republicans opposed war because they feared that the Federalists would exploit a successful war by taking actions to curtail public dissent and impede the efforts of Republicans to return to power (Levy and Mabe, 2004).

Research on the democratic peace has evolved through a number of stages during the last quarter-century. It began by describing a strong empirical regularity, and then demonstrated, at least in the eyes of its proponents, that the regularity was not simply the by-product of other factors that happen to be correlated with democracy.[59] It explored ambiguous cases in more detail to ascertain whether a more fine-grained analysis would show that they were consistent or inconsistent with the democratic peace hypothesis. After scholars reached a consensus that democracies rarely if ever go to war with each other, and that the answer had something to do with the nature of democracy rather than "spurious" influences, scholars began constructing models to explain the democratic peace. Models that generated additional predictions that run contrary to other known facts about democratic war or foreign policy behavior were rejected. The new models have generated new predictions about a wide range of other types of behavior (conflict resolution, intervention, covert action, the conduct and outcome of war, perceptions of the adversaries, etc.) that might differentiate democratic from non-democratic states, and those predictions were subject to empirical test (Russett and Starr, 2000). Scholars have yet to reach a consensus about the "true" explanation for the democratic peace, but there are clear signs of progress in the sophistication of our models.

Democratization and war

The models of the democratic peace discussed above all deal with relatively mature democracies. This raises the interesting question as to whether the model applies to new democracies, those just making the transition from authoritarian rule. If that were true, the policy implications would be enormous. Among other things, it would suggest that by promoting the development of democracies around the world the United States and other advanced democratic states could contribute to the elimination of war as well as to the establishment of liberal institutions and political freedom. In fact, in his 1994 State of the Union address President Bill Clinton justified a policy of promoting democratization around the world by referring to the absence of war among democracies.

Some researchers question this prescription, however, and argue that although well-established democratic dyads are peaceful, the *process* of transition to democracy can be a particularly destabilizing period, and that democratizing states occasionally go to war against other states and even against each other (Mansfield and Snyder, 2002, 2005). The democratization process brings new social groups with widely divergent interests into the political process at a time when the state lacks the institutional capacity to accommodate conflicting interests and respond to popular demands (Huntington, 1968). This can create enormous social conflict. This conflict can be exacerbated if democratization is coupled with the introduction of market forces into non-market economies, which leads to popular pressures for state protection against the pain of economic adjustment (Snyder, 2000). The resulting high levels of political instability can contribute to war through a number of paths, including the diversionary mechanisms discussed in the next chapter.

Democratization can be particularly destabilizing in multi-ethnic societies where ethnic groups are uncertain about how fully their rights will be protected, especially if the state in transition is too weak to maintain a monopoly of violence to protect those rights (Gurr, 2000; Ayoob, 2001). Elites competing for mass political support are tempted to make nationalist appeals and engage in external scapegoating in order to bolster their internal support. This scapegoating is particularly appealing to those elites whose interests are threatened by the democratization process and who believe that an external enemy might help reverse that process and strengthen centralized political power at home (Mansfield and Snyder, 2005). These considerations led Mansfield and Snyder (2005) to argue, supported by statistical evidence, that while it may be true that politically developed and stable democracies rarely if ever go to war with each other, states involved in transitions to democracy are actually more likely to end up in war than are other states.

The democratization and war hypothesis generated considerable scholarly debate. Critics raised questions about the case selection and research designs upon which the evidence was based, and generated new evidence that suggested that democratizing states are not more warlike (Thompson and Tucker, 1997; Ward and Gleditsch, 1998; Russett and Oneal, 2001). Mansfield and Snyder (2005) responded by arguing that it is important to distinguish between the very earliest stages of transitions away from authoritarian rule and later stages when democratic institutions have begun to consolidate. They provided evidence that war is significantly more likely in these early transitional stages than in the later ones, but that evidence and the techniques used to analyze it has been challenged by other scholars.[60]

One can certainly point to other societal-level variables contributing to the outbreak of war. Ideological, religious, ethnic, and racial differences between states are among the factors that come to mind. With respect to interstate war, these factors tend to supplement other variables surveyed in these chapters rather than serve as the primary drivers of war. Cultural differences might help to explain the identity of international rivalries, or the selection of targets for diversionary behavior. Snyder's (1991) political economy model of overexpansion incorporates the strategic use of national cultural myths to rationalize their policies to the public. Transnational, system-level norms also influence the behavior of states on issues of war and peace (Katzenstein, 1996; Finnemore, 2003; Farrell, 2005; Tannenwald, 2007). As we will see in the next chapter, ideological, religious, and cultural differences between states often contribute to misperceptions that increase the probability of interstate war.

We can also identify some historical cases in which cultural factors arguably played a primary role – religion in the early stages of the Thirty Years' War (1618–48) (Parker, 1984), for example – or a supporting role – ideology in the Cold War (Gaddis, 1997) and (to a lesser extent) race in the Pacific War between the United States and Japan (1941–5) (Dower, 1987). Some historians emphasize cultural factors in the evolution of warfare (Keegan, 1984; Lynn, 2003). We have relatively few specific theories of the causes of interstate war, however, that are built primarily around cultural variables.[61] One important exception is the "clash of civilizations" hypothesis.

Culture and War: The "Clash of Civilizations" Thesis

The "clash of civilizations" hypothesis (Huntington, 1993b; 1996) is one of the most prominent culture-based explanations for war.[62] It is also a forecast about the future. Huntington (1993b:22–3) argued that the clash of civilizations is the most recent phase in the evolution of international conflict since the Treaty of Westphalia in 1648. Until the French Revolution the primary conflicts in the world were between princes (emperors, absolute monarchs, and then constitutional monarchs) trying to expand their territory externally and their armies and bureaucracies internally. From the French Revolution in 1789 to World War I (1914–18), the primary conflicts were between nation-states. After the Russian Revolution (1917) and the reaction to it, the primary conflicts shifted from nations to ideologies. These three phases were all conflicts within Western civilization.[63]

The collapse of the Soviet Union and the end of the Cold War, Huntington argued, ended the ideological struggle between capitalism and communism and initiated a new phase of conflict. Nation-states were (and would continue to be) the most powerful actors in the global system, but the primary axes of conflict are now not ideological or economic, but instead cultural and religious. More specifically, Huntington (1993b:25) argued, "the principal conflicts of global politics will occur between nations and groups of different civilizations. The clash of civilizations will dominate global politics. The fault lines between civilizations will be the battle lines of the future." He went on to say (1993b:39) that "The next world war, if there is one, will be a war between civilizations."

Huntington (1993b:24) defined civilizations as the "the highest cultural grouping of people and the broadest level of identity people have short of that which distinguishes humans from other species." Civilizations are defined by their language, history, religion, customs, institutions, and the subjective self-identifications of peoples. They can include several states (the West) or just one (Japan). Huntington (1993b:25) identified seven or eight distinct civilizations: Western, Confucian, Japanese, Islamic, Hindu, Slavic-Orthodox, Latin American, and possibly African civilization.

Conflicts along the fault lines between civilizations have been the source of the most prolonged and most violent conflicts in history, Huntington (1993b:25–31) argued.[64] There are a number of factors that have increased the likelihood of such conflicts in the future. The end of the ideologically based divisions of the Cold War has allowed other identities to become more salient, a process that has been reinforced by a reaction against the West and its history of domination over non-Western peoples. Economic globalization and social change are weakening both national identities and local identities, and increasing interactions among people from different civilizations have heightened awareness of civilizational identities. Huntington mentioned the potential threat to Western civilization from China because of its rapid economic growth, but gave particular emphasis to the threat from Islam. Conflict between Western and Islamic civilizations has persisted for 1,300 years, in part because of its proximity to many civilizations (Western, Orthodox, Confucian, and African). With regard to the future, Huntington emphasized the destabilizing effects of the rapid growth of population in the Islamic world.[65]

The clash of civilizations thesis, published in *Foreign Affairs*, a journal perceived to be closely tied to the American foreign policy establishment, "sent shock waves around the world" (Hassner, 1996:63, quoted in Welch, 1997:198). The article further alienated much of the Islamic world by reinforcing negative images of the United States, and it led others to fear that Huntington's forecast about the future could turn into a self-fulfilling prophecy, or that it was an attempt to provide legitimacy for American aggression against Islam. The rise of anti-Western terrorism and the 9/11 attacks in particular confirmed the validity of the clash of civilizations thesis among many, and led some initial skeptics to change their views (Ajami, 1993, 2008).

Huntington's thesis also generated a strong scholarly reaction, almost all of it negative (Council on Foreign Relations, 1993). Many argued that Huntington's definition of civilization was so vague that it failed to provide the basis for the identification of specific civilizations, and that in the absence of an operational definition it is impossible to conduct an empirical assessment of the hypothesis that the primary sources of violent conflict are civilizational differences. It appears that a people's predominant religion is Huntington's primary criterion for identifying civilizations, but ethnic and linguistic similarity and even geographical proximity also appear to play a role. The lack of congruence among these criteria leads to questions about some of Huntington's classifications. Religious criteria would lead us to classify the Iran–Iraq War (1980–88) as an intra-civilizational war within Islam, while ethnic/linguistic criteria would suggest an inter-civilizational war between Persians and Arabs. Most Latin American countries have republican regimes and Christian leaders of European descent, so it is not clear why they should constitute a distinct civilization (Welch, 1997: 202–3).[66]

Scholars have also questioned whether differences between civilizations as Huntington (1993b; 1996) defined them constitute the primary determinants of conflict, and whether it is in fact true that conflicts within civilizations are as frequent as conflicts between civilizations (Kirkpatrick, 1993). Given each person's multiple identities, it is not clear why civilizational identities necessarily dominate other identities. Welch (1997:205) argued that at any level of aggregation, violence is generally more likely within a group than between groups. There is more violence within families than outside of families, within villages than between villages, within ethnic groups than between ethnic groups, and within states than between states.

This argument fits the history of modern Europe from 1500–1945, where the most destructive conflicts have been within the European system (Wright, 1965). Huntington (1993b:23) himself acknowledges this, by stating that "conflicts between princes, nation-states, and ideologies were primarily conflicts within Western civilization" and describing them as "Western civil wars." This statement clearly contradicts Huntington's (1993b:25) argument that "Over the centuries ... differences among civilizations have generated the most prolonged and the most violent conflicts."

The clash of civilizations hypothesis is also problematic for the period since 1945. The genocide in Rwanda and "Africa's World War" in the mid-1990s were among the world's bloodiest conflicts since World War II, but they were fought entirely within the African civilization identified by Huntington. The civil wars within Iraq and Afghanistan have each been fought within Islam. The US intervened militarily against Slavic Serbia in support of Islamic Bosnia, and most Arab states supported the United States in its military intervention against Iraq. Each of these actions runs diametrically opposed to Huntington's thesis.

Quantitative tests of the clash of civilizations hypothesis have reinforced empirical arguments against the clash of civilizations hypothesis. These studies have generally found that states are not more prone to militarized conflict across civilizational lines than within civilizations (Chiozza, 2002). Russett, Oneal, and Cox (2000) find that variables associated with realist theory (geographic contiguity, alliance patterns, and relative power) and with liberal theory (economic interdependence and levels of democratization) provide better explanation of occurrences of militarized interstate disputes between states than do civilizational identities.

In summary, Huntington is correct to emphasize the importance of identities in global politics, but he overestimates both the importance of civilizational identities relative to other identities and the impact of civilizational differences on militarized conflicts. His clash of civilizations hypothesis is more useful as a specification of a particular path to war than as a general theory of war.

Having surveyed a variety of nation-state level causes of war, we now turn to the role of decision-making, beginning at the individual level.

Notes

1. On religion and war, see Little (1996), Huntington (1996), and D. Martin (1997). On ideology and war, see Nelson and Olin (1979) and Haas (2005).
2. This attention was due in part to the influence of revisionism in the study of American diplomatic history, which focused on the internal social and especially economic factors driving American policy (Williams, 1962). Historical revisionism was in part a response to the Cold War, and it grew in influence in response to the Vietnam War.

3. Some Marxist–Leninists are quite explicit in describing war in Clausewitzian terms (Kubalkova and Cruickshank, 1980; Semmel, 1981).

4. For additional work in world systems theory, see Chase-Dunn and Podobnik (1995) and the brief review in Rasler and Thompson (forthcoming). In the 1970s, proponents of "dependency theory" argued that the primary explanation for the delayed development of the "South" was the structure of dominance and dependence in the global political economy and the exploitation of the South by the North (Cardoso and Faletto, 1979), though these scholars did not give much attention to the problem of war per se.

5. Similarly, while lateral pressure theory (Choucri and North, 1975) gives less emphasis to the world economy and the hierarchical structure of power, it shares with Marxist–Leninist theories the emphasis on competition for scarce resources.

6. Krasner (1978: chap. 1) calls this "structural Marxism" and distinguishes it from "instrumental Marxism," which emphasizes the hijacking of the state by the capitalist class in order to advance its own parochial class interests.

7. These different explanations are not universally accepted by all Marxist–Leninists, and in fact different variations of Marxist theory are quite critical of some other variations.

8. If the imperatives of oil drove American foreign policy, however, it would be hard to explain why the United States continues to strongly align with Israel rather than with the Arab oil-producing states.

9. Even if it were true that economic recovery was a consequence of the preparation for war, that does not necessarily imply that the goal of economic recovery was the primary goal of the war. The relative importance of different motivations needs to be established through further empirical research.

10. See the section later in this chapter on coalitional theories of war and peace.

11. The argument gained enough traction that in 1934 – with the rise of Hitler, renewed fears of another European war, and concerns (especially by increasingly influential isolationists) that armaments manufacturers might once again push the United States into war – that Congress set up a Special Senate Committee to investigate the munitions industry. The "Nye Committee," so named after its chair, held hearings for 18 months but found little evidence to support the "merchants of death" hypothesis. That finding did little, however, to dampen popular suspicions of "greedy munitions makers." See Schlesinger and Bruns (1975).

12. See Bass (1964) for a collection of alternative interpretations of American entry into World War I.

13. One significant primary difference between Marxist and non-Marxist theories of economic imperialism is that Lenin and other Marxists believed that capitalist states could not be reformed, that imperialism is inevitable, and that violent revolution is necessary for the redistribution of wealth and the elimination of imperialism. Non-Marxist critics, like Hobson and his descendants, recognized the feasibility of reform within capitalist states.

14. The monopoly stage of capitalism is defined by five basic features: the concentration of production and capital into monopolies; the merging of bank

capital with industrial capital, leading to the dominance of "finance capital" under a financial oligarchy; the distinctive importance of the export of capital as opposed to the export of commodities; the formation of international capitalist monopolies which share the world among themselves; and the territorial division of the world among the biggest capitalist powers (Lenin, [1916]1939:88–9).

15. For a class-based explanation of the Peloponnesian War, see Cornford (1971).

16. Also, recall long-cycle theory's emphasis on leadership in leading economic sectors (Modelski and Thompson, 1996).

17. The German threat and World War I did not help settle Anglo–Russian colonial disputes, as the rivalry continued after the war.

18. Analytically, this is not a useful definition, because it explicitly excludes expansionist behavior that served a useful purpose in providing protection or securing territory or trade. The definition is also circular. If imperialism is objectless by definition, then if it serves a useful function, then by definition it is not imperialism. With this definition, one could not investigate the empirical question of whether imperialism could be useful. See Doyle (1997:243).

19. Schumpeter ([1919]1951) also examined the imperialisms of Persia, Assyria, Alexander the Great, Egypt, Rome, and modern European states, each of which reflects a variation on the central theme of imperialism.

20. It is also reminiscent of interpretations of the "military revolution" in early modern Europe (Roberts, [1956]1995). A more general theoretical analysis of the mutual linkages among external threat environment, war, political organization, military organization, and political economy is provided by Levy and Thompson (2010b).

21. While some theories of the military–industrial complex give primary emphasis to the economic interests of leading firms (Domhoff, 1967), others give primary emphasis to the role of the military (Mills, 1956).

22. Snyder (1991) was responding to Kennedy's (1987) theory of "imperial overstretch." Kupchan (1994) constructs an alternative theory of overexpansion.

23. This might exclude the United States prior to the twentieth century.

24. This puts a premium on defining a "sharp" increase in threat, and on doing so independently of the government's response to the threat. Otherwise, we would be left with the meaningless statement that a sharp increase in threat (as operationally defined by a strong response to that threat) would lead to a strong response to that threat.

25. Narizny neglects the fact that on the brink of war defensive alliances can be implemented more quickly than substantial increases in armaments.

26. Haas (2005) explains these variations of policy preferences between left and right in terms of ideology. The left was more hostile to fascist Germany and more sympathetic to the Soviet Union, a potential ally of Britain's. The right was ideologically more hostile to Soviet communism than to German fascism.

27. Schweller (2006) also examines "underbalancing" in the 1930s, in an attempt to explain why Britain and France pursued such conciliatory policies in response to a rapidly growing threat. He gives less emphasis to economic factors and more attention to other political factors: the absence of elite consensus on policy preferences, the absence of elite cohesion, the political

vulnerability of the regime, and the social cohesion of the country. For a more detailed analysis of the domestic politics of grand strategy in Britain and France in the 1930s, see Imlay (2003).

28. One particular component of the national economic interest that is omitted from the Narizny (2007) and Lobell (2006) models is the creditworthiness of the state, which varies significantly across regime type and also across specific contexts. The greater the state's access to international credit markets, the more it can borrow, and the less it needs to rely on immediate taxation to fund rearmament in response to external threat (Rasler and Thompson, 1983). Democratic states tend to have greater access to credit markets than do authoritarian states, because lenders are more confident that democratic states will not default on their loans. Democracies are more likely to repay their debts because they know that democratic publics are likely to punish leaders that pursue costly economic policies, including those that weaken a state's credit rating (Schultz and Weingast, 1998).

29. Some dispute the validity of the evidence behind this quote (Blainey, 1988:76–7).

30. For a rationalist state actor interpretation of the Crimean War, see Gochal and Levy (2004). For an interpretation of the Falklands/Malvinas War that gives more attention the failure of coercive bargaining at the dyadic level, see Freedman and Gamba-Stonehouse (1990).

31. One explanation for the absence of a strong observed relationship between the political insecurity of elites emphasizes the strategic behavior between governments and adversaries. If governments are insecure and have incentives to scapegoat, adversaries recognize this and will "lie low" and not provide an easy target for scapegoating (R. Miller, 1999). This is an interesting argument and it needs further study. If a politically insecure leader is really determined to find an external scapegoat, however, a potential adversary can only back off so far before sacrificing its vital interests. Another possibility is that stronger adversaries can also threaten to escalate minor disputes to war, in an attempt to deter low-level diversionary behavior. For a game-theoretic model of diversionary behavior that emphasizes both bargaining between governments and adversaries and signaling between constituents and the government, see Tarar (2006).

32. Some scholars dispute this, however, and present evidence that scapegoating is most likely in the period immediately after elections (Gaubatz, 1999).

33. One argument is that non-democratic states have an alternative policy option that is generally not available to their democratic counterparts – direct repression of internal dissent (Enterline and Gleditsch, 2000).

34. Diversionary theory almost always assumes that the targets are external states. Governments can also engage in diversionary behavior against certain domestic groups, especially if those groups are defined as somehow different, as the "other" (Tir and Jasinski, 2008). Hitler's action against German Jews provides one example.

35. Diversionary theorists usually invoke the in-group/out-group hypothesis to explain how the use of external force increases a leader's domestic political support. Some rational choice theorists invoke a different mechanism. They

construct principal–agent models that treat the successful use of military force as a "signal" of the leader's competence, which might otherwise be in doubt if his/her policies (domestic as well as foreign) have generated internal dissatisfaction (Richards, et al., 1993; Smith, 1996). One might question, however, whether popular perceptions of a leader's competence in foreign policy translate into perceptions of competence in domestic policy (handling the economy, for example), leading to an increase in domestic support. If a leader is in real trouble domestically, however, s/he might conclude that they have nothing to lose and "gamble for resurrection" through the use of military force (Downs and Rocke, 1994).

36. Low-level diversionary actions against stronger targets might be a plausible strategy if one expects that the adversary is unlikely to respond. President Fidel Castro of Cuba has greatly enhanced his domestic support over the years by thumbing his nose at the United States, but always through actions short of military force.

37. An alternative explanation for powerful liberal democracies getting involved in large and destructive wars lies in the fact that they often take the lead in grand balancing coalitions against potential hegemonic land powers.

38. The strength of this regularity is reflected in Levy's (1989b:270) observation that "the absence of war between democratic states comes as close as anything we have to an empirical law in international relations." This probably says more about the absence of lawlike behavior in international relations than about the behavior of democracies. Still, this is the strongest empirical regularity that scholars have observed in the international relations field. For comparable claims about the "lawlike" nature of the democratic peace, see Gleditsch (1995), Chan (1997), Russett and Starr (2000), and Braumoeller and Goertz (2000).

39. As a system-level explanation, realism argues that all states respond in roughly the same way to similar threats, opportunities, and conditions. The implication is that, *ceteris parabus*, democratic dyads will go to war as often (proportionately) as any other pairs of states.

40. Similarly, the dyadic democratic peace does not imply that the international system will become more peaceful as the number of democratic states in the system increases. That would be true if there were already a substantial number of democracies in the system, but not if there were relatively few. In the latter case, adding more democracies would add more democratic–autocratic dyads, which have a higher propensity to war (Rasler and Thompson, 2005).

41. Some research has suggested that there is a "dictatorial peace" among authoritarian regimes (Peceny, Beer, and Sanchez-Terry 2002).

42. Most quantitative studies of the democratic peace use the Polity III data, which was developed by Gurr and his colleagues (Jaggers and Gurr, 1995).

43. This raises the question of whether the appropriate standard is whether states satisfy some objective set of criteria for democracy, or whether it is each state's perceptions of the democratic character of other states that matters. On the latter, see Oren (1984).

44. For more detailed discussions of these potentially anomalous cases, see Ray (1995).

45. Admittedly, the criteria for democracy are rather weak, in the sense that there is no insistence that criteria for democracy approximate the normative standard of an ideal democracy. But that is precisely the point. If we insisted on a definition of a perfect democracy, then we would conclude that there are no wars between democracies because there are few if any real democracies. That would not be an informative finding. What is so significant about the democratic peace is that even pairs of states that satisfy only the weakest criteria for democracy still rarely if ever fight each other.

46. For critiques of democratic peace theory, see Brown et al. (1996), Henderson (2002), Rosato (2003), and Rasler and Thompson (2005).

47. As we saw in chapter 3's discussion of economic interdependence and peace, a growing number of scholars now argue that the capitalist peace reinforces the democratic peace (Mousseau, 2000; Hegre, 2000; Gartzke, 2007). Some scholars also argue that international institutions also contribute to the democratic peace (Russett and Oneal, 2001).

48. This discussion draws on Levy (2002:359–61).

49. Bueno de Mesquita et al. (2003) make a similar argument.

50. The hypothesis of aversion to costly wars by democratic publics and therefore by their leaders is plausible, but it is not clear whether this is a universal generalization that applies to all democracies, or whether it is a generalization that is temporally or culturally bounded and perhaps overly influenced by contemporary Western and particularly American attitudes since the Vietnam War. Images of Pickett's charge in the American Civil War or frontal assaults by democracies against well-entrenched positions in World War I do not reflect an aversion to casualties. For empirical and experimental studies, see Gartner, Segura, and Barratt (2004) and Gartner (2008).

51. For a critique of this argument, see Rosato (2003).

52. It is sometimes argued that democratic cultures preclude democratic leaders from fighting certain types of wars. Schweller (1992), for example, argues that democracies cannot fight "preventive wars" motivated not by a current conflict of interest but rather by the fear of the adversary's rising power. There are enough exceptions, however, to seriously question this hypothesis. Examples include the Israeli attack against Iraq in 1981 and the use of preventive logic by the second Bush Administration in the United States to rationalize its 2003 war against Iraq (Levy, 2008a).

53. The impact of jingoistic publics and the press in helping to push governments into war is not confined to democratic states. In 1739, when Britain was a constitutional monarchy, both the public and the press demanded war against Spain. A reluctant First Minister Walpole agreed, leading to the "War of Jenkins' Ear" (Young and Levy, forthcoming).

54. Recall that after being soundly defeated in the 1990–91 Persian Gulf War, Saddam Hussein of Iraq stayed in power for another 12 years before he was overthrown during the 2003 American intervention in Iraq. US President George H. W. Bush was defeated in the 1992 elections, 18 months after a popular American war.

55. Although it is true that since democratic leaders are more likely to be thrown out of office after a losing war effort, and are therefore particularly sensitive to the political costs of a military defeat, authoritarian leaders have other

things to worry about. It is not just the probability of being thrown out of office but also what happens to those who are removed from office. Former democratic leaders play golf and give speeches. Disgraced authoritarian leaders often suffer a crueler fate. Some are dragged through the streets to their death. Given the greater personal costs to authoritarian leaders removed from office, they presumably base their calculations on the potential costs of negative outcomes as well as the probabilities of those outcomes (Goemans, 2000).

56. Another possible explanation of gambling by autocratic leaders, especially leaders of personalist autocratic regimes, is based on the type of leader that is likely to come to power in different types of regimes. Accession to high office in centralized authoritarian regimes often requires a risk-taking strategy. Those who take big gambles win big or lose big, and the leaders who end up on top are those who win big. This argument almost certainly applies to authoritarian leaders like Adolf Hitler and Saddam Hussein, who did not rise to power by sitting on the sidelines. It probably does not apply to leaders in collective (rather than personalist) authoritarian regimes, where the incentives point toward a more cautious strategy in the rise to power.

57. The signal is credible because it would be politically costly for the opposition to say one thing and do the other. For an influential early treatment of signaling, see Jervis (1970).

58. Lipson (2003) also emphasizes the importance of information in his explanation of the democratic peace. Democratic states can more easily reach agreements and make credible promises than can autocratic states because of democracies' higher transparency (to outsiders and to domestic publics); their greater constitutional restrictions limiting the powers of public officials and ensuring due process; their greater continuity of governance and orderly successions; the greater ability of domestic publics in democratic states to punish leaders if they break their promises; and constitutional governance. These "contracting advantages" of democracies increase the level of trust and reduce the level of uncertainty in their mutual interactions, significantly reducing the probability of war between them.

59. Others question this conclusion and argue that inferences of causality between democracy and peace at the dyadic level are spurious (Rasler and Thompson, 2005). That is, the observed relationship is due to other factors.

60. See the exchange in Wolf et al. (1996).

61. Cultural variables are more central to theories of civil war, which we examine in chapter 7. Many "constructivist" international relations theorists argue that cultural factors such as ideas and identities are the underlying factors shaping human behavior (Ruggie, 1998; Wendt, 1999; Hopf, 2002; Lebow, 2008), but they do not directly focus on war.

62. The term "clash of civilizations" was first used by Lewis (1990) in his discussion of the historical evolution of civilizational conflicts between the Muslim world and others.

63. For other, more detailed, classifications of the evolution of international conflict over the past six centuries or longer, see Howard (1976), Luard (1986), and Levy and Thompson (2010b). With respect to modern history's most destructive wars and rivalries, we question Huntington's argument that while

wars from 1648 to 1792 were primarily about territory, wars from 1792 to 1917 were fundamentally different and about clashes between nations defined as peoples, and that World War II and the Cold War were different still and primarily about ideology.

64. Huntington (1996) distinguished between fault-line conflicts and core-state conflicts. Fault-line conflicts are local, and occur between adjacent states belonging to different civilizations or within states that include peoples from different civilizations. Core-state conflicts are global and take place between the major states of different civilizations.

65. Huntington (1996) also argued that rapid population increases in the Islamic world was generating a "youth bulge" that contributes to internal conflict (through the rise of fundamentalism in Islamic societies, for example) and to external conflict as well. In a different demographic argument, Hudson and Den Boer (2005) argued that a high ratio of males to females in a country (and particularly a high proportion of unmarried males) has historically led to an increase in domestic and (to a somewhat lesser extent) international conflict. They argue that through culturally induced sex-selection, China and India are generating a disproportionately high (and historically unprecedented) proportion of low-status young males (whom the Chinese refer to as "bare branches"), with ominous implications for both domestic stability and international conflict. For other theories of demographic change and international conflict, see Krebs and Levy (2001).

66. Some question the inclusion of a distinctive Japanese civilization despite its Westernization since World War II, and others make a similar argument about Russia over a longer historical span.

5

Decision-Making: The Individual Level

War is the product of the actions of two or more states or other political organizations. It follows that to understand the outbreak of war we need to understand why states make certain decisions rather than other decisions. That leads us to an analysis of foreign policy decision-making, which focuses on the individuals and governmental organizations that are empowered to make and implement policies on behalf of the state.[1]

International relations scholars have always engaged in foreign policy analysis, but until the 1960s they had little interest in developing theories of how the foreign policy process works and how it might work differently in different kinds of political systems. Traditional approaches to the study of foreign policy generally assumed that political leaders selected those policies that they believed would do most to advance the national interest of the state, and they gave relatively little attention to the internal processes driving foreign policy.[2] This kind of analysis was based on an implicit rational model, one that was often tied to a realist conception of foreign policy based on the concepts of power and the national interest.

Growing dissatisfaction with traditional approaches, along with an increasing interest in developing more explicit conceptual frameworks for analyzing foreign policy, led to the development of the *decision-making approach* to foreign policy analysis in the early 1960s (Snyder, Bruck, and Sapin, 1962).[3] The basic premise of the decision-making approach is that an explanation of the foreign policy actions of states requires an understanding of the processes through which political leaders perceive the external world and make and then implement their decisions. The basic argument is that system-level structural theories and even societal-level theories cannot explain state foreign policies, and that it is necessary to open the "black box" of decision-making in order to understand foreign policy behavior. Decision-making theories assume that the choices made by these key individuals, groups, and organizational actors have a significant impact on state foreign policies, and that these choices are not entirely determined by underlying systemic pressures, social forces, and institutional constraints.

Of course, realists and other structural theorists recognize that in the end it is individuals in organizations who make decisions on behalf of the state. The difference between structuralists and decision-making theorists lies in the causal weight attached to decision-making variables. Structuralists assume that governmental organizations and individual decision-makers share similar perceptions of the international environment and that they respond similarly and directly to the structurally induced incentives created by that environment. For these theorists, structural factors are overpowering, and the opportunities and constraints they create translate directly into foreign policy decisions. As a result, decision-making variables themselves carry relatively little causal weight. Those variables serve as conveyor belts for causality that rests with structural factors.

Proponents of decision-making approaches, on the other hand, insist that there is no deterministic link between system structure and foreign policy action. They argue that individual worldviews and perceptions, governmental roles, and intergovernmental politics help to explain why some states in similar international positions and with similar domestic circumstances often engage in different foreign policy behaviors, or why one state in similar situations will behave differently at different times. Decision-making theorists do not deny that system structure and domestic settings frame the problem for state decision-makers, but they insist that organizational, small-group, and individual-level variables carry significant causal weight.

We begin this chapter with a discussion of a more formalized "rational model" of decision-making. The rational model is both a normative model of how decisions *ought* to be made as well as a parsimonious explanatory model of how decisions actually *are* made, and for these reasons the rational model is generally taken as the standard against which other models are compared. It is conventional to begin with an analysis of rationality for the case of a single unitary actor before moving on to the additional complications associated with the concept of organizational or collective rationality.[4] After our general discussion of rationality, we then turn to the individual level and examine psychological models of individual decision-making. In the next chapter we turn to the governmental level and focus on bureaucratic/organizational theories of decision-making. Decision-making within these formal organizations is also shaped by social–psychological dynamics within small groups, which we also consider.

Rational Models of Decision-Making

There is no single model of rational decision-making and no single conception of rationality. Most social scientists, however, conceive of rationality in terms of the maximization of values under constraints – the selection of means that will maximize previously determined goals. This is an instrumental conception of rationality. From this perspective, for the purposes of assessing rationality it does not matter what an actor's goals are, only whether that actor engages in an ends–means calculation and selects those strategies or options it anticipates will maximize its values or goals. An actor's goals might be immoral or repulsive, but that in itself does not make their behavior non-rational. Thus we can ask in principle whether Hitler behaved rationally in the pursuit of his goals, regardless of how morally repugnant his goals were.[5]

There is at least as much debate about the nature of a rational decision-making process as about the meaning of rationality itself.[6] If rationality is the maximization of goals under constraints, then central to all conceptions of rationality is the idea that an actor must begin with the identification of its goals. Since most actors have more than one goal, or "value complexity" (George, 1980), the specification of goals also requires some sense of the priorities among those goals. Since it is rare that a single strategy will maximize all goals simultaneously – just as in mathematics it is impossible to simultaneously maximize more than one variable – an actor must also have a sense of the kinds of value tradeoffs it is willing to make.

In most crises, for example, states want to maximize their interests while at the same time minimize the likelihood of escalation to an unwanted war. Some strategies might help maximize interests but simultaneously increase the risk of escalation, while other strategies might minimize the risks of escalation but only at some cost to the national interest. A fully rational decision requires a prioritization of goals so that the actor knows how much of one goal it is willing to sacrifice in order to achieve more of its other goals – or what risks it is willing to take to achieve one goal given the increased probability that it might not achieve the other goal. In addition, some strategies might bring benefits in the short term but involve costs in the long term, or vice versa, so that actors need to be clear about their time horizons.[7]

If rationality involves the selection of means to maximize one's ends, a second key element of a rational decision-making process is the specification of the set of available strategies (or policies or options), or combination of strategies, that one might adopt to advance one's goals. This involves not only an assessment of existing options, but also, to the extent that time permits, the development of new strategies to advance one's goals. Successful conflict resolution, for example, often involves the creative invention of new solutions to old problems (Bercovitch, Kremenyuk, and Zartman, 2009).

Closely related to the specification of alternative strategies is the estimation of the consequences of each of the alternatives. This is the third major element of a rational decision-making process. Given actors' multiple goals, they must calculate the consequences of each alternative for each of their goals, so they can weight the costs and benefits of each strategy by the importance they attach to each of their goals.

Estimating the likely consequences of each strategy is an extraordinarily complex process. Decisions, particularly about issues of war and peace, are made under enormous *uncertainty*. This is emphasized by Clausewitz ([1832]1976) in his concept of the "fog of war" and by game theorists in their concept of "incomplete information." One component of this uncertainty is the fact that the consequences of each strategy are determined not only by one's own actions but also by those of the adversary and other actors. In their estimations of the consequences of their actions actors must think strategically and incorporate the likely responses of the adversary and of third parties.

It is notoriously difficult to assess the intentions of the adversary (Jervis, 1976). Even if state A accurately evaluates the intentions of state B at one point in time, B might change its intentions in response to changes in its external or internal environments or even in its assessment of A's intentions. In addition, it is difficult to evaluate the adversary's capabilities, one's own capabilities, and how the capabilities of two adversaries might interact on the battlefield. Assessing the likely actions (or non-actions) of third parties, including allies and other adversaries, further complicates the problem. Relevant information is rarely fully available. An important element of this stage of the decision-making process is an *information search* to gain as much information as possible to support an informed decision.

We do not want to give the impression that this stage of a rational decision-making process requires a fully accurate assessment of the consequences of one's actions. Such an assessment is not possible. Instead, rationality is defined more by process than by outcome. The question is whether an actor makes some attempt to incorporate uncertainty and strategic interaction into its calculations. Since the world is uncertain, actors should think probabilistically rather than deterministically. They should recognize the limits of their predictive powers and the fact that they can never be certain about the consequences of their actions, and they should attempt to attach very rough probability estimates to their assessment of what is likely to happen if they take various actions. Ideally, a rational assessment of the consequences of a particular policy should take the form of a probability distribution: policy x should lead to outcome y_1 with probability p_1, outcome y_2 with probability p_2, and so on.

One sign of a non-rational process is one in which an actor estimates with 100% certainty that action x will be followed by consequence y. Certainty rarely exists in international politics. History is littered with wars that started when one state was erroneously convinced that it could achieve a rapid military victory with limited costs, or that a hardline negotiating strategy would lead with certainty to the adversary's capitulation.

Once an actor has defined its goals, identified the possible strategies for advancing its goals, estimated the consequences of each of those strategies for each of its goals, it is ready to make a decision. This raises the question of what kind of decision-rule the actor will follow. This is a complicated issue, since there are several possible decision-rules, but most rational decision theorists posit a decision-rule based on some approximation of an *expected utility* calculation. What this means is that an actor identifies all of the possible consequences for each alternative or option, assesses the probability of occurrence of each of these outcomes, evaluates the "utility" (net benefits minus costs) of each possible outcome, weights the utility of each outcome by its probability of occurrence, and calculates the weighted sum, which is the expected utility of that particular strategy.[8] The actor then selects the strategy that has the greatest expected utility.

This description of a rational decision-making process overstates the orderliness or linearity of the process. Most decisions for war are the result of a series of decisions by each adversary, and the process is an iterative one. Decisions at each stage of the process are made after observing the consequences of earlier decisions and responses. Decision-makers should learn from these observations and incorporate information about the consequences of their earlier decisions as well as other more recent information into their judgments and calculations in the next stage of decision-making. Feedback from one decision should reveal information about adversary intentions (and perhaps the intentions of third states) and possibly about relative military capabilities as well. Thus an additional element of a rational decision-making process is *learning*. One of the non-rational aspects of the US war in Iraq beginning 2003 is that as American forces were engaging the Iraqi army with the immediate goal of overthrowing Saddam Hussein, US decision-makers failed to learn from early evidence that an anti-American insurgency was forming in Iraq (Gordon and Trainor, 2006; Ricks, 2006).

It is important to note that the concept of rationality can be applied both to individuals and to collective decision-units. The application of rationality to collective decision-units raises some complicated analytic issues that we can only mention briefly here. It assumes that the collectivity (a state, for example) can be treated as if it has a single set of goals or preferences, with priorities among those goals. It also assumes that there is a consensus within the state, or at least among state decision-makers, regarding the optimal means of achieving those goals. This assumption is met if there is unanimity within the collectivity (or at least within the decision-making elite) or if there is a single dominant leader who makes decisions on behalf of the state.[9] If either of these criteria holds, we can talk about a rational and unitary actor model. Most realists and most other structural theorists make this assumption.

In the last chapter, however, we came across a number of theories that assume the existence of multiple domestic actors, each with its own parochial interests rather than a fundamental agreement on the interests of the state. Coalitional models of decision-making (Snyder, 1991; Lobell, 2006; Narizny, 2007), for example, assume that foreign policy is the product of compromises and bargains among different economically based interest groups. Each of these groups acts rationally to advance its interests, but not necessarily those of the state. Such models are rational but not unitary.[10] In the remainder of this chapter we examine non-rational models of individual decision-making, which can apply either to unitary or non-unitary models of the state. In the next chapter we focus on bureaucratic/organizational models, which are non-unitary but sometimes rational.

Psychological Models of International Conflict

Theories at the individual level trace international conflict to the behavior of key individuals in important decision-making roles.[11] These theories focus on the content of individuals' belief systems about world politics, the psychological processes through which they acquire information and make decisions, and their personalities and emotional states. These factors often lead different individuals to have different conceptions of the foreign policy goals of the state, different images of the adversary, and different beliefs as to the optimum strategies to achieve their goals and meet those threats. These variations in beliefs across individuals arise from differences in political socialization, personality, education, formative experiences and the lessons people learn from historical experience, and a host of other variables. When individual beliefs vary, different decision-makers will respond differently under similar situations, and those differences may be significant enough to have a causal impact on state decisions for war or peace (Holsti, 1967; George, 1969; Jervis, 1976; Lebow, 1981). As Hermann et al. (2001) emphasize, "who leads matters."

One important implication of most individual-level explanations is that if the individual in question had not been in power, the decision or outcome probably would have been different. The argument that Hitler was a primary cause of World War II implies that if Hitler had not been German chancellor, World War II would probably not have occurred. This is a "counterfactual" hypothesis. In an analysis of the impact of individual-level variables it is often useful to ask the counterfactual question of whether the outcome would have been different if another leader had been in power.[12]

Individual-level variables fit within the subject matter of political psychology, which falls at the intersection of social psychology and political science.[13] Social psychologists began analyzing the psychology of war and war prevention after World War I. Following Freud's emphasis on aggressive instincts as the root cause of war (Einstein and Freud, 1932), a number of scholars applied psychoanalytic perspectives drawing on Freud to the study of aggression and war (Durbin and Bowlby, 1939).[14] Psychoanalytic models are generally difficult to empirically test, however, and contemporary international relations theorists have moved away from psychoanalytic perspectives to theories that are more amenable to social scientific analysis (McDermott, 2004).[15]

Each of the psychological models discussed below is very general, and should apply to political leaders in all types of political systems – great powers, small states, ethnic groups, rebel leaders, and terrorist groups.[16] While the psychological dynamics are similar, their causal impact, relative to that of other variables, may differ in different types of regimes, depending on the constraining effects of institutions and cultures. We might predict, for example, that individuals have a greater impact in dynastic or authoritarian regimes, particularly highly centralized ("personalist") regimes and those characterized by a "cult of personality," than in liberal democracies characterized by the rule of law.

Since many (but not all) individual-level variables impact decisions for war and peace through misperceptions of the external environment, we begin with an analysis of different kinds of misperceptions and the causal paths through which they can lead to war. We then turn to a discussion of the content of individual belief systems, and then to the cognitive and emotional factors that influence how individuals process information about external threats and opportunities. After examining prospect theory, which suggests that people are particularly sensitive to losses and that they are often willing to take extreme risks to avoid any losses, we then turn to the "poliheuristic" theory of decision-making and to theories of crisis decision-making.

Paths from misperception to war

The idea that wars are caused by misperceptions is very attractive in many ways, especially for those who believe that the human and economic costs of war far outweigh any benefits that war might bring to the states that initiate them.[17] There are countless historical cases in which misperceptions are so blatant and so consequential that it is easy to conclude that war would not have occurred in their absence, so that misperceptions were a necessary cause of the war.[18]

This argument about the importance of misperceptions is reinforced by the logic of the bargaining model of war. As we noted earlier, the model suggests that if actors are rational, and if adversaries have the same information about military capabilities, they will have similar assessments of the likely outcome of the war. Those shared expectations regarding the likely outcome of war will lead them to agree to a negotiated settlement commensurate with that outcome while avoiding the costs of fighting. If misperceptions lead states to have divergent expectations about the likely outcome of war, so that at least one side expects a better outcome from war than from peace, it may be very difficult for adversaries to reach a negotiated settlement that avoids war.[19]

The analysis of the impact of misperceptions on war raises a number of difficult conceptual and methodological problems. It is extraordinarily difficult, first of all, to define what a misperception is (Jervis, 1976, 1988; Levy, 1983a). Is it the discrepancy between the way the world is perceived and the way it really is, and if so how do we know the latter? Moreover, if politics and war each involve an element of chance, at what point do we say that an erroneous judgment is a misperception? If you calculate that the odds of winning a war are 80 percent, and you initiate a war and lose, was the decision for war based on a misperception?

There is also the question of how much causal weight to attribute to misperceptions. Even if misperceptions are seen as a necessary condition for a particular war (which implies that accurate perceptions would have led to peace), it is not clear how much causal weight to attribute to misperceptions themselves and how much weight to attribute to the structural conditions, internal pressures, cultural environment, and decision-maker beliefs that generated the misperceptions in the first place. This is the sense in which some suggest that misperception is a process rather than an incorrect perception (Jervis, 1976: chap. 1). Still, it is useful to identify the various causal paths through which misperceptions might lead to war.

Another complicating issue is the fact that misperceptions can contribute to *peace* as well as to war. For example, if a state decides to forgo a preventive war strategy because it erroneously believes that the adversary is already too strong, and if an accurate assessment would have led to such a war, then the misperception causally contributed to peace.[20] The fact that misperceptions can lead to war under some circumstances but lead to peace under other circumstances makes it imperative to identify different kinds of misperceptions and the distinct causal paths through which they affect decisions for war or peace.

The most important forms of misperception are misperceptions of the capabilities and intentions of both adversaries and third parties (Levy, 1983a:282–93). Exaggeration of the hostility of the adversary's intentions is a particularly common pattern in the processes leading to war. Under rare circumstances, the erroneous belief that the adversary is about to strike can induce an actor to launch a preemptive strike of its own in order to secure first-mover advantages. At an earlier stage of the path to war, an exaggeration of the hostility of adversary intentions can lead to a military build-up or alliance as a defensive precaution, which can then lead to arms races, counter-alliances, and a conflict spiral that contributes to war. Various phases of the Arab–Israeli conflict provide good examples here.

If a state content with the status quo underestimates the adversary's hostility, that state might refrain from demonstrating its resolve or from taking countermeasures that might head off an attack in the short term.[21] In the long term, the underestimation of adversary hostility can reduce a state's incentives to build up its military capabilities. In either case, the lack of response can undermine deterrence. Alternatively, the underestimation of the adversary's resolve by an aggressive state may lead it to make more coercive military threats in the expectation that the adversary will back down, only to trigger a conflict spiral if the adversary is in fact resolved.

A state's misperceptions of its adversary's intentions may derive from secondary misperceptions of the adversary's value structure, its definition of its vital interests, its definition of the situation, its expectations about the future, and the domestic or bureaucratic constraints on its freedom of action. US misperceptions of Chinese intentions in the processes leading to the Sino–American phase of the Korean War resulted from the fact that US decision-makers failed to understand the threat that China perceived would arise if a US-backed regime were allowed to be established on Chinese borders (George and Smoke, 1974).

Misperceptions of adversary capabilities are often critical. Here we mean the evaluation of the adversary's capabilities relative to one's own, which includes both assessments of adversary capabilities, one's own capabilities, and how they are likely to interact. The underestimation of adversary capabilities generates military overconfidence and the common belief that a rapid military victory involving minimal costs is quite likely (Blainey, 1988; Johnson, 2004). This increases the probability of war, whereas an accurate assessment of a stronger adversary would have made war less likely.[22]

States can also overestimate adversary capabilities, which can lead to an unnecessary military build up that triggers an arms race and conflict spiral, along with a greater danger of war. The overestimation of the military capabilities, or rate of growth in those capabilities, of a weaker but growing state can lead to a preventive war strategy to fight now rather than later, whereas an accurate assessment of adversary capabilities would probably have not led to war. Many Americans who supported a war against Iraq in 2003 did so because of their fear of Iraq's developing program of weapons of mass destruction, whereas an accurate assessment would have led them to oppose the war. Senator Hillary Clinton, for example, said on the *Today* show in 2006, "if we knew then what we know now ... I certainly wouldn't have voted that way." A state's misperceptions of the intentions and capabilities of third states can have similar effects. The most common tendency is to exaggerate the likelihood that one's potential friends will intervene on one's behalf and the likelihood that one's potential enemies will stay neutral, either of which increases military overconfidence. Military overconfidence is further reinforced by the exaggeration of the capabilities of one's own potential allies and the underestimation of the capabilities of the adversary's potential allies.

A standard interpretation of World War I, for example, argues that German political leaders underestimated the likelihood that Britain would enter the war in defense of France in 1914, that German military leaders falsely believed that even if Britain entered the war it would be too late to make a difference, and that the war would probably not have occurred in the absence of these misperceptions (Fischer, 1988; Levy, 1990/91; Van Evera, 1999).[23] There is evidence that Saddam Hussein did not believe that the United States would intervene after an Iraqi invasion of Kuwait in 1990, that he expected the diplomatic support of Arab states, and that he certainly did not expect Arab states to align with the United States (Freedman and Karsh, 1993). The implication is that in the absence of these misperceptions Saddam would not have invaded Kuwait.

It is important to note that for the purposes of causal explanation it is not enough to demonstrate that leaders misperceive the capabilities or intentions of adversaries or third states. One must also demonstrate that these misperceptions have a causal impact on decisions for war. Misperceptions, even serious misperceptions, can occur, and war can follow, without those misperceptions playing a decisive causal role. Most scholars believe that British and French decision-makers seriously underestimated the hostility of German intentions under Hitler at the Munich conference in 1938. The argument that correct perceptions and a subsequent military build-up would have deterred war is probably incorrect, however, because there is substantial evidence to suggest that Hitler was bent on war in any case (Weinberg, 1994; Kershaw, 2000).

In addition, misperceptions that frequently lead to war can occur, but their effects are often countered by those of other variables. US and Soviet leaders made many serious misperceptions during the 1962 Cuban missile crisis, for example, but the combination of nuclear weapons, the fear of escalation, and effective crisis management strategies enabled them to overcome those misperceptions and maintain the peace. Under different conditions those same misperceptions might have led to war.

This raises a methodological problem in the study of misperception and war. If we only were to look at cases of wars and examine the role of misperceptions in the processes leading to war, we might conclude that misperceptions have an important causal impact on the processes leading to war. It is conceivable, however, that the same kinds of misperceptions are quite common in crises ending in peace. How do we assess their causal impact? We need to examine cases in which war does not occur as well as cases in which war occurs. If we were to find that misperceptions are as pronounced in non-war cases as they are in cases of wars, then we might have reasons for questioning the inference that misperceptions are an important causal variable contributing to war.[24]

It is also important to distinguish perceptions and misperceptions from *risk propensity*. Perceptions of adversary and third state capabilities and intentions help to define threats, while risk propensity combines with the assessments of the values of outcomes to shape how actors respond to threats. Sometimes it is difficult to differentiate overconfidence as a factor contributing to the initiation of a war from a willingness to take risks. Most of the evidence suggests that Japan's decision for war against the United States in 1941 was the result of a willingness to take extreme risks in a desperate situation rather than an exaggeration of Japanese military capabilities relative to those of the United States (Iriye, 1987; Taliaferro, 2004). As Japanese Prime Minister Hideki Tojo remarked a few weeks before the Japanese attack on Pearl Harbor, "There are times when we must have the courage to do extraordinary things – like jumping, with eyes closed, off the veranda of the Kiyomizu Temple" (quoted in Morgan, 1977:153).

Other leaders are much more cautious. Attitudes towards risk-taking are often the product of individual personalities. Some cultures and some ideologies are more likely to generate risk-taking leaders, as are some types of political systems. The types of leaders that generally rise to the top of highly centralized authoritarian regimes (Saddam Hussein, for example) tend to be those who are willing to take risks, because if they did not take risks they probably would not have been able to reach the top position. In other regime types, especially democratic regimes, it is more cautious individuals who avoid alienating key constituencies that are the ones more likely to end up on top. Propensities toward taking risks are also a function of the situation, as suggested by prospect theory, which we discuss later in this chapter.[25]

Now that we have seen how misperceptions lead to war, we now consider the belief systems and psychological processes that contribute to misperceptions and to other paths to war.

Beliefs and images

Individual political leaders vary widely in their personalities and belief systems, and those variations help to explain different perceptions of threats and opportunities in the international system. Beliefs are particularly important because they have a significant impact on how an individual perceives and interprets information about the adversary and about the world more generally. As we note in a subsequent section, how an individual perceives threats in a particular situation is influenced as much or more by his/her prior beliefs about the adversary and about world politics in general as by the current details of a particular situation (Jervis, 1976).

There is no consensus among scholars as to the most useful way to classify the wide variety of individual beliefs. One influential approach follows the work that originated in Leites' (1951) concept of *operational code*, which he applied to the Bolshevik ideology of Soviet political leaders. George (1969) subsequently reformulated the operational code concept and grounded it in social–psychological theories of cognition. He argued that an individual's beliefs about the political world are hierarchically organized around a small set of "master beliefs" that define the operational code. The operational code includes philosophical beliefs about the nature of politics and conflict and instrumental beliefs about the efficacy of alternative strategies for advancing one's interests. The former include questions about the fundamental nature of politics and conflict, the extent to which political outcomes are predictable or subject to chance, and the ability of political leaders to influence the flow of events. Instrumental beliefs include ideas about optimal strategies for achieving political ends, issues of timing, and conceptions of risk.

A number of scholars subsequently applied the operational code concept to a variety of political leaders, including US Secretary of State John Foster Dulles (Holsti, 1970), Henry Kissinger (Walker, 1977), George H.W. Bush and Bill Clinton (Walker, Schafer, and Young, 1999), and others.[26] One particularly interesting application of the operational code concept for the study of war and peace is Rogers' (1991) "crisis bargaining code" model, which further refined George's (1969) typology. Rogers suggested that the three most important elements of an actor's crisis bargaining code are his or her images of the adversary, crisis dynamics, and optimal bargaining strategies. Images of the adversary include beliefs about the adversary's objectives, its decision-making style, and its bargaining strategy in a crisis. Images of crisis dynamics include beliefs about the processes leading to war. Are wars usually the result of the deliberate actions of states that prefer war to peace, or are they inadvertent, resulting from an unwanted and unexpected process of escalation? Images of optimal bargaining strategies include beliefs about the relative efficacy of coercive and more conciliatory bargaining strategies. These include beliefs about whether coercive threats induce compliance or whether they provoke counter-threats and escalation, and also beliefs about the proper timing and mix of coercive and accommodative strategies.

Consider President Kennedy in the Cuban missile crisis. Kennedy's aim was to induce Soviet Premier Khrushchev to withdraw the Soviet missiles from Cuba but to do so in a way that minimized the risk of war. Kennedy believed that the sequencing of coercive and conciliatory behavior was critical in achieving his objectives. While Kennedy was quite willing to be conciliatory toward Khrushchev, the president also believed that it was essential to begin with coercive threats and actions at the onset of the crisis, in order to demonstrate his own credibility and reverse any image of weakness in the mind of the adversary – images that Kennedy believed, correctly, that Khrushchev had taken away from their June 1991 summit meeting in Vienna. Kennedy feared that a purely diplomatic strategy without coercive threats would have been more likely to escalate to risky military action (George, 1994).

The emphasis on images of the adversary can also be found in other lines of work that goes back to the 1960s. Finlay, Holsti, and Fagan (1967) wrote *Enemies in Politics* and White (1968) emphasized the importance of both adversary images (the "diabolical enemy image") and self-images, including the "virile self-image" and the "moral self-image." Lebow (1981) also emphasized the importance of images of the adversary, images of oneself, and images of the adversary's images of oneself. The latter is important in estimations of adversary intentions and of the consequences of one's own actions. An example, noted above, is President Kennedy's belief that Khrushchev perceived him as a weak leader. A different image of Khrushchev's perception might have led Kennedy to adopt a different strategy.

An individual's prior beliefs about the adversary are important in part because they shape how an individual interprets the adversary's current behavior and the possible threats the adversary poses to one's interests. We next turn to a more general discussion of factors affecting threat perception in the international system.

The psychology of threat perception

The perception and misperception of threat is shaped by causal variables at all levels of analysis.[27] System-level uncertainty leads even the most rational observers to make incorrect assessments about the capabilities and intentions of other states because they cannot distinguish meaningful "signals" from uninformative "noise" (Wohlstetter, 1962; Jervis, 1976).

This problem is compounded if the adversary engages in "strategic deception" to conceal its intentions. Bureaucratic politics and organizational processes, which we discuss in the next chapter, play an important role in shaping what information gets processed and passed on to top decision-makers, and who gets to see that information. Societal cultures, ideologies, and religions introduce an additional level of conceptual filters. It is individuals in high-level decision-making groups whose judgments about threats and opportunities determine the actual decisions for war and peace, however, and we focus here on the individual psychology of threat perception.

It is useful to distinguish two sets of biases or distortions – cognitive and motivated – that shape individuals' judgments about the world. *Cognitive biases* reflect the way the brain is "hard-wired" to process information quite independently of the impact of human emotions and motivations. Thus they are often referred to as "unmotivated" biases. The basic premise of the "cognitive" perspective is that the world is extraordinarily complex, incoherent, and changing, while people have limited information processing capabilities to comprehend that world. People try to act rationally, but they face many obstacles in approaching the ideal-type rationality described earlier in this chapter. In order to make sense of a complex and uncertain world, people adopt a number of cognitive shortcuts or heuristics (which we illustrate below) that help to simplify that world and make it more understandable. Although the use of some kind of simplifying heuristics is necessary to make sense of the external world, these heuristics can generate some important cognitive distortions (Tversky and Kahneman, 1974; Nisbett and Ross, 1980).

In contrast to cognitive biases, *motivated biases* derive from the emotional side of human beings, from their psychological needs, fears, guilt, and desires (Janis and Mann, 1977). People do not face up to information that makes them feel emotionally uncomfortable or that runs contrary to their goals, a pattern that some label "defensive avoidance." Their beliefs about the world are often convenient rationalizations for their underlying political interests or unacknowledged emotional needs, and for the policies that serve those interests and needs (Jervis, 1985; Lebow, 1981). These "motivated biases" are most likely to manifest themselves in decisions involving high stakes and important value tradeoffs. The stress inherent in these decisions often leads decision-makers to deny those threats and to deny the need to make tradeoffs between values (Holsti and George, 1975).[28]

It is important to note that each set of biases can lead either to the overestimation or the underestimation of threat, depending on circumstances. Much of the literature suggests that political leaders have a bias toward the overestimation of external threats, which increases the likelihood of conflict spirals and escalating conflict. Many similar psychological processes can, under some conditions, also lead to the underestimation of external threats, to erroneous beliefs that the adversary's intentions are benign (Johnson and Tierney, 2007). As we noted earlier, this can leave decision-makers insensitive to signals of an impending military attack.

There is also some evidence that different conditions can trigger different psychological processes, so that some conditions are conducive to overconfidence while other conditions are conducive to underconfidence. Some hypothesize that when events are uncertain and when conflict is still avoidable, people have a tendency to adopt a more deliberative mindset and carefully weigh costs and benefits. When conflict is perceived as inevitable and imminent, however, people have a tendency to switch to a different mindset, one that triggers several psychological biases that increase overconfidence (Johnson and Tierney, 2009; Heckhausen and Gollwitzer, 1987). This is an intriguing idea and needs further exploration.

We begin our discussion of the individual sources of misperception with unmotivated biases, which until recently have received most of the attention in the literature since the "cognitive revolution" in social psychology in the 1970s (Larson, 1985). One of the most important unmotivated biases involves the influence of an individual's prior beliefs on the ways in which s/he perceives and interprets information. The main hypothesis is that people have a strong tendency to see what they expect to see based on their prior beliefs. They tend to be more receptive to information that is consistent with their beliefs than to information that contradicts their beliefs. Thus there is a tendency toward *selective attention* to information. Another way of saying this is that information processing tends to be more theory driven than data driven (Jervis, 1976).

One consequence of the selective attention to information is a tendency toward *premature cognitive closure*. Instead of engaging in a complete search for information relevant to the problem at hand, there is a tendency to end the search for information after one's pre-existing views gain adequate support (Jervis 1976). These tendencies lead to the *perseverance of beliefs* beyond the point that the evidence warrants (George, 1980). These tendencies clearly violate the elements of a rational decision-making process articulated earlier.

One good illustration of the potentially paralyzing role of preexisting beliefs comes from the Israeli intelligence failure leading to the 1973 Arab–Israeli War. Israeli intelligence officers and governmental officials developed a set of conceptual guidelines to help them understand when they might anticipate a possible Arab military attack. These guidelines, known as the "Conception," specified that Egypt would not attack unless the Egyptian air force gained control of the air so that it could strike deeply into Israel, and against Israeli airfields in particular. Israel also assumed that Syria would only attack in conjunction with Egypt. There was substantial evidence of Egyptian military activity in the period leading up to the war, but Israeli intelligence discounted this information and interpreted Egyptian activity as routine military maneuvers, in part because Israeli intelligence did not believe that Egypt had the capability for a major military crossing of the Suez Canal. A standard interpretation of the Israeli intelligence failure is that the cognitive mindset formed by the "Conception" played a substantial role in shaping the perception of new information in a way that fit those preexisting beliefs, limiting Israeli intelligence analysts from thinking "outside the box" (Agranat Commission, 1974; Shlaim, 1976).

Analysts make a similar argument with regard to the American intelligence failure surrounding September 11. Although analysts attribute the failure to anticipate the 9/11 terrorist attacks to a wide range of factors, including institutional factors such as poor coordination between different intelligence agencies, many analysts argue that it was first and foremost a conceptual failure, one that derived from the intellectually constricting effects of existing mindsets. In the words of the National Commission on Terrorist Attacks Upon the United States (2004), "The most important failure was one of imagination."[29]

Some kinds of beliefs are particularly resistant to disconfirmation by new information. A good example is the dual belief that the adversary is fundamentally hostile yet at the same time responsive to external threats and opportunities. Consider the "inherent bad faith model" of the adversary (Holsti, 1970). This refers to situations in which people perceive aggressive actions by the adversary as reflecting the adversary's innate hostility, while perceiving conciliatory actions as reflecting the adversary's response to one's own resolute actions or perhaps strategic deception to induce complacency. Such beliefs are strongly resistant to change, because no matter what the adversary does its behavior reinforces one's mental model of the adversary. This can lead decision-makers to misinterpret conciliatory behavior by the adversary and consequently to miss good opportunities for conflict resolution (Tetlock, 1998).

One explanation for the tendency to perceive apparently hostile actions by the adversary as reflecting its underlying hostile intentions is provided by the *fundamental attribution theorem*, a theory in social psychology that has received substantial support from the experimental evidence (Nisbett and Ross, 1980). The theory relates to the way people explain the behavior of others. Individuals have a tendency to interpret others' behavior, particularly behavior that they regard as undesirable, as reflecting dispositional factors rather than situational factors. If the adversary adopts hardline security policies, we tend to attribute those policies to the adversary's hostile intentions or evil character, not to a threatening environment (including our own actions) that might have induced such policies. One implication is that actors tend to underestimate the effects of the security dilemma. They minimize the extent to which apparently hostile behavior by the adversary might reflect a defensive reaction to the actor's own actions that the adversary perceives as threatening.[30]

This tendency to overestimate the adversary's hostility by attributing its behavior to its evil intentions rather than to a threatening environment is compounded by actors' tendencies to explain their own behavior in terms of situational factors rather than dispositional factors, which is the "actor–observer discrepancy" (Nisbett and Ross, 1980). While we attribute the adversary's hardline strategies to his hostile intentions, we attribute our own hardline strategies to external threats and to the need to defend ourselves. Moreover, since we believe that our own actions are defensively motivated, and since we assume that the adversary understands that, we interpret the adversary's hostile behavior as evidence that it must be hostile. This leads to mutually reinforcing negative feedback and often to an escalating conflict spiral.

One important consequence of the fundamental attribution error is the tendency to perceive the adversary's regime as more centralized than it actually is, to underestimate the impact of domestic political and bureaucratic constraints on adversary leaders, and consequently to attribute too much intent to the adversary's actions (Jervis, 1976). A state may take an uncompromising position in order to pacify a domestic constituency, but its adversary tends to infer that the behavior reflects hostile intentions. Bureaucratic pressures may force a state to increase military spending, but the adversary tends to interpret the increased spending as part of a more coherent and hostile foreign policy on the adversary's part. This exaggeration of the hostility of adversary intentions can also contribute to a conflict spiral.[31]

This set of judgments and responses was quite evident for both the United States and the Soviet Union during the Cold War. Soviet officials attributed high levels of US defense spending to American ideological hostility to the Soviet Union (and to the capitalist foundations of that hostility), and US officials emphasized the role of communist ideology underlying Soviet behavior. Each downplayed the effects of its own actions and other external pressures on the actions of the other (Garthoff, 1985:903–7; Lebow and Stein, 1995).

These processes are often reinforced by a lack of empathy, or an inability to understand others' worldviews, definitions of their interests, threats to those interests, and possible strategies for neutralizing those threats (J. Stein, 1993:371). If opposing leaders have different worldviews, ideologies, cultures, or religions, they often interpret the same information differently, which increases the likelihood that a signal sent by one actor will be misinterpreted by the other. One important contributing cause of the escalation of the Korean War to a Sino–American war in 1950 was the failure of the

United States to understand how threatening a US-backed capitalist regime in North Korea would be to the communist system in China.

Ideological differences can contribute to misperceptions in other ways. Churchill warned Stalin in 1941 that Hitler was shifting his armies from the West to the East, but Stalin discounted the information in part because Churchill's liberal capitalist worldview meant that he could not be trusted. This contributed to the Soviet intelligence failure and lack of preparation for the German attack in June 1941. The larger point, however, is that Stalin was not expecting a German attack, at least not at that time, and was unreceptive to information that suggested that he might be wrong (Whaley, 1973; Bar-Joseph and Levy, 2009).

This is not to say that people never change their beliefs. Belief change is more likely if information inconsistent with existing beliefs is particularly powerful and salient, if that information arrives all at once rather than incrementally over time, if the nature of information is such that there are objective standards for assessing the accuracy of beliefs or the success or failure of existing policy, and if individuals are self-critical in their intellectual styles or organizational cultures (Jervis, 1976; George, 1980; Tetlock, 1998). Some beliefs, however, are more likely to change than others.

Psychologists have found that belief systems are organized hierarchically, with fundamental assumptions and policy objectives at the highest level, strategic policy beliefs and preferences at an intermediate level, and tactical beliefs at the bottom. If incoming information is strongly and consistently at odds with pre-existing belief systems, so that it can no longer be ignored, people first change their tactical beliefs about the best means to particular ends. If that fails to bring their beliefs into consistency with the accumulation of new information, they then change their strategic assumptions and orientation. It is only after repeated strategic failures that people reconsider their basic goals or objectives. Change in fundamental beliefs is often so psychologically difficult that it is likely to occur only in conjunction with a major political change that brings people to power that are not psychologically or politically committed to the old beliefs (Tetlock, 1991:27–31).

The perseverance of beliefs means that actors are slow to learn, slower than a rational model of learning would predict. If an actor is uncertain about adversary intentions, but believes with a given probability that the adversary has hostile intentions, then any new information about the adversary should lead the actor to "update" his probability assessment (toward a higher probability of hostile intentions if the adversary's actions are hostile, or toward a lower probability if the adversary's actions are conciliatory). Rational models of learning specify exactly how one's prior probability assessment (or "priors") should be combined with new information in a particular situation. These models are based on the logic originally suggested in the eighteenth century by the statistician Thomas Bayes. *Bayesian updating* is the standard approach to rational learning.[32]

There is substantial evidence, however, that people often depart from rational Bayesian updating. The typical pattern is to give disproportionate weight to prior beliefs relative to new information, relative to the normative Bayesian standard. Prior beliefs serve as an "anchor," and people are slow to adjust to new information. This is one of the many cognitive shortcuts or *heuristics* that people use to make sense of a complex and uncertain world, and it is sometimes referred to as the *anchoring and adjustment* heuristic (Tversky and Kahneman, 1974; Kahneman, Slovic, and Tversky, 1982).

One important source of prior beliefs is the "lessons of the past" that individuals extract from history (May, 1973). Historical events are often used as analogies to help understand the current situation and provide guidelines as to what strategies might or might not work. This *analogical reasoning* is another form of heuristic or cognitive shortcut that individuals unconsciously use to make sense of a complex world.

Analogical reasoning is often explained in terms of the *availability heuristic*. Whereas judgments of probability should be shaped by the relative frequency of occurrence of similar events, the availability heuristic suggests that judgments of probability are disproportionately influenced by events that are familiar and salient, because these are the events that easily come to mind. Most people are more fearful of dying in an airplane crash than in a car crash, even though statistics show that the latter is more likely. Pictures of airplane crashes in the newspapers or on television produce such an emotional reaction that they carry more weight than warranted by the true probabilities (Tversky and Kahneman, 1974).[33]

It is often said, for example, that generals are always fighting the last war, and that political leaders are always trying to avoid the mistakes of the past. One of the most influential analogies for the last half century of international relations was the "Munich analogy," referring to appeasement of Hitler at the 1938 Munich conference. It is associated with the perceived lesson that appeasement never works. The Munich analogy had a profound effect on American decision-making in the Korean War, the Vietnam War, and the 1990–91 Persian Gulf War (May, 1973; Khong 1992).[34]

The "Vietnam analogy," which many interpret to suggest that any US intervention involves a strong risk of ending up in a quagmire, itself had a significant impact on American foreign policy for decades.[35] The lessons of 9/11, as interpreted by the George W. Bush administration, overwhelmed the lessons of Vietnam, in part because of the analogy between Hitler and Saddam Hussein, which undoubtedly contributed to the 2003 American war in Iraq.

There are countless historical analogies from which individuals might learn. Evidence suggests, however, that there is a tendency to learn from events that have a major impact, affect the individual or her society directly, occur recently in time, and that are observed first-hand and at a formative period in a person's life (Jervis, 1976).[36] This can lead to generational effects, with successive generations, perhaps characterized by different ideological or cultural assumptions, looking back to different historical analogies and thus being influenced by different and perhaps contradictory lessons (Roskin, 2002; Jervis, 1976: chap. 3).[37] President George H.W. Bush and his advisors were significantly influenced by the Munich analogy, while Bill Clinton and his advisors were influenced more by analogies from Vietnam. The current generation is more likely to be influenced by whatever lessons are learned from 9/11 and the 2003 Iraq war, although the precise interpretation of the "lessons of Iraq" will be shaped by how the Iraqi political system evolves.

The personal experiences of decision-makers also provide a crucial source of analogies from which to draw. During the build-up to the 1991 Gulf War, President Bush and National Security Advisor Brent Scowcroft, each of whom had personal experience in the military as aviation officers, were ardent supporters of air strikes against Iraq. Generals Colin Powell and Norman Schwartzkopf, each of whose careers had been made in the US Army, were less sanguine about the potential of air strikes for degrading Iraq's then-vaunted military machine (Mintz, 1993:612).[38]

It is important to distinguish two distinct causal paths involving lessons from history and policy preferences. In one, the actor genuinely believes the lessons s/he draws from the past, and in the other the actor deliberately selects the analogies that support his/her policy preferences in order to help persuade others and advance his/her policy preferences (Jervis, 1976; Levy, 1994). In the first, historical lessons have a causal influence on policy preferences, while in the second the causal arrows are reversed, and policy preferences influence the lessons that are extracted from the past. This is the *strategic* or *rhetorical use of history*.

Although it is plausible to argue that US presidents have genuinely learned from the experience of Munich, it is also plausible that some US presidents have invoked the Munich analogy in order to enhance perceptions of external threats and give them more leverage in internal political debates. It is not an accident that Republicans and Democrats drew different lessons from Vietnam, which resulted in contradictory "lessons of Vietnam" being used in debates about whether the US should intervene in conflicts abroad. If the strategic or rhetorical use of history helps a leader to persuade others to support his/her policies, then it can still have a causal impact – but an indirect one – on decisions for war.

Both genuine learning from history and the rhetorical use of history can lead to distorted judgments and misperceptions. The problem is that the historical events from which people learn do not constitute a scientific sample for the purpose of drawing inferences, but a biased sample. In addition, as Jervis (1976:228) argues "People pay more attention to *what* has happened than to *why* it has happened. Thus learning is superficial, overgeneralized."

In other words, people look at a historical case and draw universal lessons about behavior while ignoring the contextual factors that helped to shape the historical outcome. Political leaders do not have good theories to help them predict the likely consequences of various actions (when is the use of force effective and when is it ineffective, for example), and they use the lessons of the past as cognitive shortcuts to make such causal judgments. But reasoning by analogy from the past is an inferior substitute for a good theory, and the use of misleading analogies can contribute to the processes leading to wars in situations where a more accurate assessment would have maintained the peace. The fact that a policy of appeasement failed against Hitler's Nazi Germany does not necessarily mean that a policy of appeasement will never work against any regime under any circumstances.

The preceding discussion has focused on cognitive biases, which are not motivated by one's interests or desires but which result from the use of cognitive shortcuts in an attempt to make a complex and ambiguous world more comprehensible. We now turn to *motivated biases*, which result from people's unconscious needs to maintain their own emotional well-being and to advance their interests. People are unconsciously motivated to distort information in a way that minimizes internal psychological conflict. Whereas unmotivated biases generate perceptions based on expectations, motivated biases generate perceptions based on needs or desires (Janis and Mann, 1977; Lebow, 1981). Cognitive biases lead to a tendency for people to see what they expect to see (based on their beliefs), while motivated biases lead people to see what they want to see (to avoid emotional stress or to advance their interests). This is *wishful thinking*. The tendency toward wishful thinking is exacerbated if decision-makers have an "illusion of control" (Langer, 1975) and exaggerate the degree of influence they have over the course of events.

Recall that in order to make a rational calculation of the optimal strategy for achieving one's ends, actors' assessments of the probability of an outcome must be independent of the utility of that outcome. The presence of motivated biases and wishful thinking violate that requirement, since people allow their assessment of the value of various outcomes to influence the perceived likelihood of those outcomes. Desirable outcomes are often seen as more likely to occur while undesirable outcomes are often seen as less likely. If the success of a particular strategy is seen as necessary for highly valued goals to be attained, wishful thinking can lead to an exaggeration of the probability of success of that strategy. The unconscious motivation is to reduce *cognitive dissonance*, which arises if an individual holds contradictory beliefs.

In his study of offensive military doctrines in World War I, for example, Snyder (1984) found a tendency for military organizations "to see the necessary as possible" and to inflate their estimates of the likely success of their war plans. In 1914 German leaders believed that they could only win a short war, not a long war, and their motivated biases led them to believe that the war would probably be short.[39] They had only one war plan, the Schlieffen Plan, and they unconsciously inflated the likely success of that war plan.[40]

The motivated bias hypothesis implies that actors with similar policy preferences should have similar motivated biases and thus similar biases in probability assessments. This provides one possible way for testing for the presence of these biases. We can conduct a comparative study of different actors to see if policy preferences and biases in probability assessments are correlated. This is sometimes referred to as the "third party criterion" (Lebow, 1981).[41] It is often argued, for example, that Germany's exaggerated confidence that Britain would not intervene in a European war in 1914 was due to German motivated biases: German leaders' hopes that Britain would not intervene led them to expect that Britain would not intervene. As a general explanation, the motivated bias interpretation of German misperceptions is weakened by the fact that French and Russian leaders, who were allied with Britain, who therefore hoped that Britain would intervene in the war, and who therefore (according to the motivated bias hypothesis) should have expected British intervention against Germany, were also highly uncertain about how Britain would respond (Albertini, [1942]1957).

An alternative interpretation of German behavior in 1914 is that German leaders believed that their dominant position in Europe was deteriorating rapidly enough that it was reasonable to gamble on going to war to avert that decline. This raises the issue of risk propensity. As we noted earlier, some political leaders are willing to take greater risks than are others. Hitler, against the advice of his military, who believed that Germany was unprepared for war during the mid-1930s, took enormous risks in challenging France and Britain through his aggressive foreign policies. Hitler was repeatedly vindicated by events, and his successes silenced his internal critics and reinforced his hold on power. Saddam took great risks in defying the United States in the two Persian Gulf wars, rather than playing it safe and backing off when confronted by American military threats.

Despite the importance of the risk propensities of political leaders in foreign policy behavior, international relations scholars have done relatively little theorizing about this subject (but see Kowert and Hermann, 1997).[42] Most simply acknowledge that some personalities are more willing than others to take risks. But other factors besides personality might affect a leader's willingness to take risks. Some cultures and some ideologies may encourage more risk taking than others. In addition, a substantial amount of work in social psychology suggests that certain situations (rather than certain individuals) are more likely to generate to risk-taking strategies than others. One line of research on this question is associated with "prospect theory" (Kahneman and Tversky, 1979), to which we now turn. We first describe the theory, and then consider some of its implications for international relations.

Prospect theory and risk propensity

Whereas standard economic theory suggests that value is measured in terms of net levels of wealth, prospect theory suggests that people are more sensitive to changes in wealth.[43] This leads them to define choice problems around a *reference point*. In their calculations, people give more weight to losses from that reference point than to comparable gains, which is known as *loss aversion*. Loss aversion leads people to value things in their possession more than comparable things not in their possession, which is the *endowment effect* and which makes actual losses hurt more than forgone gains (Kahneman and Tversky, 1979).[44]

This overweighting of losses helps to generate a tendency for people to engage in *risk-averse* (cautious) behavior with respect to gains and *risk-acceptant* (gambling) behavior with respect to losses. That is, given a choice between a certain gain and a gamble that might lead to either a greater gain or a lesser gain, people tend to be cautious (or at least more cautious than a rational expected-value calculation would predict) and lock in the certain gain. If, however, they are faced with a choice between a certain loss and a gamble that might lead to a greater loss or a lesser loss, they tend to take risks in an attempt to avoid the certain loss. People are so eager to avoid certain losses, or "dead losses," that they take enormous risks that often result in even greater losses, even though the expected value of the gamble may be considerably worse than the value of the certain loss.

For example, given a choice between $40 for certain or a gamble that might yield either $100 or $0, people generally prefer the risk-averse strategy of taking the sure bet of $40, even though the expected value of the gamble is greater. (The expected value, which reflects risk neutrality, is the sum of the possible outcomes weighted by their respective probabilities, or $50.) If the choice is between a certain loss of $40 and a gamble that might yield either a loss of $100 or $0, most people will take the gamble, even though the expected value of the gamble (–$50) is worse than the loss of $40.

Since gains and losses are measured with respect to deviations from a reference point, how people identify their reference points is critical. A change in reference point can lead to a change in preference (called a "preference reversal") even if the values and probabilities associated with possible outcomes remain unchanged. If people face decisions about selecting a medical treatment, for example, they are likely to respond differently if they are told they have a 90% chance of survival than if they are told that they have a 10% chance of death, although the two are mathematically equivalent. The difference lies in the reference point. A survival rate sounds like gains, which induces cautious behavior, whereas a mortality rate sounds like losses, which leads to a greater willingness to take risks on a treatment.

The identification of the reference point is known as *framing* a choice problem. In social psychology, most experimental work on the identification of the reference point focuses on the effects of framing on the choices people make rather than on the sources of framing. There has been relatively little research on the critical question of why individuals select one reference point rather than another. This is also true of most applications of prospect theory to international relations.

The most common reference point for most people in most situations, however, is the status quo. With a status quo reference point, people hesitate to take risks (or at least less inclined than a rational expected-value calculation would predict) to improve on the status quo, given risk aversion for gains with respect to their reference point. As a result, there is a *status quo bias*. If faced with possible losses from the status quo, however, individuals will prefer to gamble on risky strategies that might eliminate the loss and maintain the status quo rather than adopt a strategy that is certain to lead to that negative outcome. Given the opportunity to flip a coin for a 50 percent chance of winning $100 and a 50 percent chance of losing $100, most people will decline that opportunity and instead stay where they are.

People do not always choose the status quo as their reference point. They are sometimes influenced by expectation levels, aspiration levels, and social comparisons to select a different reference point. People tend to re-set or "renormalize" their reference points after making gains faster than they do after incurring losses (Kahneman, Knetsch, and Thaler, 1990:1342; Jervis, 1992). This implies that people tend to be prone to taking risks after suffering losses, with the aim of recovering those losses. A gambler, after suffering a string of losses, often ups the ante in an attempt to eliminate those losses. A basketball player is more likely to commit a foul after making a bad play than at other times.

Prospect theory has a number of implications for decisions for war and peace in international relations.[45] Given the overweighting of losses relative to gains and the tendencies toward risk aversion in decisions involving possible gains and risk acceptance in decisions involving possible losses, political leaders have a tendency to take more risks to maintain their international positions, reputations, and domestic political support against potential losses than they do to enhance their positions. They are more likely to fight in order to avoid losses than to make gains.[46] This helps to reinforce the argument that wars are driven more by fear than by ambition. Similarly, domestic publics punish their leaders more for incurring losses than for the failure to make gains (Nincic, 1997).

The tendency to avoid taking risks to improve the status quo in one's favor leads to a status quo bias in international relations, paralleling the general theoretical tendency described above. As Schweller (1996:99,106) argues (without referencing prospect theory), "states value what they possess more than what they covet" and "rational states do not seek relative gains so much as avoid relative losses." These are the implicit assumptions underlying defensive realism, which we discussed in chapter 2. Given the status quo bias, it is harder for conflict spirals to get started, which provides greater security for states.[47]

Standard rational economic models tell people to ignore the past, look forward rather than backward, and make decisions on the margin. This means that they should ignore past losses, or *sunk costs*. Prospect theory makes different predictions. Given the tendency to adjust to gains far more rapidly than to losses, sunk costs frequently influence decision-makers' calculations and state behavior. The losses from sunk costs persist, and they induce reference points above (superior to) the current status quo. Consequently, there is a tendency toward risk-seeking behavior to recover losses rather than to attempts to "cut one's losses." As a result, political leaders often continue to pursue costly interventions and wars, even in strategically unimportant areas, rather than risk the state's loss of power and prestige or their own loss of domestic support. This is one possible explanation for why states persist in costly interventions, as illustrated by the United States in Vietnam in the 1960s and 1970s and by the Soviet Union in Afghanistan in the 1980s (Taliaferro, 2004).

This discussion has important implications for our previous discussion of a psychological bias toward the status quo. This bias holds only if actors identify the status quo as their reference point. If an actor's reference point is a situation preferred to the status quo, so that the status quo is defined as a loss, then there is a bias away from the status quo and toward the reference point. Actors will prefer to gamble rather than accept the certainty of remaining at an unsatisfactory status quo. This might help to explain Japanese behavior in 1941. While many describe Japan's attack against the much stronger United States at Pearl Harbor as irrational, prospect theory offers a different explanation. Japan was clearly dissatisfied with the status quo and feared that the situation would only get worse. Faced with a certain loss, Japan preferred to gamble on war, in the hope of overturning an unsatisfactory status quo but recognizing that if the gamble failed the resulting situation would be even worse (Taliaferro, 2004).

Prospect theory has important implications for the strategic interaction of two states as well as for the decisions of individual states. Since those who make gains readjust their reference points and adopt risky strategies to defend those gains, and since those who suffer losses do not adjust their reference points but instead take risky actions to recover their losses, after a change in the status quo both sides engage in more risk-seeking behavior than standard rationalist expected-utility theories predict. This increases the likelihood of a conflict spiral and war. Israel is willing to take substantial risks to defend the territory it acquired in the 1967 war against possible losses, while Palestinians are willing to take substantial risks to recover the territory they lost.

Another prediction involves the consequences of coercive behavior under different circumstances. Schelling (1966: chap. 2) argued that *deterrence* is easier than *compellence*, in the sense that it is easier to deter someone from doing something than to compel them to undo something they have already done or stop what they are currently doing. Prospect theory offers a useful explanation and a modification. The reason why deterrence is easier than compellence is that deterrence involves denying the adversary gains while compellence involves forcing the adversary to accept losses by undoing past actions or stopping current actions. As a result, the adversary will take greater risks to avoid losses that it will to make gains.

This is only true, however, if the adversary defines its reference point as the status quo. If the adversary defines its reference point as a position superior to the status quo (control of territory that it had lost, for example), however, and consequently regards the present status quo as unsatisfactory, then deterrence that requires inaction involves imposing losses on the adversary rather than denying it gains. As a result, the adversary will be willing to take substantial risks to recover its losses, and deterrence is less likely to work. Thus Schelling's original hypothesis needs to be modified to incorporate the target's reference point. Coercive behavior that would deny the adversary gains (from its reference point) is more likely to succeed than coercive behavior that would force it to accept losses.

Expected utility theory and prospect theory are each *compensatory* theories of decision-making. Actors usually have multiple goals, and they must make tradeoffs across these goals. Political leaders make tradeoffs between increasing their security and promoting their ideological values, and between foreign policy goals and domestic goals. Achieving more of one goal can compensate for achieving less of another goal, though sometimes it takes a lot more of one to compensate for the loss of the other.[48] Sometimes, however, a single goal is so important that an actor refuses to make tradeoffs between that goal and other goals. Psychologists refer to this as *non-compensatory* decision-making. The most prominent theory of foreign policy decision-making based on non-compensatory decision-making is poliheuristic theory.

The Poliheuristic Theory of Decision-Making

Poliheuristic theory was developed by Mintz (1993) and Mintz and Geva (1997).[49] Consider a decision by the leader of country X to respond to a provocation by country Y. The leader of X has several policy alternatives or strategies to consider, including taking no action, responding with economic sanctions, withdrawing diplomatic relations, or authorizing a range of military responses. Each of these alternatives has consequences along several dimensions – military, economic, domestic political, reputational, etc. – reflecting the leader's multiple values or goals. It is conceivable that if one dimension or value is important enough, the leader might not give serious consideration to any strategy that might result in an unsatisfactory outcome for that dimension. If, for example, a leader is in a politically tenuous position at home and expects that a do-nothing strategy would likely come with a high political cost, s/he might eliminate that alternative outright, without even exploring the military, economic, or reputational dimensions of that alternative.

This decision-rule is non-compensatory, in that no other dimension of the do-nothing strategy can compensate the leader for the domestic political cost of that strategic option.[50] In poliheuristic theory, after an actor eliminates all strategies that might lead to unacceptable domestic costs, s/he adopts a rational, compensatory evaluation of the remaining strategic options. S/he then selects that alternative that yields the highest overall expected utility. This is a two-stage model. The first involves a non-compensatory elimination of unacceptable alternatives, and the second involves a rational expected utility calculation among remaining alternatives.

Mintz and his colleagues have utilized a computerized "decision-board" methodology to conduct a number of laboratory experiments of poliheuristic theory.[51] One such study discovered that, in a hypothetical military crisis, subjects in the control group were generally disposed towards the use of military force. This disposition did not hold in the experimental group, however, once a political dimension was added to each alternative. In the latter group, subjects tended instead to choose sanctions (Christensen and Redd, 2004). Mintz and his colleagues have also used historical case studies to explore the theoretical utility of poliheuristic theory in explaining US behavior in the Iran Hostage Crisis (Brulé, 2005), the Persian Gulf War of 1990–91 (Mintz, 1993), and the US war against Serbia in 1999 (Redd, 2005).

Poliheuristic theory is an interesting addition to the set of alternative models of decision-making, one that has important implications for the study of decisions involving war and peace. It presents an alternative to standard rational models of decision-making. The two-stage character of the model, which incorporates a non-compensatory decision-rule and an extreme form of loss aversion in the first stage and a compensatory expected-utility decision-rule in the second stage, is quite intriguing. It is particularly well suited to types of situations in which a particular value or dimension cannot be compromised, whether it be the domestic political security of a political leader or the national security of the country.

Crisis Decision-Making

The impact of the processes of judgment and decision-making surveyed in the preceding sections may vary depending on the nature of the regime, the institutional structure of the state, and the nature of the decision unit.[52] It may also vary with the type of issue involved. International relations theorists have devoted a considerable amount of time studying crisis decision-making, especially after the experience of the Cuban missile crisis in 1962. They have concluded that many aspects of decision-making in crises systematically differ from those in more routine decision contexts. Differences exist at the individual, organizational, and small-group levels of decision-making. The impact of crises on the organizational level generally parallels their impact on the individual level, and to avoid repetition we include both in this section. We leave our discussion of the small-group level of decision-making until after our survey of theories of organizational decision-making in chapter 6.[53]

We follow the scholarly consensus and define crisis as a situation that is characterized by a severe threat to important values, a high probability of war, and a finite time for coping with the threat (Brecher, 1980:1–6; Lebow, 1981:7–12).[54] Most of the literature on crisis decision-making focuses on the characteristics of decision-making during crises and how they differ from non-crisis contexts, and we share that orientation. A central assumption of most of the work on crisis decision-making is that there is a correlation between process and outcome: a flawed decision-making process increases the likelihood of lower-quality decisions. Good processes occasionally lead to bad outcomes, and flawed processes occasionally lead to good outcomes, but on average good processes are more likely to lead to good outcomes.

At the individual level, crises lead to an overload of information, an overload of tasks to be accomplished, and a restricted time frame for making decisions. Each of these characteristics increases stress. The most general finding from laboratory studies of the effects of stress is that most people perform a wide range of cognitive tasks at a suboptimal level under conditions of high stress. Some stress provides useful motivation, however, and the evidence shows that performance is most efficient at moderate levels of stress and somewhat poorer at low levels of stress.

These patterns suggest that the relationship between performance and stress follows an inverted U-shaped curve. While some level of stress may be necessary for the recognition that there is a problem and for individuals to take the appropriate problem-solving measures, high levels of stress increase cognitive rigidity, reduce the ability to make subtle distinctions, reduce creativity, and increase the selective filtering of information. Stress leads to a reduction in the number of alternative options that people consider. It also affects search, and results in the dominance of search activity by predispositions, prior images, and historical analogies rather than by a more balanced assessment of the evidence. In addition, high levels of stress reduce individuals' tolerance for ambiguity, reduce their sensitivity to others' perspectives, and increase tendencies toward scapegoating (Holsti and George, 1975; Janis and Mann, 1977; Holsti, 1989). Each of these effects detracts from a rational decision-making process. We should note that these are very general effects, which are characteristic of most humans. The nature of these effects might vary across individual personalities (Post, 1991), but the theoretical literature on crisis decision-making has given relatively little attention to the interaction of stress and personality.

Many of these individual-level patterns are reflected at the organizational level, but additional considerations emerge as we shift levels of analysis. For one thing, the nature of the decision-making unit is generally different under conditions of crisis than for more routine decisions. In crises the locus of decision-making tends to move toward the top levels of the government and away from mid-level officials in various organizations. The size of the decision-making group is usually smaller than for more routine decisions. It sometimes involves ad hoc advisory groups (such as the Ex Com during the Cuban missile crisis) rather than standard organizational units.[55] A standard argument is that the short time for decision-making usually elevates the weight given to the national interest, and in so doing diminishes the influence of parochial organizational interests, Congress or parliament, interest groups, and the public.

While these tendencies might point to greater organizational rationality for decisions in crises than at other times,[56] other characteristics of organizational decision-making during crises point in the other direction. Crisis decision-making groups consider a reduced number of alternatives, increase their reliance on ideological preconceptions and organizational routines, engage in less creative problem solving, and discount the future while attending to short-term diplomatic and political objectives (Wilensky, 1967; Holsti and George, 1975; Holsti, 1989; Brecher, 1993). The ways in which these varied patterns might affect decisions for war and peace are too varied to detail here, though certainly one path is through increasing the likelihood of misperceptions of the adversary's intentions and capabilities.

We have now completed our survey of individual-level theories of decision-making. Although individual leaders are generally less constrained in their conduct of foreign policy than they are in domestic policy, they still must rely on the information and advice provided by governmental agencies with different interests and perspectives. In the next chapter we examine theories of decision-making in organizations and the implications of those theories for issues of war and peace.

Notes

1. Although our focus on interstate war leads us to frame this analysis in terms of state decision-makers, a similar framework can be applied to most non-state actors, as we noted in chapter 1.
2. Diplomatic historians had always been more inclined than political scientists to examine "who said what to whom" and to focus on the internal processes of foreign policy (Iggers, 1994).
3. For good summaries and evaluations of the decision-making approach to the study of foreign policy, see Rosenau (1980: chap. 12) and Hudson (2002).
4. These complications include the question of how individual preferences get aggregated in collective decision-making units.
5. Some distinguish between an instrumental or "thin" conception of rationality, which consists of selecting the most efficient measures for achieving goals, and a "thick" conception of rationality, which includes both the maximization of given goals and the overall rationality of the goals themselves (Ferejohn, 1991). People generally have a hierarchy of goals, of course, and in the instrumental version, we can say that goals are non-rational if they impede the achievement of higher-level goals.
6. One of the first attempts to systematize the stages of rational decision-making was Allison (1971). Other good treatments are Steinbrunner (1974: chap. 1) and March (1994: chap. 1).
7. An actor's time horizons refer to how s/he values or discounts the future. It is often said, for example, that political leaders have short-term time horizons that extend only to the next election. Everyone understands that actors' time horizons are important, but very few theories of international relations and foreign policy formally incorporate that variable, in part because of the difficultly of empirically measuring what those time horizons are. See Streich and Levy (2007).
8. Technically, the utility of a particular outcome is also a reflection of the actor's risk propensity, which reflects the shape of an actor's utility function (Morrow, 1994: chap. 2).

9.   For a technical discussion of these requirements, see Morrow (1994: chap. 2), and for an application to the study of war, see Bueno de Mesquita (1981: chap. 2).

10. Snyder (1991) includes the use of symbolic myths to make emotional appeals to the public. This is a non-rational psychological factor.

11. We focus on the impact of individual-level psychological variables on elite behavior, because it is political elites that make decisions for war and peace. Psychological variables also influence mass behavior – including public opinion, nationalism, the formation of group identity, the construction of images of the enemy, social mobilization for war, etc. These variables are important, but they only influence decisions for war indirectly, through top decision-makers' incorporation of domestic factors into their calculations.

12. A counterfactual hypothesis takes the form "if x had not been present, the outcome would have been z rather than y." Here y is the actual outcome (World War II, in our example), and z is the hypothesized outcome (the likely avoidance of war) in the counterfactual world defined by the absence of x (Hitler as German chancellor). Counterfactual arguments, which can be stated in deterministic or probabilistic terms, raise difficult methodological issues. On criteria for evaluating the validity of counterfactual statements, see Tetlock and Belkin (1996) and Levy (2008c).

13. For a review of the literature in political psychology, see M. Hermann (1986), Monroe (2002), and Sears, Jervis, and Huddy (2003).

14. For a particularly influential psychoanalytic study of foreign policy, see George and George (1956). See also Steinberg (1996).

15. For an earlier survey of the role of personality in foreign policy decision-making, see Winter (1992). For different approaches to the assessment of political leaders, see Post (2003).

16. Social psychologists recognize that cultural differences generate significant differences in belief systems, worldviews, and emotional reactions. They generally assume, however, that the most basic processes of judgment and decision-making are universal, including the fundamental attribution error, decisional heuristics, loss aversion, and other patterns described below. Some recent research challenges this assumption (Nisbett, 2003).

17. See Stoessinger (2001) for a strong but not particularly rigorous statement of this view.

18. It is commonly argued, for example, that the United States never would have crossed the 38th parallel in Korea had American leaders anticipated Chinese military intervention and a war with China that left nearly a million people dead (George and Smoke, 1974: chap. 7; Singer and Small, 1972). Scholars have made similar arguments about the United States in the Vietnam War and the 2003 Iraq War, given the enormous costs of those wars and debatable benefits from them.

19. The bargaining model of war shifts the focus from misperception to "private information." The basic argument is similar, however, because private information often leads to misperceptions of the capabilities, interests, and likely intentions of others. Recall, however, that private information is a necessary condition only in one rationalist path to war. Rational actors can go to war

under conditions of complete information if there are expectations of shifting power that lead to commitment problems, or if there are indivisible issues.

20. In a response to the conventional wisdom that British leaders erroneously expected that a strategy of appeasement would satisfy Hitler and avoid war, Ripsman and Levy (2008) argue that the primary reason Britain did not initiate or provoke a preventive war against Germany in the mid-1930s was that Britain overestimated German military strength and concluded that it was already too late to confront Germany.

21. If, for example, Israeli leaders had recognized that Egypt and Syria were preparing for war in 1973, they probably could have deterred the surprise attack by mobilizing for war and/or gaining US diplomatic support beforehand. On the sources of the Israeli intelligence failure, see Stein (1985) and Bar-Joseph (2005).

22. Hitler was so confident of a quick victory over the Soviet Union that he did not even issue winter uniforms prior to the German invasion of Russia in 1941 (Weinberg, 1994). US political leaders anticipated a quick victory over the Iraqi army in 2003 and failed to anticipate the rise of an insurgency (Ricks, 2006), and it is reasonable to argue that accurate expectations would have led either to the absence of an American invasion or a much larger military operation.

23. For the alternative argument that German leaders hoped that Britain would stay out of the war but did not expect them to stand aside, see Trachtenberg (1990/91) and Copeland (2000).

24. Another possibility is that another factor is present in the war case but not in the non-war case, and that misperceptions contribute to war only through their interaction effects with that other variable.

25. For approaches to the study of risk, see Yates (1992). For a socio-cognitive approach, see Vertzberger (1998).

26. See Walker (2003) for a review of operational code studies.

27. This section builds on Levy (2003b: 261–9).

28. It is often not easy to distinguish between motivated and unmotivated biases on the basis of observable behavior or distortions in judgment, because these biases generate many similar behavioral patterns. Even the conceptual distinction between the two is beginning to break down. Whereas scholars had long believed that emotions detracted from rational decision-making, there is growing evidence, reinforced by new research in neuroscience, suggesting that rational cognition actually depends on emotional factors. One cannot engage in the elements of a rational decision-making calculus without some kind of emotional involvement. See Damasio (1994), Barkow, Cosmides, and Tooby (1992), Kahneman (2003), McDermott (2004), and Rosen (2005). In this section, however, we focus only on cognitive and motivated bias that detract from rational decision-making.

29. The "lack of imagination" hypothesis is difficult to evaluate. The World Trade Center had been attacked before (1993), though by different means. Moreover, American intelligence was well aware of the fact that many Muslims had been taking flight-training lessons on big jets. The larger problem was the integration and coordination of intelligence. In addition, as Wirtz (2006:63)

argues, what some see as a lack of imagination might sometimes be better interpreted as an unwillingness to respond, especially in peacetime, to threats that are imaginable but unlikely to materialize with policies that are costly.

30.   Note that the dispositional/situational dichotomy parallels our levels of analysis: dispositional is an individual or unit-level characteristic, while situational refers to external environmental factors.

31.   An adversary's build-up of military strength is often still a threat even if it is imposed on leaders who prefer more conciliatory policies. But response to the build-up might depend in part on interpretations of the intent behind the increased capabilities.

32.   For an accessible discussion of Bayesian updating, see Anderson and Holt (1996).

33.   Since politically relevant analogies often carry strong emotional impact, the availability heuristic is not purely cognitive in nature.

34.   Khong (1992:31–2) argues that "virtually all of the analysts of the Vietnam War agree that the decision-makers of the 1960s were ill-served by their historical analogies."

35.   Similarly, Saddam's belief that the United States would not intervene to drive Iraq out of Kuwait in 1990–91 was based in part on the lessons he drew from the American experience in Vietnam – that the fear of high casualties would deter the US from going to war (Freedman and Karsh, 1993).

36.   It is sometimes said that people learn more from failure than from success (J. Stein, 1994:173). This may be true, but it may also reflect a bias towards emphasizing lessons that lead to policy change and hence are more observable and salient than lessons of success that reinforce existing policy. On the need to separate learning from policy change, see Levy (1994).

37.   One thing this generational view overlooks is the fact that substantial differences arise within generations, as illustrated by the different worldviews of President Clinton and the second President Bush, who were of the same generation. We suspect that ideology plays a greater role than generational effects.

38.   We return to bureaucratic/organizational factors in the next chapter. For a study of the effectiveness of coercive bombing see Pape (1996).

39.   Recent evidence suggests that one notable exception to this belief in the "short-war illusion" was German Chief of Staff Moltke (Förster, 1999).

40.   For alternative views of the Schlieffen Plan and why the German war plan failed, see Ritter (1958) and Zuber (1999).

41.   The third-party criterion can be misleading if the different observers have access to different information, because differences in assessments might be based on informational asymmetries rather than motivated biases.

42.   Economists, on the other hand, spend an enormous amount of time studying responses to risk. People's responses to situations involving rare events are particularly interesting (Taleb, 2007). US Vice-President Dick Cheney, who talked about the danger of a "low-probability but high impact" event, was unwilling to take even a small chance that Iraq might have weapons of mass destruction. He feared both the acquisition of nuclear weapons by Iraq and a transfer of nuclear weapons to al Qaeda or another terrorist group. He said that "Even if there's just a 1 percent chance of the unimaginable coming due,

act as if it is a certainty." This became known as the "one percent doctrine" (Suskind, 2006).

43. This section builds on Levy (2000).
44. Most people, for example, get more upset when they fail to sell a stock that then goes down than when they fail to buy a stock that then goes up. The former involves real losses, while the latter involves forgone gains. Or, as the tennis player Jimmy Connors said, "I hate to lose more than I like to win."
45. For further discussion of these and other hypotheses, see Farnham (1994), McDermott (1998), Davis (2000), Levy (2000), and Taliaferro (2004). For a critique of operationalizations of risk propensity in the study of international relations, see O'Neill (2001).
46. D. Ross (1984:247), for example, argues that Soviet leaders were willing to engage in the "use of decisive and perhaps risky action far more readily for *defending* as opposed to *extending* Soviet gains."
47. For an explicit attempt to link prospect theory and defensive realism, see Taliaferro (2004).
48. The precise tradeoffs are reflected by "indifference curves" used by economists.
49. For recent summaries, see Mintz (2004a) and Brulé (2008).
50. The non-compensatory decision-rule might be seen as an extreme version of the prospect-theoretic concept of loss aversion, in the sense that losses along one dimension are regarded as infinitely harmful. The poliheuristic decision-rule is related to Tversky's (1972) "elimination by aspects" decision rule. See also Goertz (2004).
51. See Mintz (2004b) for more on the use of decision boards. For more on the decision board approach, see Mintz's "Decision Board 4.0: Computerized Decision Process Tracing," which is available at www.decisionboard.org/academic/zzzabout1.asp. For a similar decision-board methodology applied to the study of voting, see Lau and Redlawsk (2006).
52. On the importance of decision units (individual leader, group, and coalition), see M. Hermann (2001).
53. The reader should note, however, that some theories of small-group decision-making have some important implications for crisis decision-making. Group-think (Janis, 1982), for example, applies primarily to situations involving consequential decisions and high stress, which are conditions of crisis.
54. Holsti (1989:12) excludes the high-probability-of-war criterion so as to make the concept more general and applicable to non-security issues. Some add the criterion that a crisis must involve surprise (C. Hermann, 1969:414). We prefer to leave surprise out of the definition. Actions can generate threats to basic values and a high probability of war even if they are anticipated. Egypt's closing of the Straits of Tiran in May 1967 was not a surprise to Israeli decision-makers, but it precipitated a major crisis that led to the 1967 war.
55. At the peak of the Cuban missile crisis, President Kennedy even bypassed the Ex Com and used Robert Kennedy on back-channel negotiations with the Soviet Ambassador.
56. Verba (1961:158–60), for example, concludes that, "the model of means–ends rationality will be more closely approximated in an emergency when the time for careful deliberation is limited."

6

Decision-Making:
The Organizational Level

Historians have long talked about the role of "court politics" or "cabinet politics" in influencing the policies of kings and other rulers. Political scientists have for many years studied organizational behavior within the executive branch of the government (Simon, 1949; March and Simon, 1958), but they focused on the role of governmental politics in domestic policy, not in foreign policy. The underlying assumption was that foreign policy was "beyond the water's edge," and that on issues as important as foreign policy, where the national interest was at stake, governmental politics was put aside in favor of national interest calculations. Allison's *Essence of Decision* (1971, revised by Allison and Zelikow 1999) was the first systematic challenge to this assumption. It initiated a wave of research on bureaucratic/organizational influences on foreign policy decision-making (Halperin and Kanter, 1973; Halperin, 1974; Steinbrunner, 1974: chaps. 3–4).

The Bureaucratic Politics and Organizational Process Models

Allison (1971) drew on the organizational theory literature and developed two different but overlapping models of foreign policy that focused on the executive branch of the government. He called one the "organizational process" model (or "model II"), and he called the other the "governmental politics" model (or "model III"), which is also called the "bureaucratic politics" model. Allison contrasted these two models with "model I," which he described as "the Rational Model" but which is more accurately described as a rational unitary model of foreign policy ("model I").[1] Allison described the theoretical logic of each of these models and then applied all three models to the Cuban missile crisis.[2] In principle, however, the models are more general and apply to any state, or at least any state with a substantial bureaucracy.[3] We begin with model III, the governmental politics model, and then turn to the organizational process model.

The governmental politics model

Allison's (1971) governmental politics model focuses on politics within the executive branch of the government, where decisions are ultimately made. This model rejects model I's assumption that the state acts as a single unit with a well-defined set of foreign policy goals and a consensus on the best strategies for attaining those goals. Instead, the model zeros in on the inner circle of decision-makers, and assumes that if we want to understand the foreign policies made by states we need to understand who those decision-makers are, how much power they have, and how they define their interests. It recognizes that the president (or the prime minister in a parliamentary system) is the single most powerful decision-maker, but it emphasizes that the president's power is limited by the power of other actors who occupy the top positions in the primary governmental organizations involved in the making of foreign policy.[4]

In the United States, these actors include the secretaries of defense and state, the national security advisor, the chair and members of the Joint Chiefs of Staff, the head of the CIA, and usually the secretary of the treasury and a few others selected by the president. Each of these actors has two general tasks. One is to advise the president (or prime minister) as to the policies that will best serve the interests of the country as a whole. The other is to serve as manager of his/her organization and to act as advocate for the interests of the organization. Occasionally a key actor will be "minister without portfolio," without the responsibilities of representing a particular organization. For example, during the Cuban missile crisis President John Kennedy asked former Secretary of State Dean Acheson, who was widely respected for his expertise and judgment, to serve on the Ex Com during the Cuban missile crisis. Robert Kennedy, the Attorney General and the president's brother, also served on the Ex Com at the president's request, and was perhaps its most influential member because of his unique access to the president.

The bureaucratic politics model posits that the policy preferences and recommendations of each of these key actors may differ because each actor may have different perceptions of the national interest and because each represents a different organization within the government, each with its own set of interests. Different organizations within the government have different tasks, and in order to effectively deal with all of the problems it is asked to solve each organization (and sub-organization within it) generally wants to maximize the resources available to it.

The greater an organization's budget and staff, the greater is its ability to solve problems and fulfill its missions. In addition, most organizations want to maximize their political influence, prestige, and autonomy, either as ends in themselves or as means to increase their power and resources in the future. Some of these key actors may have domestic political interests, or be sensitive to the president's domestic political interests. They may also have personal interests, including career interests, their historical legacy, and business or individual financial interests. Thus the policy recommendations made to the president can reflect some combination of perception of the national interest, organizational interest, and occasionally domestic political or personal interests.

While each of these interests may influence an actor's policy preferences, a key proposition of the bureaucratic politics model is that organizational interests usually dominate. This is captured by the idea that "where you stand is where you sit" (Allison and Zelikow, 1999). The best predictor of an actor's policy preferences and thus of his/her recommendations to the president is the actor's organizational role and the organizational interests that s/he represents. One common prediction, for example, is that the defense department will push for new weapons systems and for increases in the defense budget because larger defense budgets benefit the defense department and its ability to accomplish its missions. It is also frequently argued that the Department of Defense tends to be more hawkish in its policy recommendations than are other organizations. This is often but not always the case. Of all of President Kennedy's advisors during the Cuban missile crisis, one of those most opposed to a military option and most supportive of a diplomatic solution was Secretary of Defense McNamara.

The hypothesized dominance of organizational interests in most actors' preference structures reflects either the deliberate priority individuals give to organizational interests over the national interest, or to the fact that after serving in an organization for many years the actor comes to believe that what is best for the organization is best for the country. If someone has spent most of his/her career in the navy, and becomes socialized in the worldview and culture of the navy (and perhaps of a particular branch of the navy), it is not surprising that s/he might come to believe that the best interests of the country are served by having a strong navy. When an organization advocates a budgetary level or policy that serves its narrow organizational interests but perhaps not the national interest, it is sometimes difficult to tell whether that action is based on narrow self-interest or on the genuine belief that it is acting in the best interests of the country. In either case, organizational interests have an impact on policy preferences, either directly or indirectly through shaping the mindsets of organizational actors. The first path is rationalist, while the second path involves a non-rationalist mechanism.

Key bureaucratic actors vary in their political power and influence as well as their policy preferences. The influence of each actor depends on his/her formal position in the government; control over resources, information, and policy implementation; expertise or reputation; access to the president (or prime minister); ability to mobilize external support; and political skill. Many of these factors are interrelated. An actor's formal position is by far the primary determinant of the resources at his/her disposal, control over information, and role in policy implementation. The enormous budget of the Pentagon, along with its control over vital information about the potential costs, benefits, and risks inherent in the potential use of force, give it disproportionate influence on military issues. Its ties with key committees of the Congress, with the defense industry, and with veterans' groups further increase its power in the decision-making process by giving it power to mobilize political support from outside the inner circle of decision-making. The State Department, on the other hand, has no political constituency, a smaller budget, and generally less influence (Allison and Zelikow, 1999; Halperin, 1974).

The bureaucratic politics model posits a number of different actors, each with different policy preferences and positions of unequal power within the government. The model predicts that foreign policy is the outcome of an internal political process of conflict, bargaining, and consensus building among these different actors. In this model, foreign policy choices are best conceived not as an attempt by a state to maximize its interests given external threats and opportunities, as in model I, but instead as a process of reaching a *political* resolution to a problem of internal conflict among different actors representing different organizations and advocating different policies.

One useful example of this kind of bargaining, compromise, and consensus-building is provided by Halperin (1974). In the 1960s, the United States debated whether or not to construct an anti-ballistic missile system to destroy incoming strategic missiles.[5] Two camps formed. One camp advocated a "heavy" missile system (defined by a large number of interceptor missiles) to protect the US strategic retaliatory force (rather than US cities) against a Soviet attack. The other camp advocated no missile defense. The result was a "light" missile defense to protect US cities against a Chinese attack. None of the components of the preferred positions of either of the camps entered into the final policy. It is a perfect illustration of a bureaucratic compromise driven by internal politics rather than by a primary concern for the national security interests of the country as a whole. Neither side got what it wanted, but each avoided what it regarded as the worst outcome. The result was a bureaucratic compromise resulting from battles over policy and "turf" among different organizations.

Note that in the bureaucratic politics model each actor attempts to maximize his/her interests as s/he defines them, usually based primarily on organizational interests. Thus the bureaucratic politics model (at least in most interpretations) assumes rational actors (Bendor and Hammond, 1992). Since the actors whose interests are being maximized are individuals (and the organizations they represent) rather than states, and since those interests differ, the model is a non-unitary rational actor model.

The organizational process model

Allison and Zelikow (1999) constructed an organizational process model (also described as the "organizational behavior model" or model II) as a second alternative to model I. The organizational process model also focuses on key foreign policy agencies, but less on the overtly political dimensions of organizational behavior (on fights over "turf," for example) than on standardized rules and procedures within organizations. Instead of emphasizing the interests of each organization and the attempts of those organizations to select those policies that maximize their interests, the organizational process model focuses on the *standard operating procedures* (or SOPs) that are common to all organizations.

The model posits that the decisions of organizations reflect the implementation of the organization's procedures or routines. Organizations do not analyze a particular decision problem in its entirety, consider the context in all of its details, and then make a calculated decision as to what policy is best. Rather, the organization views the situation, selects which of its pre-existing routines best fits the situation, and then implements the routine. Instead of looking forward and calculating which strategy would lead to the optimal outcome under the circumstances, as a truly rationalist model would predict, model II looks backwards to those routines that the organization set up to automatically implement certain types of policies that provide the best fit to the problem at hand. One common consequence of routine-driven behavior is *incrementalism*, which contributes to the continuity of policy. The best predictor of how an organization behaves at time t is how they behaved at time $t - 1$.

Military routines are a good example. It is often argued, for example, that one reason for the failure of the American army to win in Vietnam is that it implemented the strategies and operational methods of conventional war that had worked so effectively in the European theater during World War II but that were ill-suited to a counterinsurgency war in the jungles of Vietnam (Krepinevich, 1986). This routine-driven organizational behavior is reinforced by the role of vested interests within the military and its subunits, because there are always some sub-organizations that benefit (in terms of budgets, manpower, autonomy, and prestige) by the continuation of earlier policies, even if those policies now appear to be outdated. It is the advocates of the successful policies in one war who tend to be promoted, and who then use their influence to establish the routines for the next war. We give more examples of the impact of military routines on war later in this chapter.

Organizational theorists also emphasize that bureaucratic organizations tend to follow a distinctive type of decision rule. Recall that a rational model of decision-making predicts that actors define their goals, consider a wide range of options, estimate the consequences of each of those options, and select the option that generates the highest expected utility and is thus most likely to achieve their goals. Organizations tend to follow a different decision rule. They engage in *satisficing* (Simon, 1949). Instead of considering all options, they consider options sequentially until they find one that is good enough, that meets some pre-determined target level. They do not engage in an extensive information search on all feasible options. Instead of attempting to find the best solution under the circumstances, they are content to settle on an adequate solution.[6]

Another key concept in organizational theory is one of *factored problems* (Cyert and March, 1963). This is the idea that a given problem is often not dealt with as a whole, but parceled out to different organizations and sub-organizations with the authority and expertise to deal with its own particular aspect of the problem. The Department of Defense deals with the military dimensions of an issue, the State Department with diplomatic dimensions, the Treasury with economic dimensions, and so on. This tendency toward factored problems is enhanced by each organization's interest in maximizing its own autonomy. An important consequence of factored problems is the lack of coordination between agencies and a lack of policy integration. Often the left hand does not know what the right hand is doing, and the actions of one organization can run contrary to the actions of another organization, with too little direction and control from the top.

One can find plenty of examples of factored problems and the absence of policy coordination. In her influential interpretation of the sources of the US intelligence failure at Pearl Harbor, Wohlstetter (1962) argues that the US had plenty of information about a likely Japanese attack but that the information was spread over different organizations (the departments of the Army and the Navy). Those organizations chose not to share their information because of interservice rivalry, competition for control over intelligence, and the absence of institutionalized routines for the coordination of intelligence. Similarly, in the months leading up to the September 11, 2001, attacks against the United States, different intelligence agencies had different pieces of information, but they did not share the different pieces of the puzzle because of organizational jealousies (Zegart, 2009). A request by the FBI for a warrant to examine the computer of a suspected figure, who turned out to be a leading planner in the attack, was rejected by other agencies. Another example is the fact that the emergency response to the 9/11 attack was impeded by the lack of communications between the New York police and fire departments, in part because their radios were not compatible.

Although Allison and Zelikow (1999) distinguished between models II and III, other scholars combine the two (Halperin, 1974) and integrate both the competition and bargaining for resources and influence among actors and the influence of standardized rules and procedures. Most applications of these models to foreign policy decision-making on security issues incorporate elements from both models (Rhodes, 1989; Maoz, 1990; Zisk, 1993; Sinno, 2008). We follow that practice in our consideration of applications of bureaucratic/organizational models to issues of war and peace.

The Causal Links to War

The bureaucratic politics and organizational process models are theories of decision-making, not theories of the causes of war. Scholars have applied these models to security policy – including defense spending, military procurement, the military–industrial complex, and the conduct of war – but there have been relatively few systematic applications to the causes of war. While these models are not conducive to generating sweeping generalizations, they do highlight some causal paths involving bureaucratic politics and organizational processes that might contribute to war under certain conditions. Anyone who is familiar with these models of decision-making and who reads a historian's narrative of the causes of a particular war would undoubtedly notice some of these factors at work.

Our aim here is to identify some general causal paths through which bureaucratic politics and organizational processes contribute to the outbreak of war (or to the preservation of peace) and to illustrate each with historical examples. One involves the impact of parochial organizational interests on the formulation of state preferences and strategies. Another involves the organizationally induced distortion of information flowing up to top-level decision-makers, including the politicization of intelligence. A third involves the impact of rigidities in organizational behavior on strategy selection. In the following illustrations we combine elements from both the organizational process and bureaucratic politics models.

Impact of organizational interests on state strategies

There are a number of paths through which bureaucratic/organizational interests might contribute to the outbreak of war. One line of argument is that military organizations want war and use their influence to promote war because they believe that war serves the organizational interests of the military. We saw a form of this argument in our earlier discussion of Schumpeter's ([1919]1951) argument about military elites. Schumpeter argued that in earlier eras, when empires and then states faced many external predators, military elites had a powerful argument in support of their quest for positions of political power in society. Once in power, those military elites solidified their positions and continued to use war and the threat of war to justify their policies and maintain their dominant positions, even after earlier external security threats had diminished.

Although few scholars would argue that most contemporary states, especially advanced industrial states, are controlled by military elites, the question of the power and influence of military organizations on foreign and security policy for different kinds of states under various conditions is an important one. It is central to the bureaucratic politics approaches to war and peace. One can certainly identify some cases in which a military organization believed that its interests (or perhaps those of the state itself) would be served by war and gained a position of political power that allowed it to implement its policy preferences. One is Japan in the 1930s. Japanese military operations in China, combined with the military's manipulation of domestic politics through heavy-handed means, gave the military control over the Japanese state and played a significant role in the processes leading to the Pacific War with the United States (Ienaga, 1978).

Some make a similar argument about German foreign policy in the period leading up to World War I. They suggest that a powerful group of military and naval officers, led by the General Staff (and its chief of staff von Moltke), had gained a position of dominance over civilian authorities in the conduct of foreign policy. Some suggest that the influence of the military was further reinforced by a "social militarism" that "permeated the whole of society with its ways of thinking, patterns of behavior, and its values and notions of honor" (Wehler, 1985:156). The argument is that Germany pushed for war in 1914 because of the policy preferences and power of the German military, which had essentially hijacked the German state (Fay, 1928:38–44; Craig, 1955; Ritter, 1970; Van Evera, 1990).

This historical interpretation is controversial. In his highly influential interpretation of German behavior in 1914, Fischer (1967) argues that civilian political leaders led by Chancellor Bethmann-Hollweg were firmly in control until the very end of the July crisis, and that they differed little from the military in terms of their policy preferences. The German military may have been more sensitive than were civilians to the rise of Russian power and the risks of a two-front war in Europe (given the Franco–Russian alliance against Germany), but this is more an argument about different conceptions of the national interest than about the parochial interests of the military.

While one can find instances of militaries with preferences for war and the power to dominate the decision-making process and implement their preferences, this is almost certainly incorrect as a general statement about the causes of war in modern international history. It was Hitler and Nazi ideology that pushed for war in the 1930s, not the German military, which was far more cautious and which actually opposed Hitler at some key junctures on the road to war in the 1930s (H. Deutsch, 1974; Weinberg, 1994). Watt (1975) describes the "reluctant warriors" in all of the European capitals in the late 1930s. After World War II, it is difficult to find any trace of an eagerness for war among military organizations in the industrial states of Europe.

With respect to the United States, one of the few systematic studies of the attitudes of the American military regarding war and peace after World War II found that professional military officers have not been significantly more warlike or hawkish than their civilian counterparts. Once war is underway, however, military organizations have been more hawkish on decisions regarding the escalation of war, to finish the job they have started and to preserve the reputation of the military once its forces are engaged (Betts, 1977).[7] One implication of this is that the factors shaping the termination of war are not necessarily identical to the factors shaping the outbreak of war, contrary to Blainey (1988) and to some proponents of the bargaining model of war. New actors and new vested interests at both the bureaucratic and domestic levels come into play (Iklé, 1971).

Indeed, in most of America's recent wars, from the Korean War to the Vietnam War to the two wars against Iraq, American civilians took the lead in advocating policies that involved the use of force. In some cases these actions went against the preferences of key military leaders. Military experience and first-hand experience with the horrors of war often leads military leaders to be more cautious than civilian leaders, who lack comparable experience. Within the military, it is sometimes the "old Turks" who are more cautious than the eager younger officer corps. This pattern is often reinforced by the fact that younger leaders have career incentives to participate in combat, because distinction on the battlefield is a prime path to promotion.

Consider a few historical cases. In the Vietnam War it was the "best and the brightest" (Halberstam, 1969) of civilian defense intellectuals who were more enthusiastic than the military about the potential benefits of a dramatic American intervention in the war. In the Cuban missile crisis, although the Joint Chiefs of Staff were relatively eager to resort to a military strategy to eliminate the Soviet missiles in Cuba, Secretary of Defense McNamara (along with Robert Kennedy) played a leading role in shifting the majority opinion away from a potentially risky air strike toward a more cautious strategy of military blockade. In the 1990–91 Persian Gulf crisis, the Chairman of the Joint Chiefs of Staff, Colin Powell, argued for a continuation of economic sanctions against Iraq, at least for a time, rather than for war in January 1991 (Freedman and Karsh, 1993). As Secretary of State in George W. Bush's administration, Powell was quite skeptical of the wisdom of invading Iraq (Woodward, 2004; DeYoung, 2006:194).

Whether or not the military advocates more hardline strategies than do civilians, and in what kinds of situations and under what conditions, is an empirical question to be investigated through careful historical research rather than something to be assumed. It is surprising that scholars have devoted relatively little time to this important issue, and that applications of bureaucratic politics frameworks so often simply assume that military organizations have more hawkish policy preferences than do other governmental actors. Scholars need to make more nuanced assessments of the policy preferences of different organizations.

In addition to the direct link between military interests and decisions for war, military organizations can contribute to war through a less direct path. Military organizations do not necessarily want war, but like most organizations they generally want bigger budgets, increased manpower, and more autonomy. Moreover, by virtue of their worldviews and their training, military elites are often inclined to believe that the national interest is well served by military strength and hardline foreign policies. Some militaries (Germany before World War I, for example) rationalize their claims for resources by promulgating myths about permanent threats, intractable enemies, a glorious military past, and military honor (Van Evera, 1990; Snyder, 1991). They use their power to advance these policy preferences.

Larger military budgets often lead adversary states to increase their own military spending, which increases tensions, sometimes triggering arms races and conflict spirals, and sometimes leading to war. Military organizations also push for more technologically advanced weapons systems, which require their adversaries to do the same. This can also lead to conflict spirals and possibly war, and often more destructive wars because of the more advanced weapons.[8] Thus military organizations may not advocate war, but they often advocate policies that contribute to the processes that generate conflict spirals that can lead to war.

Another line of argument is that military organizations tend to prefer offensive doctrines and that offensive doctrines increase the likelihood of war (Posen, 1984:47–51; Snyder, 1984: chap.1; Van Evera, 1999). One reason why military organizations might prefer offensive doctrines is that the implementation of offensive doctrines and war plans requires larger numbers of troops and weapons systems, greater logistical support, and often more sophisticated military technology than do more static defensive strategies. This means larger budgets and manpower, and hence more influence for the military. A second argument is that offensive doctrines and war plans also contribute to one's ability to seize the initiative, structure the battle, and thus fight the war on one's own terms. This serves the key organizational goal of uncertainty avoidance, and it also enhances military autonomy and morale.[9]

Once in place, and whether driven by the internal interests of organizations or external national security needs, offensive doctrines and war plans contribute to the outbreak of war by increasing the incentives to strike first; fueling arms races, tensions, and conflict spirals; and encouraging aggressive policies.[10] They also increase the destructiveness of war (Posen, 1984:18–24; Van Evera, 1999). Historians have long argued that the offensive nature of military plans prior to World War I helped make that war more likely (Albertini, [1941]1957; Tuchman, 1962).[11] In fact, World War I turned out to be a long struggle defined by trench warfare and slow movement.

This leads to the puzzle of why military organizations did not anticipate this outcome, of the gap between the actual dominance of the defense and the widespread perception of the dominance of the offense in warfare (Levy, 1984:233). One argument advanced by a number of international relations theorists is that offensive war plans, and the pre-World War I "cult of the offensive" more generally, were the result of the parochial interests of military organizations and the nature of the military cultures of 1914. These offensive beliefs and doctrines were shared by the militaries of all the Continental great powers in 1914 and contributed significantly to the processes leading to war by accelerating the perceived incentives to move quickly, which minimized the opportunities for diplomatic initiatives that might diffuse the conflict (Posen, 1984; Snyder, 1984; Van Evera, 1999).[12]

This discussion of the military should not give the impression that military organizations are characterized by a homogeneity of interests and beliefs across their various subunits. Bureaucratic politics takes place within organizations as well as between them. There were some significant splits within the German military before World War I. Moltke and the army had been pushing for a preventive war at least since 1912, but Admiral Tirpitz argued strongly against that strategy on the grounds that the German navy was not yet ready (Fischer, 1967).

We can also find American examples of doctrines and strategies driven more by organizational interest than by a reasoned view of the national interest. Some have argued that one of the reasons the US Air Force recommended bombing campaigns in the Vietnam War was not because it was convinced that it was an optimal response to the existing threat to US interests, but rather because the Air Force wanted to demonstrate that there was a role for it to play in the war. Otherwise, it feared that the Air Force might be perceived as irrelevant to the new guerrilla wars of the 1960s and consequently lose resources to the other services (Gallucci, 1975). Many argue that one of the reasons for the failure of the US attempt to rescue American hostages in Iran in 1979 was because interservice rivalry led each of the military services to insist on being involved in the mission rather than allow another service to get the credit for any success, and because of the lack of tactical coordination among the military services.[13]

Internal political conflict between bureaucratic organizations can also create policy paralysis or delays that prevent a timely response to adversary actions and that under some circumstances could contribute to war. After US intelligence first discovered Soviet offensive missiles in Cuba in October 1962, a follow-up aerial surveillance mission was ordered to validate the presence of Soviet missiles. The mission was delayed for ten days, however, by turf battles between the CIA and the Air Force over which organization would conduct the mission. The outcome of the CIA–Air Force dispute was a classic bureaucratic compromise: CIA pilots flew Air Force planes (Allison and Zelikow, 1999). These delays could have been far more consequential, but fortunately the presence of the missiles was confirmed in time for the US to act. Still, the delays complicated the Kennedy Administration's efforts to manage the crisis and minimize the risk of escalation to war.[14]

Bureaucratic in-fighting and maneuvering can contribute to peace as well as to war. In the Cuban missile crisis, US decision-makers in the Ex Com defined their initial options as doing nothing, a diplomatic solution, a secret approach to Cuban Premier Fidel Castro, an air strike, an invasion, and a blockade. Initially, the majority of the Ex Com preferred an air strike option. There are a number of possible explanations as to why they eventually settled on a blockade. One was certainly Robert Kennedy's insistence that his brother would not be "another Tojo," referring to the Japanese premier who ordered the surprise attack against the United States at Pearl Harbor in 1941. This reluctance to initiate military action and to shift that burden to the Soviet Union was an important factor influencing US decision-making.

Another consideration, emphasized by Allison and Zelikow (1999) in their discussion of the bureaucratic politics model, concerned the maneuvering of Secretary of Defense McNamara. McNamara preferred a diplomatic solution. He recognized, however, that the president was quite skeptical about that strategy (perhaps for domestic political reasons) and that it would not be possible for McNamara to mobilize sufficient political support within the Ex Com around a passive strategic response to the Soviet action. For that reason, McNamara started advocating the blockade option, not because he thought it was the best for the country, but because it avoided what he regarded as the worst option (the air strike), and because he thought it might be politically feasible. McNamara calculated correctly and maneuvered skillfully.[15]

It is also possible that bureaucratic conflict can send mixed signals to adversaries (and to allies), create confusion about political leaders' intentions or resolve, and generate misperceptions that can contribute to war. In the July 1914 crisis, for example, German Chancellor Bethmann-Hollweg, after weeks of pressuring the Austrians to move against Serbia, reversed course on the night of July 29–30 and demanded that Austrian civilian authorities refrain from war. At the same time, German Chief of Staff Moltke was pressuring Conrad, his counterpart in Vienna, to move ahead with military action. This led Conrad to complain: "Who actually rules in Berlin, Bethmann or Moltke?" (Albertini, [1941]1957:673–4). These mixed signals contributed to the failure of Bethmann's last-minute efforts to preserve the peace, since it was not clear to the Austrians what Germany wanted. Admittedly, though, the chance for peace was slim by that point (Levy, 1990/91; Strachan, 2001).

Organizations and the distortion of information

Organizational interests and routines can also contribute to war (or to peace) through their impact on the flow of information within decision-making units. Organizations responsible for providing information about adversary intentions and/or capabilities to higher level decision-makers may be tempted to distort that information in a way that serves their own interests. Alternatively, their organizational structures may contribute to the inadvertent distortion of information or presentation of an incomplete picture of the information available. This can lead to a number of misperceptions that influence the likelihood of war. Many have argued, for example, that during the Vietnam War the US military, which wanted to see the war through to a successful conclusion, deliberately underestimated numbers of enemy troops and exaggerated the prospects for victory, in an attempt to persuade political authorities to continue the war through to victory (Adams, 1994).

To take another example, in the run-up to the Bay of Pigs operation in 1961, in which the United States supported an invasion of Castro's Cuba by Cuban refugees, officials in the Central Intelligence Agency deliberately overestimated the likelihood that the operation would trigger a popular uprising in Cuba. They acted so in order to obtain the political authorization for an operation to which they had become psychologically committed and which they believed would serve their organizational interests (Higgins, 1987).

These examples refer to the distortion of the information flowing up to top decision-makers by the actions of those organizations tasked with providing that information. Top political decision-makers sometimes act in a way that prevents the free flow of information, in order to structure the internal debate and provide additional leverage in mobilizing other governmental actors and the public for war. Although intelligence ought to shape policy based on the evidence, without interference from political leaders in the intelligence process, in fact policy often shapes intelligence. This is often referred to as the *politicization of intelligence* (Betts, 2007).

It is generally assumed that authoritarian regimes are more vulnerable than democratic regimes to the politicization of intelligence, because there are fewer channels for dissenting views in autocracies, because of the lack of protection for individuals under the rule of law, and because of the potentially severe personal costs of providing news the leader does not want to hear. A major reason why Saddam Hussein failed to anticipate the likelihood and consequences of an American invasion was that Iraqi military and intelligence analysts were afraid of Saddam and they felt they had no choice but to provide only good news (Woods, Lacey, and Murray, 2006). The same dynamic contributed to Stalin's failure to anticipate the German invasion in 1941. It was widely known that Stalin was a paranoid tyrant who had executed or sent to the Gulags anyone whom he suspected might challenge or undermine him. Analysts who believed that Nazi Germany might turn its armies toward the east and attack the Soviet Union did not express their concerns to Stalin for fear of the personal consequences (Bar-Joseph and Levy, 2009).

These tendencies toward the politicization of intelligence in authoritarian political systems should not blind us to the fact that political pressure on the intelligence process arises in democratic regimes as well. Intelligence officers might consciously adjust their estimates of adversary intentions or capabilities because they believe that the failure to provide "intelligence to please" might result in the loss of their jobs, the denial of a future promotion opportunity, or the loss of influence on future policy decisions.

The same outcome can emerge from more subtle pressures. In his analysis of the escalation of American involvement in the Vietnam War, for example, Thomson (1968) discusses a number of pathologies within organizations. He emphasizes the role of the "curator mentality" among mid-level officials in the departments of State and Defense. Rather than question prevailing assumptions and mindsets, individuals' career incentives led them to adopt a "don't rock the boat" orientation. They did their job within the existing set of guidelines, got their "ticket stamped," and ultimately received their promotion. While the practice of "whistle blowing" is extremely useful for organizations, it is often a bad career move for the whistle blower.

These tendencies are reinforced by what Thomson (1968) calls the "effectiveness trap." If one challenges prevailing mindsets and policies, one is likely to lose, and in the process there is a risk of suffering a loss of influence in future decisions. If one resigns in protest, one loses influence altogether. There is a temptation to go along with the consensus and to save one's "political capital" for a future issue where one might have greater impact. Such politically driven processes work to reinforce prevailing mindsets and policies. Thomson (1968) shows how these dynamics contributed to the gradual escalation of the American commitment in the Vietnam War in the 1960s by silencing dissenting voices and by limiting the range of opinions that reached political decision-makers.

Limits on the flow of information can be the result of more deliberate governmental policies. Many argue that the second Bush Administration was so committed to invading Iraq in 2003 that it deliberately distorted evidence about the possibility that Iraq had weapons of mass destruction and ties to the al Qaeda terrorist organization, in order to enhance the support for its policies in the Congress and among the public (Pillar, 2006; Rich, 2006). The administration even set up a new intelligence unit, the Office of Special Plans, in the Defense Department (Gordon and Trainor, 2006:45). There is substantial evidence that this office was designed to circumvent the CIA and produce intelligence that demonstrated both the existence of Iraqi WMD and a link between Iraq and al Qaeda, in order to provide a rationalization for a war against Iraq.[16] After his meeting with the British prime minister in 2002, the head of British intelligence concluded that "the intelligence and facts were being fixed around the policy" (Danner, 2006:89).[17]

Much of the discussion in this section deals with interesting questions in civil–military relations. Brooks (2008) provides a useful framework for analyzing the impact of civil–military relations on the assessment of the threat environment and shaping of military strategies. She identifies two key variables: the intensity of the divergence between civilian and military elites over security issues and over the institutional context for policy-making, and the balance of political power between civilian and military elites. These factors influence the extent of information sharing, strategic coordination of political and military policy, procedures for the accurate assessment of the relative strengths and weaknesses of the adversary's military organization and one's own, and the coherence of the decision-making process on questions regarding the use of force.

Brooks (2008) uses her framework to explain why Egyptian strategic assessment was so flawed under President Nasser leading up to the disastrous 1967 war with Israel, and why assessment procedures and military performance significantly improved in the period leading up to the 1973 war under President Sadat. Brooks also shows, in an analysis of Britain before and during World War I, that there can be significant variations in the quality of strategic assessment within democratic regimes.

Impact of organizational routines on policy rigidity

The standard operating procedures and vested bureaucratic interests associated with organizational behavior often affect security policy and decisions related to war and peace by reinforcing existing policies and strategies, generating policy momentum, and by denying political leaders the flexibility they need to manage crises in a way that strikes an optimum balance between preserving vital national interests while avoiding inadvertent escalation. Military organizations are well-known for the routinized nature of their military mobilization and war plans, and there have been a number of applications of organizational process models to the military.

Probably the most common explanation of how military routines contribute to the outbreak of war focuses on the momentum generated by the mobilization plans themselves. Each action in this process of incremental escalation leads logically to the next, locking in current policy and contributing to a mechanistic and practically irreversible process of escalation to war, one in which political leaders have a minimal impact because of the rigid adherence to pre-existing routines. One of the best examples of this is how it applies to World War I, which we now examine in some detail.

Many historians and political scientists have argued that the rigid military mobilization plans and railroad timetables of 1914 were an important contributory cause of World War I. This view is reflected in the title of A.J.P. Taylor's (1969) book *War by Time-table*. Once the mobilization process was initiated, the rigidity of the plans made it difficult or impossible to delay, slow, or modify a plan, or to switch from one mobilization plan to another, without creating enormous vulnerabilities. Indeed, military and political leaders believed that "mobilization means war" (Albertini, [1941]1957; Kennedy, 1979). Once the mobilization began, the process acquired a momentum of its own; the military requirements of preparing for war took precedence over political requirements of avoiding one if at all possible. Political leaders were left with few opportunities to slow or interrupt the process in order to pursue diplomatic alternatives that might preserve the peace, accentuating the slide to war.

The inexorability of the process is captured quite well by Sergei Dobrorolski, Chief of the Mobilization Section of the Russian General staff, in his description of the process a few years after the war:

> The whole plan of mobilization is worked out ahead to its end in all its details. When the moment has been chosen, one only has to press the button, and the whole state begins to function automatically with the precision of a clock's mechanism. ... The choice of the moment is influenced by a complex of varied political causes. But once the moment has been fixed, everything is settled; there is no going back; it determines mechanically the beginning of war (cited in Fay, 1928: vol. 2/481).

The impact of rigid mobilization and war plans is illustrated by the German Schlieffen Plan, which was based on the assumptions that any continental war would be a two-front war for Germany; that the slowness of the Russian mobilization (because of the size of the country and its bureaucratic inefficiency) meant that Germany could engage in an offensive in the west but a holding action in the east in an attempt to defeat France quickly; that France could be defeated only by an enveloping movement through Belgium, and that this required the preemptive seizure of Liège early in the mobilization process itself (no later than the third day); and that the assumed advantage of the offensive meant that every day's delay could be quite costly (Ritter, 1958).[18]

The Schlieffen Plan illustrates the consequences of factored problems. Military organizations tend to focus on the military aspects of policy and to minimize its political component. There is a resulting danger that military doctrine will follow a "strictly instrumental military logic" and ignore important political considerations (Posen, 1984:58), which results in a lack of congruence between foreign policy goals of the state and the military means available to achieve those ends. This is particularly likely in the absence of strong civilian intervention, which is in part a function of the bureaucratic influence of the military in the decision-making process.

By calling for a preemptive move against Liège by the third day of mobilization, the Schlieffen Plan required the violation of Belgian neutrality and significantly increased the probability that Britain would enter the war. This military policy ran contrary to the efforts of German diplomats, who were doing everything possible to try to keep the British out of the war. German foreign policy and German military policy were working at cross-purposes. As Taylor (1969:19) argues:

> Politically the plans for mobilization were all made in the void. They aimed at the best technical results without allowing for either the political conditions from which war might spring or the political consequences which might follow from any particular plan. There was little consultation between military planners and civilian statesmen. The statesmen assumed that the general staffs were doing their best to insure that they would win a war if one came and there was no speculation how policy could be seconded by military action. The dogma of the great Clausewitz ... had lost its hold.[19]

The problem of low political–military integration is compounded if political leaders are ignorant of the details of military plans, because they may not realize the extent to which they lack the military options to support their foreign policy objectives. This ignorance was an important source of escalation in 1914. Whereas the military saw mobilization as a means of preparing for a war that they perceived to be inevitable, political decision-makers generally saw it as an instrument of deterrence or coercive diplomacy. They had little conception, until it was too late, that they lacked the means to support a coercive or deterrent strategy based on a fine-tuning of military threats, or that their room to maneuver had been severely restricted. As a result, they did not realize that actions taken in all sincerity to avoid war while preserving vital interests only made war more likely. Thus Ritter (1958:90) concludes that "The outbreak of war in 1914 is the most tragic example of a government's helpless dependence on the planning of strategists that history has ever seen."

George (1991) suggests several conditions conducive to effective crisis management. In addition to the limitations of one's political objectives, these include presidential control of military options, pauses in military operations, availability of discriminating military options, coordination of military movements with political–diplomatic actions and with limited political objectives, and others. The military mobilization and war plans of 1914, and the Schlieffen Plan in particular, violated every one of these requirements. The Schlieffen Plan left German leaders with no options between a two-front war against France and Russia and no war at all. The plan would be implemented regardless of the political circumstances that might draw Germany into a war (Snyder, 1984; Van Evera, 1999). The strategy gave German leaders no intermediate military option that would allow them to demonstrate their resolve and fine-tune their threats without provoking the adversary into a dangerous escalation, which is an essential requirement for crisis management (George, 1991). World War I is only one case, but it nicely illustrates the potential causal impact of common forms of organizational behavior on decisions for war and peace.

Another key component of the bureaucratic politics/organizational process model is its focus on implementation. Political leaders do not implement their own policies, and there is often "slippage" between the foreign policy decisions of political leaders and the ways in which their decisions are actually implemented. As Harry Truman remarked as Dwight Eisenhower was about to assume the presidency, "He'll sit here, and say 'Do this! Do that!' *And nothing will happen.* Poor Ike – it won't be like the Army. He'll find it very frustrating" (quoted in Neustadt, 1991:10). Similarly, during the Cuban missile crisis President Kennedy ordered that the naval blockade be moved closer to Cuba in order to give the Soviets more time to reverse course before a collision, but the Navy did its best to resist those orders (Allison and Zelikow, 1999). Kennedy also ordered the suspension of weather-sampling flights over the Soviet Union during the crisis, to minimize the danger of dangerous misperceptions, but that order was not implemented. This led Kennedy to complain "There is always some son of a bitch who doesn't get the word" (quoted in Holsti, 1989:18).

The bureaucratic politics model sees foreign policy decision-making as a political process, defined by bargaining among actors with difference policy preferences and unequal power. The organizational behavior model broadens this conception by incorporating certain routinized forms of behavior within organizations, behavior that is driven by standard operating procedures, rules, and customs rather than explicit calculations of political interest. These models tend to minimize the genuinely social aspects of group decision-making – the interpersonal dynamics among the members of any decision-making group, whether it be a governmental organization or an informal advisory group. We now turn to the social dynamics of decision-making in small groups.

The Small-Group Level of Analysis

Social psychologists give a great deal of attention to the dynamics of small-group behavior. The small-group model that has generated the greatest interest among international relations theorists, and which in fact has become the paradigmatic theory of small-group behavior, is Irving Janis' (1982) analysis of "groupthink." Groupthink is a theory of small-group dynamics that is anchored in individual psychology.[20] It is not a theory of war, but it has a number of important implications for decision-making, especially crisis decision-making, on issues of war and peace.

Groupthink is a "concurrence-seeking tendency within cohesive groups" (Janis, 1982:7–9), a strong tendency to conform to group norms and reach a policy consensus. It is motivated not by political pressure, but by social pressure in the context of high-stakes decisions and enormous stress. Conformity with group norms and unanimity about policy maintains the integrity of the group and a sanctuary from the burdens of office, and in doing so provides psychological security for the individual, reduces anxiety, and heightens self-esteem (Janis and Mann, 1977).

Janis argues that groupthink is most likely to arise in socially cohesive groups that are relatively insulated from the government and from outside sources of intelligence, and also in situations involving significant moral dilemmas. Tendencies toward groupthink are further reinforced if the group leader actively promotes his or her preferred policy, if there is no source of contrary views or even a devil's advocate to raise unpopular arguments, if the group has recently suffered a significant failure, and if group members are particularly insecure.

Janis (1982) identifies a number of "symptoms" of groupthink, patterns associated with the tendency toward concurrence-seeking: illusions of invulnerability, unanimity, and moral superiority; discounting and rationalization of information that runs contrary to the collective beliefs of the group; and the reinforcement of these tendencies by self-appointed mindguards who work to shield the group against adverse information and to put pressure on dissenters. These tendencies generate a number of more specific patterns of group decision-making: the consideration of a limited number of policy alternatives; failure to reexamine the possible risks of a policy once it is preferred by a majority, or to reconsider the possible benefits of alternatives after they have been rejected; failure to consider what might go wrong and develop contingency plans; selective attention to information and discounting of discrepant information; lack of an attempt to acquire additional information from experts; tendency to elevate loyalty to the highest priority goal; and tendencies towards riskier courses of action (Janis, 1982; Janis and Mann, 1977:130–31).

These patterns detract from a rational decision-making process. They lead to a number of misperceptions that contribute to war through the causal paths discussed in the last chapter. As with any theory of decision-making, it is assumed that the quality of the process is probabilistically linked to the quality of the outcome, and that if the process is non-rational there is an increase in the probability of ineffective policies and bad outcomes. Janis (1982) attempts to demonstrate this in his case studies of a number of American foreign policy failures, including the Bay of Pigs and the Vietnam War. He also compares these cases of foreign policy failures with the American decision-making regarding the Marshall Plan and the Cuban missile crisis, where symptoms of groupthink are much less evident and where outcomes were quite successful for the United States.

While scholars have applauded Janis's (1982) efforts to construct a small-group model of decision-making, and welcomed it as an important contribution to our understanding of collective decision-making, they have criticized the model on a number of grounds. These criticisms have led to the development of alternative theories of small-group dynamics in foreign policy (Longley and Pruitt, 1980; 't Hart, 1990; 't Hart, Stern, and Sundelius, 1997). Most of these share many of the features of the groupthink model, and it is not necessary to provide a complete review of these theories here, but we would like to highlight three issues in particular.

First, although Janis (1982) defines groupthink in terms of concurrence-seeking within cohesive groups, it is conceivable that similar tendencies might arise in non-cohesive groups, and also that some cohesive groups might not generate such tendencies. A highly cohesive group with considerable experience working together might feel comfortable questioning each other and raising arguments that run contrary to the opinions of the majority. The greatest pressures for conformity might be in relatively newly formed, inexperienced, and weakly institutionalized groups, where individuals are most in need of the group for psychological comfort, and where many of the decision-making pathologies associated with groupthink are most likely to occur.

These considerations led Stern and Sundelius (1994) to identify a "newgroup syndrome." Stern (1997) argues that the newgroup syndrome provides a better explanation for flawed decision-making during the Bay of Pigs crisis than does Janis's (1982) groupthink model. The newgroup syndrome, if validated, has important implications for crisis decision-making on war and peace, since many international crises, particularly those involving democratic states with frequent regime changes, involve new and relatively inexperienced decision-making groups.

Second, scholars have qualified Janis's (1982) hypothesis that small-group dynamics generally lead such groups to adopt riskier courses of action than would the same individuals acting on their own, which was consistent with the longstanding *risky shift hypothesis*. New evidence suggests instead a *group polarization hypothesis*, which predicts that small groups will generate either significantly more risky or more cautious behaviors relative to what one might expect from the simple aggregation of the policy preferences of the individual members of the group (Minix, 1982; Vertzberger, 1990).

Third, in emphasizing the social–psychological dynamics leading to concurrence-seeking tendencies within small groups, Janis (1982) downplayed power-related political dynamics that might lead to several of the decisional pathologies that Janis identifies with groupthink. He also made little effort in his case studies to rule out these alternative explanations. For example, the tendency to go along with the group might be the result of political pressure or career incentives rather than the social pressures and internalized group norms. The recognition that group dynamics do not operate in a political vacuum has led 't Hart (1990) and others to try to construct a small-group theory of foreign policy decision-making that integrates political as well as social–psychological factors. This is a quite positive development in the field.

We have now covered theories of interstate war grounded in multiple levels of analysis, including systemic, dyadic, state–societal, and individual-level theories. Although all approaches to the causes of war do not fit readily into separate well-defined levels – a point to which we return in the conclusion – the levels-of-analysis framework still generates fewer problems of classification than do alternative frameworks. The application of this framework to theories of civil wars is somewhat more problematic. Distinctions among levels of analysis remain applicable, but it is much less common for theorists of civil wars than those of interstate wars to organize their analyses around these different levels. Civil war analysts are also more likely to integrate variables from multiple levels than are their counterparts who study interstate wars, though the gap is slowly closing as more of the latter integrate variables from different levels. In the next chapter we survey some of the leading theories of civil wars.

Notes

1. Allison (1971) created considerable confusion by describing model I as "the rational actor" model. This label was misleading because it implied that his other models were not based on rational actors. As we will see, especially with

respect to the governmental politics model, actors behave rationally on behalf of their interests (Bendor and Hammond, 1992). Those interests, however, are primarily organizational interests rather than the national interest. Whereas model I is a unitary rational actor model, model III is a rational but non-unitary actor model. Although some also interpret model II as a rational non-unitary model, others argue that certain aspects of the model detract from rationality, as we shall see later in the chapter. Steinbrunner (1974: chap. 3) suggested a fourth model, a "cognitive model," which is a non-rational psychological model of individual behavior.

2. Allison (1971) selected the Cuban missile crisis for a reason. This was an acute national security crisis, one that involved the risk of nuclear war. If ever we would expect a rational unitary actor model to apply, it would be in such a crisis. If Allison could show that organizational processes and bureaucratic politics played an important role in a crisis of this magnitude, we could be reasonably confident that they might play an important role in other cases where the national interest was not so directly and immediately threatened. The influence of Allison's book derived in part from this research design and case selection. The Cuban missile crisis is a "least-likely case" for the bureaucratic and organizational models (George and Bennett, 2005). The logic of least-likely case analysis involves what Levy (2008b) calls the "Sinatra inference": if I can make it there, I can make it anywhere. At the same time, the Cuban missile crisis is a "most-likely case" for the rational unitary actor model. If the case did not fit the model, it would significantly reduce our confidence in the general applicability of the model.

3. On foreign policy-making in developing states, see Vertzberger (1984), Calvert (1986), Korany (1986), and Barnett (1992).

4. One common criticism of the utility of the bureaucratic politics model for analyzing US foreign policy is that it underestimates the power of the president. After all, the president appoints (with the approval of the Congress) most of the other key actors, usually people who share his views. Another argument is that in national security crises, the effects of variables in models II and III are generally marginalized by those of the national interest calculations of model I (Krasner, 1971; Art, 1973).

5. The issue came up again in the 1980s, as the "star wars" program, and it was raised again by the second Bush Administration.

6. For an application of satisficing decision-rules, rule-driven behavior, and incrementalism to individual behavior, see Steinbrunner's (1974: chap. 3) conception of a "cybernetic model."

7. Sechser (2004) makes a different argument. In a statistical study he finds that states that lack strong civilian control tend to initiate armed conflicts much more frequently than states with stronger civilian control over their military organizations. This finding implies that the caution of the American military with respect to strategy is not generalizable to all other states. On a slightly different question, recent work has revealed an increasing ideological conservatism among American military officers relative to the views of civilians (Feaver and Kohn, 2001).

8. Recall the discussions of the spiral model and of the "steps-to-war" model in chapters 2 and 3. Scholars debate whether technologically driven "qualitative arms races" are more war-prone than are "quantitative" arms races (Huntington, 1958).

9. It is not clear that morale is greatest with offensive war plans, although that might depend on exactly how one defines morale. One thing that is clear is that soldiers tend to fight more intensely in the defense of their territory against external aggression, or perhaps in recovering lost territory, than in aggressive actions to conquer another's territory. This is consistent with evidence that people fight harder to avoid losses than to make gains, as we saw in our discussion of prospect theory and loss aversion in the last chapter.

10. One problem with these analyses is that the distinction between offensive and defensive strategies is not always clear (Levy, 1984; Lieber, 2005). Scholars often lump both incentives to striking first (preemption) and a strategy of deep territorial penetration into the same offensive category, but they are distinct. A doctrine may call for waiting for the adversary to strike first but launching a powerful counteroffensive deep into the adversary's territory if one is attacked, as illustrated by Israeli doctrine in 1973 and German military doctrine in the 1870s and 1880s.

11. For a skeptical view, see Zuber (1999), who argues that Germany did not have an offensive war plan. For responses to Zuber, see Mombauer (2001) and Strachan (2001).

12. Recent scholarship has challenged the long-held belief that all military leaders shared the belief that the war would be short. There is some evidence that Moltke believed that the war would probably be a long one (Förster, 1999).

13. McDermott (1998) suggests a prospect theory explanation based on loss aversion: US leaders recognized that they had few good options, but believed that the status quo was unacceptable, and were willing to engage in a highly risky strategy in the hope of overturning the status quo.

14. In fact, the Soviet Union had already smuggled nuclear warheads into Cuba, but US leaders were unaware of this, and in fact did not learn until years after the missile crisis (Dobbs, 2008). Thus American leaders were operating with very limited information about the magnitude of the threat to US interests. If the US had known of the presence of nuclear warheads in Cuba, they might have acted much differently in their crisis bargaining.

15. Reinforcing this argument is the fact that President Kennedy discounted the hawkish views of some in the CIA because he felt that he had been misled by the CIA in early 1961 during the Bay of Pigs crisis (Higgins, 1987).

16. It was not accidental that the analysts at OSP were selected for their job precisely because they shared the administration's assumptions.

17. This issue is quite complex. Given the inherent uncertainty about Iraqi WMD, the fact that Iraq did have WMD a decade before and provided no evidence that it had destroyed its stockpiles, and the fact that many leading Iraqi generals believed that Iraq had WMD, one can imagine intelligence analysts reaching that conclusion even in the absence of political pressure. Some leading scholars argue that the primary problem was not the assumption of Iraqi WMD, but the confidence with which it was held and the failure to

constantly question that assumption through an expanded information search and more critical perspective (Jervis, 2006; Betts, 2007).

18. Some recent research challenges conventional interpretations of the Schlieffen Plan and its impact (Zuber, 1999; Mombauer, 2001; Lieber, 2007). Moltke probably expected a long war (Förster, 1999), and it is not clear how far west the enveloping movement through Belgium was designed to go (Zuber, 1999). Still, one can make the argument that Moltke sought a quick victory against France in the west in order to position Germany for the long war to come.

19. See also Ritter (1958), Turner (1979), Snyder (1984).

20. The groupthink concept is frequently misused by journalists and some scholars, who take it out of the small-group context for which it was intended and apply it to a tendency toward conformity of thought among any level. Groupthink should be restricted to small groups and not confounded with other sources of conformity, including ideological and cultural factors.

7

Civil War

Although wars within states have always been more common than wars between states, the relative frequency of civil war to external war has increased significantly since 1945,[1] and the human costs of civil wars now exceed those of interstate wars. Data from the Correlates of War project show that in the period from 1945 to 1997 there were 23 interstate wars involving 3.3 million battle deaths and 108 civil wars involving 11.4 million deaths. On average, civil wars last four times as long as do interstate wars, and approximately three-quarters of the countries experiencing a civil war suffered from at least one additional civil war.[2] The proliferation of civil wars, the end of the Cold War and the shift in the threats to US interests, and the growing sensitivity to humanitarian concerns have all led to a proliferation of scholarly research on civil wars. Much of this research is conducted by scholars who formerly studied interstate war. It is little surprise that scholars want to be "where the action is."

This increasing attention to the phenomenon of civil war has led to a shift in the questions that scholars ask about warfare. What do the different trends in warfare mean, and what are their implications for the future? Is interstate war becoming obsolete? Is the number of civil wars escalating and spreading around the globe? Are new states doomed to state collapse and perpetual disorder as a consequence, as multiple groups compete to hijack what remains of state institutions? Along with these more macro-questions, the question of why civil wars occur in the first place has begun to receive a fair amount of explicit attention.[3] It is notable that scholars have generally concluded that civil wars work differently than interstate wars do, so that explanations for civil wars have taken a different form than explanations for interstate war.

This shift in scholarly attention and orientation has been relatively recent. Civil wars are not new, of course, nor are they completely absent from the commentaries of observers on political events from antiquity on, but studies of civil war have been something of a stepchild until lately. We have many fine histories of the more well known cases, including the English Civil War (1642–51), the American Civil War (1861–5), and the Spanish Civil War (1936–9).[4] Most of the analytical attention paid to "internal" wars in the 1960s through 1980s, however, emphasized explaining political violence in general (or the impact of modernization, as in Huntington, 1968), countering guerrilla warfare, or the more traditional interest in analyzing revolutions that have often been linked to civil wars – as attested to by the salient Mexican (1910–20), Russian (1917–21), and Chinese (1920s–40s) cases.[5]

Within the more general literature on political violence in the first generation of analysis, there are pronounced emphases on a variety of topics that have some bearing on thinking about civil wars. The work on relative deprivation (Davies, 1962; Gurr, 1970) argued that it is not the most downtrodden who should be expected to revolt, because they have to focus on day-to-day survival issues. More rebellious are populations whose living conditions have been improving up to a point and who then find further improvement blocked or conditions regressing from the level already attained.[6] Identifying relative deprivation, however, proved problematic. Some initial conceptual work (Eckstein, 1965; Tilly, 1978) was done on internal warfare without really stimulating much follow up. A number of earlier studies have also examined the relationship between inequality and revolt. Yet, no consensus ever emerged on just what the relationship is. Scholars have done interesting work on collective action problems, and a number of analyses of social movements (McAdam, Tarrow, and Tilly, 2001) have possible utility to understanding civil wars, but direct applications remain fairly rare.[7]

More recent theorizing about civil war causality has taken the form of debates about the wisdom of emphasizing the respective roles of greed, grievance, motivation, and opportunity. The greed–grievance dispute turned out to be an analytical dead end when students of civil war found little evidence that greed alone fueled civil wars (Ballentine and Sherman, 2003; Aronson and Zartman, 2008). Greed (as in making money from diamonds or opium) was not absent from domestic warfare but it was more a byproduct of rebels looking for ways to finance their activities than a primary motivation for rebelling in the first place. A motivation–opportunity dispute has largely supplanted the greed–grievance debates but the problems here are that insurgent motivations are presumably disparate and hard to pin down. Much of the evidence that might be viewed as addressing motivation also can be interpreted as representing opportunity.

A good example is the empirical finding that civil wars are more probable in poor countries than in rich ones (Collier et al., 2003). Poverty can provide a good motivation for attempting to take over states that are not addressing economic problems. Poverty also constrains the resources of the state, thereby making them more vulnerable to takeover. Poverty also creates a large pool of underemployed youth who can be lured into becoming armed dissidents. Thus, does poverty speak to motivation, opportunity, or both? If both, as is likely, the motivation–opportunity debate is not likely to be resolved.

An important conceptual issue is whether it makes sense to talk about the causes of civil war per se or whether it makes more sense to talk about specific kinds of civil war. Are civil wars involving ethnic group grievances different from those that do not involve ethnicity in some way? Should we isolate separatist wars from wars in which rebels hope to take over the state, as opposed to creating a new state? Might we gain more understanding if we distinguish between highly asymmetrical wars in which the states are stronger than the rebels and symmetrical wars in which states and rebels are roughly equal in capability? While these questions have been broached, they have not really begun to be answered.

The levels-of-analysis framework, which we found useful for classifying the causes of interstate wars, is more difficult to apply to civil wars. Analyses of interstate wars often emphasize some factor that fits in only one level – such as systemic concentration, dyadic rivalries, national regime type, organizational decision making, or individual misperception. Analyses of civil wars generally do not emphasize a privileged variable or variable at a particular level, although exceptions include research on socioeconomic inequality, weak states, or rebel group financing. The core arguments about the causes of civil war currently revolve around motive versus opportunity debates and, to a less explicit extent, onset versus duration considerations. These arguments rely on causal factors from multiple levels and do not lend themselves to neat classification within the levels-of-analysis framework.

The nature of the motive–opportunity debate will be elaborated below. Suffice it to say that most recent analyses have focused on opportunity factors – that is, what factors make it easier or more difficult to rebel for whatever reason. The lists of factors that are put forward tend to be multi-level, encompassing primarily systemic through group considerations. Motivation has been considered too difficult to capture in general terms. The onset–duration problem, most succinctly put, is that many of these opportunity factors (and motivation factors, for that matter) can be applied to explain why civil wars begin, why some become unusually protracted, or both. Although authors often specify that they are addressing either onset or duration, onset and duration still tend to become conflated. There is also a fair amount of disagreement. One person's onset factor is another person's duration factor and vice versa. We are no more likely to impose a tight order on these materials than the analysts already have, but we can try to communicate the nature of the disagreements. Thus, a different presentation strategy for civil war causes seems necessary. We will keep levels of analysis in mind but not insist that the arguments about the causes of civil war fit within them neatly.

To set the stage for discussing different interpretations of civil war causes, we need to introduce briefly the "old war/new war" debate, which we mentioned in chapter 1. Emblematic of this debate is Kaldor's (1999) perspective. Kaldor maintains that the type of warfare that became most prevalent in the past three to four centuries was closely tied to the relatively recent emergence of the nation-state organizational format. The primary goals of interstate warfare moved from a focus on territorial delineations and aristocratic inheritance squabbles to national and ideological disputes. In conjunction with these shifting goals, states became predominant and increasingly inclined to operate as blocs. Their armies transited through corresponding shifts of emphasis on mercenaries, professionals, conscripts, and back to professionals, this time with high technological proficiencies. Reliance on firearms gave way gradually to industrialized technology and successively greater lethality. All of these changes were supported by the expansion of the state's bureaucracy, increasingly effective means of mobilizing resources from the population and economy, and tighter connections between state, military, and industry.[8] Along the way and equally linked closely to the evolution of the modern state, a number of distinctions between what is public and private, internal and external, economic and political, civilian and military, and war and peace came into practice.

Kaldor's basic argument is that just as the wars with which we are most familiar were closely linked to the evolution of the modern state, the emergence of different types of political organization will lead to the supplanting of the old forms of warfare and associated conventions by new types of war and related norms. What is interesting is that the way these processes are currently working, at least in some parts of the world, is the exact opposite of the way they worked in early modern Europe. In earlier centuries, European rulers fought to establish control over specified territory and populations in order to create a fiscal foundation for state power. In doing so, they created a variety of distinctions, including one that differentiated domestic politics from the fluctuations of external politics. Maintaining this distinction meant suppressing domestic disorder, monopolizing armed forces, and staving off foreign attacks. Other things being equal, success in these endeavors led to political legitimacy within the territorial boundaries of the state, professionalized standing armies, and intermittent engagement in interstate wars.

The late twentieth century encompassed one imperial collapse (the Soviet Union), the disintegration of a number of formerly communist states, the end of the Cold War, and the failure of a large number of regimes established in the wake of the withdrawal of European empires. Further accelerating fragmentation are globalization processes that create winners (people able to participate in the new age of transnational, information technology) and losers (people excluded from participating and forced to cope on marginal local resources). All of these changes interact. The end of the Cold War and globalization were reciprocal influences on each other, with the information technology-influenced, Cold War demise knocking down the last areas attempting to remain aloof from the world economy. The collapse of the Soviet Union created a number of new states with discredited formerly Marxist regimes. The end of the Cold War diminished superpower incentives to bolster client regimes throughout the world.

In a context of economic deterioration, expanding unemployment, and growing inequalities, a number of new and some older states were beset with increasing political illegitimacy and disintegration. The new wars, focused on capturing political control largely within the disintegrating states, are increasingly privatized as state control breaks down. Thanks to an interaction between these breakdowns and globalization, the consequent political violence over claims to political control involves a confusing number of actors – including traditional armies, warlords, private and paramilitary armies, self-defense militias, mercenaries, guerrillas, criminal gangs, armed children, journalists, foreign military advisers, international organization workers, and peacekeeping forces – all usually operating somewhat independently.

The goals and tactics of the new wars have also substantially changed. Particularistic sentiments (ethnic, racial, and/or religious) are played upon (or invented) to generate rallying foci for movements stressing sub-state group identities. Political leaders of these movements can capitalize on feelings of insecurity in lieu of promising unobtainable economic gains. Leaders can stoke fear and hatred of some other group in order to enhance their own positions of power.[9] Removing the targeted group becomes the principal short-term goal. Violence is politically useful because it focuses identity differentiations more clearly. The longer term goal is the creation of a more homogenous group that encompasses fewer political opponents.

The new population displacement campaigns take place in a context of increasing economic deterioration, crime, corruption, and violence. Fighting groups pay for their activities through local predation and contributions from diasporic communities abroad (Sambanis, 2002; Collier and Hoeffler, 2004). If there are valuable resources to commandeer or to extort (diamonds, oil, drugs), contesting groups will gravitate towards them as sources of financial support (Ross, 2004).

The new wars do not begin as interstate wars in the traditional sense although they are difficult to contain and may very well spread to neighboring states.[10] Inherently, they are local or domestic wars over defining the identity of the population. Warfare is of the low-intensity, guerrilla-like, avoidance-of-battles type. Atrocities and massacres of unarmed civilians are more likely to occur than are clashes between armies. The military organizational level is generally fairly low. Equipment, training, uniforms, and discipline are likely to be relatively absent, as are heavy weapons. The economic context is equally fragmented and characterized by low rates of output. Resource mobilization for war purposes is decentralized. Fighting groups take what they can, legally or illegally.

As a consequence of this evolution in war, Kaldor (1999:100–1) notes, the military:civilian casualty ratio has literally reversed itself. In the early twentieth century, the proportion of civilian war casualties was in the neighborhood of 10–15 percent. At the end of the same century, civilian war casualties averaged roughly around 80 percent. Population displacement problems became much more severe as well. Conservative estimates of the number of refugees indicated about two and a half million people in 1975, ten and a half million in 1985, some eighteen million in 1992, and fourteen and a half million by 1995.

The contrast between the old and new wars is thus rather stark. Much of what had been proscribed in the old wars is strongly encouraged in the new wars. Most of the dominant characteristics of the old styles of warfare are entirely absent from the new style of warfare. As is often the case in the evolution of war topic, there is clear evidence that ongoing changes in the way people fight need not be progressive. It should be stressed, however, that Kaldor's perspective is geographically contained. Her new wars are located in the Balkans, the Black Sea area, Central Asia, and parts of Africa. She might also have extended them to parts of the Middle East and Latin America. Still, the point is that these new wars predominate in a territorial belt extending roughly from Tajikistan to Colombia. While new wars may or may not continue to characterize this zone, Kaldor does not appear to be arguing that the new wars necessarily will doom the old wars to extinction. The new wars are simply vastly different from the old wars.

One obvious problem with the "old war/new war" distinction is the apple/orange character of the description. The apples are old interstate wars. The oranges are civil wars taking place at the end of the twentieth century.[11] If we compared late twentieth-century internal warfare with European internal warfare of the seventeenth century, we would find the type of activities more comparable. So, in some respects, the old/new modifiers are misleading. We had become accustomed to conventional warfare between states and occasionally within states. Seemingly suddenly, few conventional wars were visible or even all that likely. What we were observing instead were unconventional and irregular warfare between small groups and, often, highly asymmetrical warfare between small groups and relatively new states – often in places where there had been little warfare in the immediate past. Yet, in a number of cases, the states involved were so weak that the conflicts were less asymmetrical than they might otherwise have been. Armies composed of children and untrained thugs and armed with automatic weapons can be quite formidable if their opponents are even fewer in number and no better trained or armed.

This larger context of "new war" novelty has stimulated a new round of theoretical arguments about why civil wars occur in the first place. Keen (1998), for one, argued that many civil wars were being waged not to defeat or capture the state but to make money.[12] Insurgents discovered that ways to finance their wars (extortion, smuggling, crime) could be lucrative in their own right. As these initially auxiliary goals became more prominent, winning civil wars became less important than maintaining the opportunity to continue making money from them. Interpretations such as this became known as *greed motivation theories* and were initially attractive to some civil war analysts as a quick handle for the "new wars" of the Balkans and sub-Saharan Africa.

Part of the attraction of the greed model was that a number of civil wars broke out in states that produced commodities such as diamonds (Angola, Democratic Republic of Congo, Liberia, Sierra Leone) and opium/cocaine (Afghanistan, Colombia). It was fairly evident that rebels were not only involved in the export of these commodities but probably also dependent on the profits to finance their rebellions. This raises the chicken–egg question. Did the rebels go to war to gain control of the diamonds and drugs or did they become dependent on the control of these "lootable" commodities in the process of waging civil war?[13] Further close examinations of key cases suggest that the resources were not part of the motivations for the onset of rebellion but did facilitate the activities of weak insurgent groups longer than might otherwise have been the case, increasing the duration of war (de Soysa, 2002; Ross, 2004).

The next development in this guide to arguments about civil war causality became known as the *greed versus grievance* debate (Ballentine and Sherman, 2003). Analysts initially attracted to the idea that greed was a strong explanation for civil war outbreaks began to compare the predictive strength of "greed" indicators with indicators of more traditional injustice-type grievances, such as socioeconomic inequality and ethnic discrimination. These studies found that "grievance" indicators had little predictive power. That is, if you knew which states were characterized by high levels of inequality or ethnic minority mistreatment, you still lacked a basis to tell which states would be engaged in civil war. At the same time, the attractions of emphasizing greed as the primary motivation had begun to wane with the realization that individual motivations were no doubt mixed and to some extent unknowable. Most civil wars were being waged for their own sake, even if some actors were simultaneously making money that they used to finance the ongoing warfare.

Focusing on Opportunity

The movement away from embracing the greed interpretation and the findings on grievance indicators led to the aphorism that grievances are more common than civil wars. Grievances can be found literally everywhere but civil wars are relatively rare, so the presence of grievances overpredicts the occurrence of civil war. This led many scholars to argue that we should ignore grievances and concentrate on opportunity. Under what circumstances do rebels think they have a reasonable chance of defeating their state targets, and through what strategies? What factors strengthen rebels? What factors strengthen states? Given the difficulties associated with generalizing about motivation, we should focus on factors that have encouraged or discouraged rebels and rebellions.

Two groups of analysts were most prominent in this emphasis on opportunity: a group of economists associated with the World Bank led by Collier,[14] and an oft-cited analysis by Fearon and Laitin (2003).[15] The first group acknowledged that all states are not equally likely to experience civil wars. Underdeveloped states with high inequality, low economic growth, and dependence on exporting raw materials, for example, face the highest risk of prolonged conflict.[16] Collier and his colleagues assumed that rebels are likely to pursue narrow group interests pertaining either to improving the group's position or ensuring that the group is not excluded by other groups from enjoying societal rewards, rather than acting for the benefit of the population as a whole.

If emphasis is placed on the organization as the level of analysis with the most explanatory payoff, the most leverage should be gained by examining rebels as military organizations with a standard slate of problems including recruitment, maintaining cohesion, acquiring equipment, surviving, and financing. Recruitment for rebel groups does not require a large population base. What is needed is a pool of young, uneducated and susceptible males for whom rebellion is more attractive than underemployment and subsistence living (Münkler, 2004:77–8). One can also draw on people seeking revenge for past attacks on their families and communities, psychopaths who enjoy violence for its own sake, and criminals with their own preferences and goals (Mueller, 2004). When all else fails, the numbers needed are so small that it is possible to coerce people to fight by giving them no choice.

Group cohesion can be gained and maintained by relying on some combination of charismatic leadership and ethnic/clan ties. The exceptions to this generalization are rebellions in societies with a large number of ethnic groups, which may require creating a multi-ethnic force. These situations, however, tend to lead to short and unsuccessful wars. States characterized by a small number of large ethnic groups have civil wars that last longer, suggesting that the duration reflects ethnic polarization and mistrust. Rebel groups with clear ethnic identities, moreover, are less likely to negotiate with states controlled by other ethnicities.[17]

Equipment became less of a problem after the collapse of the Soviet Union between 1989 and 1991 flooded the Third World with inexpensive automatic weapons. Rebel survival, in turn, depends on mountains and forests in which to hide from government forces (Sambanis, 2002; Fearon and Laitin, 2003; Hegre and Sambanis, 2006). If state populations are highly concentrated in central urban areas, less-populated peripheral areas far removed from the cities may also offer relatively safe havens. The weaker the state's military capability, of course, the easier it is to survive as a rebel.[18]

Finally, rebel organizations need financing. In Cold War days, the two superpowers were reliable sources of funding. Once the Cold War had ended, rebels had to find new sources. Nearby hostile governments, ethnic diasporas, and various extortion activities replaced the superpowers. If there were no ways to raise funds because the country was simply too poor, an outbreak of civil war was not all that likely. Poor states with easily extorted natural resources, on the other hand, were probable places for civil war outbreaks of prolonged duration because the funding for rebellious activity was readily available.

Thus, civil wars are most likely in states in which these various organizational needs are readily met. Once underway, they are not likely to end quickly, especially if the state is weak, the economy is poor and characterized by pronounced inequalities, and the social structure revolves around two to three large ethnic groups. These circumstances tend to encourage longer civil wars. Interventions by outside organizations, moreover, do not seem to make much difference. If the underlying conditions are unlikely to change and rebel organization needs are fairly low, states in which civil wars break out continue to be prone to intermittently resumed internal warfare.

The Fearon and Laitin (2003) approach is quite compatible with this emphasis on the opportunity to make civil war. They share the assumption that political grievances are more common than civil wars, but emphasize weak states as the key causal factor. Rebel insurgents practicing guerrilla war in rural areas are more likely to succeed if their state opponents are not especially strong and if they are incapable of suppressing lightly armed challengers. Various factors are likely to make rebels more potent and states less so, including recent independence, political instability, anocracy,[19] large populations, naturally protected bases, foreign government and diaspora support, and high value/low weight natural resources to exploit for financing. Low per capita income and oil exports are viewed as proxies for the probability of fairly weak regimes. Hence, the more feasible rebel operations, and the weaker the state, the more probable is insurgency or civil war.

While Collier et al. (2003) focused on the rebel organization and Fearon and Laitin (2003) emphasized the relative weakness of the state vis-à-vis the relative strength of the rebel group, Salehyan (2009) looks at political opportunity from a regional conflict cluster perspective. His main point is that many internal wars are not really waged exclusively as internal wars. Slightly more than half (55 percent) of post-1945 civil wars involved rebels engaged in some types of operations outside of their home state. They use bases in adjacent countries. They receive support from interstate rivals who exploit domestic dissidence as a proxy for interstate conflict. Alternatively, counterinsurgency programs sometimes cause problems for, and attacks on, neighboring states. Some transnational rebel groups (for instance, al Qaeda) coordinate attacks in multiple political systems. They also take advantage of refugee camps and diaspora networks outside of their home country to mobilize support and recruit manpower. Not surprisingly, then, civil wars are interdependent and occur in clusters of regionally linked conflicts. The more permissive the regional opportunity structure, the more incentive rebels have to risk taking on regimes that they hope to change or overthrow.

While some of the above-mentioned models have incorporated elements from the levels of the dyad or regional system,[20] other models give greater causal primacy to those levels, and it would be useful to look at those models more closely.

Systemic and Dyadic Influences

Hironaka (2005) adopts a systemic perspective that links weak states to fundamental changes in the international system (see also Desch, 1996). Unlike the pre-1945 process in which frequent and intense warfare, especially in Europe, created strong states and eliminated most weak states, the world after World War II operates under much different rules. Most current states were once colonies and gained their independence relatively peacefully. Meanwhile, international norms had emerged that discouraged expanding territorial boundaries by force. That meant that most states were forced to get along with whatever limited resource base they had inherited, that most states in the system would be weak and remain fairly weak, and that a mechanism that had previously eliminated weak states no longer operated. These weak states would also attempt to act, or be expected to act, like stronger and older states in providing security and welfare for their citizens even though they lacked the capacity to do so.

Strong states can contain or suppress grievances within their borders. They can also provide reasonably good governance. Weak states cannot. Thus when local grievances emerge, they are much less likely to be managed successfully in weak states. Local grievances were also exploited by the superpowers during the Cold War. Rebels were given training, weapons, and ideological justifications. Weak states were propped up by counterinsurgent interventions. The external support for ideological friends on both sides of the rebel–state equation expanded the scale and duration of internal warfare.[21] Remove the external superpower support with the demise of the Cold War and one should expect more limited scale and duration. Not surprisingly to Hironaka, the frequency of civil wars declined after 1989. But since the weak states did not disappear, civil wars continue.

Hironaka's main point is that what takes place at the local level is contingent on systemic and dyadic levels of interaction. Weak states are sustained generally by an international system and international norms that prohibit states from becoming stronger the old-fashioned way, through warfare. They have also been sustained more specifically but also temporarily by superpower aid. But as long as weak states persist, insurgents with some access to resources will be encouraged to rebel and have few incentives to negotiate. The weak states, for their part, lack sufficient resources to either appease or suppress the rebels. Civil wars, accordingly, become more probable and, in general, longer in duration after 1945 than before. They should be even more probable and longer in duration when external resources are pumped into local fights than when the local combatants are left to their own devices.[22]

Kalyvas and Balcells (2009) take Hironaka's argument a step farther. They argue that the civil war concept is overly aggregated. Civil wars are actually manifested in three different types.[23] *Asymmetric* wars in which the state is stronger than the rebels are one type and go by several names: irregular warfare, guerrilla warfare, and insurgency. A second type is the rare *conventional* civil war in which both sides are relatively equal and have relatively high levels of military technology (as in the US case in the 1860s). In these symmetric civil wars, both sides deploy regular armies wearing uniforms and using similar kinds of weaponry. In a third type of civil war the opposing sides are comparable but both sides have access to low military technology and engage in *unconventional* combat that Kaldor (1999) calls new wars. Kalyvas and Balcells (2009) argue that Cold War conditions expanded the frequency of type-one civil wars (insurgency), while the post-Cold War era has contributed to the predominance of type three (*symmetrical unconventional* wars).

Superpower aid in the Cold War, as has been noted by other scholars, bolstered both sides. Rebel capacity was enhanced in material and ideational ways. The material support encompassed weapons, training, and other types of assistance. But the assistance also came in the form of a package of beliefs and strategies for executing agrarian revolution accomplished via guerrilla warfare in the countryside that had worked in places like China and Vietnam. The capacities of weak states, at the same time, were also improved to better counter the revolutionary movements. These sorts of intervention increased the probability of insurgencies or guerrilla warfare.

With the end of the Cold War, superpower patronage of state and rebels deteriorated. The greater impact was on rebel capabilities, which meant that insurgency became somewhat less probable. Given some minimal state strength, civil war became less probable. But where states were very weak, type-three unconventional warfare was likely to increase in frequency. So, the type of civil war that was observed shifted as systemic and dyadic influences changed course.

Kalyvas and Balcells (2009) note that civil wars, for the most part, ended in Asia and Latin America after the Cold War ended. In sub-Saharan Africa and central Asia, where arguably the weakest states are concentrated, the symmetric, unconventional type of warfare increased. Only in the Middle East and North Africa did Cold War-style insurgency predominate. The first two observations are explicable in terms of their argument. The third observation on the persistence of Middle Eastern insurgency requires reference to radical Islam's ability to work as a substitute for Marxism's earlier ideational assistance for mobilizing rebel groups. That is, jihadism is an ideational resource that Muslim rebels can use to enhance their capabilities and consequent ability to engage in insurgency tactics. Jihadism also comes with the possibility of foreign bases, training and external financing.

Back to Motivation?

While Hironaka (2005) and Kalyvas and Balcells (2009) are more systemic (and dyadic) in terms of the level of analysis than Collier et al. (2003) and Fearon and Laitin (2003), they still focus on opportunity. They acknowledge motivation is important but leave it largely unexplored. Boix (2008), however, argues that we need to combine motivation and opportunity if we are to fully understand what drives civil warfare. To do this, he re-introduces inequality in a different theoretical frame. If an economy is characterized by high levels of inequality, the pressures for redistribution are likely to be equally high. In this context, wealthy members of the population have the most to lose from redistribution. They are likely to work towards maintaining authoritarian regimes that restrict either the political participation of the poor or movements to level wealth. Poorer members of the population have the most to gain from redistribution and should be expected to expand their political participation in order to tax the wealthy.

The potential polarization and conflict of rich and poor is modified by another feature of Boix's (2008) political economy model. Taxable assets are either mobile or fixed. The less mobile the assets are and the more unequal their distribution, the more likely are regimes to be authoritarian and protective of the wealthy segment's control of fixed, often agrarian, assets. Violence may be the only way to promote redistribution schemes, depending on the costs of violence. The costs of violence increase with state capacity to suppress or contain challenges. Costs decline if terrain, financing possibilities, and access to military technology favor rebels. So, if rebels perceive some chance of winning, they are more likely to respond to agrarian inequalities with force – thereby combining both opportunity and motivation.

If the economic structure becomes less unequal and/or if the main taxable assets are highly mobile (as in terms of wages/salaries and manufacturing), democratic political systems are more likely to be created and sustained. A substantial decrease in inequality means less need to resort to violence to bring about redistribution. Democracies, particularly if they are not based on agrarian economies, should therefore be less prone to civil wars (see Hegre et al., 2001; Elbadawi and Sambanis, 2002; Hegre and Sambanis, 2006).

Boix (2008) adds an additional historical element to his argument. Assuming that high levels of inequality and asset immobility remained fairly constant from the eighteenth to the twentieth centuries, he asks why have civil wars increased in frequency, duration, and intensity over that same time. His answer is that what changed was the political mobilization of peasants, who were increasingly subject to pressures from industrialization and modernization to abandon traditional passivity and political isolation. Their organization for civil war purposes also reduced the costs of taking on states.

Ethnicity and the Individual Level

Lest the preceding discussion gives the impression that civil war analysts focus only on the levels of analysis between system and organizations, two other models that highlight the other end of the levels-of-analysis ladder deserve some attention. Both focus on ethnic violence, which is not quite the same thing as civil war but certainly overlaps a great deal in the sense that ethnic conflict is frequently observed as a strong element in contemporary civil wars.[24] There are also persistent puzzles about why neighbors live peacefully for many years and then, abruptly, turn to liquidating one another in bloodbaths along the lines of the 800,000 people who died in largely Hutu–Tutsi fighting in Rwanda or the complicated fighting among Serbs, Croats, and Bosnian Muslims in the former Yugoslavia. If their killing is due to ancient hatreds, as some argue (Kaplan, 1993), why is the violence so intermittent? Another way of putting that is how can these groups co-exist for centuries, turn on each other for relatively brief interludes, and, in some cases, return to some semblance of co-existence after the fighting stops? Part of the answer may lie at the psychological level.

Petersen's (2001) perspective on emotions, without doubt, is the one approach to civil wars that is most clearly linked to the individual level.[25] The basic assumption is that everyone desires some central goals along the lines of security, wealth, and status. Different circumstances cause one or more of the goals to be elevated in importance through the mechanism of emotion. For example, the perception of threat generates fear (an emotion), which makes security more important than wealth or status. If we add to these processes the notion of ethnic identity, which must be learned and which often is linked to a sense of ethnic status hierarchy, all one needs are some environmental shocks to cause psychological problems. These shocks can build up gradually (as in modernization and globalization pressures) or abruptly as in the collapse of a political system. The point is that the individuals see the environmental changes and realize that the landscape is in flux. New perceived threats may be emerging. Traditional status hierarchies may be deteriorating. Individual concerns with their personal security, wealth, or status are likely to be heightened.

In this context, some central emotions (fear, hatred, resentment) are likely to be aroused. Fear makes it more likely that some other ethnic group, perceived as threatening, will be attacked. Hatred can be channeled into attacking some group that had often been a target in the past. If some group seems to be moving up the status hierarchy at another group's expense, resentment can trigger attacks in the direction of some other that can safely be targeted.

Petersen's (2002) model combines environmental changes with individual responses that are translated into intergroup conflict. Hence, his approach is just as multi-level as the other ones we have reviewed. The levels chosen, however, are a bit different and the outcomes are more variegated as well. The model does not merely predict increased ethnic group conflict. It also specifies what paths the increased ethnic group conflict might take given which intermediary emotions are involved.

Exactly how one should best pin down which emotions are in play and when, however, is not all that clear. It is easy to imagine civil war situations in which all three are operative simultaneously. One group sees another expanding its size and claim on governmental offices and services. It resents the loss of status in the present, fears what might take place in the future, and hates the agents believed responsible for the present and future downward transition of their own group.

This emphasis on the emotions involved in ethnic conflict can be paired readily with Stuart Kaufman's (2001) stress on symbolism in generating warfare between ethnic groups. The Kaufman model is quite compact. He establishes three preconditions for escalation to ethnic warfare: (1) a mythology justifying hostility between or among ethnic groups; (2) fears on the part of one or more ethnic groups that their existence is threatened; and (3) political opportunities to mobilize the myths and the threat perception. The conjuncture of the three preconditions creates an ethnic group security dilemma in which groups begin working harder at preserving their security and status.[26] In the process of preserving their own welfare, their actions threaten the security and status of other groups. Political entrepreneurs can exploit these potentially escalatory situations to their own advantage, as well, by drawing attention to the myths and the threats in electoral rhetoric. The outcome is increased hostility among ethnic groups, which may only need some trigger to break out into civil war.

Conceptual Issues

The arguments on civil wars that we have reviewed are of recent origin and reflect ongoing analytical disputes about the proper focus of scholarly attention. Motivation and opportunity go together naturally. Civil wars do not occur randomly. The people that fight them have reasons for engaging in fairly risky activities. If we could capture their motivation in general terms, it should help to delineate where civil wars are most likely to occur. At the same time, people do not usually go to war against their own states unless they think they have some chance of winning. In this respect, the distinction between motivation and opportunity tends to blur. Circumstances that bolster rebel chances of winning (or states' chances of losing) will presumably increase the chances of rebellion. Weak states are often associated with bad governance, corruption, and less-than-successful repression, and rulers of weak states do not rule as much as they attempt to stay in power however they can. Civil wars are fought ostensibly to remove weak rulers and regimes. Is that motivation at work? Or, is it that many of these weak states can be defeated with hit and run tactics, as long as one has somewhere to run to? Even if they are not susceptible to being defeated and overthrown in the near term, the weakness of such regimes makes it possible for armed dissidents to survive for long periods of time on limited resources. Is this simply opportunity at work?

Motive and opportunity are obvious concepts to explain why people sometimes take on their own states. But they also represent an operational conundrum. How does one systematically distinguish between them? If one thinks that they both need to be present to adequately explain the onset of civil war, the theoretical conundrum is what set of explanatory foci will accomplish this task? As we have seen, analysts continue to disagree about what the best set of explanatory factors might be.

These theoretical disagreements about causality are compounded by problems encountered in distinguishing between explanations of the onset and duration of civil wars. It is conceivable that some factors are distinctively associated with one or the other but not both, though it is exceedingly difficult to imagine such a variable. Most, if not all, factors that are thought to dispose societies toward civil war are also likely to contribute to the prolongation of those wars. Examples include societal inequality, weak states, and rough terrain, to mention just a few. Some variables affecting both the onset and duration of war may have a greater impact on one than on the other. As we noted earlier, although the presence of lootable resources affects both the onset and duration of war, it probably has a greater impact on the latter. This differential impact would affect the relative causal weights given to such variables in each model, but not the structure of the explanatory models themselves. Thus it might or might not be worth distinguishing between explanations of the onset and duration of war.

Explaining civil wars is not, or should not be, an intractable analytical problem. But it is a more complex problem than it might seem to be. As in the case of interstate wars, it is characterized by disagreements about what matters most in accounting for the outbreak of warfare. It is less than clear that all warfare is sufficiently similar to treat every civil war as if they were similar phenomena. But if we need to make distinctions among types of civil wars, then we also need to make distinctions about the causal factors that lead to insurgency versus those that lead to classical, conventional warfare, or ethnic versus non-ethnic wars. It is possible that contextual conditions change over time – as exemplified by the coming and going of the Cold War. Yet for every analysis that has found the Cold War to be a significant factor in explaining the onset of war, there is another analysis that finds it insignificant. It is also possible that contextual conditions vary over space, and that African civil wars are somehow different than Asian or Latin American civil wars. But if this is the case, it remains to be seen precisely what is it about "Africa" that might differentiate it from "Asia" or "Latin America." In other words, it will take time to sort out our many theoretical and empirical puzzles about the etiology of civil warfare.

Notes

1. Two important factors underlying this trend are the period of decolonization after World War II and the expansion of the number of states in the international system (Levy and Thompson, 2010b).

2. See www.correlatesofwar.org. The frequency of civil wars peaked in the 1990s and has declined since then but the frequency of interstate wars has declined even more rapidly. For a summary of these trends see Mason (2009). For case studies of civil wars, see Collier and Sambanis (2005). Peaks in civil war activity depend on how one counts them (number of new wars in a given period, number of ongoing wars, or various battle death thresholds), whether the series is smoothed by some type of temporal aggregation, and whether one controls for the number of states in the system. For examples, see Collier et al. (2003:94), Hironaka (2005:4), Lacina and Gleditsch (2005), and Mack (2007: chap. 3).

3. Scholars have addressed three other general questions in addition to those about the causes of civil wars. One is why some civil wars are brief and others are protracted (Walter, 2002; Collier, Hoeffler, and Soderbom, 2004; Fearon, 2004; Fortna, 2008). Another is why some civil wars are very intense and kill large numbers of people while others are less deadly (see, for instance, Kalyvas, 2006; 2008; Weinstein, 2007). The final question in this trio focuses on the consequences of civil war (Licklider, 1995; Zartman, 1995; Ghobarah, Huth, and Russett, 2003; Kang and Meernik, 2005; Lacina and Gleditsch, 2005; Hoddie and Smith, 2009). How many people die? How can people learn to live together in the same country after killing each other (a problem generally not faced after an interstate war)? What are the implications for economic development? Is it possible to construct post-civil war contexts that make renewed civil war less likely? These are all worthwhile questions but, as in earlier chapters, we will focus almost exclusively on the question of the causes of civil war, though this will necessitate some discussion of the question of the duration of war.

4. There is an enormous literature on the American Civil War. Even here, however, studies of the causes of the war lag far behind descriptions of battles and social histories of the participants.

5. Good places to pursue the question of theorizing about how revolutions work include Moore (1966), Skocpol (1979), Goldstone (1991), Wickham-Crowley (1992), and Goodwin (2001).

6. Note the link with prospect theory in theories of relative deprivation. People whose poor conditions have started to improve often define their reference points in terms of their aspiration levels for the future, or in terms of a level of progress that was achieved before subsequent backtracking. They see their current situation as one of losses from those reference points, and engage in highly risky behaviors to overcome those losses. The downtrodden without hope for the future identify the status quo as their reference points and are not willing to take great risks to improve their situation.

7. The older literature examining inequality includes Russett (1964), Muller (1985), Muller and Seligson (1987), Midlarsky (1988), and Lichbach (1989). Collective action problems emphasize incentives for individuals to "free ride" on the actions of others. Why join a rebellion for the collective good if you can get the same benefits from a successful rebellion by sitting on the sidelines and avoiding the risks (Lichbach, 1995)?

8. On the increasing severity of war in the West, see Rogers (1995), Lynn (1996), and Levy and Thompson (2010b).

9. See the discussion of diversionary theory in chapter 4.
10. A good example is the war in the Congo in the mid-1990s, which grew out of the Rwandan genocide and expanded into what many have called "Africa's World War" (Prunier, 2009).
11. Münkler (2004:8) contrasts the older "state-building" wars of Europe with the newer "state-disintegrating" wars in the Third World, but switches the emphasis to the effects of the war and continues to conflate the type of "fruit" with which we are dealing. Europe certainly experienced intrastate warfare but it is their external wars that are usually remembered and credited with state building. Whether European intrastate wars were more state-building than they were state-disintegrating would make an interesting research question in itself.
12. See Berdal and Keen (1997), Keen (1998), and Keen (2000). Ballentine (2003) and Ballentine and Sherman (2003) are good places to start for criticism of the greed motivation approach.
13. Ross (2003) distinguishes between lootable and unlootable natural resources and between separatist and non-separatist civil conflicts. He concludes that lootable resources (i.e., gemstones, drugs) are more likely to prolong non-separatist conflicts, while unlootable resources (i.e., oil) appear to increase the chances of separatist conflict by fostering grievances over resource income distribution.
14. It was these economists who were initially attracted to the greed motivation but then gradually distanced themselves from the emphasis on greed. See, for instance, Collier et al. (2003).
15. These are both rationalist approaches. For critiques of rational choice approaches to the study of ethnic conflict, see C. Kaufman (2005) and S. Kaufman (2006).
16. These hypotheses are quite plausible, but they raise questions. Ross (2004:338,fn.2) points out that the Angolan economy was relatively diversified and characterized by high growth rates from 1960 to 1974. The onset of civil war in 1975 led to a collapse of the economy and industrial production, which meant that Angola had been transformed into a country highly dependent on raw material exports by, in part, civil war.
17. On ethnic polarization, see Reynal-Querol (2002), Collier et al. (2003), and Toft (2003).
18. Gates (2002) argues that rebellions which are concentrated in a smaller geographic area are better able to discipline their members to avoid defection. Geographic distribution issues (and fears of defection) can be overcome by non-pecuniary ethnic and/or ideological "payments" to members.
19. An "anocracy" is a regime that has a mixture of democratic and autocratic elements (Jaggers and Gurr, 1995).
20. Other analysts who pursue various dimensions of external linkages in civil war settings include Modelski (1961), Mitchell (1970), Midlarsky (1992), Lake and Rothchild (1998), Regan (2000), and Saideman (2001).
21. Hironaka (2005) notes that while external interventions certainly occurred prior to the Cold War, the earlier interventions tended to be more one-sided on behalf of defending the status quo and, therefore, suppressing revolts.

(Examples might be the interventions of the Concert of Europe in the early nineteenth century.) Such external interventions were more decisive, other things being equal, than the Cold War interventions on both sides more or less simultaneously.

22. Another system-level factor contributing to both internal and external conflict, particularly in Africa and the Middle East, is the fact that state boundaries were set during the colonial period by European powers for their own convenience. As a result, state boundaries often diverge from the boundaries of ethnic, linguistic, and religious groups. This creates an incongruence or imbalance between the state and the nation, which can be a potent source of conflict by creating incentives for separatist movements or for attempts to incorporate a "displaced" identity group beyond a state's borders (Miller, 2007). In addition, European powers played an important role in fanning the flames of sectarian tension between Maronite Christians, Sunni, and Sh'ia in nineteenth-to-twentieth-century Lebanon, which set the stage for the 1975–90 civil war (Makdisi, 2000).

23. These types emerge from a structured comparison of state and rebel military capabilities. High state and rebel military capability leads to symmetrical, conventional warfare. Low state and rebel military capability leads to symmetrical, unconventional warfare. High state and low rebel capability generates irregular warfare. Kalyvas and Balcells (2009) say that a fourth type (low state and high rebel capability) is associated with military coups. There are probably other examples as well, including the current war (as of Spring 2009) between the government of Afghanistan and the Taliban rebels.

24. Scholars debate whether ethnic civil wars should be treated separately from non-ethnic civil wars (Sambanis, 2001; Reynal-Querol, 2002). Toft (2003:3), however, maintains that two-thirds of all armed conflict involves some ethnic component.

25. Note that the civil war literature tends to look at rebels rather than rebel leaders at the individual level. This focus marks a departure from the interstate war literature in which the individual of analysis is often targeted on state decision-makers.

26. The application of the security dilemma concept to civil wars is one of those areas in which interstate and intrastate conflict explanations overlap quite concretely (Posen, 1993; Lake and Rothchild, 1998).

8

Conclusion: Reflections on Levels, Causes, and War

We have now completed our review of some of the leading theories of war and peace. *Causes of War* makes no attempt to be exhaustive and incorporate all theories of war. That would be a near-impossible task, given the voluminous scholarship produced on the subject in many disciplines and in many countries over the centuries. Rather, we have focused on some of the most influential theories of the causes of war and the conditions for peace advanced by international relations theorists, and supplemented that with a discussion of some related work from other disciplines. We have organized our survey of theories around a levels-of-analysis framework. For each level of analysis, we summarized the major theories, identified key variables and the causal paths through which they contribute war or to peace, suggested some historical examples, and noted some of the evidentiary and analytic problems raised by these theories.

At the system level, we began with an overview of realism, including its classical, structural, and neoclassical variants. Each of these realist theories incorporates some form of balance of power theory, which we then examined in some detail. After contrasting balance of power theories and hegemonic theories, we then analyzed two of the leading forms of hegemonic theory – power transition theory and long-cycle theory. Shifting from the overall structure of the international system to the dyadic interactions between pairs of states, we examined the rivalry approach to the study of international conflict, the "steps-to-war" model, the "bargaining model of war," and theories of economic interdependence and peace.

Our next task was to look inside the state and analyze several theories of war that give causal primacy to state- and societal-level factors. We began with a brief survey of Marxist–Leninist international theories and the argument that imperialism and war are driven by the interests of the capitalist class. That led to an examination of Schumpeter's argument that state policy was controlled not by a capitalist class, for which war is costly, but by military elites whose primary goal is maintaining their own position of power. Next was a survey of various coalitional theories, which emphasize that state grand strategies are each the product of bargaining between opposing coalitions of economically self-interested domestic groups. The discussion of societal-level theories continued with an examination of the "diversionary theory of war," the "democratic peace," and the "clash of civilizations" thesis.

Turning to decision-making at the individual, organizational, and small-group levels, we began our discussion of individual-level theories with an analysis of rational decision-making. We then considered a variety of psychological models that depart from one or more elements of an ideal-type rational decision-making process. After emphasizing the importance of misperceptions by tracing the causal paths through which they can lead to war, we analyzed how the content of individual belief systems and the nature of information processing (including the impact of both cognitive and emotional factors) help to generate those misperceptions. We described prospect theory and the sources of propensities toward taking risks, examined poliheuristic theory, and ended with a discussion of crisis decision-making.

In our survey of decision-making at the organizational level, we focused on theories of bureaucratic politics and organizational processes. We then took a closer look at how the key variables in these general theories of decision-making might contribute to the processes leading to war. We examined the impact of bureaucratic politics on state strategies and on the distortion of information, and the impact of organizational routines on policy rigidity. Our review of decision-making theories ended with a discussion of the dynamics of small-group behavior and its implications for international conflict.

We followed this analysis of theories of interstate war with a brief survey of some of the leading theories of civil war. This survey began with a discussion of the debate about "old wars" and "new wars," which provided a useful transition from the earlier focus on interstate wars. We examined economic theories of civil wars and then the "greed versus grievance" debate, giving attention both to the opportunities for war and the motivations for war. We also looked at systemic and dyadic effects, including the ways in which the post-1945 international systems created an environment that was conducive to the survival of weak states, which are those most prone to civil war.

Reflections on the Levels of Analysis

Since *Causes of War* relies upon the levels-of-analysis framework to organize the presentation of theories of the causes of war, it would be useful to reflect on the utility of that framework. The levels of analysis have generally served us well in our survey of the causes of interstate war, by helping us to group similar causal factors in the same category for the purposes of organizing our review.[1] We find it more useful than alternative organizing schemes, such as one distinguishing realist and liberal frameworks or rationalist and constructivist approaches.[2] Among other things, none of these organizing frameworks makes it easy to incorporate decision-making theories at the individual, organizational, and small-group levels. Of the approaches mentioned above, only constructivist approaches really allow for non-rationalist influences on decision-making, and many constructivists ignore psychological variables altogether.[3]

As we noted in chapter 1, the levels-of-analysis framework works better as a system for classifying variables than for classifying theories. Many theories incorporate variables from more than one level of analysis, and many theories have important variations, each of which gives causal priority to variables at different levels. The most influential variant of the liberal theory of economic interdependence and peace, for example, gives causal priority to the dyadic interactions of states, but the theory also incorporates hypotheses about the structure of the international political economy and the role of domestic political pressure groups. Neoclassical realist theories include both system-level and nation-state level causal factors.

For this reason, the levels-of-analysis typology works particularly well for "monocausal" theories that emphasize a single causal variable or at least one dominant concept,[4] such as economic class in Marxist–Leninist theory or disagreements about relative power in Blainey's (1988) theory.[5] The framework also works well for theories that emphasize a set of interrelated causal variables from a single level of analysis. There is little ambiguity, for example, in classifying balance of power theory at the system-level (global or regional), the influence of regime type at the state and societal level, or psychological theories at the individual level of causation.

At first, many applications of the levels-of-analysis framework to questions of war and peace or foreign policy behavior focused on the question of "which level is most important?" or the related question of "what is the relative contribution of different levels to the outbreak of war?" This question reflected the variable-oriented rather than the theory-oriented bias of the levels-of-analysis framework. Several decades of theoretical and empirical analysis, however, have not led to any consensus among scholars on the relative importance of causal variables at different levels of analysis. Both statistical studies of large numbers of cases and comparative historical studies of a more modest number of cases have failed to identify any single causal variable that can explain a substantial amount of the variance in war and peace.[6] Most correlations between causal variables and the outbreak of war are modest at best (Bennett and Stam, 2004).

For the handful of hypotheses where empirical correlations are high, such as the near absence of wars between democracies, there is often little agreement on precisely *how* to explain the empirical regularity, on the precise causal mechanism(s) leading from one variable to the other, or even on the direction of causality. The interdemocratic peace thus remains a strong empirical regularity in search of a theory to explain it. As we noted earlier, claims that the democratic peace is the closest thing we have to an empirical law in international relations says as much or more about the state of international theory and the complexity of the world as it does about the democratic peace.

There are other hypotheses for which the empirical findings of scholars using a particular method are mutually reinforcing, but completely at odds with the empirical findings of scholars using a different method. Consider empirical research on the diversionary theory of war. Historical case studies generally find that external scapegoating is frequently important in the processes leading to war, whereas statistical studies find no strong relationship between a leader's domestic political security and the probability that s/he will initiate a war.

This lack of scholarly consensus about the causes of war and the relative importance of different levels of analysis is the product of several factors. These include the enormous complexity of the phenomenon we are trying to analyze, the different theoretical questions that scholars ask, the different types of wars they want to explain, the different theoretical preconceptions and methodological preferences that drive their research, and the often hidden assumptions in their approaches to the study of war.

We first consider the complexity of the problem, which has many dimensions. First of all, war is the outcome of the interactions of two or more states (or other politically organized groups), and the actions of two adversaries may be driven by different causal factors at different levels of analysis. How do we combine these into a single summary statement specifying that one level of analysis is more important than another? Waltz (1959) framed his distinction among three different images around the question of the causes of *war*. War, however, is a dyadic- or systemic-level outcome in terms of the unit of analysis, and the levels-of-analysis framework is not ideally suited to an analysis of strategic interaction. The framework is most useful as a typology for classifying causal variables influencing state foreign policies, which is a state-level unit of analysis. That is one reason we have included the dyadic unit of analysis and also the dyadic level of analysis. An explanation for war requires the inclusion of the variables affecting each state's decision-making along with an explanation of the nature of the strategic interaction between the two states in the crisis.

Even within a single state, however, it may be difficult to say with confidence that one level of analysis is more important than others. In terms of more general theories of policy-making, scholars have long recognized that the relative importance of different levels of analysis can vary by issue-area (Rosenau, 1980:chap. 17). The impact of factors from different levels may vary significantly between domestic and foreign policy issues and between security issues and different kinds of foreign policy issues. Individual political leaders usually have a greater influence on foreign policy than on domestic policy.[7] Within foreign policy issues, we might hypothesize that domestic groups generally have a greater impact on international economic, environmental, and human rights policies than on security policies. Within security policy issues, which are the primary concerns here, we might hypothesize that societal and bureaucratic factors probably have a greater impact on decisions regarding the size or allocation of the defense budget than on decisions to use military force. These are hypotheses to be tested, however, rather than confirmed empirical generalizations.

With respect to war, it is conceivable that different types of war have different causes, and that different causal variables have a different impact on different types of wars. Societal-level variables probably have a greater impact on the onset of civil wars and colonial wars than on interstate wars, while system-level and individual-level factors probably have a greater impact on interstate wars than they do on civil wars (though recall the argument about system-level selection of weak states out of the system before 1945 but not after that, and the impact of emotions on the outbreak of civil wars). Within the category of interstate wars, system-level variables probably have a greater impact on great power wars between the leading states in the system than on wars between weaker states, and on general or global wars than on other great power wars.[8] Each of these statements, however, should be considered a hypothesis to be investigated rather than a well-confirmed research finding. If the relative impact of different levels of analysis were found to vary for different types of wars, however, the implication would be that we would need different types of theories for different types of wars – or, ideally, a more complex theory that specified what factors are most important for what kinds of wars.[9]

The importance of level of analysis also varies by regime type and by level of economic development (Rosenau, 1980:chap. 17). Individual political leaders have a greater impact on foreign policy in autocratic regimes than in democratic regimes, in personalist regimes than in oligarchic regimes, and in presidential regimes than in parliamentary regimes. Individual leaders probably have a less influential role in advanced industrial states than they do in developing states. The relationship gets more complicated still, as regime type interacts with level of economic development. Economic development promotes democracy (Lipset, 1959), and democracy (and especially the property rights that tend to be associated with it) tends to promote economic development (North and Weingast, 1989).

The regime type example is a good illustration of the fact that the causal importance of variables at one level of analysis may be a function of the values of variables at other levels of analysis. The likelihood of a dyadic rivalry emerging between two states often depends on the structure of regional and global systems in which it is embedded. If the two states are the two strongest states in a region, in adjacent regions, or in the global system, they are likely to become rivals. The likelihood of a particular rivalry leading to war may be significantly influenced by variables at the state and societal level of analysis, including the domestic political security of state leaders and their willingness to manipulate the rivalry to enhance their domestic political support (Colaresi, 2005).[10]

To take another example, hypotheses on preventive war emphasize a state's perception of the rising power of an adversary, the anticipation of a significant shift in relative power, and the fear of a risk of war under worse circumstances later, which generate an incentive for a preventive war strategy based on better-now-than-later logic. Although conditions like this arise fairly frequently, states only occasionally resort to preventive war strategies. Adverse power shifts do not automatically lead to war (Lemke, 2003). To explain when they do and when they do not requires the incorporation of political leaders' calculations of the costs, risks, and benefits of war now and the costs, risks, and benefits of war later. These calculations often involve leaders' domestic political security, their time horizons, and their propensities for risk taking (Levy, 2008a). Time horizons and attitudes toward risk are particularly difficult to evaluate. Such calculations are common in many or most situations involving decisions for war, but the stark choices in preventive war situations make them all the more salient.

The need to incorporate factors from different levels of analysis is based on the need for a logically complete theory as well as on the goal of increasing the amount of variance explained. Some hypotheses about the relationship between the polarity of the international system and the stability of the system, for example, suggest that one key intervening variable is the responses of states to uncertainty (Bueno de Mesquita and Lalman, 1992). The argument that the clarity of a bipolar world reduces the danger of war implies that uncertainty promotes misperceptions and war, whereas the argument that multipolarity deters aggression because it increases the number of possible coalitions that might form against an aggressor implies that uncertainty induces caution. A theoretically complete explanation of polarity and stability thus requires the incorporation of responses to uncertainty, which derives from the individual or possibly state level of analysis.

Complicating things still further, especially for the purposes of developing a general theory of war or even of great power war, is the fact that the causes of war may vary across historical periods.[11] Economic factors might have been more important in the seventeenth and eighteenth century than in the nineteenth century, in part because of mercantilist ideology (Luard, 1986; K. Holsti, 1991). The distribution of power in the system has a different impact on the probability of great power war in the nuclear era than in previous historical eras, because nuclear deterrence provides weaker nuclear states a degree of protection against stronger nuclear states that weaker states did not previously possess, and more generally because military power does not translate quite as directly into political influence in the nuclear era as it did in earlier eras. Deterrence has also been reinforced by the "taboo" that has developed against the use of nuclear weapons (Tannenwald, 2007). Individual political leaders probably had a greater impact on the onset of great power war several centuries ago, before the rise of bureaucratic state structures and mass politics, while the influence of societal factors has probably increased with the rise of mass politics in the nineteenth and twentieth centuries.

This last example suggests another dimension of complexity: a given variable, broadly defined, might influence war through different mechanisms in different periods. Economic factors may influence war and peace in different ways in mercantilist systems and in liberal free-trade systems. Deterrence may work differently in the pre-nuclear era than in the nuclear era. Although the coercive use of force has always been an instrument of policy, deterrence through the threat of punishment is more powerful in the nuclear era than it was in previous eras.

Leaving macro-historical changes aside, causal variables at different levels of analysis can vary over time in the processes leading to specific wars. Most wars do not arise out of the blue but instead reflect a process that plays out over time. Conflicts of interest can lead to rivalry, the combination of both can lead to disputes, disputes lead to crises, and crises sometimes escalate to war (Bremer and Cusack, 1995). A given causal variable, or different combinations of causal variables, may have a different impact at different stages of escalation, and the same variable can have the opposite effects at different times. A state facing a stronger adversary in an ongoing rivalry might build up its armaments in the early stages of a dispute, which can trigger a conflict spiral that increases the risks of war, while the same state might behave in a more conciliatory fashion as war draws closer, in the hope of heading off the war. In either situation, however, the outcome is dependent on the strategic reaction of the adversary.[12]

One way of thinking about the different stages of conflict escalation is to differentiate between proximate (or immediate) causes and distant (or remote or underlying) causes, a distinction first suggested by Aristotle. In the aggregate, broad system-, economic-, or societal-level forces probably have a greater impact than particular individuals on the formation of rivalries and/or on the underlying processes leading to war, while the impact of individuals, including their misperceptions of the adversary's capabilities and intentions, usually increases as a dispute or crisis moves closer to final decisions for war.

In the 1990–91 Gulf War, for example, system-level strategic and economic factors had a strong impact on the US decision to send troops to Saudi Arabia in response to Iraq's invasion of Kuwait in August 1990, in order to contain the Iraqi threat to the stability of the balance of power in the Middle East and to world oil markets.[13] Individual-level factors, in the form of President George H.W. Bush's belief system, probably had a lesser impact. Individual factors probably played a more significant role in the US decision to initiate the air war and then ground war against Iraq in January 1991. There is a high probability that most any other American president would have taken strong action in response to the initial Iraqi invasion. There is a lower probability that another president would have decided on an air war in January 1991, rather than first wait to see if economic sanctions would work to induce Iraq to withdraw from Kuwait.

It is not always true, however, that individual-level factors are more important than system-level factors in the immediate processes leading to war. System structures not only generate rivalries between states, and arms races between rivals; they may also induce a state to undertake a preemptive or preventive attack in a crisis situation. Cultural and religious differences between states can also help generate interstate rivalries, while also creating images of the inevitability of war that lead to preemption or prevention. Xenophobic public opinion can both preclude leaders from making important compromises that might avert or resolve a dispute in its early stages, and push leaders into a war that they prefer to avoid at the peak of a crisis.

In addition, individuals sometimes play a key role in the early stages of a conflict episode by making decisions that send a state down the path to war. A good test of this hypothesis, at least in individual historical cases, is an analysis of the counterfactual question of whether the war would still have occurred if another leader had been in power. Most analysts argue, for example, that if Al Gore rather than George W. Bush had been president at the time of the September 11, 2001, terrorist attacks on the United States, the US would probably not have invaded Iraq in 2003 or begun planning such an invasion over a year in advance.[14]

For all of these reasons, most international relations analysts have shifted away from the question of "which level is most important?" They have increasingly come to believe that theories of war and peace and other phenomena in international politics need to draw on variables from multiple levels of analysis.[15] This raises the question of exactly how variables from different levels of analysis (or from the same level, for that matter) combine to increase the probability of war or to promote peace. International relations scholars are not always careful to specify exactly what forms these combinations take or to carefully think through whether their statistical models of conflict accurately reflect the actual combinations in the real world.

Multiple paths to war

Implicit in our discussion of theories of the causes of war, and in our reflections on the "which-level-is-most-important?" question guiding many applications of the levels-of-analysis framework, is the likelihood that no single theory is correct and that there are multiple causal paths through which war can occur. The primary process leading to one war might be a conflict spiral generated by security fears (the 1967 Arab–Israeli War, for example), while the primary factors leading to other wars might be fears of an adverse shift in relative power (the 431 BCE Peloponnesian War), external scapegoating to divert public attention from domestic problems (the 1982 Falklands/Malvinas War), the ambitions of an individual leader (Hitler and World War II), and so on. The possibility that the same outcome can arise from different causal paths is known as *equifinality*.

International relations scholars have increasingly come to recognize the existence of *multiple paths to war*. Rationalists recognize three distinct rationalist paths to war,[16] and many rationalists concede that some wars might occur through non-rationalist processes. Senese and Vasquez (2008) construct a steps-to-war model of war but state explicitly that this is only one of many paths to war. Some more qualitatively oriented international relations scholars have begun to adopt the notion of *multiple conjunctural causation* (Ragin, 1987), which suggests that causation is the product of combinations of variables and that different combinations can lead to the same outcome.[17]

The concept of multiple causal paths raises additional complications in the study of war. Among other things, while scholars have increasingly acknowledged the existence of multiple paths to war, they have yet to define the concept. Social scientists interested in theorizing about empirical regularities or patterns of behavior will presumably not equate a path to war with a series of events, but instead will want to define the concept of causal path in terms of a distinctive combination of causal variables that lead to a particular outcome. But how broadly should a path be defined? In Senese and Vasquez's (2008) steps-to-war model, for example, do territorial disputes constitute one path to war, territorial disputes between rivals another, territorial disputes between rivals drawing in allies still another, and so on, or do all possible combinations of each of these variables, which they call the "realist road to war," constitute a single path to war? Is there a general "domestic path to war," or do diversionary behavior, pressure from influential economic groups, and ideological hostility constitute distinct paths to war? Is a particular combination of variables enough to define a path to war, or is the temporal sequence of variables important?[18]

The more narrowly we define a path to war, the more paths to war we find. The more paths we identify, the further we move (after a point) away from theory and the closer to the view of most historians that each war (or other historical episode) is unique.[19] The question is not how many paths to war there "really are," but what conceptual definition is most useful in helping us understand the causes of war. Another question is how "complete" a causal path must be. Should a causal path include *all* the factors that "cause" the war to occur, and by that do we mean the complete set of conditions and processes that are jointly sufficient for war? Or should we define a causal path as a set of factors that make war highly probable? If the latter, what threshold of probability is appropriate?

These questions illuminate an important divide between researchers in different methodologically defined research communities, particularly one between those whose primary aim is to develop theoretical generalizations about war and peace and those whose primary aim is to provide the "best" interpretation of a particular war or the absence of war.

Theoretical Generalization and Historical Interpretation

It is useful to begin with an important disciplinary distinction between historians and political scientists. Most historians are primarily interested in explaining particular historical events or temporally-bounded sequences of events, while most political scientists are primarily interested in constructing and testing theoretical generalizations (Levy, 2001).[20] These differences derive in part from professional training and in part from different conceptions of how the world works and how best to study it. Most historians tend to see historical events as unique and aim to provide "total" explanations of individual cases. They tend to be relatively uninterested in constructing general theories and skeptical about the very possibility of a single, widely applicable theory.[21]

Most political scientists (and other social scientists) see patterns as well as idiosyncrasies. They are more interested in testing theoretical generalizations about these patterns than in explaining particular historical episodes. Many political scientists recognize that there is some element of unpredictability in the world, and they model theories in probabilistic terms, test those theories with statistical methods, and include an "error term" that incorporates other variables that might affect some outcomes but that are not systematically important enough to include in their models.[22] Researchers using statistical methods generally seek to estimate the average effects of different variables in large numbers of cases, not to fully explain the outcomes in any particular case (King, Keohane, and Verba, 1994).[23] They try to explain as much of the variance in war as possible, or to generate the best predictions of the likelihood of war under different conditions, and to do so with a modest number of theoretical variables. Statistical models use statistical criteria to assess whether the increase in explanatory power generated by adding more variables is warranted by the additional complexity of the model, assuming that for a given level of explanatory power the fewer the number of a model's assumptions the better.[24]

While many political scientists use statistical methods, many others prefer to do historical case studies. They fall somewhere between statistically oriented political scientists and historians. They have a social science orientation, and their ultimate aim is often to contribute to the development of theory and not just to explain a particular historical episode. But they often view the explanation of a small set of individual cases as a useful first step in the theory-building process. Their immediate aim is to explain the case, using the leverage provided by the comparative method to do so.[25]

Historically oriented political scientists often start with a preliminary theory to guide their case studies. They then often use the findings from their case studies to modify their theories, and they then move on to other cases (George and Smoke, 1974; George and Bennett, 2005). They recognize, however, that the cases they select for the next test of the theory must include data that are different from the data that were used to generate the theory (Lakatos, 1970; Elman and Elman, 2003).

In the process of explaining particular historical events or temporally bound series of events, case study researchers usually insist on providing complete explanations rather than probabilistic explanations. These explanations generally involve the specification of the conditions that are necessary for a particular outcome and those that are jointly sufficient for the outcome. As Mahoney, Kimball, and Koivu (2009:117) write, reflecting an increasingly common view among qualitative methodologists, in "historical explanation … researchers tend to view causes as necessary and/or sufficient for outcomes of interest."[26] Thus statistical methods and historical methods generally involve different conceptions about the nature of causality.[27]

One can certainly find interpretations of the causes of individual wars that specify one or more necessary conditions.[28] It is relatively rare, however, that an interpretation specifies that a particular factor was sufficient for a particular war. Although underlying structural conditions and relationships, both international and domestic, might lead to the prediction that war is very likely, the tipping point in many decisions for war might be the idiosyncrasies of individual political leaders or internal political calculations that are not easily predicted.

It might be possible to add variables to cover all of the factors that make war almost certain in a given case, but that would make the explanation far less generalizable to other cases. This tradeoff between providing a detailed explanation of an individual case and one that is generalizable beyond a particular case or set of cases is always present, but it is particularly acute if the aim is specifying conditions that are sufficient for war.

A related problem with any approach that relies on a combination of necessary and sufficient conditions is that it assumes that both the outcome variable and the explanatory variables are dichotomous – a condition is either present or it is not.[29] This is reasonable enough for war as the outcome variable, and also for some explanatory variables (territorial dispute/no dispute, alliance/no alliance, etc.), but it is much more problematic for many of the variables posited in our leading theories of war – the distribution of power in the system, perceptions of a rising adversary, external scapegoating, degree of ideological or religious hostility, etc. In addition, unlike statistical models, which facilitate the attribution of relative causal weight to various causal variables, models specifying necessary or sufficient conditions cannot easily do this (Thompson, 2003).

This is not to say that statistical models are superior to individual or comparative case studies (whether or not the latter posit necessary or sufficient conditions), only that each is most useful in answering slightly different questions.[30] Statistical models are particularly useful for testing theoretical generalizations about the conditions under which war is likely to occur, provided that it is possible to measure key variables in a large number of cases. They are less useful, however, in helping to explain individual historical events.

Historical case studies are particularly useful for explaining the outbreak of individual wars, but they are less useful for generalizing beyond a specific case to wars in general. Historical case studies can serve a useful "hypothesis-generating" function, however, and in fact many important theoretical ideas originate from detailed historical case studies.[31] Those hypotheses can then be tested by statistical methods or perhaps comparative methods, and in this way historical case studies can serve as a key component of a larger research strategy.

Case studies can also serve in a hypothesis-testing capacity, but some kinds of case studies are more useful than others for this purpose, given the difficulties in generalizing from a small number of cases to a larger population.[32] The detailed elaboration of the processes leading from a crisis to war (*process tracing*) can often reveal whether the empirical regularities identified by statistical methods reflect a genuine causal relationship. A careful comparison of two very similar crises, one of which leads to war and one of which does not, can identify causal factors that co-vary with war and peace, ruling out those that are constant across cases. This method is often referred to as "controlled comparison," "paired comparison," "structured, focused comparison," or "matching." Finally, if we have good theoretical reasons to believe that a particular case should not fit a theory (a "hard" or "least-likely" case), and it is demonstrated that the case does in fact fit the theory, our confidence that the theory is more generally valid is greatly enhanced. Similarly, cases that should fit a theory ("easy" or "most-likely" cases) but that are falsified by the data significantly reduce our confidence in the validity of the theory.[33]

It is important to note that explanations of variations in war and peace and explanations for the outbreak (or not) of individual wars provide answers to slightly different questions about the causes of war. Different still are explanations for the constant recurrence of war over human history, which is a more abstract philosophical question. Waltz (1988:20) recognized this distinction when he stated that neorealist theory could explain "war's dismal recurrence through the millennia" but "not ... why particular wars are fought." This suggests that the question of what causes war can be "unpacked" into three different but overlapping questions: (1) what causes the constant recurrence of war? (2) what causes variations in war and peace, or under what conditions does war occur? (3) what causes particular wars? (Suganami, 1996: chap. 1; Black, 1998:13–14; Levy, 2002:352).

These different questions that people ask about war lead scholars to frame the problem in different ways, to begin their research with different preconceptions about what is important, and to adopt different methodologies and construct different research designs. To answer the question of what caused the 2003 Iraq war with the answer "human nature" would not be very satisfying. Explanations based on "human nature," evolutionary processes, or international anarchy might help to explain the constant recurrence of war in world politics, but they cannot explain either variations in war and peace or the outbreak of particular wars. A historical explanation of a particular war might be compelling, but it can almost certainly not be generalized as a theory of the conditions under which war is most likely to occur or as an explanation for the constant recurrence of war. Strong empirical regularities might be revealing about the conditions under which war is likely to occur, but many scholars would not accept that as a fully satisfactory explanation of the outbreak a particular war, especially of the precise timing of the war. While many scholars accept the finding that democracies rarely if ever fight each other, we would probably not be content with that as a complete explanation for why Anglo–American crises during a period of power transition in the 1890s did not lead to war.

We do not mean to suggest that the slight differences in the questions that scholars in different research communities ask about war preclude them from learning from each other or from combining multiple approaches in their study of war. Quite to the contrary, differences between approaches make such an integration between them all the more necessary, as long as scholars understand the nature of their differences. Social scientists are increasingly coming around to the view that the application of several different methods to a given question is likely to likely to increase our understanding of a phenomenon. Each method has its own distinctive strengths and limitations, and the use of multiple methods allows us to use the strengths of each to compensate for the weakness of the other.[34] If a hypothesis is confirmed by the applications of different methods, our confidence in the hypothesis is increased. Despite this agreement in principle on the benefits of methodological pluralism, there is less agreement on the question of exactly *how* different methods can be combined with optimum effect. Recently, however, this question has begun to attract attention from political methodologists and applied researchers (George and Bennett, 2005; Fearon and Laitin, 2008).

Now that the reader has waded through a few hundred pages on the causes of war, s/he might be discouraged to realize that this book has generated more questions than answers. We have emphasized that scholars have identified relatively few strong patterns in the processes leading to war or sustaining peace. Where there are strong patterns – democracies rarely if ever fight each other, most wars involve territorial disputes but most territorial disputes do not to lead to war, most wars are between strategic rivals, strong imbalances of power between two states is associated with peace between them – our theoretical explanations for these patterns are often weak. Where our theoretical explanations are plausible, they concern pieces of the puzzle of war rather than an integrated theory of war.

The search for a comprehensive theory of war has been an elusive task. Some continue to seek an overarching theory of war – for example, a realist theory based on state power and interest or a rationalist bargaining model of war. Others have recognized that perhaps a more realistic goal, at least in the short term, is a number of more limited theories, with the hope that the accumulation of such theories might eventually lead to a grand theory of war, but with the recognition that even limited theory improves our understanding. This parallels Guetzkow's (1950) argument – with respect to international relations theory as a whole – that our immediate aim should be "islands of theory." In the six decades since Guetzkow's plea, however, as a field, we have only a limit number of islands of theory, or at least islands of empirically confirmed theory. As Vasquez (2000:367) notes, the state of our knowledge of war and peace is better described as "islands of findings."

Some will attribute the limitations in our knowledge to the lack of imagination of scholars in constructing theories, or perhaps to limitations in existing methodologies for testing our theories. That may be true to some extent, as the development in the last three decades of more rigorous theories and more sophisticate methodologies – both quantitative and qualitative – for testing those theories has contributed to an increased understanding of war. The fact that our understanding is still limited, however, reflects the complexity of the world we are trying to explain as much as limitations in our theory and methodologies.

Einstein might have been right that "God does not play dice with the universe." We suspect, however, that Bernstein et al. (2000) are right that "God gave physics the easy problems," and that the social world is even more complex than the physical world. War is hardly an exception. Clausewitz ([1832]1976) was right that there is a "fog of war," and a fog of peace as well. That fog complicates the conduct of war and impedes our comprehension of war, particularly its causes. The collective efforts of scholars in recent decades have helped to dissipate the fog to some extent. Further progress is anticipated, warranted, and needed, but it is not clear that the fog of war will ever lift completely. An appreciation of the nature of past efforts to make sense of the causes of war is a necessary but not sufficient foundation for further progress, and for further efforts to reduce the incidence of war and to mitigate its effects. We hope that this book has contributed to that foundation.

Notes

1. Recall that the levels-of-analysis framework is a system for classifying causal variables, not a theory of war.
2. After the "realist–idealist" debate following World War II (Carr, 1940; Herz, 1951), the most common paradigmatic distinction in the international relations field was between realist, liberal, and Marxist approaches (Gilpin, 1975), and then just realism and liberalism (Baldwin, 1993). By 2000 or so, that distinction had generally been supplanted by the distinction between rationalist and constructivist approaches (Ruggie, 1998; Fearon and Wendt, 2002). For a critical view of the common conception of the history of the field as a series of great debates, see Schmidt (2002).
3. Until recently most constructivist approaches gave relatively little importance to individual-level factors. Early constructivist approaches emphasized structural determinants of *social* constructions of reality and minimized the effects of individual agency. Wendt (1999) quite self-consciously presented a structural/ideational theory of international politics. It is important to note that constructivists are less accepting of the analytic distinction among levels of analysis. They emphasize instead that structure and agency are mutually constituted and incapable of really being defined without the other. We, on the other hand, argue that it is useful to analytically distinguish between different levels, and then to analyze the causal (as opposed to constitutive) relationship between variables at different levels.
4. As we have repeated many times, however, any individual- and state/societal-level theory of war must include some dyadic or systemic component in order to explain war as a product of the interaction of states. This does not necessarily mean, however that the system or dyadic component carries the greatest causal weight. A variable x may be a necessary condition for outcome y, but

that does not mean that x is the primary cause of y (Goertz and Levy, 2007: chap. 2). Any explanation of the 2003 Iraq War, for example, must include Iraqi as well as American behavior and the bargaining between the two states, but in most interpretations the greatest causal weight goes to individual and nation-state level variables on the American side.

5.   Bargaining takes place between and within organizations, state agencies, states, and within international organizations, and thus applies to several different units of analysis.

6.   Individual empirical studies may emphasize the key role of a particular variable, but such studies are usually contradicted by other studies of the same phenomenon.

7.   It is sometimes said that this helps to explain why, after coming to power, some US presidents whose greatest expertise had been on domestic policy soon gravitate towards foreign policy.

8.   Of course, internal economic and political factors influence which states become great powers in the first place.

9.   This relates to the debate on the question of whether we need different theories for "big" wars than for "little" wars (Midlarsky, 1990).

10.   If a variable at one level of analysis takes on an extreme value, then variables at other levels of analysis may be less important. In situations involving extreme external threat, a state's response is less likely to reflect the idiosyncrasies of individual political leaders or the particular characteristics of the regime. Iraq's invasion of Kuwait and threat to Middle East oil supplies in 1990 would have led to a strong US response regardless of who was president. Similarly, if an individual political leader has an extremely high propensity for taking risks, s/he is less likely to be constrained by systemic-, dyadic-, or societal-level factors. This is illustrated by the role of Hitler in Germany in the 1930s.

11.   This reflects the fact that different historical periods are defined by different conditions and characteristics – structural, technological, political, social, and cultural.

12.   These variations across the stages of conflict escalation have important implications for the consequences of different definitions of a historical case for the purposes of analyzing the causes of a particular war. The more narrow the temporal boundaries that a researcher uses to define a case, the greater the weight that s/he is likely to attribute to decision-making factors. The broader a researcher defines such temporal boundaries, the greater the weight that s/he is likely to attribute to underlying structural, social, and cultural factors. A study of the causes of World War I that begins with the unification of Germany in 1871 (as many do) is likely to give more weight to structural changes in the international system and the international political economy and less weight to decision-making than would a study that focuses on the July 1914 crisis, though there are exceptions (Levy, 1990/91).

13.   This is in addition to the important but often neglected impact on American strategy of the end of the Cold War and the collapse of the Soviet Union, which eliminated the risk of Soviet intervention in response to the US air war and/or ground war.

14. A counterfactual hypothesis or argument specifies what would happen in an alternative world defined by a hypothetical change in one or more of the conditions in the real world. The validity of a counterfactual statement is difficult to evaluate, since the counterfactual world does not actually exist and consequently we cannot know for sure if that world would have turned out as predicted. That said, we can evaluate counterfactuals in term of the clarity of their predictions, the plausibility of the hypothesized antecedent, and the conditional probability of the hypothesized consequent given the antecedent (Levy, 2008c). The plausibility of the antecedent is often evaluated in terms of the "minimal rewrite of history" rule: the fewer things one has to change to get from the real world to the counterfactual world, the better the counterfactual. The Gore counterfactual is a good one because only a minuscule change in the number of votes in the 2000 election would have led to a Gore victory, and because it is quite likely, given what we know about Gore's belief system and those of the kinds of advisors he was most likely to select, that he would have acted differently than Bush after the 9/11 attacks and not authorized the invasion of Iraq. For a different view, see Harvey (2008).

15. It is not just a matter of adding variables, but adding them in a way that creates a logically consistent and theoretically integrated model of war. Some scholars argue that since bargaining takes place at multiple levels, a rational/strategic bargaining model might provide a framework for unifying processes at different levels (Milner, 1991; Wagner, 2007). Others emphasize the utility of a cultural framework (Lebow, 2008).

16. The three rationalist paths to war are private information and incentives to misrepresent that information, commitments problems, and indivisible issues. We might add a fourth, by incorporating domestic processes into a rational but non-unitary actor model. One effort in this direction is Tarar (2006).

17. This concept has been particularly influential in comparative politics, and has led to research designs based on Boolean or fuzzy-set methods (Ragin, 1987; 2000).

18. Recall that Senese and Vasquez (2008) specify different combinations of variables but not the different sequences in which a given combination might appear.

19. This view is shared by radical constructivists, who question the very possibility of a theory that can be tested against a theoretically neutral body of evidence.

20. Students might reflect on whether their own experience in history and political science courses is consistent with this generalization.

21. These are broad generalizations. We recognize that differences within each discipline are often greater than differences between them.

22. Some argue that in the end the difference between war and peace are random factors captured by the error term. If the bargaining model of war is correct, and if political leaders understand that model, they will have already taken into account the all of the factors specified in the model, and adjusted their bargaining strategies accordingly. Thus "war is in the error term" (Gartzke, 1999).

23. The use of statistical methods in the study of political history was influential at one time (e.g., Fogel, 1964), but the influence of such methods subsequently declined.

24. This is the definition of parsimony: explaining more with less.

25. As Mahoney, Kimball, and Koivu (2009:216) argue, in historical explanation, the explanation of specific past occurrences is primary, and "the question of whether and how the resulting explanation might then be generalized is a secondary concern."

26. A *sufficient condition* takes the form "if x, then y." To say that a causal factor is sufficient for war means that if the factor is present war will follow, regardless of what other factors are present or absent. A *necessary condition* takes the form "if not x, then not y." To say that a causal factor is necessary for war means that in the absence of that factor war will not occur. Note that statements of necessary conditions are often expressed in different ways: a particular factor was a "permissive condition," that it "made the outcome possible," or that "absent x, y would not have occurred."

27. Statistically oriented researchers generally adopt a "regularity" conception of causation, which is most commonly associated with the philosopher David Hume ([1748]1902) and which associates causality with "constant conjunction" (or correlation), temporal precedence, and non-spuriousness (ensuring that observed correlations are truly causal and that they are not the product of third variables that co-vary with both the independent variable and the causal variable). Case study researchers tend to conceive of causality in terms of necessary condition counterfactuals, an approach that is associated with D. Lewis (1973). See also Mahoney and Goertz (2006) and Goertz and Levy (2007:10–15). On the nature of historical explanation, see Dray (1957).

28. An example is Lebow's (2000/01) argument that World War I was the product of the confluence of several underlying structural conditions and the assassination of the Austrian Archduke. Lebow argues each was a necessary condition for the war and that both the unstable international structure and the spark provided by the assassination were equally important for Europe to explode into a continental war. For an argument that structural conditions are generally more important than catalysts, and that in the absence of one catalyst another will probably arise and lead to the same outcome, see Thompson (2003). For an argument that German leaders wanted a continental war and that in the absence of the assassination they would have found another way to provoke a war before 1917, see Levy (1990/91; 2008c:640).

29. For a more probabilistic approach to the analysis of necessary and sufficient conditions, one that uses "fuzzy" set logic, see Ragin (2000).

30. The different aims of quantitative and qualitative researchers reflect differences in professional training and also different conceptions of what constitutes a good theory, particularly the optimum tradeoffs between the analytic power and predictive utility of parsimonious theories and the descriptive richness of more complex theories.

31. Details about the role of rigid railway time-tables and military plans in World War I, for example, helped to generated hypotheses about the impact of organizational routines on war.

32. On the hypothesis-testing role of case studies, see George and Bennett (2005) and Levy (2008b).

33. As we noted in chapter 5, the fact that Allison and Zelikow (1999) could demonstrate that the Cuban missile crisis – which should be an easy case for the rational state actor model and a difficult case for the organizational/ bureaucratic model – raised substantial doubts about the generalizability of the former and provided enormous plausibility for the latter. On "easy" and "hard" cases, see Van Evera (1997), George and Bennett (2005), and Levy (2008b:12–13).

34. Two issues that have successfully been examined through a combination of statistical and case study methods and formal game-theoretic models are the democratic peace and the diversionary theory of war.

References

Adams, Sam (1994) *War of Numbers: An Intelligence Memoir.* South Royalton, VT: Steerforth Press.

Agranat Commission (1974) *The Agranat Report* (in Hebrew). Tel Aviv: Am Oved.

Ajami, Fouad (1993) "The Summoning." *Foreign Affairs,* 72, 4: 2–9.

Ajami, Fouad (2008) "The Clash." *New York Times,* January 6, 2008, section A.

Albertini, Luigi ([1942]1957) *The Origins of the War of 1914,* Vol. III, trans. Isabella M. Massey. London: Oxford University Press.

Allison, Graham T. (1971) *Essence of Decision.* New York: Longman.

Allison, Graham T., and Philip Zelikow (1999) *Essence of Decision,* 2nd ed. New York: Longman.

Anderson, Lisa R., and Charles A. Holt (1996) "Classroom Games: Understanding Bayes' Rule." *Journal of Economic Perspectives,* 10, 4 (Spring): 179–87.

Andreas, Peter (2008) *Blue Helmets and Black Markets: The Business of Survival in the Siege of Sarajevo.* Ithaca, NY: Cornell University Press.

Angell, Norman ([1910]1972) *The Great Illusion: A Study of the Relation of Military Power to National Advantage.* London: Garland.

Archer, Christon, John R. Ferris, Holger H. Herwig, and Timothy H.E. Travers (2002) *World History of Warfare.* Lincoln: University of Nebraska Press.

Aron, Raymond (1968) "War and Industrial Society." In Leon Bramson and George W. Goethals, eds., *War.* New York: Basic Books, pp. 359–402.

Aron, Raymond (1985) *Clausewitz,* trans. Christine Booker and Norman Stone. Englewood Cliffs, NJ: Prentice Hall.

Aronson, Cynthia J., and I. William Zartman, eds. (2008) *Rethinking the Economics of War: The Intersection of Need, Creed, and Greed.* Baltimore: Johns Hopkins University Press.

Art, Robert J. (1973) "Bureaucratic Politics and American Foreign Policy: A Critique." *Policy Sciences,* 4: 467–90.

Avant, Deborah D. (2005) *The Market for Force: The Consequences of Privatizing Security.* New York: Cambridge University Press.

Axelrod, Robert (1984) *The Evolution of Cooperation.* New York: Basic Books.

Ayoob, Mohammed (2001) "State Making, State Breaking, and State Failure." In Chester A. Crocker, Fen Osler Hampson, and Pamela Aall, eds., *Turbulent*

Peace: The Challenges of Managing International Conflict. Washington: United States Institute of Peace Press, pp. 127–42.

Babst, Dean (1972) "A Force for Peace." *Industrial Research*, April: 55–8.

Baldwin, David A. (1993) *Neorealism and Neoliberalilsm: The Contemporary Debate.* New York: Columbia University Press.

Ballentine, Karen (2003) "Beyond Greed and Grievance: Reconsidering the Economic Dynamics of Armed Conflict." In Karen Ballentine and Jake Sherman, eds., *The Political Economy of Armed Conflict: Beyond Greed and Grievance.* Boulder, CO: Lynne Rienner.

Ballentine, Karen, and Jake Sherman (2003) "Introduction." In Karen Ballentine and Jake Sherman, eds., *The Political Economy of Armed Conflict: Beyond Greed and Grievance.* Boulder, CO: Lynne Rienner.

Baran, Paul A., and Paul Sweezy (1966) *Monopoly Capital: An Essay on the American Economic and Social Order.* New York: Monthly Review Press.

Barbieri, Katherine (2002) *The Liberal Illusion: Does Trade Promote Peace?* Ann Arbor, MI: University of Michigan Press.

Barbieri, Katherine, and Jack S. Levy (1999) "Sleeping With the Enemy: Trade Between Adversaries During Wartime." *Journal of Peace Research*, 36, 4: 463–79.

Bar-Joseph, Uri (2005) *The Watchman Fell Asleep: The Surprise of Yom Kippur and Its Sources.* Albany, NY: State University of New York Press.

Bar-Joseph, Uri, and Jack S. Levy (2009) "Conscious Action and the Study of Intelligence Failure." *Political Science Quarterly*, 124, 3 (Fall): 461–88.

Barkow, Jerome H., Leda Cosmides, and John Tooby, eds. (1992) *The Adapted Mind: Evolutionary Psychology and the Generation of Culture.* Oxford: Oxford University Press, 1992.

Barnett, Michael N. (1992) *Confronting the Costs of War: Military Power, State, and Society in Egypt and Israel.* Princeton, NJ: Princeton University Press.

Barnett, Michael N., and Jack S. Levy (1991) "Domestic Sources of Alliances and Alignments: The Case of Egypt, 1962–1973." *International Organization*, 45, 3 (Summer): 369–95.

Bass, Herbert J. (1964) *American Entry into World War I: Submarines, Sentiment, or Security?* New York: Holt, Rinehart, and Winston.

Bendor, Jonathan, and Thomas H. Hammond (1992) "Rethinking Allison's Models." *American Political Science Review*, 86, 2 (June): 301–22.

Bennett, D. Scott (1997) "Democracy, Regime Change and Rivalry Termination." *International Interactions*, 22: 369–97.

Bennett, D. Scott (1998) "Interpreting and Testing Models of Rivalry Data." *American Journal of Political Science*, 42: 1200–32.

Bennett, D. Scott, and Allan C. Stam III (2004) *The Behavioral Origins of War.* Ann Arbor, MI: University of Michigan Press.

Benoit, Kenneth (1996) "Democracies Really Are More Pacific (in General)." *Journal of Conflict Resolution*, 40, 4: 309–41.

Bercovitch, Jacob, Victor Kremenyuk, and I. William Zartman, eds. (2009) *Handbook of Conflict Resolution.* London: Sage.

Berdal, Mats, and David Keen (1997) "Violence and Economic Agendas in Civil Wars: Some Policy Implications." *Millennium*, 26, 3: 795–818.

Berghahn, Volker R. (1973) *Germany and the Approach of War in 1914*. New York: St. Martin's.

Berghahn, Volker R. (1982) *Militarism: The History of an International Debate, 1816–1979*. New York: St. Martins.

Bernstein, Steven, Richard Ned Lebow, Janice Gross Stein, and Steven Weber (2000) "God Gave Physics the Easy Problems: Adapting Social Science to an Unpredictable World." *European Journal of International Relations*, 6, 1 (March): 43–76.

Betts, Richard K. (1977) *Soldiers, Statesmen, and Cold War Crises*. Cambridge, MA: Harvard University Press.

Betts, Richard K. (1999) "Must War Find a Way?" *International Security*, 24 (Fall): 166–98.

Betts, Richard K. (2007) *Enemies of Intelligence: Knowledge and Power in American National Security*. New York: Columbia University Press.

Black, Jeremy (1998) *Why Wars Happen*. New York: New York University Press.

Black, Jeremy (2008) *Great Powers and the Quest for Hegemony: The World Order since 1500*. New York: Routledge.

Blainey, Geoffrey (1988) *The Causes of War*, 3rd ed. New York: Free Press.

Bodin, Jean ([1576]1955) *Six Books of the Commonwealth*, trans. Michael Tooley. Oxford: Basil Blackwell.

Boix, Carles (2008) "Civil Wars and Guerrilla Warfare in the Contemporary World: Toward a Joint Theory of Motivations and Opportunities." In Stathis N. Kalyvas, Ian Shapiro, and Tarek Masoud, eds., *Order, Conflict, and Violence*. Cambridge: Cambridge University Press.

Boulding, Kenneth (1962) *Conflict and Defense*. New York: Harper.

Boulding, Kenneth Ewart (1978) *Stable Peace*. Austin, TX: University of Texas Press.

Braumoeller, Bear, and Gary Goertz (2000) "The Methodology of Necessary Conditions." *American Journal of Political Science*, 44, 4: 844–58.

Brecher, Michael (1980) *Decisions in Crisis*. Berkeley: University of California Press.

Brecher, Michael (1993) *Crisis in World Politics: Theory and Reality*. New York: Pergamon.

Bremer, Stuart A. (1992) "Dangerous Dyads: Conditions Affecting the Likelihood of Interstate War, 1816–1965." *Journal of Conflict Resolution*, 36, 2: 309–41.

Bremer, Stuart A. (2000) "Who Fights Whom, When, Where, and Why?" In John A. Vasquez, ed., *What Do We Know About War?* Lanham, MD: Rowman & Littlefield, pp. 23–36.

Bremer, Stuart A., and Thomas R. Cusack, eds. (1995) *The Process of War: Advancing the Scientific Study of War*. Luxembourg: Gordon and Breach.

Brewer, Anthony (1980) *Marxist Theories of Imperialism*. London: Routledge & Kegan Paul.

Brooks, Risa A. (2008) *Shaping Strategy: The Civil–Military Politics of Strategic Assessment*. Princeton, NJ: Princeton University Press.

Brooks, Stephen G. (1997) "Dueling Realisms." *International Organization*, 51 (Summer): 445–78.

Brooks, Stephen G. (2005) *Producing Security: Multinational Corporations, Globalization, and the Changing Calculus of Conflict*. Princeton, NJ: Princeton University Press.

Brooks, Stephen G., and William C. Wohlforth (2008) *World Out of Balance: International Relations and the Challenge of American Primacy*. Princeton, NJ: Princeton University Press.

Brown, Michael E., Sean M. Lynn-Jones, and Steven E. Miller, eds. (1996) *Debating the Democratic Peace*. Cambridge, MA: MIT Press.

Brown, Michael E., Owen R. Coté, Jr., Sean M. Lynn-Jones, and Steven E. Miller, eds. (2004) *Offense, Defense, and War*. Cambridge, MA: MIT Press.

Brulé, David J. (2005) "Explaining and Forecasting Foreign Policy Decisions: A Poliheuristic Analysis of the Iran Hostage Rescue Decision." *International Studies Perspectives*, 6, 1: 99–113.

Brulé, David J. (2008) "The Poliheuristic Research Program: An Assessment and Suggestions for Further Progress." *International Studies Review*, 10, 2: 266–93.

Bueno de Mesquita, Bruce (1981) *The War Trap*. New Haven: Yale University Press.

Bueno de Mesquita, Bruce (2003) "Neorealism's Logic and Evidence: When Is a Theory Falsified?" In John A. Vasquez and Colin Elman, eds., *Realism and the Balancing of Power: A New Debate*. Saddle River, NJ: Prentice Hall.

Bueno de Mesquita, Bruce, and David Lalman (1992) *War and Reason*. New Haven: Yale University Press.

Bueno de Mesquita, Bruce, and Randolph M. Siverson (1995) "War and the Survival of Political Leaders: A Comparative Study of Regime Types and Political Accountability." *American Political Science Review*, 89, 4: 841–55.

Bueno de Mesquita, Bruce, James D. Morrow, Randolph M. Siverson, and Alastair Smith (2003) *The Logic of Political Survival*. Cambridge, MA: MIT Press.

Bull, Hedley (1977) *The Anarchical Society*. New York: Columbia University Press.

Buzan, Barry (1984) "Economic Structure and International Security: The Limits of the Liberal Case." *International Organization*, 38: 597–624.

Buzan, Barry, Charles Jones, and Richard Little (1993) *The Logic of Anarchy*. New York: Columbia University Press.

Calvert, Peter (1986) *The Foreign Policy of New States*. Brighton, UK: Wheatsheaf Books.

Cardoso, Fernando Henrique, and Enzo Faletto (1979) *Dependency and Development in Latin America*, trans. Marjory Mattingly Urguidi. Berkeley: University of California Press.

Carr, Edward Hallett (1940) *The Twenty Years' Crisis, 1919–1939*. London: Macmillan & Co.

Centeno, Miguel Angel (2002) *Blood and Debt: War and the Nation State in Latin America*. University Park, PA: Pennsylvania State University Press.

Cetinyan, Rupen (2002) "Ethnic Bargaining in the Shadow of Third-Party Intervention." *International Organization*, 56, 3 (Summer), 645–77.

Chan, Steven (1997) "In Search of Democratic Peace: Problems and Promise." *Mershon International Studies Review*, 41, 1: 59–91.

Chase-Dunn, Christopher, and Bruce Podobnik (1995) "The Next World War: World-System Cycles and Trends." *Journal of World-Systems Research*, 1, 6.

Chiozza, Giacomo (2002) "Is There a Clash of Civilizations? Evidence from Patterns of International Conflict Involvement, 1946–97." *Journal of Peace Research*, 39, 6 (November): 711–34.

Choucri, Nazil, and Robert North (1975) *Nations in Conflict: National Growth and International Violence*. San Francisco: W.H. Freeman.

Christensen, Thomas J. (1996) *Useful Adversaries: Grand Strategy, Domestic Mobilization, and Sino–American Conflict, 1947–1958*. Princeton, NJ: Princeton University Press.

Christensen, Eben J., and Steven B. Redd (2004) "Bureaucrats vs. the Ballot Box in Foreign Policy Decision Making: An Experimental Analysis of the Bureaucratic Politics Model and the Poliheuristic Theory." *Journal of Conflict Resolution*, 48, 1: 69–90.

Churchill, Winston S. (1948) *The Second World War*, Vol. 1: *The Gathering Storm*. Boston, MA: Houghton Mifflin.

Cioffi-Revilla, Claudio (2000) "Ancient Warfare: Origins and Systems." In Manus I. Midlarsky, ed., *Handbook of War Studies II*. Ann Arbor, MI: University of Michigan Press.

Claude, Inis L., Jr. (1962) *Power & International Relations*. New York: Random House.

Claude, Inis L., Jr. (1971) *Swords into Plowshares*, 4th ed. New York: Random House.

Clausewitz, Carl von ([1832]1976) *On War*, ed. and trans. Michael Howard and Peter Paret. Princeton, NJ: Princeton University Press.

Cobden, Richard ([1903]1969). *The Political Writings of Richard Cobden*. London: Unwin.

Cohen, Arthur A. (1991) "The Sino-Soviet Border Crisis of 1969." In Alexander L. George, ed., *Avoiding War: Problems of Crisis Management*. Boulder, CO: Westview.

Cohen, Benjamin J. (1973) *The Question of Imperialism*. New York: Basic.

Cohn, Carol (1987) "Sex and Death in the Rational World of Defense Intellectuals." *Signs: Journal of Women in Culture and Society*, 12: 687–718.

Colaresi, Michael (2001) "Shocks to the System: Great Power Rivalry and Leadership Long Cycle." *Journal of Conflict Resolution*, 45: 569–93.

Colaresi, Michael (2004) "When Doves Cry, International Rivalry, Un-reciprocated Cooperation, and Leadership Turnover." *American Journal of Political Science*, 48: 555–70.

Colaresi, Michael (2005) *Scare Tactics: The Politics of International Rivalry*. Syracuse, NY: Syracuse University Press.

Colaresi, Michael, and William R. Thompson (2002) "Hot Spots or Hot Hands? Serial Crises Behavior, Escalating Risks and Rivalry." *Journal of Politics*, 64: 1175–98.

Colaresi, Michael, Karen Rasler, and William R. Thompson (2007) *Strategic Rivalry: Space, Position and Conflict Escalation in World Politics*. Cambridge: Cambridge University Press.

Collier, Paul, and Anke Hoeffler (2004) "Greed and Grievance in Civil War." *Oxford Economic Papers*, 56: 563–95.

Collier, Paul, Anke Hoeffler, and Mans Soderbom (2004) "On the Duration of Civil War." *Journal of Peace Research*, 41, 3: 253–73.

Collier, Paul, and Nicholas Sambanis (2005) *Understanding Civil War: Evidence and Analysis*. Vol. 1: *Africa*; Vol. 2: *Europe, Central Asia, and Other Regions*. Washington, DC: World Bank Publications.

Collier, Paul, V.L. Elliott, Håvard Hegre, Anke Hoeffler, Marta Reynal-Querol, and Nicholas Sambanis (2003) *Breaking the Conflict Trap: Civil War and Development Policy*. Washington, DC: The World Bank and Oxford University Press.

Copeland, Dale C. (1996) "Economic Interdependence and War: A Theory of Trade Expectations." *International Security*, 20, 4: 5–41.

Copeland, Dale C. (2000) *The Origins of Major Wars*. Ithaca: Cornell University Press.

Cornford, Francis M. (1971) *Thucydides Mythhistoricus*. Philadelphia, PA: Pennsylvania University Press.

Coser, Lewis (1956) *The Function of Social Conflict*. New York: Free Press.

Council on Foreign Relations (1993) *The Clash of Civilizations? The Debate. A Foreign Affairs Reader*. New York: Council on Foreign Relations.

Craig, Gordon A. (1955) *The Politics of the Prussian Army, 1940–1945*. Oxford: Oxford University Press.

Crawford, Timothy W. (2003) *Pivotal Deterrence: Third-Party Statecraft and the Pursuit of Peace*. Ithaca: Cornell University Press.

Crescenzi, Mark J.C. (2005) *Economic Interdependence and Conflict in World Politics*. Lanham, MD: Lexington Books.

Crescenzi, Mark J.C. (2007) "Reputation and Interstate Conflict." *American Journal of Political Science*, 51, 2 (April): 382–96.

Cyert, R. M., and James G. March (1963) *A Behavioral Theory of the Firm*. Englewood Cliffs, NJ: Prentice Hall.

Daase, Christopher (2007) "Clausewitz and Small Wars." In Hew Strachan and Andreas Herberg-Rothe, eds., *Clausewitz in the Twenty-First Century*. Oxford: Oxford University Press, pp. 182–95.

Dahrendorf, Ralf (1959) *Class and Conflict in Industrial Society*. Stanford, CA: Stanford University Press.

Damasio, Antonio. R. (1994) *Descartes' Error: Emotion, Reason, and the Human Brain*. New York: G. P. Putnam's Sons.

Danner, Mark (2006) *Secret Way to War: The Downing Street Memo and the Iraq War's Buried History*. New York: New York Review Books.

Davies, James C. (1962) "Toward a Theory of Revolution." *American Sociological Review*, 29: 5–19.

Davis, James W., Jr. (2000) *Threats and Promises*. Baltimore: Johns Hopkins University Press.

DeRouen, Karl, Jr., and Jacob Bercovitch (2008) "Enduring Internal Rivalries: A New Framework for the Study of Civil War." *Journal of Peace Research*, 45: 55–74.

Desch, Michael C. (1996) "War and Strong States, Peace and Weak States?" *International Organization*, 50, 2 (Spring): 237–68.

Desch, Michael C. (2008) *Power and Military Effectiveness: The Fallacy of Democratic Triumphalism*. Baltimore: Johns Hopkins University Press.

de Soysa, Indra (2002) "Paradise is a Bazaar? Greed, Creed, and Governance in Civil War, 1989–1999." *Journal of Peace Research*, 39: 395–416.

Deutsch, Harold C. (1974) *Hitler and His Generals: The Hidden Crisis, January–June 1938*. Minneapolis, MN: University of Minnesota Press.

Deutsch, Karl W., and J. David Singer (1964) "Multipolar Power Systems and International Stability." *World Politics*, 16: 390–406.

DeYoung, Karen (2006) *Soldier: The Life of Colin Powell*. New York, NY: Alfred A. Knopf.

DiCicco, Jonathan M., and Jack S. Levy (2003) "The Power Transition Research Program: A Lakatosian Analysis." In Colin Elman and Miriam Fendius Elman, eds., *Progress in International Relations Theory: Appraising the Field*. Cambridge, MA: MIT Press, pp. 109–57.

Diehl, Paul F. (1983) "Arms Races and Escalation: A Closer Look" *Journal of Peace Research*, 20: 205–12.

Diehl, Paul F. (1998) *The Dynamics of Enduring Rivalries*. Urbana: University of Illinois Press.

Diehl, Paul F., and Gary Goertz (2000) *War and Peace in International Rivalry*. Ann Arbor, MI: University of Michigan Press.

Dixon, William J. (1994) "Democracy and the Peaceful Settlement of International Conflict." *American Political Science Review*, 88, 1: 14–32.

Dobbs, Michael (2008) *One Minute to Midnight: Kennedy, Khrushchev, and Castro on the Brink of Nuclear War*. New York: Knopf.

Domhoff, William G. (1967) *Who Rules America?* Englewood Cliffs, NJ: Prentice Hall.

Doran, Charles F. (1991) *Systems in Crisis: New Imperatives of High Politics at Century's End*. Cambridge: Cambridge University Press.

Dower, John W. (1987) *War without Mercy: Race & Power in the Pacific War*. New York: Pantheon.

Downes, Alexander (2009) "How Smart and Tough are Democracies? Reassessing Theories of Democratic Victory in War." *International Security*, 33, 4 (Spring): 9–51.

Downs, George W., and David M. Rocke (1994) "Conflict, Agency, and Gambling for Resurrection: The Principal–Agent Problem Goes to War." *American Journal of Political Science*, 38 (May): 362–80.

Doyle, Michael (1983) "Kant, Liberal Legacies, and Foreign Affairs," Parts I & II. *Philosophy & Public Affairs*, 12 (Fall): 205–35, 323–53.

Doyle, Michael W. (1997) *Ways of War and Peace*. New York: W.W. Norton.

Doyle, Michael (2008) *Striking First: Preemption and Prevention in International Conflict*, ed. Stephen Macedo. Princeton, NJ: Princeton University Press.

Dray, William H. (1957) *Laws and Explanation in History*. London: Oxford University Press.

Dreyer, David R., and William R. Thompson (<forthcoming>) *Handbook of Interstate Rivalries*. Washington, DC: Congressional Quarterly Press.

Durbin, E.F.M., and Bowlby, J. (1939) *Personal Aggressiveness and War*. London: Kegan Paul.

Duyvesteyn, Isabelle, and Jan Angstrom, eds., (2005) *Rethinking the Nature of War*. London: Frank Cass.

Easton, David (1953) *The Political System*. New York: Knopf.

Eckstein, Harry (1965) "On the Etiology of Internal Wars." *History and Theory*, 4: 133–63.

Einstein, A., and Freud, S. (1932) *Why War?* Paris: International Institute of Intellectual Cooperation.

Elbadawi, Ibrahim, and Nicholas Sambanis (2002) "How Much War Will We See? Explaining the Prevalence of Civil War." *Journal of Conflict Research*, 46: 307–34.

Ellsberg, Daniel (1972) "The Quagmire Myth and the Stalemate Machine." In Daniel Ellsberg, *Papers on the War*. New York: Simon & Schuster, pp. 42–135.

Elman, Colin (1996) "Why *Not* Neorealist Theories of Foreign Policy?" *Security Studies*, 6, 1 (Autumn): 7–53.

Elman, Colin (2004) "Extending Offensive Realism: The Louisiana Purchase and America's Rise to Regional Hegemony." *American Political Science Review*, 98, 4 (November): 563–76.

Elman, Colin, and Miriam Fendius Elman, eds. (2003) *Progress in International Relations Theory*. Cambridge, MA: MIT Press.

Elman, Miriam Fendius (2000) "Unpacking Democracy: Presidentialism, Parliamentarism, and Theories of Democratic Peace." *Security Studies*, 9, 4 (Summer): 91–126.

Elshtain, Jean Bethke (1987) *Women and War*. New York: Basic Books.

English, Robert (2000) *Russia and the Idea of the West: Gorbachev, Intellectuals, and the End of the Cold War*. New York: Columbia University Press.

Enterline, Andrew J., and Krisian S. Gleditsch (2000) "Threats, Opportunity, and Force: Repression and Diversion of Domestic Pressure, 1948–1982." *International Interactions*, 26, 1: 21–53.

Farber, Henry S., and Joanne Gowa (1995) "Politics and Peace." *International Security*, 20, 2 (Fall): 123–46.

Farnham, Barbara (1994) *Taking Risks/Avoiding Losses*. Ann Arbor, MI: University of Michigan Press.

Farrell, Theo (2005) *The Norms of War: Cultural Beliefs and Modern Conflict*. Boulder, CO: Lynne Rienner.

Fay, Sidney B. (1928) *The Origins of the World War*, 2 vols. New York: Macmillan.

Fearon, James D. (1995) "Rationalist Explanations for War." *International Organization*, 49, 3: 379–414.

Fearon, James D. (1998) "Commitment Problems and the Spread of Ethnic Conflict." In David A. Lake and Donald Rothchild, eds., *The International Spread of Ethnic Conflict*. Princeton, NJ: Princeton University Press, pp. 107–26.

Fearon, James D. (2004) "Why Do Some Civil Wars Last So Longer Than Others?" *Journal of Peace Research*, 41: 275–301.

Fearon, James D., and David D. Laitin (1996) "Explaining Interethnic Cooperation." *American Political Science Review*, 90, 4 (December): 715–35.

Fearon, James D., and David D. Laitin (2003) "Ethnicity, Insurgency and Civil War." *American Political Science Review*, 97: 75–90.

Fearon, James D., and David D. Laitin (2008) "Integrating Qualitative and Quantitative Methods." In Janet Box-Steffensmeier, Henry Brady, and David Collier, eds., *Oxford Handbook of Political Methodology*. New York: Oxford University Press, pp. 756–76.

Fearon, James, and Alexander Wendt (2002) "Rationalism vs. Constructivism: A Skeptical View." In Walter Carlsnaes, Thomas Risse, and Beth A. Simmons, eds., *International Relations*. London: Sage, pp. 52–72.

Feaver, Peter, and Richard Kohn, eds. (2001) *Soldiers and Civilians: The Civil–Military Gap and American National Security*. Cambridge, MA: MIT Press.

Ferejohn, John (1991) "Rationality and Interpretation: Parliamentary Elections in Early Stuart England." In Kristen Redwick Monroe, ed., *The Economic Approach to Politics: A Critical Reassessment of the Theory of Rational Action.* New York: HarperCollins.

Ferguson, R. Brian (1999) "A Paradigm for the Study of War and Society." In Kurt Raaflaub and Nathan Rosenstein, eds., *War and Society in the Ancient and Medieval Worlds.* Cambridge, MA: Harvard University Press, pp. 389–437.

Ferrill, Arther (1997) *The Origins of War: From the Stone Age to Alexander the Great*, 2nd ed. Boulder, CO: Westview.

Finlay, David J., Ole R. Holsti, and Richard R. Fagan (1967) *Enemies in Politics.* Chicago: Rand McNally.

Finnemore, Martha (2003) *The Purpose of Intervention: Changing Beliefs about the Use of Force.* Ithaca, NY: Cornell University Press.

Fischer, Fritz (1967) *Germany's Aims in the First World War.* New York: W.W. Norton.

Fischer, Fritz (1974) *World Power or Decline*, trans. L.L. Farrar et al. New York: Norton.

Fischer, Fritz (1975) *War of Illusions*, trans. Marian Jackson. New York: Norton.

Fischer, Fritz (1988) "The Miscalculation of English Neutrality." In Solomon Wank, et al., eds., *The Mirror of History.* Santa Barbara, CA: ABC-Clio, pp. 369–93.

Fogel, Robert William (1964) *Railroads and American Economic Growth.* Baltimore: Johns Hopkins University Press.

Fordham, Benjamin O. (1998) *Building the Cold War Consensus: The Political Economy of U.S. National Security Policy, 1949–51.* Ann Arbor, MI: University of Michigan Press.

Förster, Stig (1999) "Dreams and Nightmares: German Military Leadership and the Images of FutureWarfare, 1871–1914." In Manfred F. Boemeke, Roger Chickering, and Stig Förster, eds., *Anticipating Total War: The German and American Experiences, 1871–1914.* Washington, DC: German Historical Institute, pp. 343–76.

Fortna, Virginia Page (2008) *Does Peacekeeping Work? Shaping Belligerents' Choices after Civil War.* Princeton, NJ: Princeton University Press.

Freedman, Lawrence, and Virginia Gamba-Stonehouse (1990) *Signals of War: The Falklands Conflict of 1982.* London: Faber and Faber.

Freedman, Lawrence, and Efraim Karsh (1993) *The Gulf Conflict, 1990/91.* Princeton, NJ: Princeton University Press.

Gaddis, John Lewis (1987) *The Long Peace.* New York: Oxford University Press.

Gaddis, John Lewis (1992/93) "International Relations Theory and the End of the Cold War." *International Security*, 17, 3 (Winter): 5–58.

Gaddis, John Lewis (1997) *We Now Know: Rethinking Cold War History.* Oxford: Clarendon Press.

Gagnon, V.P., Jr. (2004) *The Myth of Ethnic War: Serbia and Croatia in the 1990s.* Ithaca, NY: Cornell University Press.

Gallucci, Robert I. (1975) *Neither Peace Nor Honor.* Baltimore: Johns Hopkins University Press.

Ganguly, Sumit (2002) *Conflict Unending: India–Pakistan Tensions Since 1947.* New Delhi: Oxford University Press.

Garthoff, Raymond (1985) *Deterrence and Confrontation: American–Soviet Relations from Nixon to Reagan*. Washington DC: Brookings.

Gartner, Scott Sigmund (2008) "The Multiple Effects of Casualties on Public Support for War: An Experimental Approach." *The American Political Science Review*, 102, 1: 95–106.

Gartner, Scott Sigmund, Gary M. Segura, and Bethany Barratt (2004) "War Casualties, Policy Positions, and the Fate of Legislators." *Political Research Quarterly*, 53, 3: 467–77.

Gartzke, Erik (1999) "War Is in the Error Term." *International Organization*, 53, 3 (Summer): 567–87.

Gartzke, Erik (2000) "Preferences and the Democratic Peace." *International Studies Quarterly*, 44, 2 (June): 191–212.

Gartzke, Erik (2007) "The Capitalist Peace." *American Journal of Political Science*, 51, 1 (January): 161–91.

Gartzke, Erik, Quan Li, and Charles Boehmer (2001) "Investing in the Peace: Economic Interdependence and International Conflict." *International Organization*, 55, 2: 391–438.

Gartzke, Eric, and Michael Simon (1999) "Hot Hand: A Critical Analysis of Enduring Rivalries." *Journal of Politics*, 61: 777–98.

Gat, Azar (2006) *War in Human Civilization*. New York: Oxford University Press.

Gates, Scott (2002) "Recruitment and Allegiance: the Microfoundations of Rebellion." *Journal of Conflict Resolution*, 46, 1 (February): 111–30.

Gaubatz, Kurt (1999) *Elections and War*. Stanford, CA: Stanford University Press.

Geddes, Barbara (2003) *Paradigms and Sandcastles: Theory Building and Research Design in Comparative Politics*. Ann Arbor, MI: University of Michigan Press.

Gelpi, Christopher (1997) "Democratic Diversions: Governmental Structure and the Externalization of Domestic Conflict." *Journal of Conflict Resolution*, 41, 2: 255–82.

George, Alexander L. (1969) "The 'Operational Code': A Neglected Approach to the Study of Political Leaders and Decisionmaking." *International Studies Quarterly*, 13, 2 (June): 190–222.

George, Alexander L. (1980) *Presidential Decisionmaking in Foreign Policy: The Effective Use of Information and Advice*. Boulder, CO: Westview.

George, Alexander L., ed. (1991) *Avoiding War: Problems of Crisis Management*. Boulder, CO: Westview.

George, Alexander L. (1994) "The Cuban Missile Crisis: Peaceful Resolution Through Coercive Diplomacy." In George and William R. Simons, eds., *The Limits of Coercive Diplomacy*, 2nd ed. Boulder, CO: Westview, pp. 111–32.

George, Alexander L., and Andrew Bennett (2005) *Case Studies and Theory Development in the Social Sciences*. Cambridge, MA: MIT Press.

George, Alexander L., and Juliette L. George (1956) *Woodrow Wilson and Colonel House: A Personality Study*. New York: John Day.

George, Alexander L., and Richard Smoke (1974) *Deterrence in American Foreign Policy*. New York: Columbia University Press.

Ghobarah, Hazem, Paul Huth, and Bruce Russett (2003) "Civil Wars Kill and Maim People – Long after the Shooting Stops." *American Political Science Review*, 97: 189–202.

Gibler, Douglas M. (2000) "Alliances: Why Some Cause War and Others Cause Peace." In John A. Vasquez, ed., *What Do We Know About War?*" Lanham, MD: Rowman & Littlefield, pp. 145–64.

Gibler, Douglas M. (2007) "Bordering on Peace: Democracy, Territorial Issues and Conflict." *International Studies Quarterly*, 51 (September): 509–32.

Gibler, Douglas, Toby J. Rider, and Marc L. Hutchison (2005) "Taking Arms Against a Sea of Troubles: Conventional Arms Races During Periods of Rivalry." *Journal of Peace Research*, 42: 131–47.

Gilpin, Robert (1975) *U.S. Power and the Multinational Corporation: The Political Economy of Foreign Direct Investment*. New York: Basic Books.

Gilpin, Robert (1981) *War and Change in World Politics*. New York: Cambridge University Press.

Gilpin, Robert (1986) "The Richness of the Tradition of Political Realism." In Robert O. Keohane, ed., *Neorealism and Its Critics*. New York: Columbia University Press, pp. 301–21.

Glaser, Charles L. (1997) "The Security Dilemma Revisited." *World Politics*, 50, 1: 171–201.

Glaser, Charles L. (2004) "When Are Arms Races Dangerous: Rational versus Suboptimal Arming." *International Security*, 28, 4 (Spring): 44–84.

Gleditsch, Nils Petter (1995) "Geography, Democracy, and Peace." *International Interactions*, 20: 297–323.

Gleditsch, Nils Petter (2008) "The Liberal Moment Fifteen Years On." *International Studies Quarterly*, 52, 4 (December): 691–712.

Gochal, Joseph R., and Jack S. Levy (2004) "Crisis Mismanagement or Conflict of Interests? A Case Study of the Crimean War." In Zeev Maoz, Alex Mintz, T. Clifton Morgan, Glenn Palmer, and Richard J. Stoll et al, eds., *Multiple Paths to Knowledge in International Relations: Methodology in the Study of Conflict Management and Conflict Resolution*. Lexington, MA: Lexington Books, pp. 309–42.

Goemans, H.E. (2000) *War & Punishment: The Causes of War Termination and the First World War*. Princeton, NJ: Princeton University Press.

Goertz, Gary (2004) "Constraints, Compromises and Decision Making." *Journal of Conflict Resolution*, 48, 1: 14–37.

Goertz, Gary, and Paul Diehl (1995) "The Initiation and Termination of Enduring Rivalries: The Impact of Political Shocks." *American Journal of Political Science*, 39: 30–52.

Goertz, Gary, and Jack S. Levy (2007) "Causal Explanation, Necessary Conditions, and Case Studies." In Gary Goertz and Jack S. Levy, eds., *Explaining War and Peace: Case Studies and Necessary Condition Counterfactuals*. New York: Routledge, pp. 9–45.

Goldstein, Joshua S. (1988) *Long Cycles*. New Haven: Yale University Press.

Goldstein, Joshua S. (2001) *War and Gender*. New York: Cambridge University Press.

Goldstone, Jack A. (1991) *Revolution and Rebellion in the Early Modern World*. Berkeley, CA: University of California Press.

Goodwin, Jeff (2001) *No Other Way Out: States and Revolutionary Movements, 1945–1991*. Cambridge: Cambridge University Press.

Gordon, Michael R., and General Bernard E. Trainor (2006) *Cobra II: The Inside Story of the Invasion and Occupation of Iraq*. New York: Pantheon Books.

Gowa, Joanne (1994) *Allies, Adversaries, and International Trade*. Princeton, NJ: Princeton University Press.

Gowa, Joanne (1999) *Ballots and Bullets*. Princeton, NJ: Princeton University Press.

Grieco, Joseph M. (1990) *Cooperation Among Nations*. Ithaca, NY: Cornell University Press.

Guetzkow, Harold (1950) "Long Range Research in International Relations." *American Perspective*, 4: 421–40.

Gulick, Edward V. (1955) *Europe's Classical Balance of Power*. Ithaca, NY: Cornell University Press.

Gurr, Ted Robert (1970) *Why Men Rebel*. Princeton, NJ: Princeton University Press.

Gurr, Ted Robert (2000). *People Versus States: Minorities at Risk in the New Century*. Washington, DC: United States Institute of Peace.

Haas, Jonathan (1999) "The Origins of War and Ethnic Violence." In John Carman and Anthony Harding, eds., *Ancient Warfare: Archaeological Perspectives*. Gloucestershire, UK: Sutton Publishing.

Haas, Mark L. (2005) *The Ideological Origins of Great Power Politics, 1789–1989*. Ithaca, NY: Cornell University Press.

Haass, Richard N. (2009) *War of Necessity, War of Choice: A Memoir of Two Iraq Wars*. New York: Simon & Schuster.

Haftendorn, Helga, Robert O. Keohane, and Celeste A. Wallander, eds. (1999) *Imperfect Unions: Security Institutions over Time and Space*. Oxford: Oxford University Press.

Haggard, Stephan, and Robert R. Kaufman (1995) *The Political Economy of Democratic Transitions*. Princeton University Press.

Halberstam, David (1969) *The Best and the Brightest*. Greenwich, CT: Fawcett.

Halperin, Morton H. (1974) *Bureaucratic Politics and Foreign Policy*. Washington, DC: Brookings.

Halperin, Morton, and Arnold Kanter, ed. (1973) *Readings in American Foreign Policy*. Boston, MA: Little Brown.

Harbom, Lotta, and Ralph Sundberg, eds. (2008) *States in Armed Conflict 2007*. Uppsala, Sweden: Uppsala University, Department of Peace and Conflict Research, Research Report 83.

Hart, Paul 't (1990) *Groupthink in Government: A Study of Small Groups and Policy Failure*. Amsterdam: Swets and Zeitlinger.

Hart, Paul 't, Eric K. Stern, and Bengt Sundelius, eds. (1997) *Beyond Groupthink: Political Group Dynamics and Foreign Policy-making*. Ann Arbor, MI: University of Michigan Press.

Harvey, Frank P. (2008) *"President Al Gore and the 2003 Iraq War: A Counterfactual Critique of Conventional Wisdom."* Calgary, Alberta: Canadian Defence and Foreign Affairs Institute. www.cdfai.org

Haslam, Jonathan (2002) *No Virtue like Necessity: Realist Thought in International Relations since Machiavelli*. New York: Cambridge University Press.

Hassner, Pierre (1996) "Morally Objectionable, Politically Dangerous." *The National Interest*, 46 (Winter): 63–9.

Heckhausen, Heinz, and Peter M. Gollwitzer (1987) "Thought Contents and Cognitive Functioning in Motivational Versus Volitional States of Mind." *Motivation and Emotion*, 11, 2: 101–20.

Hegre, Håvard (2000) "Development and the Liberal Peace: What Does it Take to Be a Trading State?" *Journal of Peace Research*, 37, 1: 5–30.

Hegre, Håvard, and Nicholas Sambanis (2006) "Sensitivity Analysis of Empirical Results on Civil War Onset." *Journal of Conflict Resolution*, 50: 508–35.

Hegre, Håvard, Tanja Ellingsen, Scott Gates, and Nils Petter Gleditsch (2001) "Towards a Democratic Civil Peace: Democracy, Democratization, and Civil War, 1834–1992." *American Political Science Review*, 95, 1 (March), 33–48.

Henderson, Errol A. (2002) *Democracy and War: The End of an Illusion?* Boulder, CO: Lynne Rienner.

Hensel, Paul R. (1994) "One Thing Leads to Another: Recurrent Militarized Disputes in Latin America, 1816–1986." *Journal of Peace Research*, 31: 281–98.

Hensel, Paul R. (2000) "Theory and Evidence on Geography and Conflict." In John A. Vasquez, ed., *What Do We Know About War?*" Lanham, MD: Rowman & Littlefield, pp. 57–84.

Hensel, Paul, and Gary Goertz (2000) "The Democratic Peace and Rivalries." *Journal of Politics*, 62: 1173–88.

Hermann, Charles F. (1969) *Crises in Foreign Policy*. Indianapolis: Bobbs-Merrill.

Hermann, Margaret G. (1986) *Political Psychology*. San Francisco: Jossey-Bass.

Hermann, Margaret G. (2001) "How Decision Units Shape Foreign Policy: A Theoretical Framework." *International Studies Review*, 3, 2 (Summer): 47–82.

Hermann, Margaret G., Thomas Preston, Baghat Korany, and Timothy M. Shaw (2001) "Who Leads Matters: The Effects of Powerful Individuals." *International Studies Review*, 3, 2 (Summer): 83–132.

Herz, John H. (1951) *Political Realism and Political Idealism: A Study in Theories and Realities*. Chicago: University of Chicago Press.

Herz, John H. (1959) *International Politics in the Atomic Age*. New York: Columbia University Press.

Hewitt, J. Joseph, Jonathan Wilkenfeld, and Ted Robert Gurr (2008). *Peace and Conflict 2008*. Boulder, CO: Paradigm.

Higgins, Trumbull (1987) *The Perfect Failure: Kennedy, Eisenhower, and the CIA at the Bay of Pigs*. New York: Norton.

Higgs, Robert (2006) *Depression, War, and Cold War*. New York: Oxford University Press.

Hilferding, Rudolph ([1910]1981) *Finance Capital: A Study of the Latest Phase of Capitalist Development*, trans. Morris Watnick and Sam Gordon, ed. Tom Bottomore. London and Boston: Routledge & Kegan Paul.

Hinde, Robert A. (1993) "Aggression and War: Individuals, Groups and States." In Philip E. Tetlock, Jo L. Husbands, Robert Jervis, Paul C. Stern, and Charles Tilly, eds., *Behavior, Society, and International Conflict*, Vol. III. New York: Oxford University Press, pp. 8–70.

Hinsley, F. H. (1967) *Power and the Pursuit of Peace: Theory and Practice in the History of Relations between States*. London: Cambridge University Press.

Hiro, Dilip (1991) *The Longest War: The Iran–Iraq Military Conflict*. New York: Routledge.

Hironaka, Ann (2005) *Neverending Wars: The International Community, Weak States, and the Perpetuation of Civil War*. Cambridge, MA: Harvard University Press.

Hirschman, Albert O. ([1945]1980) *National Power and the Structure of Foreign Trade*. Berkeley: University of California Press.

Hobson, J.A. ([1902]1965) *Imperialism*. Ann Arbor, MI: University of Michigan Press.

Hoddie, Mathew, and Jason M. Smith (2009) "Forms of Civil War Violence and Their Consequences for Future Public Health." *International Studies Quarterly*, 53: 175–202.

Hoffmann, Stanley (1963) "Rousseau on War and Peace." *American Political Science Review*, 57: 137–333.

Holsti, Kalevi J. (1991) *Peace and War: Armed Conflicts and International Order, 1648–1989*. New York: Cambridge University Press.

Holsti, Kalevi J. (1996) *The State, War, and the State of War*. New York: Cambridge University Press.

Holsti, Ole R. (1967) "Cognitive Dynamics and Images of the Enemy." In John Farrell and Asa Smith, eds., *Image and Reality in World Politics*. New York: Columbia University Press, pp. 16–39.

Holsti, Ole R. (1970) "The 'Operational Code' Approach to the Study of Political Leaders: John Foster Dulles' Philosophical and Instrumental Belief." *Canadian Journal of Political Science*, 3: 123–57.

Holsti, Ole R. (1989) "Crisis Decision-Making." In Philip E. Tetlock, Jo L. Husbands, Robert Jervis, Paul C. Stern, and Charles Tilly, eds., *Behavior, Society, and Nuclear War*, Vol. 1. New York: Oxford University Press, pp. 8–84.

Holsti, Ole R., and Alexander L. George (1975) "The Effects of Stress on the Performance of Foreign Policy-Makers." In C. P. Cotter, *Political Science Annual*. Indianapolis, IN: Bobbs-Merrill, pp. 255–319.

Holsti, Ole R., P.T. Hoppman, and J.D. Sullivan (1973) *Unity and Disintegration in International Alliances*. New York: John Wiley.

Hopf, Ted (2002) *Social Construction of International Politics: Identities and Foreign Policies, Moscow, 1955 and 1999*. Ithaca, NY: Cornell University Press.

Horowitz, Donald L. (1985) *Ethnic Groups in Conflict*. Berkeley, CA: University of California Press.

Howard, Michael (1976) *War in European History*. Oxford: Oxford University Press.

Howard, Michael (1983) *Clausewitz*. Oxford: Oxford University Press.

Hudson, Valerie M. (2002) "Foreign Policy Decision-Making: A Touchstone for International Relations Theory in the Twenty-first Century." In Richard C. Snyder, H.W. Bruck, and Burton Sapin, *Foreign Policy Decision-Making (Revisited)*. New York: Palgrave, pp. 1–20.

Hudson, Valerie M., and Andrea M. Den Boer. (2005) *Bare Branches: The Security Implications of Asia's Surplus Male Population*. Cambridge, MA: MIT Press.

Hui, Victoria Tin-bor (2004) *War and State Formation in Ancient China and Early Modern Europe*. Cambridge University Press.

Hull, Isabel V. (2005) *Absolute Destruction: Military Culture and the Practices of War in Imperial Germany.* Ithaca, NY: Cornell University Press.

Human Security Centre (2005) *Human Security Report 2005: War and Peace in the 21st Century.* New York: Oxford University Press.

Hume, David ([1748]1902) *An Enquiry Concerning Human Understanding,* ed. L. A. Selby-Bigge. Oxford: Clarendon Press.

Hunt, Gaillard, ed. (1906) *The Writings of James Madison:* Vol. VI: 1790–1802. New York: G.P. Putnam's Sons.

Huntington, Samuel P. (1958) "Arms Races: Prerequisites and Results." *Public Policy,* 8: 41–86.

Huntington, Samuel P. (1968) *Political Order in Changing Societies.* New Haven, CT: Yale University Press.

Huntington, Samuel P. (1993a) "Why International Primacy Matters." *International Security,* 17, 4 (Spring): 68–83.

Huntington, Samuel P. (1993b) "The Clash of Civilizations?" *Foreign Affairs,* 72, 3 (Summer): 22–9.

Huntington, Samuel P. (1996) *The Clash of Civilizations and the Remaking of World Order.* New York: Simon & Schuster.

Huth, Paul (1996a) "Enduring Rivalries and Territorial Disputes, 1950–1990." *Conflict Management and Peace Science,* 15: 7–41.

Huth, Paul K. (1996b) *Standing Your Guard: Territorial Disputes and International Conflict.* Ann Arbor, MI: University of Michigan Press.

Huth, Paul K. (2000) "Territory: Why Are Territorial Disputes between States a Central Cause of International Conflict?" In John A. Vasquez, ed., *What Do We Know About War?"* Lanham, MD: Rowman & Littlefield, pp. 85–110.

Ienaga, Saburo (1978) *The Pacific War, 1931–1945.* New York: Pantheon.

Iggers, George G. (1994) *New Directions in European Historiography,* rev. ed. Middletown, CT: Wesleyan University Press.

Ikenberry, G. John. (2000) *After Victory: Institutions, Strategic Restraint, and the Rebuilding of Order After Major Wars.* Princeton, NJ: Princeton University Press.

Ikenberry, G. John (2002) "Introduction." In G. John Ikenberry, ed., *America Unrivaled.* Ithaca, NY: Cornell University Press.

Ikenberry, G. John, David A. Lake, and Michael Mastanduno (1988) "Introduction: approaches to explaining American foreign economic policy." *International Organization,* 42, 1 (Winter), pp. 1–14.

Ikenberry, G. John, Michael Mastanduno, and William C. Wohlforth (2009) "Introduction: Unipolarity, State Behavior, and Systemic Consequences." *World Politics,* 61, 1 (January): 1–27.

Iklé, Fred C. (1971) *Every War Must End.* New York: Columbia University Press.

Imlay, Talbot C. (2003) *Facing the Second World War: Strategy, Politics, and Economics in Britain and France, 1938–1940.* New York: Oxford University Press.

Iriye, Akira (1987) *The Origins of the Second World War in Asia and the Pacific.* New York: Longman.

Jaggers, Keith, and Ted Robert Gurr (1995) "Tracking Democracy's Third Wave with the Polity III Data." *Journal of Peace Research,* 32: 469–82.

James, Patrick (1995) "Structural Realism and the Causes of War." *Mershon International Studies Review*, 39: 181–208.

James, Patrick, and Glenn E. Mitchell II (1995) "Targets of Covert Pressure: The Hidden Victims of the Democratic Peace." *International Interactions*, 21, 1: 85–107.

James, Patrick, and John R. Oneal (1991) "The Influence of Domestic and International Politics on the President's Use of Force." *Journal of Conflict Resolution*, 35 (June): 307–32.

Janis, Irving L. (1982) *Groupthink: Psychological Studies of Policy Decisions and Fiascoes*, 2nd ed. Boston, MA: Houghton Mifflin.

Janis, Irving L., and Leon Mann (1977) *Decision Making: A Psychological Analysis of Conflict, Choice, and Commitment*. New York: Free Press.

Jervis, Robert (1970) *The Logic of Images in International Relations*. Princeton, NJ: Princeton University Press.

Jervis, Robert (1976) *Perception and Misperception in International Politics*. Princeton, NJ: Princeton University Press.

Jervis, Robert (1978) "Cooperation under the Security Dilemma." *World Politics*, 30, 2: 186–213.

Jervis, Robert (1982) "Security Regimes." *International Organization*, 36 (Spring): 357–78.

Jervis, Robert (1985) "Perceiving and Coping with Threat." In Robert Jervis, Richard Ned Lebow, and Janice Gross Stein, *Psychology and Deterrence*. Baltimore: Johns Hopkins University Press, pp. 13–33.

Jervis, Robert (1988) "War and Misperception." *Journal of Interdisciplinary History*, 18, 4 (Spring): 675–700.

Jervis, Robert (1989) *The Meaning of the Nuclear Revolution*. Princeton, NJ: Princeton University Press.

Jervis, Robert (1992) "Political Implications of Loss Aversion." *Political Psychology*, 13, 2 (June): 187–204.

Jervis, Robert (1998) "Realism in the Study of World Politics." *International Organization*, 52, 4 (Autumn): 971–91.

Jervis, Robert (2002) "Theories of War in an Era o Leading-Power Peace." *American Political Science Review*, 96, 1 (March): 1–14.

Jervis, Robert (2006) "Reports, Politics, and Intelligence Failure: The Case of Iraq." *The Journal of Strategic Studies*, 29, 1 (February): 3–52.

Johnson, Dominic D.P. (2004) *Overconfidence and War: The Havoc and Glory of Positive Illusions*. Cambridge, MA: Harvard University Press.

Johnson, Dominic D.P., and Dominic Tierney (2006) *Failing to Win: Perceptions of Victory and Defeat in International Politics*. Cambridge, MA: Harvard University Press.

Johnson, Dominic D.P., and Dominic Tierney (2007) "We Shall be Smashed: The Munich Crisis, Underconfidence, and War." Unpublished manuscript.

Johnson, Dominic D.P., and Dominic Tierney. (2009) "The Rubicon Model of War." Unpublished manuscript.

Johnston, Alastair Iain (1995) *Cultural Realism: Strategic Culture and Grand Strategy in Chinese History*. Princeton, NJ: Princeton University Press.

Joll, James (1984) *The Origins of the First World War*. London: Longman.

Jones, Daniel M., Stuart A. Bremer, and J. David Singer (1996) "Militarized Inter-state Disputes, 1816–1992: Rationale, Coding Rules, and Empirical Patterns." *Conflict Management and Peace Science*, 15, 2 (June): 163–213.

Kacowicz, Arie Marcelo, Yaacov Bar-Siman-Tov, Ole Elgstrom, and Magnus Jerneck (2000) *Stable Peace Among Nations*. Lanham, MD: Rowman & Littlefield.

Kadera, Kelly M. (2001) *The Power–Conflict Story: A Dynamic Model of Interstate Rivalry*. Ann Arbor, MI: University of Michigan Press.

Kagan, Donald (2003) *The Peloponnesian War*. New York: Viking.

Kahneman, Daniel (2003) "Maps of Bounded Rationality: Psychology for Behavioral Economics" *American Economic Review*, 93 (December): 1449–75.

Kahneman, Daniel, and Amos Tversky (1979) "Prospect Theory: An Analysis of Decision Under Risk." *Econometrica*, 47, 2 (March): 263–91.

Kahneman, Daniel, Jack L. Knetsch, and Richard H. Thaler (1990). "Experimental Tests of the Endowment Effect and the Coase Theorem." *Journal of Political Economy*, 98, 6 (December): 1325–48.

Kahneman, Daniel, Paul Slovic, and Amos Tversky (1982) *Judgment Under Uncertainty: Heuristics and biases*. New York: Cambridge University Press.

Kaiser, David E. (1983) "Germany and the Origins of the First World War." *Journal of Modern History*, 55 (September): 442–74.

Kaldor, Mary (1999) *New and Old Wars: Organized Violence in a Global Era*. Stanford, CA: Stanford University Press.

Kalyvas, Stathis N. (2001) " 'New' and 'Old' Civil Wars: A Valid Distinction?" *World Politics*, 54, 1: 99–118.

Kalyvas, Stathis N. (2006) *The Logic of Violence in Civil War*. New York: Cambridge University Press.

Kalyvas, Stathis N. (2008) "Promises and Pitfalls of an Emerging Research Program: The Microdynamics of Civil War." In Stathis N. Kalyvas, Ian Shapiro, and Tarek Masoud, eds., *Order, Conflict and Violence*. Cambridge: Cambridge University Press, pp. 397–421.

Kalyvas, Stathis N., and Laia Balcells (2009) "International System and Technologies of Rebellion: How the Cold War Shaped Internal Conflict." Unpublished paper: Yale University.

Kang, Seonjou, and James Meernik (2005) "Civil War Destruction and the Prospects for Civil War Growth." *Journal of Politics*, 67: 88–109.

Kant, Immanuel ([1795]1949) "Eternal Peace." In C.J. Frederich, ed., *The Philosophy of Kant* New York: Modern Library, pp. 430–76.

Kaplan, Robert D. (1993) *Balkan Ghosts*. New York: Vintage.

Kassimeris, George, ed. (2006) *The Barbarization of Warfare*. New York: New York University Press.

Katzenstein, Peter J., ed. (1996) *The Culture of National Security: Norms and Identity in World Politics*. New York: Columbia University Press.

Kaufman, Chaim (2004) "Threat Inflation and the Failure of the Marketplace of Ideas: The Selling of the Iraq War." *International Security*, 29, 1 (Summer): 5–48.

Kaufman, Chaim (2005) "Rational Choice and Progress in the Study of Ethnic Conflict." *Security Studies*, 14, 1 (January–March): 178–207.

Kaufman, Stuart J. (2001) *Modern Hatreds: The Symbolic Politics of Ethnic War*. Ithaca, NY: Cornell University Press.

Kaufman, Stuart J. (2006) "Symbolic Politics or Rational Choice? Testing Theories of Extreme Ethnic Violence." *International Security*, 30, 4 (Spring): 45–86.

Kaufman, Stuart J., Richard Little, and William C. Wohlforth (2007) *The Balance of Power in World History*. New York: Palgrave Macmillan.

Kautsky, Karl ([1914]1970) "Ultra-Imperialsim." *New Left Review*, 59 (January–February).

Keegan, John (1984) *A History of Warfare*. New York: Vintage.

Keeley, Lawrence H. (1996) *War Before Civilization: The Myth of the Peaceful Savage*. New York: Oxford University Press.

Keen, David (1998) *The Economic Functions of Violence in Civil Wars*, Adelphi Paper number 320. Oxford: IISS/Oxford University Press.

Keen, David (2000) "Incentives and Disincentives for Violence." In Mats Berdal and David Malone, eds., *Greed and Grievance: Economic Agendas in Civil Wars*. Boulder, CO: Lynne Rienner.

Kegley, Charles W., ed. (1991) *The Long Postwar Peace*. Glenview, IL: Scott, Foresman.

Kegley, Charles W., Jr., and Gregory A. Raymond (1990) *When Trust Breaks Down: Alliance Norms & World Politics*. Columbia, SC: University of South Carolina Press.

Kennan, George F. (1951) *American Diplomacy, 1900–1950*. New York: New American Library/Mentor.

Kennedy, Paul M., ed. (1979) *The War Plans of the Great Powers 1880–1914*. Boston, MA: George Allen & Unwin.

Kennedy, Paul (1982) *The Rise of the Anglo–German Naval Rivalry, 1860–1914*. London: Allen & Unwin.

Kennedy, Paul (1983) "Arms Races and the Causes of War, 1850–1945." In Paul Kennedy, ed., *Strategy and Diplomacy, 1870–1945*. London: George Allen & Unwin, chap. 6.

Kennedy, Paul (1987) *The Rise and Fall of the Great Powers: Economic Change and Military Conflict from 1500 to 2000*. New York: Random House.

Keohane, Robert O. (1984) *After Hegemony: Cooperation and Discord in the World Political Economy*. Princeton, NJ: Princeton University Press.

Keohane, Robert O. (1986a) "Realism, Neorealism, and the Study of World Politics." In Robert O. Keohane, ed., *Neorealism and Its Critics*. New York: Columbia University Press, pp. 1–26.

Keohane, Robert O., ed. (1986b) *Neorealism and Its Critics*. New York: Columbia University Press.

Keohane, Robert O., and Lisa L. Martin (1995) "The Promise of Institutionalist Theory." *International Security*, 20, 1: 39–51.

Kernell, Samuel (1978) "Explaining Presidential Popularity." *American Political Science Review*, 72: 506–22.

Kerr, Eckart (1965) *Der Primat der Innenpolitik*. Berlin: Walter de Gruyter.

Kershaw, Ian (2000) *Hitler 1936–1945: Nemesis*. New York: Norton.

Keshk, Omar M.G., Brian M. Pollins, and Rafael Reuveny (2004) "Trade Still follows the Flag: The Primacy of Politics in a Simultaneous Model of Interdependence and Armed Conflict." *Journal of Politics*, 66: 1155–79.

Khong, Yuen Foong (1992) *Analogies at War*. Princeton, NJ: Princeton University Press.

Kindleberger, Charles P. (1973) *The World in Depression, 1929–1939*. Berkeley, CA: University of California Press.

King, Gary, Robert O. Keohane, and Sidney Verba (1994) *Designing Social Inquiry*. Princeton, NJ: Princeton University Press.

Kirkpatrick, Jeane J. (1993) "The Modernizing Imperative." *Foreign Affairs*, 72, 4: 22–6.

Kirshner, Jonathan (2007) *Appeasing Bankers: Financial Caution on the Road to War*. Princeton, NJ: Princeton University Press.

Klein, James P., Gary Goertz, and Paul F. Diehl (2006) "The New Rivalry Dataset: Procedures and Patterns." *Journal of Peace Research*, 43: 331–48.

Knievel, Timothy M. (2008) "Presidents and 'Problems from Hell': Executive Decision-Making and the Interpretation of Two-Level Ethnic Entrepreneurial Games." Unpublished paper.

Knorr, Klaus (1966) *On the Uses of Military Power in the Nuclear Age*. Princeton, NJ: Princeton University Press.

Koch, H.W. (1984) "Social Darwinism as a Factor in the 'New Imperialism.'" In H.W. Koch, ed., *The Origins of the First World War*, 2nd ed. London: Macmillan, pp. 319–42.

Korany, Bahgat (1986) *How Foreign Policy Decisions Are Made in the Third World*. Boulder, CO: Westview.

Kowert, Paul A., and Margaret G. Hermann (1997) "Who Takes Risks? Daring and Caution in Foreign Policy Making." *Journal of Conflict Resolution*, 41: 611–37.

Krasner, Stephen D. (1971) "Are Bureaucracies Important? (Or Allison Wonderland)." *Foreign Policy*, 7: 159–79.

Krasner, Stephen D. (1978) *Defending the National Interest*. Princeton, NJ: Princeton University Press.

Krebs, Ronald R., and Jack S. Levy (2001) "Demographic Change and the Sources of International Conflict." In Myron Weiner and Sharon Stanton Russell, eds., *Demography and National Security*. New York: Berghahn Books, pp. 62–105.

Krepinevich, Andrew F., Jr. (1986) *The Army and Vietnam*. Baltimore: Johns Hopkins University Press.

Kubalkova, V., and A.A. Cruickshank (1980) *Marxism–Leninism and Theory of International Relations*. London: Routledge & Kegan Paul.

Kugler, Jacek, and Douglas Lemke, eds. (1996) *Parity and War*. Ann Arbor, MI: University of Michigan Press.

Kugler, Jacek, and Douglas Lemke (2000) "The Power Transition Research Program: Assessing Theoretical and Empirical Advances." In Manus I. Midlarsky, ed., *The Handbook of War Studies II*. Ann Arbor, MI: University of Michigan Press, pp. 129–63.

Kuhn, Thomas (1962) *The Structure of Scientific Revolutions*. Chicago: University of Chicago Press.

Kupchan, Charles A. (1994) *The Vulnerability of Empire*. Ithaca, NY: Cornell University Press.

Kydd, Andrew (1997) "Sheep in Sheep's Clothing: Why Security Seekers Do Not Fight One Another." *Security Studies*, 7, 1: 114–54.

Labs, Eric J. (1997) "Beyond Victory: Offensive Realism and the Expansion of War Aims." *Security Studies*, 6, 4: 1–49.

Lacina, Bethany, and Nils Petter Gleditsch (2005) "Monitoring Trends in Global Combat: A New Data Set of Battle Deaths." *European Journal of Population*, 21: 145–66.

Laitin, David D. (2007) *Nations, States, and Violence*. New York: Oxford University Press.

Lakatos, Imre (1970) "Falsification and the Methodology of Scientific Research Programmes." In Imre Lakatos and Alan Musgrave, eds., *Criticism and the Growth of Knowledge*. New York: Cambridge University Press, pp. 91–196.

Lake, David A. (1992) "Powerful Pacifists: Democratic States and War." *American Political Science Review*, 86, 1 (March): 24–37.

Lake, David A. (2009) *Hierarchy in International Relations*. Ithaca, NY: Cornell University Press.

Lake, David A., and Patrick M. Morgan, eds. (1997) *Regional Orders: Building Security in a New World*. University Park, PA: Pennsylvania State University Press.

Lake, David A., and Robert Powell (1999) "International Relations: A Strategic Choice Approach." In David Lake and Robert Powell, eds., *Strategic Choice and International Relations*. Princeton, NJ: Princeton University Press.

Lake, David A., and Donald Rothchild, eds. (1998) *The International Spread of Ethnic Conflict: Fear, Diffusion, and Escalation*. Princeton, NJ: Princeton University Press.

Langer, Ellen J. (1975) "The Illusion of Control." *Journal of Personality and Social Psychology*, 32, 2: 311–28.

Larson, Deborah (1985) *Origins of Containment*. Princeton, NJ: Princeton University Press.

Lau, Richard R., and David P. Redlawsk (2006) *How Voters Decide: Information Processing and Election Campaigns*. New York: Cambridge University Press.

Layne, Christopher (2006) *The Peace of Illusions: American Grand Strategy from 1940 to the Present*. Ithaca, NY: Cornell University Press.

Layne, Christopher (2008) "Security Studies and the Use of History: Neville Chamberlain's Grand Strategy Revisited." *Security Studies*, 17, 3: 397–437.

Lebow, Richard Ned (1981) *Between Peace and War*. Baltimore, MD: Johns Hopkins University Press.

Lebow, Richard Ned (2000/01) "Contingency, Catalysts, and International System Change." *Political Science Quarterly*, 115, 4 (Winter): 591–616.

Lebow, Richard Ned (2001) "Thucydides the Constructivist." *American Political Science Review*, 95, 3 (September): 547–60.

Lebow, Richard Ned (2008) *A Cultural Theory of International Relations*. New York: Cambridge University Press.

Lebow, Richard Ned, and Janice Gross Stein (1995) *We All Lost the Cold War*. Princeton, NJ: Princeton University Press.

Leeds, Ashley Brett (2003) "Do Alliances Deter Aggression? The Influence of Military Alliances on the Initiation of Militarized Interstate Disptues." *American Journal of Political Science*, 47 (July): 427–39.

Leites, Nathan (1951) *The Operational Code of the Politburo*. New York: McGraw-Hill.

Lemke, Douglas (2001) *Regions of War and Peace*. Ann Arbor, MI: University of Michigan Press.

Lemke, Douglas (2003) "Investigating the Preventive Motive for War." *International Interactions*, 29, 4: 273–92.

Lenin, V.I. ([1916]1939) *Imperialism*. New York: International Publishers.

Leng, Russell (1983) "When Will They Ever Learn? Coercive Bargaining in Recurrent Crises." *Journal of Conflict Resolution*, 27: 379–419.

Leng, Russell J. (1993) *Interstate Crisis Behavior, 1816–1980: Realism Versus Reciprocity*. New York: Cambridge University Press.

Leng, Russell (2000) *Bargaining and Learning in Recurring Crises: The Soviet–American, Egyptian–Israeli and Indo–Pakistan Rivalries*. Ann Arbor, MI: University of Michigan Press.

Levy, Jack S. (1983a) "Misperception and the Causes of War: Theoretical Linkages and Analytical Problems." *World Politics*, 36, 1 (October): 76–99.

Levy, Jack S. (1983b) *War in the Modern Great Power System, 1495–1975*. Lexington, KY: University Press of Kentucky.

Levy, Jack S. (1984) "The Offensive/Defensive Balance of Military Technology: A Theoretical and Historical Analysis." *International Studies Quarterly*, 28, 2 (June): 219–38.

Levy, Jack S. (1989a) "The Diversionary Theory of War: A Critique." In Manus I. Midlarsky, ed., *Handbook of War Studies*. Boston: Unwin Hyman, pp. 259–88.

Levy, Jack S. (1989b) "The Causes of War: A Review of Theories and Evidence." In Philip Tetlock, Jo L. Husbands, Robert Jervis, Paul C. Stern, and Charles Tilly, eds., *Behavior, Society, and Nuclear War*, Vol. 1. New York: Oxford University Press, pp. 209–333.

Levy, Jack S. (1990/91) "Preferences, Constraints, and Choices in July 1914." *International Security*, 15, 3: 151–86.

Levy, Jack S. (1994) "Learning and Foreign Policy: Sweeping a Conceptual Minefield." *International Organization*, 48, 2 (Spring): 279–312.

Levy, Jack S. (2000) "The Implications of Framing and Loss Aversion for International Conflict." In Manus I. Midlarsky, ed., *Handbook of War Studies II*. Ann Arbor, MI: University of Michigan Press, pp. 193–221.

Levy, Jack S. (2001) "Explaining Events and Testing Theories: History, Political Science, and the Analysis of International Relations." In Colin Elman and Miriam Fendius Elman, eds., *Bridges and Boundaries: Historians, Political Scientists, and the Study of International Relations*. Cambridge: MIT Press, pp. 39–83.

Levy, Jack S. (2002) "War and Peace." In *Walter Carlsnaes*, Thomas Risse, and Beth A. Simmons, eds., *Handbook of International Relations*, London: Sage, pp. 350–68.

Levy, Jack S. (2003a) "Balances and Balancing: Concepts, Propositions, and Research Design." In John A. Vasquez and Colin Elman, eds., *Realism and the*

Balancing of Power: A New Debate. Englewood Cliffs, NJ: Prentice Hall, pp. 128–53.

Levy, Jack S. (2003b) "Political Psychology and Foreign Policy." In David O. Sears, Leonie Huddy, and Robert Jervis, eds., *Oxford Handbook of Political Psychology.* New York: Oxford University Press, pp. 253–84.

Levy, Jack S. (2008a) "Preventive War and Democratic Politics." *International Studies Quarterly*, 52, 1 (March 2008): 1–24.

Levy, Jack S. (2008b) "Case Studies: Types, Designs, and Logics of Inference." *Conflict Management and Peace Science*, 25, 1: 1–18.

Levy, Jack S. (2008c) "Counterfactuals and Case Studies." In Janet Box-Steffensmeier, Henry Brady, and David Collier, eds., *Oxford Handbook of Political Methodology.* New York: Oxford University Press, pp. 627–44.

Levy, Jack S., and William F. Mabe, Jr. (2004) "Politically Motivated Opposition to War." *International Studies Review*, 6: 65–83.

Levy, Jack S., and William R. Thompson (2005) "Hegemonic Threats and Great Power Balancing in Europe, 1495–2000." *Security Studies*, 14, 1 (January–March): 1–30.

Levy, Jack S., and William R. Thompson (2010a) "Balancing at Sea: Do States Ally Against the Leading Global Power?" Unpublished paper.

Levy, Jack S., and William R. Thompson (2010b) *The Arc of War.* Unpublished book manuscript.

Levy, Jack S. and Lily I. Vakili (1992) "External Scapegoating in Authoritarian Regimes: Argentina in the Falklands/Malvinas Case." In Manus I. Midlarsky, ed., *The Internationalization of Communal Strife.* London: Routledge, pp. 118–46.

Lewis, Bernard (1990) "The Roots of Muslim Rage." *The Atlantic Monthly*; 266, 3 (September): 47–60.

Lewis, David (1973) *Counterfactuals.* Cambridge, MA: Harvard University Press.

Liberman, Peter (1996) *Does Conquest Pay? The Exploitation of Occupied Industrial Societies.* Princeton, NJ: Princeton University Press.

Lichbach, Mark I. (1989) "An Evaluation of 'Does Economic Inequality Breed Political Conflict?' Studies." *World Politics*, 41: 431–70.

Lichbach, Mark I. (1995) *The Rebel's Dilemma.* Ann Arbor, MI: University of Michigan Press.

Licklider, Roy (1995) "The Consequences of Negotiated Settlements in Civil Wars, 1945–1993." *American Political Science Review*, 89, 3 (September): 681–90.

Lieber, Keir A. (2005) *War and the Engineers: The Primacy of Politics over Technology.* Ithaca, NY: Cornell University Press.

Lieber, Keir A. (2007) "The New History of World War I and What It Means for International Relations Theory." *International Security*, 32, 2 (Fall): 155–91.

Lieber, Keir, and Gerard Alexander (2005) "Waiting for Balancing: Why the World Is Not Pushing Back" *International Security*, 30, 1 (Summer): 109–39.

Lipset, Seymour Martin (1959) "Some Social Requisites of Democracy: Economic Development and Political Legitimacy." *American Political Science Review*, 53, 1 (March): 69–105.

Lipson, Charles (2003) *Reliable Partners: How Democracies Have Made a Separate Peace.* Princeton, NJ: Princeton University Press.

Little, David (1996) "Religious Militancy." In Chester A. Crocker and Fen Osler Hampson, with Pamela Aall, eds., *Managing Global Chaos*. Washington, DC: United States Institute of Peace Press, chap. 5.

Little, Richard (2007) *The Balance of Power in International Relations: Metaphors, Myths and Models*. New York: Cambridge University Press.

Lobell, Steven E. (2006) "The Political Economy of War Mobilization: From Britain's Limited Liability to a Continental Commitment." *International Politics*, 43, 283–304.

Lobell, Steven E., Norrin M. Ripsman, and Jeffrey W. Taliaferro, eds. (2009) *Neoclassical Realism, the State, and Foreign Policy*. New York: Cambridge University Press.

Logevall, Fredrik (1999) *Choosing War: The Lost Chance for Peace and the Escalation of War in Vietnam*. Berkeley, CA: University of California Press.

Longley, J., and Dean Pruitt (1980) "Groupthink: A Critique of Janis' Theory." In L. Wheeler, ed. *Review of Personality and Social Psychology*, 1 (1980): 74–93. Beverly Hills, CA: Sage.

Luard, Evan (1986) *War in International Society*. London: I.B. Tauris.

Luxemburg, Rosa ([1913]1964) *The Accumulation of Capital*. New York: Monthly Review Press.

Lynn, John A. (1996) "The Evolution of Army Style in the Modern West, 800–2000." *The International History Review*, 18 (August): 505–45.

Lynn, John A. (2003) *Battle: A History of Combat and Culture*. Boulder, CO: Westview.

Lynn-Jones, Sean M. (1995) "Offense–Defense Theory and Its Critics." *Security Studies*, 4, 1: 660–91.

McAdam, Doug, Sidney Tarrow, and Charles Tilly (2001) *Dynamics of Contention*. Cambridge: Cambridge University Press.

McDermott, Rose (1998) *Risk-Taking in International Politics: Prospect Theory in American Foreign Policy*. Ann Arbor, MI: University of Michigan Press.

McDermott, Rose (2004) *Political Psychology and International Relations*. Ann Arbor, MI: University of Michigan Press.

McDonald, Patrick J. (2009) *The Invisible Hand of Peace: Capitalism, The War Machine, and International Relations Theory*. New York: Cambridge University Press.

Mack, Andrew (2007) *Human Security Brief 2007*. Vancouver, Canada: Simon Fraser University.

Magdoff, Harry (1969) *The Age of Imperialism*. New York: Monthly Review Press.

Mahoney, James, and Gary Goertz (2006) "A Tale of Two Cultures: Contrasting Qualitative and Quantitative Research." *Political Analysis*, 14: 227–49.

Mahoney, James, Erin Kimball, and Kendra L. Koivu (2009) "The Logic of Historical Explanation in the Social Sciences." *Comparative Political Studies*, 42, 1: 114–46.

Makdisi, Ussama (2000) *The Culture of Sectarianism: Community, History, and Violence in Nineteenth-Century Ottoman Lebanon*. Berkeley, CA: University of California Press.

Malešević, Siniša (2008) "The Sociology of New Wars? Assessing the Causes and Objectives of Contemporary Violent Conflicts." *International Political Sociology*, 2, 2 (June): 97–112.

Malinowski, Bronislaw ([1941]1968) "An Anthropological Analysis of War." *American Journal of Sociology*, 46, 4: 521–50.

Mann, James (2004) *Rise of the Vulcans: The History of Bush's War Cabinet*. New York: Viking/Penguin.

Mansbach, Richard W., and John A. Vasquez (1981) *In Search of Theory*. New York: Columbia University Press.

Mansfield, Edward D., and Brian M. Pollins, eds. (2003) *Economic Interdependence and International Conflict*. Ann Arbor, MI: University of Michigan Press.

Mansfield, Edward D., and Jack Snyder (2002) "Democratic Transitions, Institutional Strength, and War." *International Organization*, 56, 2 (Spring): 297–337.

Mansfield, Edward D., and Jack Snyder (2005) *Electing to Fight: Why Emerging Democracies Go to War*. Cambridge, MA, and London: MIT Press.

Maoz, Zeev (1990) *National Choices and International Processes*. New York: Cambridge University Press.

Maoz, Zeev (1997) "The Debate Over the Democratic Peace: Rearguard Action or Cracks in the Wall?" *International Security*, 32: 162–98.

Maoz, Zeev, and Ben Mor (2002) *Bound by Struggle: The Strategic Evolution of Enduring International Rivalries*. Ann Arbor, MI: University of Michigan Press.

March, James G. (1994) *A Primer on Decision Making: How Decisions Happen*. New York: Free Press.

March, James G., and Herbert A. Simon (1958) *Organizations*. New York: Wiley.

Martel, William C. (2007) *Victory in War: Foundations of Modern Military Policy*. New York: Cambridge University Press.

Marten, Kimberly (2006/07) "Warlordism in Comparative Perspective." *International Security*, 31, 3 (Winter): 41–73.

Martin, David (1997) *Does Christianity Cause War?* Vancouver, British Columbia: Regent College Publishing.

Mason, T. David (2009) "The Evolution of Theory on Civil War and Revolution." In Manus I. Midlarsky, ed., *Handbook of War Studies III*. Ann Arbor, MI: University of Michigan Press.

May, Ernest (1961) *Imperial Democracy*. New York: Harper & Row.

May, Ernest R. (1973) *"Lessons" of the Past: The Use and Misuse of History in American Foreign Policy*. New York: Oxford University Press.

Mayer, Arno (1977) "Internal Crises and War since 1870." In Charles Bertrand, ed., *Revolutionary Situations in Europe, 1917–1922*. Concordia University and University of Quebec and Montreal, pp. 201–33.

Mead, Margaret (1940) "Warfare: Only an Invention, Not a Biological Necessity." *Asia*, 40: 402–5.

Mearsheimer, John J. (1994/95) "The False Promise of International Institutions." *International Security*, 19, 3: 5–49.

Mearsheimer, John J. (1995) "A Realist Reply." *International Security*, 20, 1 (Summer): 82–93.

Mearsheimer, John J. (2001a) *The Tragedy of Great Power Politics*. New York: W.W. Norton.

Mearsheimer, John. J. (2001b) "The Future of the American Pacifier." *Foreign Affairs*, 80, 5 (September/October): 46–61.

Mearsheimer, John J., and Stephen M. Walt (2007) *The Israeli Lobby and U.S. Foreign Policy*. New York: Farrar, Straus and Giroux.

Meernick, James David (2004) *The Political Use of Military Force in US Foreign Policy*. Burlington, VT: Ashgate.

Melman, Seymour (1970) *Pentagon Capitalism: The Political Economy of War*. New York: Oxford University Press.

Mercer, Jonathan (1995) "Anarchy and Identity." *International Organization*, 49, 2 (Spring): 229–52.

Mercer, Jonathan (1996) *Reputation and International Politics*. Ithaca, NY: Cornell University Press.

Midlarsky, Manus I. (1988) "Rulers and Ruled: Patterned Inequality and the Onset of Mass Political Violence." *American Political Science Review*, 82: 491–509.

Midlarsky, Manus I., ed. (1990) "Big Wars, Little Wars: A Single Theory?" *International Interactions*, Special Issue, 16, 3: 157–224.

Midlarsky, Manus I., ed. (1992) *The Internationalization of Communal Strife*. New York: Routledge.

Miller, Benjamin (2007) *States, Nations, and the Great Powers: The Sources of Regional War and Peace*. New York: Cambridge University Press.

Miller, Ross (1999) "Regime Type, Strategic Interaction, and the Diversionary Use of Force." *Journal of Conflict Resolution*, 43, 3 (June): 388–402.

Mills, C. Wright (1956) *The Power Elite*. London: Oxford University Press.

Milner, Helen (1991) "The Assumption of Anarchy in International Relations Theory: A Critique." *Review of International Studies*, 17, 1: 67–85.

Milward, Alan (1977) *War, Economy, and Society, 1939–1945*. Berkeley, CA: University of California Press.

Minchinton, Walter E. (1969) *Mercantilism: System or Expediency?* Lexington, MA: D.C. Heath.

Minix, D.G. (1982) *Small Groups and Foreign Policy Decision-Making*. Washington, DC: University Press of America.

Mintz, Alex (1993) "The Decision to Attack Iraq: A Noncompensatory Theory of Decision Making." *Journal of Conflict Resolution*, 37: 595–618.

Mintz, Alex (2004a) "How Do Leaders Make Decisions? A Poliheuristic Perspective." *Journal of Conflict Resolution*, 48, 1: 3–13.

Mintz, Alex (2004b) "Foreign Policy Decision Making in Familiar and Unfamiliar Settings: An Experimental Study of High Ranking Military Officers." *Journal of Conflict Resolution*, 48, 1: 91–104.

Mintz, Alex, and Nehemia Geva (1997) "The Poliheuristic Theory of Foreign Policy Decisionmaking." In Alex Mintz and Nehemia Geva, eds., *Decision-making on War and Peace: The Cognitive–Rational Debate*. Boulder, CO: Lynne Rienner Publishers.

Mitchell, Christopher (1970) "Civil Strife and the Involvement of External Parties." *International Studies Quarterly*, 14: 166–94.

Mitchell, Sara McLoughlin, and Brandon Prins (2004) "Rivalry and Diversionary Uses of Force." *Journal of Conflict Resolution*, 48: 937–61.

Modelski, George (1961) *The International Relations of Internal War*. Princeton, NJ: Princeton University Center for International Studies.

Modelski, George, and William R. Thompson (1996) *Leading Sectors and World Powers: The Coevolution of Global Politics and Economics*. Columbia, SC: University of South Carolina Press.

Mombauer, Annika (2001) *Helmuth von Moltke and the Origins of the First World War*. New York: Cambridge University Press.

Mombauer, Annika (2002) *The Origins of the First World War: Controversies and Consensus*. London: Pearson.

Monroe, Kirsten R. (2002) *Political Psychology*. Mahwah, NJ: Lawrence Erlbaum.

Montesquieu, Charles de Secondat, baron de ([1750]1989) *The Spirit of the Laws*, trans. and ed. Anne M. Cohler, Basia Carolyn Miller, and Harold Samuel Stone. New York: Cambridge University Press.

Moore, Barrington (1966) *Social Origins of Dictatorship and Democracy: Lord and Peasant in the Making of the Modern World*. Boston, MA: Beacon Press.

Morgan, Patrick (1977) *Deterrence: A Conceptual Analysis*. Beverly Hills, CA: Sage.

Morgan, T. Clifton (1994) *Untying the Knot of War: A Bargaining Theory of International Crises*. Ann Arbor, MI: University of Michigan Press.

Morgan, T. Clifton, and Kenneth Bickers (1992) "Domestic Discontent and the External Use of Force." *Journal of Conflict Resolution*, 36 (March): 25–52.

Morgan, T. Clifton, and Sally Howard Campbell (1991) "Domestic Structure, Decisional Constraints, and War: So Why Kant Democracies Fight?" *Journal of Conflict Resolution*, 35 (June): 187–211.

Morgan, T. Clifton, and Jack S. Levy (1990) "Base Stealers versus Power Hitters: A Nation-State Level Analysis of the Frequency and Seriousness of War." In Charles S. Gochman and Alan Ned Sabrosky, eds., *Prisoners of War?* Lexington, MA: Lexington Books, pp. 43–56.

Morgenthau, Hans J. (1967) *Politics Among Nations*, 4th ed. New York: Knopf.

Morrow, James D. (1989) "A Twist of Truth: A Reexamination of the Effects of Arms Races on the Occurrence of War." *Journal of Conflict Resolution*, 33: 500–29.

Morrow, James D. (1994) *Game Theory for Political Scientists*. Princeton, NJ: Princeton University Press.

Morrow, James D. (1999) "How Could Trade Affect Conflict?" *Journal of Peace Research*, 36, 4: 481–9.

Morrow, James D. (2003) "Assessing the Role of Trade as a Source of Costly Signals." In Edward D. Mansfield and Brian Pollins, eds., *Economic Interdependence and International Conflict: New Perspectives on an Enduring Debate*. Ann Arbor, MI: University of Michigan Press, pp. 89–95.

Morrow, James D., Randolph M. Siverson, and Tressa E. Tabares (1998) "The Political Determinants of Trade: The Major Powers, 1907–1990." *American Political Science Review*, 92, 3: 649–61.

Most, Benjamin A., and Harvey Starr (1987) "International Relations Theory, Foreign Policy Substitutability, and 'Nice' Laws." *World Politics*, 36 (April): 383–406.

Mousseau, Michael (2000) "Market Prosperity, Democratic Consolidation, and Democratic Peace." *Journal of Conflict Resolution*, 44, 4 (August): 472–507.

Mousseau, Michael (2009) "The Social Market Roots of Democratic Peace." *International Security*, 33, 4: 52–86.

Mousseau, Michael, and Yuhang Shi (1999) "A Test for Reverse Causality in the Democratic Peace Relationship." *Journal of Peace Research*, 36, 6: 639–65.

Mousseau, Michael, Håvard Hegre, and John Oneal (2003) "How the Wealth of Nations Conditions the Liberal Peace." *European Journal of International Relations*, 9, 2: 277–314.

Mueller, John (1973) *War, Presidents, and Public Opinion*. New York: John Wiley.

Mueller, John (1989) *Retreat from Doomsday: The Obsolescence of Major War*. New York: Basic.

Mueller, John (2004) *The Remnants of War*. Ithaca, NY: Cornell University Press.

Muller, Edward N. (1985) "Income Inequality, Regime Repressiveness, and Political Violence." *American Sociological Review*, 50: 47–61.

Muller, Edward N., and Mitchell Seligson (1987) "Inequality and Insurgency." *American Political Science Review*, 81: 425–51.

Münkler, Herfried (2004) *The New Wars*. Oxford: Oxford University Press.

Murray, Williamson (1984) *The Change in the European Balance of Power, 1938–1939: The Path to Ruin*. Princeton, NJ: Princeton University Press.

Nakdimon, Shlomo (1987) *First Strike*, trans. Peretz Kidron. New York: Summit Books.

Narizny, Kevin (2007) *The Political Economy of Grand Strategy*. Ithaca, NY: Cornell University Press.

National Commission on Terrorist Attacks Upon the United States (2004) *The 9/11 Commission Report: Final Report of the National Commission on Terrorist Attacks Upon the United States*. New York: W.W. Norton.

Neff, Stephen C. (2005) *War and the Law of Nations: A General History*. New York: Cambridge University Press.

Nelson, Keith L., and Spencer C. Olin, Jr. (1979) *Why War? Ideology, Theory, and History*. Berkeley: University of California Press.

Neustadt, Richard E. (1991) *Presidential Power and the Modern Presidents: the Politics of Leadership from Roosevelt to Reagan*. New York: Simon & Schuster.

Nincic, Miroslav (1997) "Loss Aversion and the Domestic Context of Military Intervention." *Political Research Quarterly*, 50: 97–120.

Nisbett, Richard E. (2003) *The Geography of Thought: How Asians and Westerners think Differently ... and Why*. New York: Free Press.

Nisbett, Richard, and Lee Ross (1980) *Human Inference: Strategies and Shortcomings of Social Judgment*. Englewood Cliffs, NJ: Prentice Hall.

North, Douglass C., and Barry R. Weingast (1989) "Constitution and Commitment: The Evolution of Institutional Governing Public Choice in Seventeenth-Century England." *Journal of Economic History*, 49, 4: 803–32.

O'Connell, Mary Ellen (2005) *International Law and the Use of Force: Cases and Materials*. New York: Foundation Press.

Olson, Mancur, Jr. (1971) *The Logic of Collective Action*. Cambridge, MA: Harvard University Press.

O'Neill, Barry (2001) "Risk Aversion in International Relations Theory." *International Studies Quarterly*, 45, 4 (August): 617–40.

Oren, Ido (1984) "The Subjectivity of the Democratic Peace: Changing U.S. Perceptions of Imperial Germany." *International Security*, 20, 2 (Fall): 147–84.

Oren, Ido (1990) "The War Proneness of Alliances." *Journal of Conflict Resolution*, 34 (June): 208–33.

Oren, Michael (2002) *Six Days of War: June 1967 and the Making of the Modern Middle East*. New York: Oxford University Press.

Organski, A.F.K. (1958) *World Politics*. New York: Knopf, chap. 14.

Organski, A.F.K., and Jacek Kugler (1980) *The War Ledger*. Chicago: University of Chicago Press.

Owen, John IV (1997) *Liberal Peace Liberal War: American Politics and International Security*. Ithaca, NY: Cornell University Press.

Paine, Thomas ([1791/92]1969) *Rights of Man*, ed. H. Collins. Baltimore, MD: Penguin.

Palmer, Glenn, and T. Clifton Morgan (2006) *A Theory of Foreign Policy*. Princeton, NJ: Princeton University Press.

Papayoanou, Paul A. (1999) *Power Ties: Economic Interdependence, Balancing, and War*. Ann Arbor, MI: University of Michigan Press.

Pape, Robert A. (1996) *Bombing to Win: Air Power and Coercion in War*. Ithaca, NY: Cornell University Press.

Pape, Robert Anthony (2005a) "Soft Balancing Against the United States." *International Security*, 30, 1: 7–45.

Pape, Robert A. (2005b) *Dying to Win: The Strategic Logic of Suicide Terrorism*. New York: Random House.

Paret, Peter (1976) *Clausewitz and the State*. New York: Oxford University Press.

Parker, Geoffrey (1984) *The Thirty Years' War*. London: Routledge & Kegan Paul.

Paul, T.V. (2005a) "Soft Balancing in the Age of U.S. Primacy." *International Security*, 30, 1: 46–71.

Paul, T.V., ed. (2005b) *The Indo–Pakistan Conflict: An Enduring Rivalry*. Cambridge: Cambridge University Press.

Paul, T.V., James Wirtz, and Michel Fortmann, eds. (2004) *Balance of Power Revisited: Theory and Practice in the 21st Century*. Stanford, CA: Stanford University Press.

Peceny, Mark, Caroline C. Beer, and Shannon Sanchez-Terry (2002) "Dictatorial Peace?" *American Political Science Review*, 96, 1 (March): 15–26.

Petersen, Roger (2001) *Resistance and Rebellion: Lessons from Eastern Europe*. Cambridge: Cambridge University Press.

Petersen, Roger (2002) *Understanding Ethnic Violence: Fear, Hatred and Resentment in Twentieth Century Eastern Europe*. Cambridge: Cambridge University Press.

Pevehouse, Jon, and Bruce Russett (2006) "Democratic International Governmental Organizations Promote Peace." *International Organization*, 60, 4 (Fall): 969–1000.

Pfiffner, James P., and Mark Phythian, eds. (2008) *Intelligence and National Security Policymaking on Iraq: British and American Perspectives*. College Station, TX: Texas A&M Press.

Pickering, Jeffrey, and Emizet F. Kisangani (2005) "Democracy and Diversionary Military Intervention: Reassessing Regime Type and the Diversionary Hypothesis." *International Studies Quarterly*, 49, 1 (March): 23–44.

Pillar, Paul R. (2006) "Intelligence, Politics, and the War in Iraq." *Foreign Affairs*, 85 (March–April): 17–25.

Polachek, Soloman W. (1980) "Conflict and Trade." *Journal of Conflict Resolution*, 24, 1: 55–78.

Polybius (1960) *The Histories*, Vol. I, trans. W. R. Paton. Cambridge, MA: Harvard University Press.

Popper, Karl R. (1989) *The Logic of Scientific Discovery*. New York: Harper Torchbacks.

Posen, Barry R. (1984) *The Sources of Military Doctrine*. Ithaca, NY: Cornell University Press.

Posen, Barry R. (1993) "The Security Dilemma and Ethnic Conflict." *Survival*, 35: 103–24.

Posen, Barry R. (2003) "Command of the Commons: The Military Foundation of U.S. Hegemony." *International Security*, 28, 1 (Summer): 5–46.

Post, Jerrold M. (1991) "The Impact of Crisis-Induced Stress on Policy Makers." In Alexander L. George, ed., *Avoiding War*. Boulder, CO: Westview, chap. 20.

Post, Jerrold M., ed. (2003) *The Psychological Assessment of Political Leaders*. Ann Arbor, MI: University of Michigan Press.

Powell, Robert (1991) "Absolute and Relative Gains in International Relations Theory." *American Political Science Review*, 85, 4 (December), 1303–20.

Powell, Robert (1999) *In the Shadow of Power*. Princeton, NJ: Princeton University Press.

Powell, Robert (2002) "The Bargaining Model of War." *Annual Review of Political Science*, 5: 1–30.

Powell, Robert (2006) "War as a Commitment Problem." *International Organization*, 60, 1 (Winter): 169–204.

Press, Daryl (2005) *Calculating Credibility: How Leaders Assess Military Threats*. Ithaca, NY: Cornell University Press.

Pressman, Jeremy (2008) *Warring Friends: Alliance Restraint in International Politics*. Ithaca, NY: Cornell University Press.

Prunier, Gérard (2009) *Africa's World War: Congo, the Rwandan Genocide, and the Making of a Continental Catastrophe*. New York: Oxford University Press.

Ragin, Charles C. (1987) *The Comparative Method: Moving Beyond Qualitative and Quantitative Strategies*. Berkeley, CA: University of California Press.

Ragin, Charles C. (2000). *Fuzzy-Set Social Science*. Chicago: University of Chicago Press.

Rapkin, David P., and William R. Thompson (2003) "Power Transition, Challenge, and the (Re)Emergence of China." *International Interactions*, 29 (October–December).

Rapkin, David P., and William R. Thompson (2006) "Economic Interdependence and the Emergence of China and India in the 21st Century." In Ashley Tellis and Michael Wills, eds., *Strategic Asia 2006–07: Trade, Interdependence and Security*. Seattle, WA: National Bureau of Asian Research.

Rapkin, David P., and William R. Thompson, with Jon A. Christopherson (1979) "Bipolarity and Bipolarization in the Cold War Era: Conceptualization, Measurement, and Validation." *Journal of Conflict Resolution*, 23: 261–95.

Rasler, Karen A., and William R. Thompson (1983) "Global Wars, Public Debts and the Long Cycle." *World Politics*, 35 (July): 489–516.

Rasler, Karen A., and William R. Thompson (1989) *War and State Making*. Boston, MA: Unwin Hyman.

Rasler, Karen A., and William R. Thompson (1994) *The Great Powers and Global Struggle, 1490–1990*. Lexington, KY: The University Press of Kentucky.

Rasler, Karen, and William R. Thompson (2000a) "Explaining Escalation to War: Contiguity, Space and Position in the Major Power Subsystem." *International Studies Quarterly*, 44: 503–30.

Rasler, Karen, and William R. Thompson (2000b) "Global War and the Political Economy of Structural Change." In Manus I. Midlarsky, ed., *Handbook of War Studies II*. Ann Arbor, MI: University of Michigan Press, pp. 301–33.

Rasler, Karen A., and William R. Thompson (2005) *Puzzles of the Democratic Peace: Theory, Geopolitics and the Transformation of World Politics*. New York: Palgrave-Macmillan.

Rasler, Karen A., and William R. Thompson (forthcoming) "Systemic Theories of Conflict." *International Studies Compendium*.

Ray, James Lee (1995) *Democracy and International Conflict*. Columbia, SC: University of South Carolina Press.

Ray, James Lee (2000) "Democracy: On the Level(s), Does Democracy Correlate with Peace." In John A. Vasquez, ed., *What Do We Know About War?* Lanham, MD: Rowman & Littlefield, pp. 299–316.

Redd, Steven B. (2005) "The Influence of Advisers and Decision Strategies on Foreign Policy Choices: President Clinton's Decision to Use Force in Kosovo." *International Studies Perspectives*, 6: 129–50.

Regan, Patrick (2000) *Civil Wars and Foreign Powers: Interventions and Intrastate Conflicts*. Ann Arbor, MI: University of Michigan Press.

Reiter, Dan (1995) "Exploding the Powder Keg Myth: Preemptive Wars Almost Never Happen." *International Security*, 20, 2: 5–34.

Reiter, Dan, and Allan C. Stam III (2002) *Democracies at War*. Princeton, NJ: Princeton University Press.

Reuveny, Rafael, and Heejoon Kang (1996) "International Trade, Political Conflict/Cooperation, and Granger Causality." *American Journal of Political Science*, 40, 3: 943–70.

Reynal-Querol, Marta (2002) "Ethnicity, Political Systems, and Civil Wars." *Journal of Conflict Resolution*, 46: 29–54.

Rhodes, Edward (1989) *Power and MADness*. New York: Columbia University Press.

Rich, Frank (2006) *The Greatest Story Ever Sold*. New York: Penguin.

Richards, Diana, et al. (1993) "Good Times, Bad Times, and the Diversionary Use of Force." *Journal of Conflict Resolution*, 37, 3 (September): 504–35.

Richardson, Lewis F. (1960) *Arms and Insecurity*. Pittsburgh, PA: Boxwood.

Ricks, Thomas E. (2006) *Fiasco: The American Military Adventure in Iraq*. New York: Penguin.

Ripsman, Norrin M., and Jean-Marc F. Blanchard (1996/97) "Commercial Liberalism under Fire: Evidence from 1914 and 1936." *Security Studies*, 6, 2: 4–50.

Ripsman, Norrin M., and Jack S. Levy (2007) "The Preventive War that Never Happened: Britain, France, and the Rise of Germany in the1930s." *Security Studies*, 16, 1 (January–March): 32–67.

Ripsman, Norrin M., and Jack S. Levy (2008) "Wishful Thinking or Buying Time? The Logic of British Appeasement in the 1930s." *International Security*, 33, 2 (Fall): 148–81.

Risse-Kappen, Thomas (1995) "Democratic Peace – Warlike Democracies? A Social Constructivist Interpretation of the Liberal Argument." *European Journal of International Relations*, 1, 4: 491–517.

Ritter, Jeffrey M. (2000) "Know Thine Enemy: Information and Democratic Foreign Policy." In Bernard I. Finel and Kristin M. Lord, eds., *Power and Conflict in the Age of Transparency*. New York: Palgrave, pp. 83–113.

Ritter, Gerhard (1958) *The Schlieffen Plan*. New York: Praeger.

Ritter, Gerhard (1970) *The Sword and the Scepter*, 4 vols, trans. Heins Norden. Coral Gables, FL.: University of Miami Press.

Roberts, Michael ([1956]1995) "The Military Revolution, 1560–1660." In Clifford J. Rogers, ed., *The Military Revolution Debate: Readings on the Military Transformation of Early Modern Europe*. Boulder, CO: Westview, pp. 13–35.

Robinson, Ronald, and John Gallagher. (1950) "The Imperialism of Free Trade." *Economic History Review*, Second Series, 6: 1–15.

Rogers, J. Philip (1991) "Crisis Bargaining Codes and Crisis Management." In Alexander L. George, ed., *Avoiding Inadvertent War: Problems of Crisis Management*. Boulder, CO: Westview, pp. 413–42.

Rogers, Clifford J., ed. (1995) *The Military Revolution Debate: Readings on the Military Transformation of Early Modern Europe*. Boulder, CO: Westview.

Rogowski, Ronald (1989) *Commerce and Coalitions: How Trade Affects Domestic Political Alignments*. Princeton, NJ: Princeton University Press.

Rosato, Sebastian (2003) "The Flawed Logic of Democratic Peace Theory." *American Political Science Review*, 97, 4 (November): 585–602.

Rose, Gideon (1998) "Neoclassical Realism and Theories of Foreign Policy." *World Politics*, 51, 1 (October): 144–72.

Rose, William (2000) "The Security Dilemma and Ethnic Conflict: Some New Hypotheses." *Security Studies*, 9, 4 (Summer): 1–51.

Rosecrance, Richard (1986) *The Rise of the Trading State: Commerce and Conquest in the Modern World*. New York: Basic Books.

Rosen, Steven (1973) *Testing the Theory of the Military–Industrial Complex*. Lexington, MA: D.C. Heath.

Rosen, Stephen Peter (2005) *War and Human Nature*. Princeton, NJ: Princeton University Press.

Rosenau, James N. (1966) "Pre-Theories and Theories of Foreign Policy." In R. B. Farrell, ed., *Approaches to Comparative and International Politics*. Evanston, IL: Northwestern University Press, pp. 27–92.

Rosenau, James N. (1980) *The Scientific Study of Foreign Policy*. London: Frances Pinter.

Roskin, Michael (2002) "From Pearl Harbor to Vietnam: Shifting Generational Paradigms and Foreign Policy." In G. John Ikenberry, ed., *American Foreign Policy: Theoretical Essays*. 4th ed. New York: Longman, pp. 298–319.

Ross, Dennis (1984) "Risk Aversion in Soviet Decisionmaking." In Jiri Valenta and William Potter, eds., *Soviet Decisionmaking for National Security*. London: Allen & Unwin, pp. 237–51.

Ross, Michael L. (2003) "Oil, Drugs and Diamonds: The Varying Roles of Natural Resources in Civil War." In Karen Ballentine and Jack Sherman, eds., *The Political Economy of Armed Conflict: Beyond Greed and Grievance*. Boulder, CO: Lynne Rienner Publishers, pp. 47–70.

Ross, Michael L. (2004) "What Do We Know About Natural Resources and Civil War?" *Journal of Peace Research*, 41, 3: 337–56.

Ruggie, John Gerard (1998) *Constructing the World Polity: Essays on International Institutionalization*. New York: Routledge.

Rummel, R.J. (1995a) "Democracies ARE Less Warlike Than Other Regimes." *European Journal of International Relations*, 1, 4: 457–79.

Rummel, Rudolph J. (1995b) "Democracy, Power, Genocide, and Mass Murder." *Journal of Conflict Resolution*, 39, 1 (March): 3–26.

Russett, Bruce M. (1964) "Inequality and Instability." *World Politics*, 16: 442–54.

Russett, Bruce M. (1990) "Economic Decline, Electoral Pressure, and the Initiation of International Conflict." In Charles Gochman and Alan Sabrosky, eds., *The Prisoners of War*. Lexington, MA: D.C. Heath, pp. 123–40.

Russett, Bruce (1993) *Grasping the Democratic Peace*. Princeton, NJ: Princeton University Press.

Russett, Bruce, and John R. Oneal (2001) *Triangulating Peace: Democracy, Interdependence, and International Organization*. New York: W.W. Norton.

Russett, Bruce M., and Harvey Starr (2000) "From the Democratic Peace to Kantian Peace: Democracy and Conflict in the International System." In Manus I. Midlarsky, ed., *Handbook of War Studies II*. Ann Arbor, MI: University of Michigan Press, pp. 93–128.

Russett, Bruce M., John R. Oneal, and Michaelene Cox (2000) "Clash of Civilizations, or Realism and Liberalism Deja Vu? Some Evidence." *Journal of Peace Research*, 37, 5 (September): 583–608.

Sabrosky A., ed. (1985) *Polarity and War*. Boulder, CO: Westview.

Sagan, Scott D. (1988) "The Origins of the Pacific War." *The Journal of Interdisciplinary History*, 18, 4 (Spring): 893–922.

Saideman, Stephen (2001) *The Ties that Divide: Ethnic Politics, Foreign Policy and International Conflict*. New York: Columbia University Press.

Salehyan, Idean (2009) *Rebels Without Borders: Transnational Insurgencies in World Politics*. Ithaca, NY: Cornell University Press.

Sambanis, Nicholas (2001) "Do Ethnic and Non-ethnic Civil Wars have the Same Causes? A Theoretical and Empirical Inquiry (Part I)." *Journal of Conflict Resolution*, 45: 259–82.

Sambanis, Nicholas (2002) "A Review of Recent Advances and Future Directions in the Literature on Civil Wars." *Defense and Peace Economics*, 13, 2: 215–43.

Sambanis, Nicholas (2004) " "What Is Civil War?' Conceptual and Empirical Complexities of an Operational Definition." *Journal of Conflict Resolution*, 48, 6 (December): 814–58.

Sample, Susan G. (2000) "Military Buildups: Arming and War." In John A. Vasquez, ed., *What Do We Know about War?* Lanham, MD: Rowman & Littlefield, pp. 165–96.

Sample, Susan G. (2002) "The Outcomes of Military Buildups: Minor States vs. Major Powers." *Journal of Peace Research*, 39, 6 (November): 669–91.

Sarkees, Meredith Reid, Frank Weylon Wayman, and J. David Singer (2003) "Inter-State, Intra-State, and Extra-State Wars: A Comprehensive Look at their Distribution over Time, 1816–1997." *International Studies Quarterly*, 47, 1 (March): 49–70.

Schelling, Thomas C. (1960) *The Strategy of Conflict*. Cambridge, MA: Harvard University Press.

Schelling, Thomas C. (1966) *Arms and Influence*. New Haven, CT: Yale University Press.

Schlesinger, Arthur M., Jr., and Roger Bruns, eds. (1975) *Congress Investigates: A Documented History, 1792–1974*. New York: Chelsea House Publishers.

Schmidt, Brian C. (2002) "On the History and Historiography of International Relations." In Walter Carlsnaes, Thomas Risse, and Beth A. Simmons, eds., *Handbook of International Relations*. London: Sage, pp. 3–22.

Schneider, Gerald, Katherine Barbieri, and Nils Petter Gleditsch, eds. (2003) *Globalization and Armed Conflict*. Lanham, MD: Rowman & Littlefield.

Schroeder, Paul W. ([1976] 2004) "Alliances, 1815–1945: Weapons of Power and Tools of Management." In Paul W. Schroeder, ed., *Systems, Stability, and Statecraft: Essays on the International History of Modern Europe*. Co-edited by David Wetzel, Robert Jervis, and Jack S. Levy. New York: Palgrave, pp. 195–222.

Schroeder, Paul W. (1994) *The Transformation of European Politics, 1763–1848*. New York: Oxford University Press.

Schroeder, Paul W. (2001) "International History: Why Historians Do It Differently than Political Scientists." In Colin Elman and Miriam Fendius Elman, eds., *Bridges and Boundaries: Historians, Political Scientists, and the Study of International Relations*. Cambridge, MA: MIT Press, pp. 403–16.

Schultz, Kenneth A. (2001) *Democracy and Coercive Diplomacy*. Princeton, NJ: Princeton University Press.

Schultz, Kenneth A., and Barry R. Weingast (1998) "Limited Governments, Powerful States." In Randolph M. Siverson, ed., *Strategic Politicians, Institutions, and Foreign Policy*. Ann Arbor, MI: University of Michigan Press, pp. 15–49.

Schumpeter, Joseph A. ([1919]1951) *Imperialism and Social Classes*. Oxford: Oxford University Press.

Schweller, Randall L. (1992) "Domestic Structure and Preventive War: Are Democracies More Pacific?" *World Politics*, 44, 2: 235–69.

Schweller, Randall L. (2006) *Unanswered Threats: Political Constraints on the Balance of Power*. Ithaca, NY: Cornell University Press.

Schweller, Randolph M. (1996) "Neorealism's Status Quo Bias: What Security Dilemma?" *Security Studies*, 5, 3: 90–121.

Sears, David O., Leonie Huddy, and Robert Jervis, eds. (2003) *Oxford Handbook of Political Psychology*. New York: Oxford University Press.

Sechser, Todd S. (2004) "Are Soldiers Less War-Prone than Statesmen?" *Journal of Conflict Resolution*, 48, 5, 746–74.

Segev, Tom (2007) *1967: Israel, the War, and the Year that Transformed the Middle East*. New York: Metropolitan Books/Henry Holt.

Semmel, Bernard, ed. (1981) *Marxism and the Science of War*. New York: Oxford University Press.

Senese, Paul D., and John A. Vasquez (2008) *The Steps to War: An Empirical Study*. Princeton, NJ: Princeton University Press.

Shakespeare, William ([1596]1845) *Henry IV, Part I*. London: Shakespeare Society.

Sheehan, Michael (1996) *The Balance of Power: History and Theory*. London: Routledge.

Shlaim, Avi (1976) "Failures in National Intelligence Estimates: The Case of the Yom Kippur War." *World Politics*, 28: 348–80.

Silberner, Edmund ([1946]1972) *The Problem of War in Nineteenth Century Economic Thought*, trans. Alexander H. Krappe. Princeton, NJ: Princeton University Press.

Simmel, George (1898) "The Persistence of Social Groups." *American Journal of Sociology*, 3, 5: 662–98; 3, 6: 829–36.

Simon, Herbert A. (1949) *Administrative Behavior: A Study of Decision Making Processes in Administrative Organization*. New York: Free Press.

Singer, J. David (1961) "The Levels of Analysis Problem in International Relations." *World Politics*, 14, 1 (October): 77–92.

Singer, J. David (1991) "Peace in the Global System: Displacement, Interregnum or Transformation?" In Charles W. Kegley, Jr., ed., *The Long Postwar Peace*. Glenview, IL: Scott, Foresman, pp. 56–84.

Singer, J. David, and Melvin Small (1968) "Alliance Aggregation and the Onset of War, 1815–1945." In J. David Singer, ed., *Quantitative International Politics*. New York: Free Press, 1968, pp. 247–86.

Singer, J. David, and Melvin Small (1972) *The Wages of War, 1816–1965*. New York: Wiley.

Singer, J. David, and Melvin Small (1976) "The War-Proneness of Democratic Regimes, 1816–1965." *Jerusalem Journal of International Relations*, 1: 50–69.

Sinno, Abdulkader H. (2008) *Organizations at War in Afghanistan and Beyond*. Ithaca, NY: Cornell University Press.

Sisk, Timothy D. (2009). *International Mediation in Civil Wars: Bargaining with Bullets* London: Routledge.

Siverson, Randolph M. (1995) "Democracies and War Participation: In Defense of the Institutional Constraints Argument." *European Journal of International Relations*, 1 4: 481–9.

Skocpol, Theda (1979) *States and Social Revolutions: A Comparative Analysis of France, Russia, and China*. Cambridge: Cambridge University Press.

Slantchev, Branislav L. (2003) "The Principle of Convergence in Wartime Negotiations." *American Political Science Review*, 97, 4 (November): 621–32.

Smith, Alastair (1996) "Diversionary Foreign Policy in Democratic Systems." *International Studies Quarterly*, 40, 1: 133–53.

Smoke, Richard (1977) *War: Controlling Escalation*. Cambridge, MA: Harvard University Press.

Snidal, Duncan (1991) "Relative Gains and the Pattern of International Cooperation." *American Political Science Review*, 85, 3 (September): 701–26.

Snyder, Glenn H. (1997) *Alliance Politics*. Ithaca, NY: Cornell University Press.

Snyder, Glenn, and Paul Diesing (1977) *Conflict Among Nations*. Princeton, NJ: Princeton University Press.

Snyder, Jack (1984) *The Ideology of the Offensive*. Ithaca, NY: Cornell University Press.

Snyder, Jack (1991) *Myths of Empire: Domestic Politics and International Ambition*. Ithaca, NY: Cornell University Press.

Snyder, Jack L. (2000) *From Voting to Violence: Democratization and Nationalist Conflict*. New York: W.W. Norton.

Snyder, Jack, and Robert Jervis (1999) "Civil War and the Security Dilemma." In Barbara F. Walter and Jack Snyder, eds., *Civil Wars, Insecurity, and Intervention*. New York: Columbia University Press, pp. 15–37.

Snyder, Richard C., H. W. Bruck, and Burton Sapin, eds. (1962) *Decision-Making as an Approach to the Study of International Politics*. New York: Free Press of Glencoe.

Solingen, Etel (1998) *Regional Orders at Century's Dawn: Global and Domestic Influences on Grand Strategy*. Princeton, NJ: Princeton University Press.

Spruyt, Hendrik (1996) *The Sovereign State and Its Competitors*. Princeton, NJ: Princeton University Press.

Stein, Arthur A. (1993) "Governments, International Interdependence, and Cooperation." In Philip E. Tetlock, Jo L. Husbands, Robert Jervis, Paul C. Stern, and Charles Tilly, eds., *Behavior, Society, and International Conflict*. New York: Oxford University Press, pp. 241–324.

Stein, Janice Gross (1985) "Calculation, Miscalculation, and Conventional Deterrence, II: The View from Jerusalem." In Robert Jervis, Richard Ned Lebow, and Janice Gross Stein, eds., *Psychology and Deterrence*. Baltimore: Johns Hopkins University Press, pp. 60–88.

Stein, Janice Gross (1991) "The Arab–Israeli War of 1967: Inadvertent War Through Miscalculated Escalation." In Alexander L. George, ed., *Avoiding War: Problems of Crisis Management*. Boulder, CO: Westview, pp. 126–59.

Stein, Janice Gross (1993) "Building Politics into Psychology: The Misperception of Threat." In Neil J. Kressel, *Political Psychology*. New York: Paragon House, pp. 367–92.

Stein, Janice Gross (1994) "Political Learning by Doing: Gorbachev as Uncommitted Thinker and Motivated Learner." *International Organization*, 48, 2 (Spring): 155–84.

Steinberg, Blema S. (1996) *Shame and Humiliation: Presidential Decision-Making on Vietnam-A Psychoanalytic Interpretation*. Pittsburgh, PA: University of Pittsburgh Press.

Steinbrunner, John D. (1974) *The Cybernetic Theory of Decision*. Princeton, NJ: Princeton University Press.

Stern, Erik K. (1997) "Probing the Plausibility of Newgroup Syndrome: Kennedy and the Bay of Pigs." In Paul 't Hart, Eric K. Stern, and Bengt Sundelius, eds., *Beyond Groupthink: Political Group Dynamics and Foreign Policy-making*. Ann Arbor, MI: University of Michigan Press, pp. 153–89.

Stern, Eric K., and Bengt Sundelius (1994) "The Essence of Groupthink." *Mershon International Studies Review*, 1: 101–8.

Stevenson, David (1996) *Armaments and the Coming of War: Europe 1904–1914*. New York: Oxford University Press.

Stevenson, David (2004) *Cataclysm: The First World War as Political Tragedy*. New York: Basic Books.

Stoessinger, John G. (2001) *Why Nations Go to War*. 8th ed. Pacific Grove, CA: Wadsworth.

Strachan, Hew (2001) *The First World War*, Vol. 1: *To Arms*. New York: Oxford University Press.

Strachan, Hew, and Andreas Herberg-Rothe (2007) *Clausewitz in the Twenty-First Century*. Oxford: Oxford University Press.

Streich, Philip, and Jack S. Levy (2007) "Time Horizons, Discounting, and Intertemporal Choice." *Journal of Conflict Resolution*, 51, 2 (April): 199–226.

Suganami, Hidemi (1996) *On the Causes of War*. New York: Oxford University Press.

Sun Tzu (1963) *The Art of War*, trans. Samuel B. Griffith. New York: Oxford University Press.

Summers, Harry G. (1984) *On Strategy*. New York: Dell.

Suskind, Ron (2006) *The One Percent Doctrine: Deep Inside America's Pursuit of Its Enemies Since 9/11*. New York: Simon & Schuster.

Taleb, Nassim Nicholas (2007) *The Black Swan: The Impact of the Highly Improbable*. New York: Random House.

Taliaferro, Jeffrey W. (2004) *Balancing Risks: Great Power Intervention in the Periphery*. Ithaca, NY: Cornell University Press.

Tammen, Ronald L., et al. (2000) *Power Transitions: Strategies for the 21st Century*. New York: Chatham House Publishers.

Tannenwald, Nina (2007) *The Nuclear Taboo: The United States and the Non-Use of Nuclear Weapons Since 1945*. New York: Cambridge University Press.

Tansill, Charles Callan (1938) *America Goes to War*. Boston, MA: Little Brown.

Tarar, Ahmer (2006) "Diversionary Incentives and the Bargaining Approach to War." *International Studies Quarterly*, 50, 1: 169–88.

Taylor, A.J.P. (1954) *The Struggle for Mastery in Europe, 1848–1918*. Oxford: Oxford University Press.

Taylor, A.J.P. (1961) *The Origins of the Second World War*, 2nd ed. Greenwich, CT: Fawcett.

Taylor, A.J.P. (1969) *War by Time-table*. London: Macdonald.

Tetlock, Philip E. (1991) "Learning in U.S. and Soviet Foreign Policy: In Search of an Elusive Concept." In George Breslauer and Philip Tetlock, eds., *Learning in U.S. and Soviet Foreign Policy*. Boulder, CO: Westview, pp. 20–61.

Tetlock, Philip E. (1998) "Social Psychology and World Politics." In D. Gilbert, S. Fiske, and G. Lindzey, eds., *Handbook of Social Psychology*, 4th ed. New York: McGraw-Hill, pp. 868–912.

Tetlock, Philip E., and Aaron Belkin, eds. (1996) *Counterfactual Thought Experiments in World Politics*. Princeton, NJ: Princeton University Press.

Thies, Cameron G. (2004) "State Building, Interstate and Intrastate Rivalry: A Study of Post-Colonial Developing Country Extractive Efforts, 1975–2000." *International Studies Quarterly*, 48: 53–72.

Thompson, William R. (1983) "Succession Crises in the Global System: A Test of the Transition Model." In Albert Bergesen, ed., *Crises in the World System*. Beverly Hills, CA: Sage, pp. 93–116.

Thompson, William R. (1988) *On Global War*. Columbia, SC: University of South Carolina Press.

Thompson, William R. (1996) "Democracy and Peace: Putting the Cart before the Horse?" *International Organization*, 50 (Winter): 141–74.

Thompson, William R. (1999) *Great Power Rivalries*. Columbia, SC: University of South Carolina Press.

Thompson, William R. (2001a) "Identifying Rivals and Rivalries in World Politics." *International Studies Quarterly*, 45: 557–86.

Thompson, William R. (2001b) "Expectancy Theory, Strategic Rivalry Descalation, and the Evolution of the Sino–Soviet Case." In William R. Thompson, eds., *Evolutionary Interpretations of World Politics*. New York: Routledge, pp. 218–39.

Thompson, William R. (2003) "A Streetcar Named Sarajevo: Catalysts, Multiple Causation Chains, and Rivalry Structures." *International Studies Quarterly*, 47, 3 (September): 453–74.

Thompson, William R., and Richard Tucker (1997) "A Tale of Two Democratic Peace Critiques." *Journal of Conflict Resolution*, 41, 3 (June): 428–54.

Thomson, James C. (1968) "How Vietnam Happened? An Autopsy." *Atlantic Monthly*, April: 47–53.

Thucydides (1996) *History of the Peloponnesian War*. Edited by Robert B. Strassler, *The Landmark Thucydides*. New York: Free Press.

Tickner, J. Ann (2001) *Gendering World Politics*. New York: Columbia University Press.

Tilly, Charles (1975) "Reflections on the History of European State Making." In Charles Tilly, ed., *The Formation of National States in Western Europe*. Princeton, NJ: Princeton University Press.

Tilly, Charles (1978) *From Mobilization to Revolution*. Reading, MA: Addison-Wesley.

Tilly, Charles (1990) *Coercion, Capital, and European States, AD 990–1990*. Cambridge, MA: Basil Blackwell.

Tir, Jaroslav, and Michael Jasinski (2008) "Domestic-Level Diversionary Theory of War: Targeting Ethnic Minorities." *Journal of Conflict Resolution*, 52, 5: 641–64.

Tocqueville, Alexis de ([1835]1975) *Democracy in America*, Vol. I. New York: Vintage.

Toft, Monica Duffy (2003) *The Geography of Ethnic Violence: Identity, Interests and the Indivisibility of Territory*. Princeton, NJ: Princeton University Press.

Trachtenberg, Marc (1990/91) "The Meaning of Mobilization in 1914." *International Security*, 15, 3: 120–50.

Trachtenberg, Marc (1999) *A Constructed Peace: The Making of the European Settlement, 1945–1963*. Princeton, NJ: Princeton University Press.

Tremblay, Reeta Chowdhari, and Julian Schofield. (2005) "Institutional Causes of the India–Pakistan Rivalry." In T.V. Paul, ed., *The India–Pakistan Conflict: An Enduring Rivalry*. Cambridge: Cambridge University Press, pp. 225–48.

Tuchman, Barbara W. (1962) *The Guns of August*. New York: Dell.

Turner, L.C.F. (1979) "The Significance of the Schlieffen Plan." In Paul M. Kennedy, ed., *The War Plans of the Great Powers, 1880–1914*. Boston: George Allen & Unwin, pp. 199–221.

Tversky, Amos (1972) "Elimination by Aspects: A Theory of Choice." *Psychological Review*, 79 (July): 281–99.

Tversky, Amos, and Daniel Kahneman (1974) "Judgment under Uncertainty: Heuristics and Biases." *Science*, New Series, 185, 4157 (September 27): 1124–31.

Vagts, Alfred (1959) *A History of Militarism*, rev. ed. New York: Free Press.

van Creveld, Martin (1991) *The Transformation of War*. New York: Free Press

Van Evera, Stephen (1990) "Primed for Peace." *International Security*, 15, 3: 7–57.

Van Evera, Stephen (1997) *Guide to Methods for Students of Political Science*. Ithaca, NY: Cornell University Press.

Van Evera, Stephen (1999) *Causes of War*. Ithaca, New York: Cornell University Press.

Vasquez, John A. (1993) *The War Puzzle*. New York: Cambridge University Press.

Vasquez, John A. (1996) "Distinguishing Rivals That Go To War From Those That Do Not: A Quantitative Case Study of the Two Paths to War." *International Studies Quarterly*, 40: 531–58.

Vasquez, John A. (1997) "The Realist Paradigm and Degenerative versus Progressive Research Programs: An Appraisal of Neotraditional Research on Waltz's Balancing Proposition." *American Political Science Review*, 91, 4 (December): 899–912.

Vasquez, John A. (1998a) "The Evolution of Multiple Rivalries Prior to the Second World War in the Pacific." In Paul F. Diehl, ed., *The Dynamics of Enduring Rivalries*. Urbana: University of Illinois Press, pp. 191–223.

Vasquez, John A. (1998b) *The Power of Power Politics: From Classical Realism to Neotraditionalism*. Cambridge: Cambridge University Press.

Vasquez, John A. (2000) "What Do We Know about War?" In Vasquez, ed., *What Do We Know about War?* Lanham, MD: Rowman & Littlefield, pp. 335–70.

Vasquez, John A., and Colin Elman, eds. (2003) *Realism and the Balancing of Power: A New Debate*. Saddle River, NJ: Prentice Hall.

Vattel, Emmerich de ([1758]1916) *The Law of Nations*, trans. Charles Fenwick. Washington, DC: Carnegie Institution.

Veblen, Thorstein ([1915]1966) *Imperial Germany and the Industrial Revolution*. Ann Arbor, MI: University of Michigan Press.

Verba, Sidney (1961) "Assumptions of Rationality and Non-Rationality in Models of the International System." *World Politics*, 14, 1 (October): 93–117.

Vertzberger, Yaacov (1984) "Bureaucratic-organizational Politics and Information Processing in a Developing State." *International Studies Quarterly*, 28, 1 (March): 69–95.

Vertzberger, Yaacov Y.I. (1990) *The World in their Minds*. Stanford, CA: Stanford University Press.

Vertzberger, Yaacov Y.I. (1998) *Risk Taking and Decisionmaking: Foreign Military Intervention Decisions*. Stanford: Stanford University Press.

Viner, Jacob (1948) "Power Versus Plenty as Objectives of Foreign Policy in the Seventeenth and Eighteenth Centuries" *World Politics*, 1, 1 (October): 1–29.

Wæver, Ole (1998) "The Sociology of a Not So International Discipline: American and European Developments in International Relations." *International Organization*, 52, 4: 687–727.

Wagner, R. Harrison (2000) "Bargaining and War." *American Journal of Political Science*, 44, 3: 469–84.

Wagner, R. Harrison (2007) *War and the State*. Ann Arbor, MI: University of Michigan Press.

Walker, Stephen G. (1977) "The Interface Between Beliefs and Behavior: Henry Kissinger's Operational Code and the Vietnam War." *Journal of Conflict Resolution*, 21 (March): 129–68.

Walker, Stephen G. (2003) "A Cautionary Tale: Operational Code Analysis as a Scientific Research Program." In Colin Elman and Miriam Fendius Elman, eds., *Progress in International Relations Theory*. Cambridge, MA: MIT Press, pp. 245–76.

Walker, Stephen G., Mark Schafer, and Michael D. Young (1999) "Presidential Operational Codes and Foreign Policy Conflicts in the Post-Cold War World." *The Journal of Conflict Resolution*, 43, 5 (October): 610–25.

Walker, Thomas C. (2000) "The Forgotten Prophet: Tom Paine's Cosmopolitanism and International Relations." *International Studies Quarterly*, 44, 1 (March): 51–72.

Walker, Thomas C., and Jeffrey S. Morton (2005) "Re-Assessing the 'Power of Power Politics' Thesis: Is Realism Still Dominant?" *International Studies Review*, 7, 2 (June): 341–56.

Wallace, Michael (1982) "Armaments and Escalation: Two Competing Hypotheses." *International Studies Quarterly* 26, 1: 37–51.

Wallerstein, Immanuel (1984) "Three Instances of Hegemony and the History of the World Economy." *International Journal of Comparative Sociology*, 24: 100–108.

Walt, Stephen M. (1987) *The Origins of Alliances*. Ithaca, NY: Cornell University Press

Walt, Stephen M. (2002) "The Enduring Relevance of the Realist Tradition." In Ira Katznelson and Helen V. Milner, eds., *Political Science: State of the Discipline*. New York: W.W. Norton, pp. 197–230.

Walt, Stephen M. (2005) *Taming American Power: The Global Response to US Primacy*. New York: W.W. Norton.

Walter, Barbara (2002) *Committing to Peace: The Successful Settlement of Civil Wars*. Princeton, NJ: Princeton University Press.

Waltz, Kenneth N. (1959) *Man, the State, and War*. New York: Columbia University Press.

Waltz, Kenneth N. (1979) *Theory of International Politics*. Reading, MA: Addison-Wesley.

Waltz, Kenneth N. (1988) "The Origins of War in Neorealist Theory." *Journal of Interdisciplinary History*, 18, 4: 615–28.

Waltz, Kenneth N. (2000) "Structural Realism after the Cold War." *International Security*, 25, 1 (Summer): 5–41.

Ward, Michael D., and Kristian S. Gleditsch (1998) "Democratizing for Peace." *American Political Science Review*, 92, 1: 51–62.

Watt, Donald Cameron (1975) *Too Serious a Business: European Armed Forces and the Approach to the Second World War*. Berkeley, CA: University of California Press.

Weart, Spencer R. (1989) *Nuclear Fear: A History of Images*. Cambridge, MA: Harvard University Press.

Weede, Erich (2003) "Globalization: Creative Destruction and the Prospect of a Capitalist Peace." In Gerald Schneider, Katherine Barbieri, and Nils Petter Gleditsch, eds., *Globalization and Armed Conflict*. Lanham, MD: Rowman & Littlefield, pp. 311–23.

Weeks, Jessica L. (2008) "Autocratic Audience Costs: Regime Type and Signaling Resolve." *International Organization*, 62, 1 (Winter): 35–64.

Wehler, Hans-Ulrich (1985) *The German Empire 1871–1918*, trans. Kim Traynor. Dover, NH: Berg Publishers.

Weinberg, Gerhard L. (1994) *A World at Arms*. New York: Cambridge University Press.

Weinstein, Jeremy M. (2007) *Inside Rebellion: The Politics of Insurgent Violence*. Cambridge: Cambridge University Press.

Welch, David A. (1997) "The 'Clash of Civilizations' Thesis as an Argument and as a Phenomenon." *Security Studies*, 6, 4 (Summer): 197–216.

Wendt, Alexander (1999) *Social Theory of International Politics*. New York: Cambridge University Press.

Whaley, Barton (1973) *Codeword Barbarossa*. Cambridge, MA: MIT Press.

White, John Albert (1964) *The Diplomacy of the Russo–Japanese War*. Princeton, NJ: Princeton University Press.

White, Robert H. (1968) *Nobody Wanted War*. Garden City, NY: Doubleday/ Anchor.

Wickham-Crowley, Timothy (1992) *Guerrillas and Revolution in Latin America: A Comparative Study of Insurgents and Regimes Since 1956*. Princeton, NJ: Princeton University Press

Wilensky, H. (1967) *Organizational Intelligence*. New York: Basic Books.

Williams, William Appleman (1962) *The Tragedy of American Diplomacy*. New York: Dell.

Williamson, Samuel R., Jr., and Ernest R. May (2007) "An Identity of Opinion: Historians and July 1914." *The Journal of Modern History*, 79 (June): 335–87.

Winter, David G. (1992) "Personality and Foreign Policy: Historical Overview of Research." In Eric Singer and Valerie Hudson, eds., *Political Psychology and Foreign Policy*. Boulder, CO: Westview, pp. 79–101.

Wirtz, James J. (2006) "Responding to Surprise." *Annual Review of Political Science*, 9: 45–65.

Wohlforth, William C. (1994/95) "Realism and the End of the Cold War." *International Security*, 19, 2 (Winter): 91–129.

Wohlstetter, Roberta (1962) *Pearl Harbor*. Stanford, CA: Stanford University Press.

Wolf, Reinhard, Erich Weede, Andrew J. Enterline, Edward D. Mansfield, and Jack Snyder (1996) "Democratization and the Danger of War." *International Security*, 20, 4 (Spring): 176–207.

Wolfers, Arnold (1962) *Discord and Collaboration*. Baltimore: Johns Hopkins University Press.

Woods, M. Kevin, James G. Lacey, and Williamson Murray (2006) "Saddam's Delusions: The View From The Inside." *Foreign Affairs*, 85 (May/June): 2–26.

Woodward, Bob (2004) *Plan of Attack*. New York: Simon & Schuster.

Woodward, Susan L. (1995) *Balkan Tragedy*. Washington, DC: Brookings Institution.

Worchel, Stephjen, and William G. Austin, eds. (1986) *Psychology of Intergroup Relations*. Chicago: Nelson-Hall.

Wrangham, Richard (2006) "Why Apes and Humans Kill." In Martin Jones and A.C. Fabian, eds., *Conflict*. New York: Cambridge University Press, pp 43–62.

Wrangham, Richard, and Dale Peterson (1996) *Demonic Males: Apes and the Origins of Human Violence*. Boston: Houghton Mifflin/Mariner Books.

Wright, Quincy ([1942]1965) *A Study of War*. Chicago: Chicago University Press.

Yates, J. Frank, ed. (1992) *Risk-Taking Behavior*. New York: Wiley.

Young, Patricia, and Jack S. Levy (forthcoming) "Domestic Politics and Commercial Rivalry: Explaining the War of Jenkins' Ear, 1739–1748." *European Journal of International Relations*.

Zakaria, Fareed (1992) "Realism and Domestic Politics." *International Security*, 17, 1: 177–98.

Zakaria, Fareed (1998) *From Wealth to Power*. Princeton, NJ: Princeton University Press.

Zakaria, Fareed (2001) "America's New Balancing Act." *Newsweek*, 6 August.

Zartman, I. William (1995) *Elusive Peace: Negotiating an End to Civil Wars*. Washington, DC: Brookings.

Zegart, Amy B. (2009) *Spying Blind: The CIA, the FBI, and the Origins of 9/11*. Princeton, NJ: Princeton University Press.

Zhang, David D., Peter Brecke, Harry F. Lee, Yuan-Quin He, and Jane Zhang (2007) "Global Climate Change, War, and Population Decline in Recent Human History." *Proceedings of the National Academy of Sciences of the U.S. (PNAS)*, 104, 49 (December 4): 19214–19.

Zisk, Kimberly Marten. (1993) *Engaging the Enemy: Organization Theory and Soviet Military Innovation, 1955–1991*. Princeton, NJ: Princeton University Press.

Zuber, Terence (1999) "The Schlieffen Plan Reconsidered." *War in History*, 6, 3 (July): 262–305.

Index

Note: "n." after a page reference indicates the number of a note on that page.